Frontiers of Labor

THE WORKING CLASS IN AMERICAN HISTORY

A list of books in the series appears at the end of this book.

Frontiers of Labor

Comparative Histories of the United States and Australia

Edited by

GREG PATMORE AND
SHELTON STROMQUIST

1 2 3 4 5 C P 5 4 3 2 1
∞ This book is printed on acid-free paper.
Printed and bound in Great Britain by
Marston Book Services Ltd, Oxfordshire

Library of Congress Control Number: 2017055613
ISBN 978-0-252-04183-9 (hardcover)
ISBN 978-0-252-08345-7 (paperback)
ISBN 978-0-252-05050-3 (e-book)

Contents

PART 5. ECONOMIC DEMOCRACY AND WORKING-CLASS INSTITUTIONS

PART 6. TRANSNATIONAL WORKING-CLASS POLITICS

Acknowledgments

This book is the product of a unique set of collaborations that stretched across the vast Pacific Ocean and more time zones than we can remember. In many ways it embodies the transnationalism that is also the book's subject. We have known each other for many years and have sojourned at each other's institutions, and we developed the idea for the volume out of a session on comparative Australian and US labor history that we organized for the national conference of the Labor and Working-Class History Association (LAWCHA) held in New York City in June 2013.

With support from both LAWCHA and the Australian Association for the Study of Labour History, we conceived a conference on comparative and transnational Australian and US labor history to be held at the University of Sydney in January 2015. We recruited a first-rate program committee—Braden Ellem, Rae Frances, Jim Gregory, Harry Knowles, Melanie Nolan, Fran Shor, and Kerry Taylor—that reviewed dozens of paper proposals under a very tight deadline.

With strong institutional support from the Work and Organisational Studies (WOS) discipline, the Business and Labour History Group (BLHG), and the University of Sydney Business School, a wonderful staff, including Andre Pinto (WOS), Yasmin Rittau and Merilyn Bryce (BLHG), and Mark Nearhos (University of Sydney Business School), helped organize and manage the very fine conference. The presentations and lively discussions produced the essays that comprise this volume.

We are especially grateful for the patience and excellent work of the contributors through multiple rounds of revision and for the excellent and instructive comments on the essays by Nick Fischer (Monash University) and another anonymous reviewer. Financial assistance for publication has been provided by the BLHG, LAWCHA, and Elizabeth Malcolm and Bradley Bowden.

At the University of Iowa History Department, Patricia Goodwin and Sheri Sojka provided valuable help in producing a final manuscript. And at the University of Illinois Press, James Engelhardt and Laurie Matheson gave tremendous support to the project, and Ellen Goldlust provided excellent copyediting of the manuscript.

Finally, we thank our families for their patience and perseverance. In particular, our spouses, Helen Warner and Ann Stromquist, have again showered us with more love and support than we probably deserve.

Greg Patmore and Shelton Stromquist

Frontiers of Labor

US and Australian Labor

A Comparative and Transnational Perspective

GREG PATMORE
SHELTON STROMQUIST

Australia and the United States have long been recognized as fertile fields for comparative history. Both the American and Australian colonies were "frontier societies" with considerable natural resources and without a feudal heritage.[1] Their patterns of European settlement at the expense of indigenous peoples, their early colonial heritage, the imprint of Anglo-Saxon law and custom, and the development of liberal democratic institutions are obvious points of comparison. Transportation and extractive industries of continental scope played a significant role in the economic development and class formation of both.

Despite their similarities, the histories of Australia and the United States are also marked by striking divergences, notably in the composition of their working classes, their labor relations, and their politics. Recent studies that examine not only race, gender, ethnicity, and class but also the politics of reform and institutions of social amelioration have, on the whole, complicated those comparisons. Divergences in social structure, cultural life, and political development bring into focus differences that illuminate both histories. The essays in this volume contribute significantly to a more complex set of comparisons even as they emphasize the transnational influences that cross-fertilized the histories of the two countries.

Working-class history has flourished in both the United States and Australia in recent decades, drawing on new insights that highlight race and gender as significant features of class formation.[2] But to a large extent, those developments have been bounded by their respective national histories and historiographical traditions. That has now begun to change as a result of transnational impulses within the discipline. Although comparative and transnational analysis has animated new work in labor history, specific comparisons of the United States and Australia remain relatively underdeveloped.[3]

The essays in this volume break new ground in comparative and transnational history. As a whole, they offer considerable evidence to support the general proposition that despite similarities in the development of their economies and in the fabric of their democratic institutions, the labor histories of Australia and the United States manifest notable differences. The long period of industrialization in the United States was marked by intense and frequently violent class and race polarization—a by-product of its legacy of slavery and an employing class determined to resist unionization. While Australia also witnessed significant conflict as its economy industrialized, its working class was less racially/ethnically diverse and benefited from a government-regulated system of labor arbitration that provided a degree of security for most organized workers and a measure of relative industrial peace that was largely absent in the United States. While Australian employers initially opposed state intervention through industrial arbitration, they realized that such intervention had advantages. While reducing employers' flexibility, the industrial tribunals could discipline labor with fines, union deregistration, and even jail and could impose restraints on wages during periods of inflation.

Nevertheless, since the end of World War II, labor relations in the two societies have grown more similar, at least to a degree. Postwar declines in Australian union densities, following the model of the United States, and sharp reductions in strikes and violence in American industrial relations have produced a degree of convergence. Australian employers, influenced by the rise of "free market" models and the increasing international competition, supported the weakening and even abolition of industrial arbitration. The rise of neoliberal ideology and international competitiveness have influenced US industrial relations, while the weakening of the National Labor Relations Board and recent attacks on public employee unions have accelerated the decline in union strength.[4]

The essays in this volume make significant contributions to these and other comparative aspects of Australian and US labor history. They examine several themes: the divergent impact of World War I on the fortunes of labor and socialist movements, the history of coerced labor, patterns of ethnic and class identification, the forms of working-class collective action and institution building, struggles over trade union democracy, and the viability of independent working-class politics. In addition, several essays explore the ways in which radical labor and political activists from both countries developed transnational ties that cross-fertilized their respective trade union and political cultures.

In these centennial years of World War I, several essays in this collection consider the many ways the Great War provides a crucible for examining the contrasting patterns of social and political mobilization for war, opposition to conscription and the war itself, and the repression of dissent in the two countries. While significant segments of the socialist movement in both countries maintained a distinctive and principled opposition to the war, only in Australia were the labor movement and the dominant faction of the Labor Party able to defeat proposed conscription in two referenda. Women in both countries played central roles in the opposition to war and conscription. And although the war brought significant state repression of wartime dissent on both sides of the Pacific, the tides of repression that swept across independent labor and socialist political movements in the United States ultimately proved more disabling to the socialist movement. The experience of wartime repression and the postwar Red Scare in the United States did not have parallels in Australia. As a consequence of their wartime experiences, the labor and socialist movements in the two countries entered the 1920s in dramatically different conditions. While the Labor Party split over conscription and did not regain control of the Australian federal government until 1929, it held office at the state level for varying periods in key states such as Queensland and New South Wales, where significant legislation reduced working hours and workers' compensation. While trade union membership in the United States fell from 19 percent in 1920 to 10 percent a decade later, trade union membership in Australia peaked at 47 percent in 1927.[5]

A second area of comparison examined in this book is the coerced labor embedded in the early settlement of both countries through varying forms of indentured service, convict labor, and slavery. The mark of race and inherited forms of labor regulation produced a dramatic divergence in the two countries' early histories of dependent labor. Large agriculturalists in Australia treated dependent labor with a degree of humanity that was much less common in the United States, and in Australia, unlike the United States, the colonial states claimed jurisdiction to regulate the conditions of labor. In more recent times, coercive forms of employer antiunionism, especially in the US context, have narrowed the realm of union employment and given new scope to more widespread employer coercion through increased casual and contingent labor and the weakening of state regulation. These patterns have also infected Australian labor relations in more recent times.[6]

Third, the impact of immigration on labor movements has been of interest to labor historians in both countries. Early comparisons between unionism in Australia and the United States claimed that ethnic homogeneity explained the strength of the Australian labor movement. At the end of the nineteenth century, W. E. Murphy, a former secretary of the Melbourne Trades Hall, blamed ethnic divisions within US labor for the failure to achieve the eight-hour day. Labor theorists in the 1950s and the 1960s argued that one of the reasons for the growth of "group consciousness" among US workers was the disappearance of ethnicity as a divisive force. However, more recent work demonstrates that ethnic diversity does not necessarily inhibit unionism. Direct workplace experiences rather than premigration cultures largely shaped workers' industrial behavior. Opportunities to join unions, however, were limited by state, management, and organized labor policies toward minorities. The state on occasion threatened immigrant workers with deportation or enforced racial segregation. Employers also exacerbated ethnic divisions within the workforce by organizing employees along ethnic lines and establishing ethnically stratified wage scales and working conditions. Racist ideologies and fears of economic competition led some unions to exclude ethnic minorities.[7] Two essays in this collection examine the different ways in which Irish ethnicity functioned in the class milieus of the two countries to both promote and inhibit class and racial identification and the politics of reform. A strong legacy of racial and ethnic polarization and the pull of Irish republican ideology created more volatile conditions for Irish workers in the United States than did the lingering effects of empire and church on the position of the Irish in Australian society.[8]

A fourth area of comparison illustrates the variety of forms working-class collective action has taken in each country. While extraordinary levels of violence and repression have at times marked US labor relations, the overall trajectories of union growth and decline have followed a similar arc to those of Australia, punctuated by significant advances (and retreats) in state regulation. These essays seek new explanations for patterns of labor conflict and repression: in the structure of global labor and commodity markets, in state wartime policies, and in workers' rights to collective bargaining and state social provision. The timing of advance and retreat varied, but long-term convergence—declining strike rates, diminished violence, and weakened union strength—has produced greater similarity in recent years. Fueling this convergence, as noted previously, has been the adoption of neoliberal policies since the administrations of President Ronald Reagan and Prime Minister Bob Hawke; the decline of the manufacturing sector, with a loss of jobs offshore in both countries; and the growth of international competition with reductions in tariff protection.[9]

Fifth, a renewed interest among labor historians in the institutions of working-class life and how they function constitutes a related area of comparative investigation. Whether it is national unions and their practice of democracy, labor's role in the politics of social reform, or working-class support for consumer cooperatives under changing market conditions, these comparisons highlight differences in national historical contexts and political cultures that account in significant measure for the different histories and behavior of these institutions.[10]

Finally, the contrasting course of working-class politics in the two countries has been a long-standing point of comparison. And while the question of why no viable labor party ever arose in the United States (like the "why no socialism in the United States" question) has generated considerable interest, the answers turn out to be more complicated than previously thought. New studies of transnational influences have found considerable circulation of ideas and organizational models between the working-class movements of Australia and the United States. The Knights of Labor, syndicalist miners' unionism, the Industrial Workers of the World, philosophical anarchism, and waterfront workers' job control represent important sites of transnational influence that connect the histories of the two countries.[11]

Australian and US Labor: Historical Contexts

The European settlement of Australia did not begin until 1788, and the country remains sparsely populated compared to the United States. Australian settlers found less arable land than did their American counterparts. Only the United States bore the legacy of slavery, and the enslavement of Africans produced a lasting racial imprint on the American working class and American society more generally. Both countries, however, experienced other forms of dependent labor—most notably, convicts and indentured servants. Although immigration fed population growth in both countries, immigrants to Australia came disproportionately from the British Isles prior to 1945, whereas almost from the outset, the United States drew a far more diverse immigrant working-class population. Interethnic differences in the United States reinforced divisions between skilled and unskilled workers, particularly in the era of mass production, and inhibited the forging of a homogeneous class culture.[12] The smaller Australian domestic market has historically meant that manufacturing is based on batch production rather than mass production, resulting in a larger component of skilled labor.[13]

Although labor conflict has been present in both countries, levels of violent employer and state repression have been higher in the United States.[14] While the use of blacklisting and management espionage against labor is not unknown in Australia, employer repression has been more pervasive in the United States.[15] As Badger has argued in the United States, "Before the New Deal the coercive power of the state has largely been arrayed against labor."[16] At all levels of government, public officials showed a willingness to use force against union activists and strikers. Local government officials tended to act as an arm of employers, and state governors reinforced this bias by calling out the National Guard "ostensibly to maintain law and order, in practice to protect scabs, keep plants open, and break strikes."[17] In the 20 April 1914 Ludlow massacre, for example, the Colorado National Guard and company guards attacked a camp for striking miners, torching tents and ultimately leaving six men, two women, and eleven children dead.[18]

Three specific differences mark the labor histories of the United States and Australia: the level of unionization, the rise of the Australian Labor Party, and the role of the state in labor relations. Australia's earliest trade unions date from the late 1820s, when they were small, mainly confined to skilled tradesmen, and based in one locality. During the second half of the nineteenth century, trade unionism spread to miners, transport workers, shearers, and factory workers. Australian workers formed peak union councils in most major cities and began holding Intercolonial Trade Union Congresses from 1879. By 1891 more than 20 percent of workers were organized in the two largest colonies, New South Wales and Victoria.[19]

In the United States, trade union organizing occurred predominantly among artisans in the first half of the nineteenth century but accelerated in the aftermath of the Civil War with the formation and consolidation of unions in metals, textile manufacturing, railroad operations, factory-based shoemaking, and cigar making that affiliated with the National Labor Union. Following the collapse of unions in the depression of 1873–78, a massive wave of unionization occurred under the auspices of the Knights of Labor between 1878 and 1893, with union density peaking at more than 20 percent in the mid-1880s. The Knights declined rapidly as a consequence of fierce employer resistance, state hostility, and internal political divisions. In the 1890s, competing craft and general union tendencies in the labor movement pitted the fledgling American Federation of Labor (AFL) against rival industrial unions on the rails, in coal and hard-rock mining, and in a host of other trades at the heart of the transition to mass production (machinists, iron- and steelworkers, meatpackers, shoemakers, clothing workers).[20]

Comparing trade union densities for the United States and Australia poses some technical difficulties. Nevertheless, it is clear that until recently, the level of union membership has been higher in Australia than the United States, although the gap has narrowed. While US trade unions formed a national federation, the AFL, in 1886, no equivalent emerged in Australia until the 1927 formation of the Australian Council of Trade Unions.[21]

A major issue in comparing the working classes of Australia and the United States is the viability of independent labor politics. The United States saw the early appearance of mass political parties. By the mid-nineteenth century, universal suffrage for free white males outside the South was the norm, with property and taxation qualifications largely removed. Mass political parties emphasized neighborhood, ethnic, and religious ties and hinged on political patronage within an urban party system. These parties, which predated the rise of an industrial working class, were not primarily based on class.[22] Nonetheless, a series of class-based political movements emerged in the late nineteenth century and vied for political power, most successfully at the municipal level: these movements included the Greenback-Labor Party (1877–79), the Union Labor Party (1886–88) and the Populist Party (1892–96).[23]

The 1890s marked a turning point in the attitudes of both Australian and US unions toward politics. Both had to face a state acting on behalf of employers in major industrial disputes. The AFL under Samuel Gompers chose the path of "pure and simple unionism," which involved no explicit political alignment for organized labor and a nonpartisan approach to electoral activity, at least until 1908. Although the AFL and by the 1930s the rival Congress of Industrial Organizations (CIO) in practice aligned with the Democratic Party, neither the separate organizations nor the merged AFL-CIO after 1955 consistently supported a separate Labor Party at the national level. By contrast, Australian unionists took the view that employers' undue influence on the state would end only if labor directly won representation in parliament.[24]

The various state Labor Parties in Australia had mixed success at first. In New South Wales, the Labor Party won 35 of the 141 seats in the Legislative Assembly in the 1891 elections, but splits over protectionism and other issues soon weakened the party. Working-class activists made several attempts to form a Labor Party in Victoria, and Labor formed alliances with radical liberals in Queensland and South Australia. The party broadened its base beyond trade unions and appealed to Catholics and small farmers to gain electoral support, but trade unions still saw their affiliation with the Labor Party as an important means of improving wages and conditions. While socialist ideas abounded within the Labor Party, it did not fundamentally challenge capitalism. In 1910, the party won majority governments both in New South Wales and federally. The Australian Labor Party has been particularly successful at the state level, where trade unions have won major improvements in working conditions through legislation rather than industrial action.[25]

Robin Archer has argued that a number of reasons account for the absence of a US labor party, among them the level of state repression of the labor movement, the impact of religion on politics, and socialist sectarianism. Ethnic and racial division has also significantly constrained labor's ability to organize politically, especially in the South. While industrial unionism in the United States may have been episodic and limited to certain sectors before the 1930s, unions in Australia covered large numbers of unskilled and semiskilled workers, particularly agricultural workers in rural areas. Although the AFL feared that partisan politics would undermine union solidarity, a vibrant socialist movement before the Great War and the emergence of the CIO in the 1930s challenged those views, with some success.[26]

Australian trade unions also grew reliant on the state through the process of conciliation and arbitration. Liberals saw state intervention as an answer to major industrial confrontations and economic depression during the 1890s, promoting the early legislation for compulsory arbitration and viewing trade union recognition as an essential feature of the system. In the United States, progressive reformers favored some limited forms of arbitration but were constrained by their own antistatism and the labor movement's fears of an employer-dominated state.[27] State intervention on behalf of employers had been amply demonstrated in the nineteenth and early twentieth centuries through court injunctions prohibiting various forms of collective action and state and federal military intervention to break local as well as national strikes that enjoyed some success.[28] While the 1935 Wagner Act created machinery to determine whether US workers would choose union representation, Australia's analogous legislation presumed that workers would prefer union representation. Compulsory arbitration assisted union growth and gave unions a role in the determination of legally binding awards covering wages and conditions. Nevertheless, the role of unions in industrial regulation in Australia has weakened since the 1980s with the rise of enterprise bargaining and recognition of nonunion collective bargaining. Scholars have argued that the Australian unions' focus on compulsory arbitration and parliamentarianism had a number of long-term negative implications for the labor movement, including weakening union organization in the workplace.[29]

US and Australian labor were not completely isolated from one another, however, as the exchange of ideas and individuals' migration and communication linked labor and social movements in the two countries.[30] While Australians and New Zealanders evidenced interest in the organizational strategies embodied in the Knights of Labor and the Industrial Workers of the World in the United States, the Australian experience with compulsory arbitration and independent labor politics also drew significant attention.[31] As Lloyd Churchward has noted, "the reformist drive of the New Deal" and its agencies such as the Tennessee Valley Authority and the Civilian Conservation Corps aroused "considerable interest and even enthusiasm" within Australia.[32]

These essays bring together historians and scholars who explore the new comparative and transnational landscapes of labor history in both Australia and the United States. This volume joins a wider movement toward a more global labor history.[33] By opening new territory and new questions for comparative and transnational labor history of Australia and the United States, the essays that follow promise to stimulate a new round of comparisons in both national contexts.

Notes

1. Greg Patmore, "Australian Labor Historiography: The Influence of the USA," *Labor History* 37 (1996): 530–34.

2. For the United States, see, for example, David Roediger, *Working toward Whiteness: How America's Immigrants Became White* (New York: Basic Books, 2005); Alice Kessler Harris, *Gendering Labor History* (Urbana: University of Illinois Press, 2007). See also Marilyn Lake, "The White Man under Siege: New Histories of Race in the Nineteenth Century and the Advent of White Australia," *History Workshop Journal* 58 (2004): 41–62.

3. For transnational and comparative tendencies in labor history, see Leon Fink, ed., *Workers across the Americas: The Transnational Turn in Labor History* (New York: Oxford University Press, 2011). For North America and Australia, see Gregory S. Kealey and Greg Patmore, eds., *Canadian and Australian Labour History: Towards a Comparative Perspective* (Sydney: Australian Society for the Study of Labour History, 1990).

4. Christopher Wright, *The Management of Labour: A History of Australian Employers* (Melbourne: Oxford University Press, 1995), 53–54, 197, 213; Joseph A. McCartin, *Collision Course: Ronald Reagan, the Air Traffic Controllers, and the Strike That Changed America* (Oxford: Oxford University Press, 2011).

5. Helen Nelson, "Legislative Record 1925–27: How Radical?," in *Jack Lang*, ed. Heather Radi and Peter Spearritt (Sydney: Hale and Iremonger, 1977), 79–87; Greg Patmore, *Worker Voice. Employee Representation in the Workplace in Australia, Canada, Germany, the UK, and the US, 1914–1939* (Liverpool: Liverpool University Press, 2016), 39; Leo Troy, *Trade Union Membership, 1897–1962* (New York: National Bureau of Economic Research, 1965). These contrasting wartime experiences and outcomes are explored in chapters in this volume by Robin Archer, Verity Burgmann and Jeffrey Johnson, and Shelton Stromquist. Diane Kirkby's chapter examines the key role played by working-class women in the movements against war and repression in the United States and Australia.

6. On contrasting patterns of dependent labor in the United States and Australia, see Jennie Jeppesen, this volume. For the undermining of union representation in the United States, see Lawrence Richards, *Union-Free America: Workers and Antiunion Culture* (Urbana: University of Illinois Press, 2008); McCartin, *Collision Course*; Rosemary Feurer and Chad Pearson, eds., *Against Labor: How U.S. Employers Organized to Defeat Union Activism* (Urbana: University of Illinois Press, 2017). See also Marjorie Jerrard and Patrick O'Leary, this volume.

7. Albert Blum, "Why Unions Grow," *Labor History*, 9, no. 1 (1968): 39–72; Constance Lever-Tracy and Michael Quinlan, *A Divided Working Class* (London: Routledge, 1998), 309; W. E. Murphy, *History of the Eight Hours' Movement* (Melbourne: Picken, 1900), 3–4,

39. For a case study of the role of ethnicity in labor conflict, see James R. Green, *Death in Haymarket: A Story of Chicago, the First Labor Movement, and the Bombing That Divided Gilded Age America* (New York: Pantheon, 2006).

8. See Dianne Hall and Elizabeth Malcolm, this volume; James R. Barrett, this volume.

9. For comparative studies of collective action, labor conflict, and labor regulation, see Bradley Bowden and Peta Stevenson-Clarke, this volume. For the novel realm of military service, see Nathan Wise, this volume. For discussion of the convergence of Australian and US industrial relations in recent years at an industry level, see Marjorie Jerrard and Patrick O'Leary, this volume.

10. See, for example, Scott Stephenson, this volume. Ben Huf, this volume, identifies a more advanced position on social provision in the 1930s United States than Australia. Greg Patmore and Nikola Balnave, this volume, find a generally more robust cooperative movement in the United States than in Australia.

11. The most recent influential contribution to these comparative questions is Robin Archer, *Why Is There No Labor Party in the United States?* (Princeton: Princeton University Press, 2007). Studies of transnational influence include those of Robert H. Weir and Fran Shor. And on the multidirectional transnational flow of political ideas, see Robert Cherny, this volume; Peter Clayworth, this volume; Tom Goyens, this volume.

12. See, for example, David Brody, *Steelworkers in America: The Nonunion Era* (New York: Harper and Row, 1969); James R. Barrett, *Work and Community in the Jungle: Chicago's Packinghouse Workers, 1894–1922* (Urbana: University of Illinois Press, 1987). For a contemporary study, see Isaac Hourwich, *Immigration and Labor* (New York: Putnam's, 1912).

13. Wright, *Management of Labour*, 16.

14. For comparative strike data, see Malcolm Waters, *Strikes in Australia: A Sociological Analysis of Industrial Conflict* (Sydney: Allen and Unwin, 1982). For the United States, see P. K. Edwards, *Strikes in the United States, 1881–1974* (New York: St. Martin's, 1981). For qualitative studies, see, for example, David Montgomery, "The 'New Unionism' and the Transformation of Workers' Consciousness in America, 1909–1922," *Journal of Social History* 7 (1974): 510–29; Ian Turner, *Industrial Labour and Politics: The Dynamics of the Labour Movement in Eastern Australia, 1900–1921* (Sydney: Hale and Iremonger, 1979).

15. Rae Cooper and Greg Patmore, "Private Detectives, Blacklists, and Company Unions: Anti-Union Employer Strategy and Australian Labour History," *Labour History* 97 (2009): 4–5; Joseph McCartin, "'An American Feeling': Workers, Managers, and the Struggle over Industrial Democracy in the World War I Era," in *Industrial Democracy in America: The Ambiguous Promise*, ed. Nelson Lichtenstein and Howell Harris (Cambridge: Cambridge University Press, 1993), 81–82; Stephen Norwood, "Ford's Brass Knuckles: Harry Bennett, The Cult of Muscularity, and Anti-Labor Terror—1920–1945," *Labor History* 37 (1996): 367. For a discussion of more contemporary tactics, see Marjorie Jerrard and Patrick O'Leary, this volume.

16. Anthony Badger, *The New Deal: The Depression Years, 1933–1940* (Chicago: Dee, 1989), 119. See also David Montgomery, *Citizen Worker: The Experience of Workers in the*

United States with Democracy and the Free Market in the Nineteenth Century (Cambridge: Cambridge University Press, 1993).

17. Badger, *New Deal*, 119. See also Anthony DeStefanis, "Guarding Capital: Soldier Strikebreakers on the Long Road to the Ludlow Massacre" (PhD diss., College of William and Mary, 2004); James R. Green, *The Devil Is Here in These Hills: West Virginia's Coal Miners and Their Battle for Freedom* (New York: Grove, 2015).

18. Thomas Andrews, *Killing for Coal: America's Deadliest Labor War* (Cambridge: Harvard University Press, 2008); Jonathan Rees, "Beyond Body Counts: A Centennial Rethinking of the Ludlow Massacre," *Labor: Studies in Working-Class History of the Americas* 11 (2014): 107–15. See also George McGovern and Leonard Guttridge, *The Great Coalfield War* (Boulder: University of Colorado Press, 1996), 210–35.

19. Greg Patmore, *Australian Labour History* (Melbourne: Longman Cheshire, 1991), 36–39, 56–63. For an overview of Australian trade unions, see Bradley Bowden, "The Rise and Decline of Australian Unionism: A History of Industrial Labour from the 1820s to 2010," *Labour History* 100 (2011): 51–82.

20. For overviews of trade union developments, see David Montgomery, *Beyond Equality: Labor and the Radical Republicans, 1862–1872* (New York: Knopf, 1967) (on the National Labor Union); Robert E. Weir, *Beyond Labor's Veil: The Culture of the Knights of Labor* (University Park: Penn State University Press, 1996) and Robert E. Weir, *Knights Unhorsed: Internal Conflict in a Gilded Age Social Movement* (Detroit: Wayne State University Press, 2000) (on the Knights of Labor); John H. M. Laslett, *Labor and the Left: A Study of Socialist and Radical Influences in the American Labor Movement, 1881–1894* (New York: Basic Books, 1970). See also Shelton Stromquist, "United States of America," in *The Formation of Labour Movements, 1870–1914: An International Perspective*, ed. Marcel van der Linden and Jürgen Rojahn (Leiden: Brill, 1990), 543–77.

21. Patmore, "Australian Labor Historiography," 522–23. For data on Australian unions after 1980, see Australian Bureau of Statistics survey data; for the United States after 1982, see the US Bureau of Labor Statistics. For a comprehensive overview of the Australian Council of Trade Unions, see Jim Hagan, *The History of the ACTU* (Melbourne: Longman Cheshire, 1981). On the early history of the AFL, see Stuart B. Kaufman, *Samuel Gompers and the Origins of the American Federation of Labor, 1848–1896* (Westport, Conn.: Greenwood, 1973).

22. Alexander Keyssar, *The Right to Vote: The Contested History of Democracy in the United States* (New York: Basic Books, 2009); Archer, *Why Is There No Labor Party?*, 74; Theda Skocpol, *Protecting Soldiers and Mothers: The Political Origins of Social Policy in the United States* (Cambridge: Harvard University Press, 1995), 44–46; Christopher Tomlins, *The State and the Unions: Labor Relations, Law and the Organised Labor Movement in America, 1880–1960* (Cambridge: Cambridge University Press, 1985), 21–23.

23. See Leon Fink, *Workingmen's Democracy: The Knights of Labor and American Democracy* (Urbana: University of Illinois Press, 1983); Richard Schneirov, Shelton Stromquist, and Nick Salvatore, eds., *The Pullman Strike and the Crisis of the 1890s: Essays on Labor, Politics, and the State* (Urbana: University of Illinois Press, 1999). On the AFL's political

evolution, see Julie Greene, *Pure and Simple Politics: The American Federation of Labor and Political Activism, 1881–1917* (New York: Cambridge University Press, 1998).

24. Greene, *Pure and Simple Politics*; David Brody, *In Labor's Cause: Main Themes on the History of the American Worker* (New York: Oxford University Press, 1993), 51–70; Peter Shergold, "Comparative Labor Movements: An Australian Perspective," *Labour Studies Journal* 10 (1985): 65–66; R. H. Zeiger, *American Workers, American Unions*, 2nd ed. (Baltimore: Johns Hopkins University Press, 1994), 20–24, 114–22.

25. Patmore, *Australian Labour History*, 74–82.

26. Archer, *Why Is There No Labor Party?*, 232–43. See also Greene, *Pure and Simple Politics*; Steve Fraser, *Labor Will Rule: Sidney Hillman and the Rise of American Labor* (New York: Free Press, 1991); James Weinstein, *The Decline of Socialism in America, 1912–1925* (New York: Vintage, 1967).

27. See Daniel Rodgers, *Atlantic Crossings: Social Politics in a Progressive Age* (Cambridge: Harvard University Press, 1998); Skocpol, *Protecting Soldiers and Mothers*; Shelton Stromquist, *Reinventing "the People": The Progressive Movement, the Class Problem, and the Origins of Modern Liberalism* (Urbana: University of Illinois Press, 2006).

28. Notable cases of intervention by the courts and military include the Homestead Steel Strike (1892), the Pullman Boycott (1894), and the Great Steel Strike (1919).

29. Bowden, "Rise and Decline," 64; Greg Patmore, "A Voice for Whom? Employee Representation and Labour Legislation in Australia," *University of New South Wales Law Review* 29 (2006): 18–21. For a comprehensive discussion of the history of the federal system of industrial arbitration, see Joe Isaac and Stuart Macintyre, eds., *The New Province for Law and Order: 100 Years of Industrial Conciliation and Arbitration* (Cambridge: Cambridge University Press, 2004).

30. Raymond Markey, "The Australian Place in Comparative Labour History," *Labour History* 100 (2012): 177.

31. Ian Bedford, "The Industrial Workers of the World in Australia," *Labour History* 13 (1967): 40–46; Robert E. Weir, *Knights Down Under: The Knights of Labour in New Zealand* (Newcastle: Cambridge Scholars, 2009); Francis Shor, "Left Labor Agitators in the Pacific Rim of the Early Twentieth Century," *International Labor and Working-Class History* 67 (2005): 148–63; Verity Burgmann, *Revolutionary Industrial Unionism in Australia. The Industrial Workers of the World in Australia* (Melbourne: Cambridge University Press, 1995), 27–31; Frank Cain, *Wobblies at War: A History of the IWW and the Great War in Australia* (Melbourne: Spectrum, 1993), chaps. 1, 11; Lloyd Churchward, *Australia and America, 1788–1972: An Alternative History* (Sydney: Alternative Publishing, 1979), 258–70.

32. Churchward, *Australia and America*, 140. See also Ben Huf, this volume.

33. See Marcel van der Linden, *Workers of the World: Essays toward a Global Labor History* (Leiden: Brill, 2008); Jan Lucassen, ed., *Global Labour History: A State of the Art* (New York: Lang, 2006); van der Linden and Rojahn, *Formation of Labour Movements*.

PART 1

The Great War: Repression and Political Countermobilization

Quite Like Ourselves

Opposition to Military Compulsion during the Great War in the United States and Australia

ROBIN ARCHER

> But we are told, Australia is democratic, quite like ourselves, and Australia has dedicated its youth to training in arms. . . . [W]hy should we not be like Australia? Surely there's no militarism there?
>
> —Oswald Garrison Villard, *United Mine Workers Journal*, 6 July 1916

> In only one country has there been a genuine test vote upon military conscription and to the everlasting credit of self-governing Australia the proposal was rejected.
>
> —Editorial, *Coast Seamen's Journal*, 11 April 1917

Two waves of opposition arose during the First World War, and labor and socialist movements were central to both. The first—opposition to the war itself—took place in all belligerent countries on the eve of their entry into the war. The second—opposition to the introduction of conscription—was peculiar to the English-speaking world, where this practice had long been anathema. The United States and Australia were each unique in one of these respects. The

United States was the only belligerent in which the main labor-based party maintained its uncompromising opposition to the war even after the country had entered the conflict.[1] Australia was the only belligerent in which opposition to the introduction of conscription succeeded.

Indeed, these two countries stood at opposite ends of the spectrum of outcomes in both respects. In the United States, opposition to entry into the war was the most substantial of any of the belligerents—it kept the country out of the war for the first two and half years, and the president had just been reelected by emphasizing his responsibility for this; while Australia had minimal opposition on the eve of entry into the war. Yet their location on the poles reversed with respect to conscription. In Australia, opposition to conscription was so great that it proved impossible to introduce, while the United States introduced conscription more quickly than did any other English-speaking country—almost immediately after the Americans entered the war.[2]

To what extent were Americans and Australians interested in each other's experiences during this great formative period? And in particular, to what extent did the opponents of war and conscription pay attention the experiences of their counterparts across the Pacific? The answer is something of a surprise. During the early 1890s, a good deal of mutual interest had existed.[3] But as might be expected, given the size of the United States and its political and ideological influence, Australians manifested substantially more interest in American developments than vice versa. However, during the First World War, this changed. Indeed it reversed itself. Australian interest in American developments declined markedly, while American interest in Australian developments reached a new peak.

This essay examines these changes in the level of transnational interest. I begin by considering the extent of interest in each case and the reasons why it increased or decreased. I then offer some suggestions about the possible effects of these changes. Finally, I turn from a transnational inquiry to a comparative question, and set out some preliminary thoughts about why the outcome of the conflict over conscription was so different in these two similar New World societies.

Underpinning the potential for mutual interest were a number of fundamental similarities in the underlying social and political structures of the United States and Australia. Economically, both countries had very high living standards, jostling with each other for the accolade of having the highest average living standards in the world. Politically, both were among the handful of precocious democracies that had removed property qualifications for suffrage more than half a century earlier. Militarily, both countries' continental geopolitical situation left them basically secure and isolated from the main sources of Great

Power conflict. And culturally, the two countries shared an English-speaking heritage of institutions and values as well as language and ideas.

Of course, these similarities did not mean that either was the most important point of reference for the other. On the contrary, their common cultural heritage meant that Britain was the most important source of reference for both. And both also had other New World reference points. During this period, as we will see, this was especially true of Canada.

Australian Interest in the United States

In the late nineteenth century, Australian labor leaders and progressive intellectuals often argued that the New World was blessed with more egalitarian and democratic social and political structures that were far more hospitable to liberty than were the aristocratic and hierarchical structures of the Old World. Prior to the First World War, the standard point of reference for these arguments was the United States. The idea that Australia had the potential to be "another America" and the practice of looking there for inspiration was already well established in the early 1890s. Within the labor movement, left-wing reform thought emanating from the United States was particularly influential, and important labor papers drew inspiration from populist experiments in the United States. Indeed, the spelling of the Australian Labor Party's name may well testify to this American influence.[4]

However the dilemmas facing labor anticonscriptionists in the sharp and defining conflicts that wracked Australia prior to the first referendum on conscription in October 1916 made these activists wary of looking to the United States for lessons. Partly this was simply a consequence of censorship, which made access to some US journals difficult and reprinting US articles risky. But in addition, with the United States remaining neutral and Wilson campaigning for reelection on a "He Kept Us out of the War" platform, appealing to American experience threatened to damage the anticonscription cause by confusing it with an antiwar stance.[5]

Some references to the United States still appeared in the Australian labor press but these were limited to brief updates on American labor, socialist, or political news. US attitudes toward the war were occasionally smuggled in via short notes or cartoons included without comment.[6] But developments in the United States were almost never cited as a model or made part of an argument by analogy about what Australia ought to do.

Rather, Canada now loomed large. For Canada seemed to have rejected conscription.[7] Statements in parliament by Canada's Conservative prime minister,

Robert Borden, and Liberal opposition leader, Wilfrid Laurier, that neither had any intention of introducing conscription were repeated over and over again in Australia: If "loyal Canada . . . declines to put on the shackles of militarism," why should Australia do so?[8] This, said one Australian anticonscriptionist, was their "best argument."[9]

"Canada's common sense" was invoked repeatedly in the labor press, by socialist and Christian peace activists, at major rallies, and every week during the referendum campaign itself. Other British dominions provided additional points of reference, but many of these had problems of their own, and none was invoked as repeatedly as the Canadian case.

Unlike appeals to the United States, the "Canadian common sense" argument minimized the target that anticonscriptionists presented to their loyalist opponents. By limiting the grounds on which they would be susceptible to attack, opponents of conscription avoided opening up distracting extra fronts. The argument could appeal to both British tradition and the superior liberalism of the New World. Canada could be seen as a British as well as a New World model.[10]

US Interest in Australia

Americans were already interested in Australia before the United States entered the war. Australia was seen not only as a similar country but also as a more advanced one and perhaps even the most advanced one, a social laboratory providing a model for how America might itself develop in the near future.

This general perception of Australia was apparent in both the leading journals of progressive and liberal opinion and in the labor and socialist press. The *Nation* noted that men "have won in Australia the most favorable working conditions known." The *New Republic* argued that Australia and New Zealand are "self governing communities of a democratic type which . . . is of so advanced a character that it represents the *ultima Thule* of many social reformers in other lands." In a debate on German socialism for the *Intercollegiate Socialist*, one participant (described later as an apologist for the nationalist wing of the German Social Democratic Party) argued that "it is well known that the socialization of national life has reached a higher degree in Germany than in any other country except Australia and New Zealand." His opponent did not demur, adding only that "the equally advanced and efficient State Socialism of Australia" is "built upon a purely democratic foundation."[11]

Interest in Australian experiments in socialization and regulation can be found in various socialist and union journals. The *United Mine Workers Journal* reported on the workings of the state employment bureau, the *Coast Seaman's Journal* on the Commonwealth clothing factory, and the *Appeal to Reason* on Queensland's experiments in the grain and meat industries. A feature article on state socialism in Australia for the *New York Call*'s Sunday magazine concluded that "these measures put Australia a century ahead of England."[12]

Similar perceptions continued after the United States entered the war. A review of Ernest Scott's *Short History of Australia* for the *Nation* noted that "labor has perhaps more power [in Australia] than in any other country." A review of another book soon thereafter commented that "Australians are much more 'American' in temperament than the English from whom they spring." And commenting on a visit to the United States by William Arthur Holman, the Labor premier of New South Wales, the *New Republic* argued that "Australia represents even better than the United States the democratic ideal upon which our national life rests."[13]

This interest was also reflected in the reprinting of Australian articles in the labor and socialist press, as a survey of September 1916–March 1917 publications demonstrates. Articles from the *Australian Worker* (especially those written by its editor, Henry Boote), the *Queensland Worker*, and less frequently the *Labour Call* can be found in major union papers—both the *Coast Seaman's Journal* and others that largely supported Gompers's leadership of the AFL and the *United Mine Workers Journal* and others that were critical. Similar articles were also reprinted in the socialist press—including both the *Appeal to Reason*, which had the largest circulation of any socialist paper in the United States, and the *New York Call*, which was the most important socialist daily. In addition, the *United Mine Workers Journal* and the *New York Call* ran special articles from their "Australian correspondent"—usually Francis Ahern. These four journals alone carried at least twenty-four such reprinted or special articles in this six-month period.

Interest in Australia was especially notable among progressives—a wide range of whom, from liberal reformers through to socialists, were attracted to one or more of the social experiments taking place there. And yet for many American progressives, Australia was also something of mixed blessing. For example, socialists' enthusiasm for what they saw as socialist or protosocialist experiments was tempered by doubts about the Labor government and especially about its enthusiastic support for the war under Prime Minister Billy Hughes.[14] But this ambivalence was not limited to socialists. In 1916 and early 1917 (that is, in the year or so before American entry into the war), highly charged debates focused attention on two specific Australian experiments and heightened interest in (and ambivalence toward) Australia still further.

Compulsory Military Training

One of these concerned the demand for universal military training or service or what in Australia was called, somewhat more accurately, compulsory military training (CMT). This was the central goal of the American preparedness movement, whose main organization, the National Service League, was founded in December 1914.[15] Blocking this push was the central goal of American peace activists and antimilitarists, who came together in the American Union against Militarism in November 1915, following President Wilson's sudden change of tack and partial embrace of the preparedness movement demand for military expansion.[16] Wilson's continued resistance to the core demand for CMT, even when that stance led to the resignation of Secretary of War Lindley Miller Garrison, suggested limits to the pressure that preparedness advocates could exert.[17] But the anxieties of the peace camp were further aroused by state legislative initiatives, especially in New York, where the 1916 Welsh-Slater Act required all boys between ages eight and nineteen undertake CMT, as well as by a supposedly innocent amendment to federal legislation, the so-called Hayden joker, that appeared to allow the president to introduce conscription in certain circumstances.[18]

The inspiration for the preparedness movement came from the British National Service League and its leading figure, General Frederick Sleigh Roberts. But Australia and Switzerland were the key examples to which preparedness advocates turned for support. Australia and New Zealand were the only English-speaking countries that had broken with the long tradition of hostility toward military compulsion and (again taking inspiration from British National Service League) introduced CMT. Moreover, like the United States, Australia was a democratic society without a feudal hierarchy or property qualifications for voting. And better yet, CMT had been introduced by a Labor government.[19]

The Australian example was invoked from the outset by the chief American advocate of CMT, General Leonard Wood.[20] Like Britain's Roberts, Wood was a former army chief who presided over an organization whose supporters came largely from elite social circles.[21] And like Roberts, who feted Hughes, long a key Australian supporter of CMT, Wood seized on the Australian example. The example was widely cited, especially by progressive proponents of universal military training in the *New Republic* and elsewhere.[22] Among socialists, too, proponents—though few in number—rested their argument on a distinction between the Swiss and Australian "democratic" version of universal military training and the European "autocratic" version.[23]

Thus, as issues of war and peace came to the center of public debate in late 1915 and early 1916, Australia was ever more frequently cited. But for the extensive ranks of liberal, socialist, and labor antimilitarists and peace activists, Australia became a negative model. Australian developments were a weapon in the hands of opponents that had to be somehow disposed of or set aside.

A pamphlet for the American Union against Militarism by one of its leading figures, publisher Oswald Garrison Villard, argued that compulsory military service would foster the kind of subservience that is inimical to democracy. After supporting his case with examples from Europe, he turned his attention to Australia: "But we are told, Australia is democratic, quite like ourselves, and Australia has dedicated its youth to training in arms. . . . [W]hy should we not be like Australia? Surely there's no militarism there?" He replied by pointing to intense opposition in Australia and the thousands of boys that he said had been punished for noncompliance.[24] The preamble to the Socialist Party's 1916 election platform was also amended (by a membership vote) to emphasize that "we must refuse to put into the hands of [the capitalist] enemy an armed force even under the guise of a 'democratic army,' as the workers of Australia and Switzerland have done."[25] The AFL also rejected preparedness arguments at its November 1916 convention, reversing the previous year's decision and despite AFL President Gompers's ongoing support for them. And various articles in union journals referred to the Australian model in the wake of this.[26]

Industrial Arbitration

The other debate that increased interest in Australia concerned the growing calls for greater state involvement in the regulation of industrial disputes and especially for some form of compulsory arbitration. This was the approach favored by many industrial relations experts and more generally by many of the highly influential "progressive" intellectuals such as academic pioneer John Commons and *New Republic* editor Walter Lippmann.[27]

Again Australia (and New Zealand) provided these advocates with their prime example. Established in 1904, the Commonwealth Court of Conciliation and Arbitration had become one of Australia's most distinctive institutions. As the editor of one union journal pointed out, "For years the advocates of compulsory arbitration in the United States have sung the praises of the personal-relations laws in Australia." He then went on to argue that a current Australian miners' strike showed that American labor was right to "set its face against this form of legislation."[28]

The arguments about compulsory arbitration received heightened attention in the period before the United States entered the war. One reason for this was the introduction of laws in Colorado and Canada as well as a forthcoming US Supreme Court case regarding the constitutionality of compulsory arbitration.[29] Another reason was the push by some delegates at the November 1916 AFL convention to over turn opposition to eight-hour-day laws and other forms of government intervention, including arbitration.[30]

But any such move was anathema to many in the AFL and especially Gompers. For the federation's longstanding president, such efforts represented a fundamental assault on the voluntarist system of industrial relations to which he was committed and ultimately on American freedom. He responded with "repeated denunciations of the Arbitration laws of New Zealand and Australia."[31] Three of the five times that the AFL's official monthly journal referred to Australia in 1914 concerned critiques of the arbitration system, as did all five of the times Australia was mentioned in 1916.[32] Commenting on a visit to the United States by Justice H. B. Higgins, the president and presiding spirit of the Australian Arbitration Court from 1907 to 1921 and formerly the attorney general in the first Australian Labor government in 1904, Gompers juxtaposed democratic American methods with paternalistic Australian ones. "Red-blooded Americans," he later said, would not allow the law to prevent them from striking.[33]

Indeed, Gompers adamantly opposed any sort of compulsion in labor relations—not just compulsory arbitration but also general laws limiting the workday to eight hours as well as proposals for social insurance.[34] Yet he was quick to join the preparedness bandwagon and throw his support behind compulsory military service. However, despite their common support for CMT, there was quite a gulf between the arguments of Gompers and those of Hughes (himself a former union leader). While Gompers argued for radical voluntarism in all matters except conscription, Hughes's campaign on behalf of conscription increasingly argued that compulsion was the essence of unionism.

Thus, as the issue of compulsory arbitration came to the fore in 1916, it produced a second wave of American commentary about Australia. But for many unionists, it again offered a negative model.[35]

The Conscription Referendum

In late 1916 and early 1917, the interest generated by these debates was augmented and eventually superseded by a new wave of interest in Australia following the country's decision to hold a referendum on conscription. And during this period, much of the earlier progressive ambivalence subsided. The referendum generated unprecedented American interest in Australia. Major newspapers covered it in detail, and the outcome was reported in scores of other newspapers—large and small—across the country. The level of interest was all the more remarkable because the referendum coincided with the final days of the US presidential election.[36]

The labor, progressive, and socialist press also provided extensive coverage of the referendum. The level of interest was not uniform. The *American Federationist*, for example, chose to ignore it, as did the *United Mine Workers Journal* despite its more oppositional stance. Moreover, some accounts could be misleading. Prowar socialist William English Walling attributed the result—Billy Hughes style—to the Catholic Church, farmers, and other "sinister forces." And in the *New York Call*, Ahern let wishful thinking get the better of him and argued that the referendum "may mean war's end."[37] Nevertheless, there was widespread US interest in the referendum, its result, and the subsequent split in the Labor Party, and most reports were thoughtful and reasonably accurate.[38] Commentators were particularly struck by the extraordinary nature of the referendum: "Modern history knows no other election like this," reported the *New York Call*, while the *Intercollegiate Socialist* thought it was "probably the most interesting experiment that has ever been made in a political democracy."[39]

Most saw the result as offering lessons for democracies in general and the United States in particular. According to the *Coast Seamen's Journal*, the result represented "the first break in the world-wide drift toward compulsory military servitude." The *Intercollegiate Socialist* suggested that "the result seems to prove that a modern democracy will not sanction the compulsion of men to bear arms except in the immediate defense of the state against invasion." A more qualified editorial in the *New York Call* agreed that it was a "pointer as to how the people of the United States would vote" but concluded that the closeness of the result showed that although conscription would have "no chance" while the country was at peace, it would be likely to win if the United States were threatened by a powerful enemy. The *Nation* argued that "the Australian election adds to the general assurance that the great self-governed Dominions will not act as Prussianism would have them do" and that "the social progressiveness of the [Australian] continent will be felt to be vindicated." And even the *New Republic*, though it soon changed its position, concluded that "what Canada and Australia still refuse to do, Americans will not do . . . whatever the theoretical advantages of conscription may be."[40]

Interest in the Australian conscription referendum quickly flared back to life in early 1917 as the Wilson administration moved toward entering the war and deciding what recruitment methods would be required. From early February to early April, debate focused on whether to enter the war; then for the rest of April and into May, the focus switched to whether to introduce conscription. The Australian experience now became Exhibit A in the struggle against conscription—a struggle that now drew together the vast majority of socialists, trade unionists, liberal antimilitarists, and peace activists, though not prowar liberal progressives like those associated with the *New Republic,* the handful of prowar socialist intellectuals, or Gompers, who briefly found himself isolated from most of his supporters in the AFL.

Interest in the Australian referendum must be seen against the background of preexisting demands for a war referendum in socialist and peace movement circles. As Woodrow Wilson moved the United States toward entry into the war following the renewed threat of submarine attacks on US commercial shipping on 31 January 1917, the demand for a referendum became the centerpiece of a last-ditch emergency campaign to keep the United States out of the war.[41]

The demand for a war referendum reflected the basic analysis of the British war skeptics who had established the Union for Democratic Control, albeit in the idiom of American-style direct democracy. That analysis had been popularized in the United States in the books of Allan Benson and was central to the Socialist Party's 1916 election platform and to Benson's selection as the party's presidential candidate.[42] The demand for a war referendum became a constant refrain in the *Appeal to Reason* throughout February and March and was taken up by a number of union leaders and activists.[43] And test referenda were conducted nationally by the American Union against Militarism and locally, often by congressmen, in a number of cities and states.[44] But the appeal of a war referendum extended far beyond socialist and union circles. Its most influential proponent was William Jennings Bryan, Wilson's erstwhile secretary of state, a three-time presidential candidate, and probably the second-most-powerful man in the Democratic Party, who made it the focus of a huge antiwar rally in Madison Square Garden in New York on 3 February 1917.[45] Following the breaking of diplomatic ties with Germany, nine resolutions calling for an advisory war referendum were introduced in Congress between 9 and 23 February.[46]

However, while American socialists adopted a striking (and internationally unusual) stance of full-throated opposition to the war even after the United States had entered it, many unions exhibited a general fatalism as soon as entry came to seem likely.[47] And in a way that was quite similar to that of their Australian counterparts in August 1914, this resigned acceptance became nearly universal after war had in fact been declared. Gompers took the lead, convening a special meeting of union leaders on 12 March 1917 that unanimously endorsed a resolution offering wartime support in return for guarantees about working conditions and a greater voice for labor in government.[48] But fatalism manifested itself throughout the union movement, even among those unions that at first opposed US involvement. For example, the seamen's union and its long-standing leader, Andrew Furuseth, though usually loyally aligned with Gompers, strongly opposed the AFL's proposed resolution (although Furuseth did not vote against it). Yet once the United States entered the war, the seamen rallied to the government. Similarly, the United Mine Workers, which had frequently been in conflict with Gompers, opted out of the special meeting altogether. The miners' president, John P. White, wrote to Gompers that he was "against the whole scheme of war and preparedness." Yet the miners also quickly rallied to the government once war was joined.[49]

Unions may have been fatalistic about the war, but they typically remained adamantly opposed to conscription—at least prior to its introduction. On this question, socialists, peace activists, and unionists were as one.[50] In contrast to Gompers's efforts to lead the union movement to accept entry into the war, any suggestion that unions should accept the introduction of conscription ran into widespread suspicion and resistance. The AFL's special 12 March meeting had already made clear that compulsory military service was "repugnant to the Constitution of the United States and the genius of our republic," and the AFL's Executive Council voted overwhelmingly to oppose compulsory military service.[51] Ambiguity in Gompers's public statements on the question elicited immediate public challenges in the labor press.[52] And a survey of two hundred American labor papers "failed to reveal a single favorable expression for compulsory military training or conscription" but found much opposition.[53]

Following the declaration of war on 6 April, opponents made an eleventh-hour bid to block conscription by again rallying around the demand for a referendum. The Socialist Party was particularly quick off the mark, and even the minority report of the prowar socialists had called for a conscription referendum.[54] Some months later, the Socialist National Executive Committee was still calling for Fourth of July demonstrations to focus on the demand for a "referendum on conscription."[55] A reorganized peace movement also made a conscription referendum a central demand.[56] And some unions appealed to the Australian precedent and suggested that at the very least a referendum should be held among AFL members.[57]

This was the context in which the Australian referendum returned to the center of public debate. After all, as the *Coast Seamen's Journal* argued, "in only one country has there been a genuine test vote upon military conscription and to the everlasting credit of self-governing Australia the proposal was rejected."[58]

Congressional Debate

These unusually high levels of interest in Australia also manifested themselves in the congressional debate about the introduction of conscription. Secretary of War Newton Baker had formally forwarded a draft bill to Congress for the immediate introduction of conscription the day after war was declared. The House Military Affairs Committee voted 13–8 against the president's bill and instead forwarded a bill proposed by committee chair Hubert Dent that sought to give voluntary recruitment a proper trial while allowing the administration to establish the infrastructure for a draft. The Senate Military Affairs Committee, however, voted 10–7 in favor of the president's proposal, leaving the Senate committee's minority, led by Kenneth McKellar, to propose an amendment along the lines of the Dent bill.[59] A highly charged debate began in both chambers on 21 April and lasted for a week.[60]

Consider the debate in the Senate. Nine of those who spoke against conscription invoked the example of Australia. Proponents on the other hand largely ignored it. Only two of them mentioned Australia at all, although one, the chair of the Military Affairs Committee, George Chamberlain, whose bill was before the Senate, felt it necessary to address what he described as the "partially true" argument from Australia in some detail when replying to critics toward the end of the debate. Those who invoked Australia regularly invoked Canada in the same breath; indeed, Canada often received precedence.[61] Eight of the nine opponents who invoked Australia also invoked Canada. Australia was invoked because it had rejected conscription, whereas Canada was invoked because it had not yet even proposed it. These were not the only comparative reference points. Examples from American history, especially the Civil War experience, were extensively discussed on all sides, while proponents regularly raised Britain's decision to opt for conscription as well as the experience of some other countries, notably France. But outside the United States, Australia and Canada were the favorite examples of the opponents. According to Senator Robert La Follette, "We should look to England's liberty-loving colonies rather than to England herself for our example."[62] "They have not applied the conscription system to their brave people," said Senator James A. Reed, "Why, then, should we be asked to apply it?"[63]

Two main lessons were drawn from the Australian and Canadian examples. The first concerned the success of the voluntary system of recruitment and the quality of the soldiers that it was said to produce. Six of the nine opponents who invoked Australia made this case, which of course reflected the centrality of the argument that voluntary recruitment should be tried first—the basic proposition of those opposing the president's bill. In a typical example, Senator Jacob H. Gallinger said that Australia and Canada had "no trouble in getting the very best soldiers the world has ever seen."[64] Likewise, according to Senator William E. Borah, their enthusiasm as volunteers made Australians and Canadians "the most effective fighters."[65]

The second lesson concerned the enduring relevance of the Anglo-American liberal tradition in those societies that most closely resembled the United States. This idea, too, was integral to the arguments made by opponents, whose amendment stated explicitly that "the traditions and history of our people favor the volunteer system." And this point was also raised by six of the nine opponents who appealed to the example of Australia. In a typical example, Senator Thomas W. Hardwick urged, "You must remember that we are talking about our kinsfolk, the English-speaking people, the same blood that we have, the same devotion to the ideals of English liberty and American liberty that our people entertain."[66] Likewise, Reed argued, "We are now asked to reverse the traditional policies of our country as they have existed from the first—nay more, the traditional policies of the English-speaking people as they have existed for a thousand years."[67]

The debate occasionally betrayed some misunderstandings. A couple of contributors claimed that conscription had been rejected by an overwhelming majority in Australia, though Senator Chamberlain corrected this.[68] And two others thought that conscription had been rejected in New Zealand as well as Australia.[69] In addition, some speakers tended to partake in the mythologization of the military prowess of the Australian and Canadian volunteers, proclaiming that they had been "at the forefront of every battle," had "probably saved the cause of the allies," and had "distinguished themselves in every field."[70]

The strength of the arguments based on appeals to the Australian and Canadian examples can be seen in the frequency with which the proponents of conscription conceded their significance. This is especially clear with respect to the argument about the enduring relevance of the Anglo-American liberal tradition. Senator William J. Stone, for example, argued in favor of conscription while conceding that "to me the principle involved in such a law is obnoxious."[71] And Senator Frank Kellogg advocated support for conscription while admitting that the very word "is odious to the American people."[72]

Eventually the House rejected the Dent bill by a 279–98 vote on 28 April and then approved the draft 397–24. And on the same day, the Senate rejected the McKellar amendment 69–18 and finally voted in favor of the draft, 81–8. These votes represented a major shift in opinion: at the beginning of April, it had not been at all clear that a majority supported the president's bill.

A final round of congressional debate about Australia took place on 1 May, during Senator La Follette's eleventh-hour effort to amend the conscription bill by including a provision requiring an advisory referendum on conscription.[73] The example of Australia's referendum lay at the heart of the proposed amendment, and the wording was modeled directly on it. The proposed question was, said La Follette, "exactly the question which was presented in Australia."[74] But the principle of conscription had by now been accepted by both houses, and the amendment was defeated by a 68–4 vote (with 24 senators not voting).

Transnational Effects

What was the effect of these changes in transnational interest? What was the effect of reduced Australian interest in the United States? And what was the effect of increased American interest in Australia?

By its very nature, the reduction in Australian interest meant that US developments had little immediate effect in Australia. In particular, little evidence suggests that the earlier calls for a war referendum provision in the United States had much impact in Australia. The Australian labor press made only a handful of references to such calls and at most one or two tentative suggestions that they might be relevant in Australia.[75] In general, Australian anticonscriptionists did not look to the United States for inspiration.[76] Indeed, anticonscriptionists in the two countries had fundamentally different attitudes toward the desirability of referenda . In the United States, opponents of conscription sought a referendum to block its introduction, while in Australia, proponents sought a referendum to circumvent parliamentary opposition and keep alive the possibility of introducing conscription. Most Australian anticonscriptionists did not want a referendum since they believed they would likely lose.[77]

However, the reduced interest in the United States may still have had some effect on the conscription conflict. After all, the change in part reflected a strategic decision by anticonscriptionists in response to the surge of (British empire) loyalism. By closing off some avenues of criticism to the supporters of conscription, the lack of attention to the United States may have played a role (alongside many other factors) in conscription's narrow October 1916 defeat.

In the longer term, in the decades following the war, this implicit settlement on a kind of British parochialism may have had more significant consequences. Observers have often noted that the First World War marked the end of the period of social experimentation in Australia, experimentation that drew the sustained attention of a number of reform-minded scholars and activists in the United States and Europe. But it also coincided with reduced horizons within Australia itself. Australia's intense conflicts over conscription may have bolstered the Labor left but overall these conflicts left behind a political culture of heightened British loyalism that narrowed the terms of public debate and limited the viability of appealing to the most influential model of the promise and problems of the New World.[78]

What about the effect on the United States? It is difficult to determine the overall influence of the increased American interest in Australia because the different sources of this interest pulled in such different directions. Interest in Australian developments was at a peak, but the effect of this interest may not have been great, since the reasons for it tended to neutralize each other.

For CMT advocates it meant one thing; for antimilitarists another. For industrial relations experts it meant one thing; for many AFL leaders another. For labor party advocates it meant one thing, for pure and simple unionists another. For some socialists it meant one thing, for other socialists another. And for anticonscriptionists it began meaning one thing before later meaning another. In the first two years of the war, Australia started as one of the main positive models for proponents of military compulsion, only to become one of the main positive models for opponents of conscription in late 1916 and early 1917.

Moreover, the highest level of US politics—the office of the president—apparently had little interest in Australian developments. The index to the multivolume Woodrow Wilson papers lists only a handful of references to Australia in 1916 and 1917—a sketch of Billy Hughes and comments on Australian concerns about Pacific territories and the lack of shipping for wheat. But the Australian conscription conflict is not mentioned.[79]

After the war, interest in Australia soon returned to its normal low level. Indeed, it soon returned to a lower level than before the war, as Australian social experimentation petered out and international interest waned. Moreover, with the First World War putting a seal on its Great Power status, the United States had little need or inclination to attend to those developments that did take place in Australia. However, in the longer term, the period of increased interest in Australia during the First World War may have helped strengthen the idea of a fraternity of English-speaking nations, an idea that in turn underwrites the deep and enduring levels of cooperation evident to the present day.

War is a quintessentially transnational activity, and in the twenty-first century, no closer transnational ties exist than those among English-speaking countries, embedded as they are in a kind of "deep state" agreement on security and intelligence—the so-called five eyes agreement between the United States, Britain, Canada, Australia, and New Zealand.

Comparing Outcomes

Why was it harder to block the introduction of conscription in the United States than it was in Australia? After all, looking beyond the underlying economic, political, military, and cultural similarities between the two countries, American opponents of conscription seemed to have a number of significant advantages over their Australian counterparts. The United States had no formal or symbolic ties to the British Empire and its monarchy; on the contrary, the United States had a history of military conflict with Britain. There was a strong general US sentiment in favor of neutrality, and it had just been reinforced during a presidential election campaign in which that had been a central issue. The United States had much larger Scandinavian and especially German and Austro-Hungarian immigrant communities that had particular reasons to support neutrality. And there had been no prior acceptance of the campaign for CMT, even after the war in Europe had broken out. In addition, the example of the Australian referendum itself provided a powerful warning to those who imagined that sentiment could easily be rallied on behalf of conscription in a historically liberal English-speaking society, even in the midst of war.

A number of differences suggest potential explanatory factors. As Diane Kirkby observes elsewhere in this volume, the existence of women's suffrage in Australia may have amplified the voices of women peace activists there (even though their American sisters were arguably more prominent and numerous among the high leadership of peace and anticonscription organizations) as politicians sought to factor in women's opinions. However, where the weight of women's attitudes toward conscription actually lay remains unclear.[80] Support for conscription by American Catholic cardinal James Gibbons may have had some influence, although the anticonscription role of his (soon-to-be) Australian counterpart, coadjutor archbishop Daniel Mannix, in the first Australian referendum was limited, and a range of attitudes existed among the church hierarchy in both countries.[81] The preemptive German attacks on American commercial shipping while the United States was still neutral had no counterpart in Australia, although by the time of the first referendum, Australians had of course suffered far more extensive losses. And the extraordinary sui generis dispute over former president Theodore Roosevelt's efforts to raise a volunteer force under his command and President's Wilson's determination to stop it may have helped to scuttle opposition by leading some Democratic congressmen otherwise cautious about conscription to favor it as a way of keeping Roosevelt contained.[82]

However, two differences especially stand out. The first concerns the precocious political strength of the labor movement in Australia. Australia entered the war with the world's most electorally powerful labor movement, and within weeks of the outbreak of war, the Labor Party retook control of the federal government, receiving 50.9 percent of the vote, forty-two of the seventy-five seats in the House of Representatives, and thirty-one of the thirty-six seats in the Senate.[83] In the United States, most union leaders continued to oppose the establishment of a labor-based party, and in the 1916 elections, the Socialist Party candidate received just 3.2 percent of the presidential vote and the party held one seat in the House of Representatives and no seats in the Senate.[84]

Initially, members of the US Congress, especially Democrats, also expressed widespread initial opposition to conscription. Yet what seemed like an anti-conscription majority in Congress in early April 1917 melted away within three weeks. On its face, this seems paradoxical. The US president, in a system with notoriously weak party discipline, was able to get many opponents within his party to toe his line, while the Australian prime minister, despite a far stronger system of party discipline, was not. But the paradox was only apparent. What mattered was who controlled the party machinery. And in Australia, at least on this issue, anticonscriptionist MPs, the extraparliamentary party, and the unions that had established it gained the upper hand. In both cases (as in Britain), the ruling party was divided. President Wilson had to rely on his Republican opponents to bring his bill to the floor of the House. But Labor's supermajority in the Australian Senate placed opponents in an unusually strong position. Even with the support of the opposition Liberals, Hughes could not command a majority in the Senate.

The second factor that stands out is the temporal compression of developments in the United States. In Australia, the debate over CMT was in full swing at least half a dozen years before war broke out; the decision to support the war took place in the days before its outbreak; and the debate about whether to introduce conscription began about one year into the war and culminated more than a year later. In the United States, all these developments took place well after the outbreak of the war within a much shorter period of time.

As a result, Americans had far longer to mobilize opposition to the war than Australians—two and half years rather than three or four days. But Australians had far longer to mobilize opposition to conscription (in the period following the decision to enter the war and before the legislative preferences of the country's top leader were declared)—more than two years rather than two days. In addition, although a related movement of opposition to CMT and preparedness had been organized in the United States since the early months of 1915, Australian anticonscriptionists could build on a movement against CMT that had been gathering momentum since its enactment in 1909.

Note the speed with which events unfolded in the United States—all just after the country had reelected a president for keeping it out of the war. On 31 January 1917, Germany announced the resumption of submarine attacks against neutral ships bound for Britain or France. On 3 February, diplomatic relations with Germany were ended. By mid-March, four commercial ships had been sunk. On 2 April, Wilson asked Congress for a declaration of war and foreshadowed his intention to ask for conscription. On 4 April, Congress voted to enter the war. On 6 April, war was declared and legislation to introduce conscription was sent to Congress. In three weeks, it was all over. On 28 April, both houses passed a version of the president's bill. By 18 May, the slight differences—and the wild-card problem of Theodore Roosevelt—had been settled and the act was signed into law. On 5 June, all men aged twenty-one to thirty were required to register.

John Spargo's minority report to the Socialist Party's St. Louis Convention on 7 April contained some hint of the potential for an Australian-style prowar but anticonscription campaign.[85] And more generally, many activists agreed with the *Appeal to Reason* that "now that war has been declared the fight of the liberal forces must be directed against conscription and censorship."[86] But major anticonscription forces, including the Socialist Party, (understandably) remained focused on opposing entry into the war itself. Indeed to settle the debate between pro-and antiwar socialists, the party held a referendum of members whose outcome was announced on 7 July. Socialists, unionists, and antimilitarists and peace activists did not have time to give up on opposing the war and reorganize around opposing conscription before it had been enacted.

Comparison with the United States also points to the importance of timing in the success of the Australian anticonscription campaign. Early in the war, the newly elected Labor government had no difficulty in passing sweeping measures like the War Precautions Act. A similar "early war" frame of mind is apparent in the US Congress in the months after American entry into the war, when both the Espionage Act and conscription passed.[87] And the US experience provides some support for the claim that if the Australian government had demanded conscription soon after the outbreak of war, the parliament might well have passed it.

In some ways, legislative opposition in the two countries was more similar than it at first seems. In both cases, a number of opponents were looking for a compromise with the pro-conscription leadership of their party. Indeed, some may have been more concerned with avoiding responsibility for the introduction of conscription than with opposing it.[88] The compromise sought by American congressional opponents—a voluntary recruitment trial alongside the establishment of the machinery for conscription should the president deem it necessary—was similar to the compromise offered by the Australian proponent-in-chief, Prime Minister Hughes (a further trial of the voluntary system plus a referendum to establish acceptance of the principle of conscription). That Hughes was forced to offer something similar to what congressional opponents sought testifies, however, to the greater strength of the Australian anticonscription movement and its hold within the parliamentary Labor Party.

Comparison also highlights the importance of the "Billy-free months" in the first half of 1916 when the prime minister was away in Britain. These months were marked by both uncertainty and growing suspicion of the government's intentions—and especially those of the prime minister. That period enabled opponents of conscription to take the initiative and gave them the time to build a powerful movement of opposition in the Labor Party and the trade unions.

In short, American activists had time to build an antiwar movement but not an anticonscription movement, while Australian activists had time to build an anticonscription movement but not an antiwar movement. Like the precocious political strength of the Australian labor movement, this forms only part of the explanation for the different outcomes in the two countries. But it does help to explain both why opposition to the war was far more developed in the United States and why opposition to conscription was far more developed in Australia.

More particularly, it helps to explain why two such similar historically liberal New World societies ended up at opposite poles in the struggle against conscription. Alone among the belligerents, the English-speaking countries began the war without conscription and with a strong tradition of opposition to it. In most of these countries, conscription was eventually introduced, but not until well into the war and after a long period of anguished debate: first in Britain in early 1916, then in New Zealand in late 1916, and finally in Canada in late 1917. Only in the United States was it introduced almost immediately after entering the war. And only in Australia was opposition strong enough to stop it from ever being introduced.

Notes

1. Of course, smaller groups in most of the belligerents maintained some opposition to the war even after their entry into conflict, and that opposition tended to grow in importance later in the conflict.

2. Robin Archer, "Stopping War and Stopping Conscription: Australian Labour's Response to World War I in Comparative Perspective," *Labour History* 106 (2014): 43–67; Robin Archer, Joy Damousi, Murray Goot, and Sean Scalmer, eds., *The Conscription Conflict and the Great War* (Melbourne: Monash University Press, 2016).

3. Robin Archer, *Why Is There No Labor Party in the United States?* (Princeton: Princeton University Press, 2007).

4. For more on the influence of American left-wing reform thought, see Archer, *Why Is There No Labor Party?*, 17, 163, 209–14.

5. Wariness about appealing to American experience continued after the United States entered the war, not now because of its antiwar stance, but because of its immediate embrace of conscription.

6. See, for example, the small reprinted cartoons from the US labor press, especially the *Masses*, that sometimes appeared.

7. Canada in fact did introduce a conscription bill in May 1917, but there was no indication that it would do so prior to Australia's 1916 referendum. See Jack Granatstein and J. M. Hitsman, *Broken Promises: A History of Conscription in Canada* (Toronto: Oxford University Press, 1977).

8. See T. J. Miller, "Conscription—Its Effects on Industry and Business," Riley Papers, MS 759, folder 6/3, National Library of Australia.

9. *Labor Call*,14 September 1916.

10. For a fuller account of this argument and its supporting evidence, see Robin Archer, "Liberty and Loyalty: The Great War and Labour's Conscription Dilemma," *Australian Journal of Politics and History*, forthcoming.

11. *Nation*, 9 November 1916; *New Republic*, 12 February 1916; *Intercollegiate Socialist*, December 1915–January 1916.

12. *United Mine Workers Journal*, 14 September 1916; *Coast Seaman's Journal*, 1 November 1916; *Appeal to Reason*, 16, 23 December 1916, 24 March 1917; *New York Call*, 3 September 1916.

13. *Nation*, 17 May, 12 July 1917; *New Republic*, 22 September 1917.

14. On Hughes, see *United Mine Workers Journal*, 6 July 1916.

15. John Whiteclay Chambers, *To Raise an Army* (New York: Free Press, 1987), 81.

16. Ibid., 103, 109; Ernest C. Bolt, *Ballots before Bullets* (Charlottesville: University Press of Virginia, 1977), 10.

17. David M. Kennedy, *Over Here: The First World War and American Society* (Oxford: Oxford University Press, 1980), 18.

18. For American Union against Militarism pamphlets on New York and a similar initiative in New Jersey, see *The Bloody Fire, New Jersey Says: No!, New York's Sober Second Thoughts*, all in PE.036, Printed Ephemera Collection of Organizations, Box 10, American Union against Militarism Folder, Tamiment Library. See also Allan Benson in *Appeal to Reason*, 22 July 1916; *Coast Seaman's Journal*, 20 September 1916.

19. On CMT in Australia, see Thomas W. Tanner, *Compulsory Citizen Soldiers* (Sydney: Alternative Publishing, 1980); John Barrett, *Falling In: Australians and "Boy Conscription," 1911–1915* (Sydney: Hale and Iremonger, 1979).

20. See, for example, Leonard Wood, *Our Military History* (Chicago: Reilly and Britton, 1916), 193–213; Leonard Wood, statements regarding universal military training, 18 December 1916, in *Universal Military Training: Statements Made by Maj. Gen. Leonard*

Wood before the Senate Subcommittee on Military Affairs and the House Committee on Military Affairs (Washington, D.C.: U.S. Government Printing Office, 1917).

21. Chambers, *To Raise an Army*, 78–82. Wood had served as the US Army chief of staff from 1910 to 1914.

22. See "The Plattsburg Idea," *New Republic*, 9 October 1915; *Nation*, 17 May 1917 ("Australia has led the way on compulsory military service."); *Nation*, 12 July 1917.

23. See "Does Universal Military Training Educate?," *Intercollegiate Socialist*, December 1916–January 1917.

24. See *Universal Military Training: Our Latest Cure-All*, PE.036, Printed Ephemera Collection of Organizations, Box 10, American Union against Militarism Folder, Tamiment Library; reprinted in *United Mine Workers Journal*, 6 July 1916.

25. See Alexander Trachtenberg, *The American Socialists and the War* (New York: Rand School of Social Science, 1917), 28; cf. *Socialist Handbook, Campaign 1916* (Chicago: Socialist Party, 1916), 12, copy in PE.032, Printed Ephemera Collection for Organizations, Box 13, Socialist Party (US) Election Campaign Handbooks, Tamiment Library.

26. See, for example, *Coast Seaman's Journal*, 10 January, 28 February 1917. On Gompers's support for ("democratic") preparedness, see Samuel Gompers, *The Samuel Gompers Papers*, ed. Peter J. Albert and Grace Palladino (Urbana: University of Illinois Press, 2007), 9:329–31, 346, 364–65, 524, 10:38 (though he makes no mention of Australia).

27. See the debate with Commons in *American Federationist*, January 1917, 21–25; Lippmann's critique of the National Association of Manufacturers' rejection of the Australian compulsory arbitration, *New Republic*, 3 July 1915. See also "Experiments in Industrial Arbitration," *Nation*, 17 August 1916.

28. *Coast Seaman's Journal*, 20 December 1916. See also *Coast Seaman's Journal*, 31 January, 7 February 1917.

29. On Colorado and Canada, see *American Federationist*, October 1916, January 1917; *Coast Seaman's Journal*, 7 February 1917. On the Supreme Court decision (which ultimately upheld the constitutionality of compulsory arbitration by a 5–4 vote), see *American Federationist*, April 1917.

30. For this (unsuccessful) push, see *New Republic*, 2 December 1916.

31. Ibid.

32. See *American Federationist*, vols. 21, 23.

33. See "Compulsory Arbitration's Latest Evangelist," *American Federationist*, September 1914; *American Federationist*, January 1917. See also "Freedom Gives National Virility," *American Federationist*, February 1917.

34. For Gompers's rejection of a law to implement the eight-hour day, see "Regulation by Law! Law!! Law!!," *American Federationist*, March 1916. On social insurance, see his debate with Socialist congressman Meyer London, *American Federationist*, June 1916; "Not Even Compulsory Benevolence Will Do," *American Federationist*, January 1917.

35. Australia was also a problematic example for the Gompers-led AFL because his hostility to independent labor politics—conflict over which had been a defining issue in the 1890s—had hardened into an inflexible dogma by the early twentieth century. See

Archer, *Why Is There No Labor Party?* But for the one-third or so of AFL union leaders and delegates who had never accepted Gompers's position, Australia seemed to provide a standing counterexample, not least when the Labor Party returned to power in September 1914. However, the AFL seems to have decided to almost entirely ignore Labor's election victory. This was certainly not because Gompers was unaware of Australian developments. Indeed, he not only received delegations from the Australian labor movement but also made a point of following the Australian labor press, as he had since the 1880s. See *American Federationist,* September 1914 (on the US visit of Australian union leader Albert Hinchcliffe); Gompers to Henry Boote, 9 March 1915 (Boote's "delightful 'Touchstone' articles had afforded me so much pleasure"), Henry Boote Papers, MS 2070, Series 1, Correspondence, National Library of Australia. On Gompers's interest since the late nineteenth century, see Archer, *Why Is There No Labor Party?*

36. For a full analysis of why the referendum was held and the arguments that led so many Labor MPs to oppose conscription, see Robin Archer, "Labour and Liberty: The Origins of the Conscription Referendum," in *The Conscription Conflict and the Great War* (Melbourne: Monash University Press, 2016), 37–66.

37. For Walling, see *Intercollegiate Socialist,* April–May 1917. For Ahern, who also wrote for the *Australian Worker,* see *New York Call,* 4 March 1917.

38. For some of the more detailed accounts, see *Nation,* 21 September, 2, 9, 23 November 1916; *Intercollegiate Socialist,* February–March 1916, especially the long analysis by Vance Palmer; *New York Call,* 29, 31 October, 7 November 1916, 4, 6 March 1917.

39. *New York Call,* 29 November 1916; *Intercollegiate Socialist,* February–March 1917.

40. *Coast Seaman's Journal,* 8 November 1916; *Intercollegiate Socialist,* February–March 1917; *New York Call,* 31 October 1916; *Nation,* 9 November 1916; *New Republic,* 13 January 1917.

41. Bolt, *Ballots before Bullets,* 29–87.

42. Allan Benson, *A Way to Prevent War* (Girard, Kans.: Appeal to Reason, 1915); Trachtenberg, *American Socialists,* 26, 29. The platform demanded that foreign policy be exercised in public and by Congress rather than the executive and "that no war shall be declared or waged by the United States without a referendum vote of the entire people, except for the purpose of repelling invasion."

43. See, for example, letter to the *United Mine Workers Journal,* 22 March 1917; *Coast Seaman's Journal,* 14 February 1917 (both endorsing the war referendum and drawing a direct analogy to the Australian referendum).

44. Bolt, *Ballots before Bullets,* 49–52, 70.

45. *New York Call,* 3 February 1917.

46. Bolt, *Ballots before Bullets,* 52–70. Most were not granted a committee hearing, and none were reported out of committee.

47. For the majority and minority reports of the Socialist Party's emergency St. Louis Convention held during the week after the Congress declared war, see Trachtenberg, *American Socialists,* 38–45; *Appeal to Reason,* 14 April 1917.

48. Gompers, *Samuel Gompers Papers,* 10:17–45; *American Federationist,* April 1917.

49. See Kennedy, *Over Here*, 28, Philip S. Foner, *History of the Labor Movement in the United States*, vol. 7, *Labor and World War I* (New York: International, 1987), 101–9; John Laslett, *Labor and the Left* (New York: Basic Books, 1970), 221. For elements of fatalism in these unions even before US entry, see *Coast Seaman's Journal*, 7 February, 4 April 1917, *United Mine Workers Journal*, 8, 22 March, 5 April 1917. For White, see Gompers, *Samuel Gompers Papers*, 10:22.

50. See *Appeal to Reason*, 21 April 1917. Even progressive proponents of conscription acknowledged that theirs was a difficult position and that they were transgressing some basic values and traditions. It was, said proponents in the *New Republic*, "autocratic, unfair and ruthless"; "an evil but the lesser evil." See *New Republic*, 14 April, 5 May 1917.

51. Foner, *History*, 159–61.

52. *Coast Seaman's Journal*, 4, 18 April 1917; *United Mine Workers Journal*, 12 April 1917.

53. *Coast Seaman's Journal*, 25 April 1917.

54. See Bolt, *Ballots before Bullets*, 71; for Spargo's minority report, see *Appeal to Reason*, 21 April 1917.

55. Trachtenberg, *American Socialists*, 45–47.

56. Bolt, *Ballots before Bullets*, 71–87.

57. *Coast Seaman's Journal*, 4 April 1917.

58. Ibid., 11 April 1917.

59. Chambers, *To Raise an Army*, 153, 160–61.

60. For the debate in the House of Representatives, see *Congressional Record*, vol. 55, pts. 1–2, 866–67, 959–89, 1027–68, 1091–1148, 1181–1292, 1368–1432, 1502–57; for the Senate, see 829, 902, 907–21, 928, 930–51, 994–1024, 1071–87, 1150–80, 1295–1367, 1437–1501.

61. See especially ibid., 1076, 1322,.

62. Ibid., 1354.

63. Ibid., 1084.

64. Ibid., 915–16.

65. Ibid., 1446.

66. Ibid., 1323.

67. Ibid., 1072.

68. Ibid., 1218, 1323, 1342.

69. Ibid., 1193, 1076, 1084.

70. Ibid., 916.

71. Ibid., 1177.

72. Ibid., 1317; see also 1446, 1331.

73. Ibid., 1616–24.

74. Ibid., 1623.

75. See, for example, letter by F. W. Armstrong, *Australian Worker*, 14 September 1916.

76. The more obvious point of reference for the Australian labor movement were the unsuccessful 1911 and 1913 referenda to give the commonwealth control of trusts and prices and Labor's promise to hold another referendum, which Hughes abandoned as soon as he became prime minister, ostensibly in the interest of maintaining wartime unity. See

Ian Turner, *Industrial Labour and Politics* (Sydney: Hale and Iremonger, 1965), 77; Nick Dyrenfurth, *Heroes and Villains: The Rise and Fall of the Early Labor Party* (Melbourne: Australian Scholarly, 2011): 153–54, 185–86.

77. For more on the parliamentary arithmetic in Australia, see Archer, "Stopping War," 57–59, 66; Archer, "Labour and Liberty."

78. Robin Archer and Sean Scalmer, introduction to *Conscription Conflict and the Great War*, ed. Archer et al., 1–12.

79. See Woodrow Wilson, *Papers of Woodrow Wilson*, ed. Arthur S. Link, vols. 37–42 (Princeton: Princeton University Press, 1982–83). However, the index to the *Papers* may not tell the full story: the index to the *Congressional Record* also shows just a handful of references to Australia, yet there were multiple references in the actual debates..

80. In addition, some US suffrage activists pledged loyalty to the war effort in hopes of gaining support for their cause after the war.

81. On Gibbons, see Chambers, *To Raise an Army*, 158; "Would Christ Conscript?," *Appeal to Reason*, 21 October 1916. On the opinions within the hierarchy, see Patrick O'Farrell, *The Catholic Church and Community* (Sydney: New South Wales University Press, 1992), 324–26.

82. Chambers, *To Raise an Army*, 136–41, 167–70; Kennedy, *Over Here*, 148–49.

83. Archer, "Stopping War"; Colin A. Hughes and B. D. Graham, *A Handbook of Australian Government and Politics 1890–1964* (Canberra: Australian National University Press, 1968), 310.

84. Foner, *History*, 21. The Labor Party also governed all but one of the Australian states by mid-1915. As Stromquist shows elsewhere in this volume, the Socialist Party did have substantial support in local elections in some parts of the United States.

85. See Trachtenberg, *American Socialists*; *Appeal to Reason*, 21 April 1917.

86. *Appeal to Reason*, 21 April 1917.

87. Though while considering the Espionage Act, the Senate did vote 39–38 to strike a censorship clause (*Coast Seaman's Journal*, 23 May 1917).

88. Chambers, *To Raise an Army*, 154–55.

Workers against Warfare

The American and Australian Experiences before and during World War I

VERITY BURGMANN
JEFFREY A. JOHNSON

Before and during World War I, the Far Left in Australia and the United States campaigned against militarism and involvement in the Great War in differing circumstances. Australia's immediate involvement from 4 August 1914 came considerably before the U.S. entry into the war, which did not occur until 6 April 1917, so American agitation against "preparedness" formed a long period of antimilitarist shadowboxing before the real bout commenced. On the two home fronts, the Industrial Workers of the World (IWW), a syndicalist or revolutionary industrial unionist organization popularly known as the Wobblies, played contrasting roles. The American IWW was cautious, while the Australian IWW largely led the antimilitarist forces. This difference had significant ramifications for how the respective antimilitarist movements developed and presented themselves and the outcomes they achieved. Finally, wartime divisions in Australia developed not just within the wider society but also within the ruling Labor Party, causing it to split over the issue of conscription. However, the situations in the two countries were similar in one important respect: both were governed by parties that traditionally had qualms about militarist exploits abroad but threw aside these reservations to bring their nations enthusiastically into the fray.

The Australian Labor Party was committed programmatically to the cultivation of "Australian national sentiment," toying even with republican notions.

Nonetheless, Labor leaders had become more acquiescent toward Britain and the empire, a process especially apparent during Labor's 1910–13 stint in government. This transition away from customary Labor Party wariness about British imperialism was confirmed by Labor leader Andrew Fisher when he announced on 31 July 1914 that should the mother country become embroiled in war, "Australians will stand beside our own to help and defend her to our last man and our last shilling." Robin Archer argues that the Australian Labor Party's position stemmed from its precocious strength as a political party already capable of forming a government and therefore eager to hold the support of the median voter—in comparison with other labor and social democratic parties that opposed the drift to war.[1] Douglas Newton deems Fisher's speech a calculated political tactic to protect against the accusation that the Labor Party, filled with Catholic supporters of Irish home rule, was unfit to govern if war broke out.[2] The tactic worked. The election held a month after the outbreak of war convincingly returned a Labor government, judged by the nation at large in this period of patriotic fervor as competent to conduct the war effort. Yet many within the party, both in parliament and among the rank and file, especially in the trade unions, were hostile to the war, influenced still by labor movement traditions of antimilitarism and anti-imperialism—and fearful that workers' lives would be wasted and their livelihoods worsened. A moderate weekly labor newspaper in Melbourne commented at the outbreak of war, "The workers have nothing to gain in the evidently coming slaughter, but all to lose."[3] As its truth became ever more apparent, this position grew increasingly popular within the labor movement.

In the United States, governing Democrats were solidly isolationist until external exigencies prompted them to reverse more than a century of this strongly valued national tradition. Although progressive "liberal internationalists" argued for the necessity of foreign intervention to advance liberal causes, a broader American isolationism dated back to Thomas Jefferson's 1801 inaugural address, in which he warned that the United States should avoid Europe's "entangling alliances." When World War I broke out, the United States stood committed against involvement. American reluctance on the road to war is not surprising, given the attitudes of its citizenry and leadership. Most Americans felt Europe's quarrels were its own, and specific immigrant communities had compelling reasons why America should stay out of such conflicts. Irish Americans, for example, did not care to help England and so opposed engagement, while thousands of German Americans did not want to fight their countrymen. One of the more popular songs of 1915, "Don't Take My Darling Boy Away," encapsulated these broader American isolationist attitudes. Isolationism was a long-standing and valued American tradition, yet the preparedness movement swelled.[4]

During 1915, preparedness strengthened. Former president Theodore Roosevelt and others argued that a large and ready military remained critical to international prowess. Nonetheless, the current president, Woodrow Wilson, and the Americans who broadly supported nonintervention adhered to a neutralist course for almost three years. Wilson, a late-career politician with considerably more experience domestically (as governor of New Jersey) than internationally, typified isolationist feelings. "It would be the irony of fate if my administration had to deal chiefly with foreign affairs," he joked to a friend. However, he and his secretary of state, William Jennings Bryan, also a pacifist with little foreign policy experience, were consumed by foreign policy questions and the war. Even after the *Lusitania* attack, Wilson maintained in his declaration on neutrality that the United States "must be neutral in fact as well as in name during these days that are to try men's souls." And Wilson won reelection in 1916 with the campaign slogan "He Kept Us out of the War."[5]

However, President Wilson's positions had begun to shift, particularly in light of the threats posed by U-boat attacks and the Mexican Revolution. As US involvement seemed increasingly unavoidable, preparedness advocates claimed that a strong defense network, particularly a ready army and navy, mattered. The 1916 National Defense Act and organizations such as the Navy League and the National Security League institutionalized military and national readiness. Local branches of the Chamber of Commerce also supported preparedness in many communities. Returning from the East Coast, E. D. Horkheimer, secretary and treasurer of the Balboa Amusement Producing Company, announced in the *Los Angeles Herald*, "Preparedness is in the air." A witness to President William McKinley's 1901 funeral, the 1898 declaration of war against Spain, and world's fairs, Horkheimer believed that "nothing to date in our country has caused the people to rally like these preparedness demonstrations." Preparedness parades sprung up across the nation. In May 1916, 135,000 people marched down New York City's Fifth Avenue as part of a twelve-hour demonstration of preparedness. Another 130,000 took to Chicago's streets on 3 June.[6]

Such public displays became increasingly common. On 14 June 1916, Wilson headed Washington's Preparedness Parade in front of an estimated 60,000 men, women, and children. Papers billed it "the most remarkable patriotic spectacle the capital has even seen." By presidential order, all federal offices closed for the day as a wide array of individuals joined the march, among them cabinet officials, members of Congress, scientists, suffragists, and Boy Scouts. The president carried an American flag over his shoulder. Handlers released several hundred carrier pigeons into the air in front of the president "to take the message of preparedness all over the capital." Across the nation, parades and rallies celebrated American preparedness and patriotism.[7]

Because Wilson took considerably longer than his Australian counterparts to lead his country into the war, antimilitarist agitation in the United States focused much longer on campaigning against preparedness. For many—indeed, most—on the U.S. left, preparedness represented militarism run amok. In this campaign against preparedness, the Left, dominated by the Socialist Party of America (SPA), was careful to distinguish its position from simple American isolationism. Socialist ideology had never fit with militarism. For example, the 1912 platform of the Socialist Party of Washington State outlined formal objections to the Boy Scouts and the organization's militaristic lessons. In 1917 the Washington branch similarly adopted resolutions against compulsory military training in the state's high schools. Anarchists and syndicalists were also hostile to militarism and US involvement in the conflagration in Europe. Emma Goldman, for example, warned of the dangers in antiwar addresses across the country under titles such as "Preparedness: The Road to Universal Slaughter."[8] But American socialists led the charge. Without question, they proved the most unabashed and outspoken critics of US potential and actual involvement in the European war.

The SPA's Marxist interpretation of the war in Europe was clear: capitalism inevitably evolves into imperialism, as countries must expand beyond their boundaries; imperialism continues until capitalist nations confront each other's economic interests, and these confrontations inevitably result in war. "Every intelligent workingman and woman," announced the *International Socialist Review* in 1914, "is opposed to all capitalist wars." Socialists also stressed that workers provided the bulk of armies; war would therefore disproportionately waste working-class lives.[9]

Left-wing newspapers printed graphic reports, such as the atrocities at Verdun, to provide evidence for avoiding warfare. A French captain dramatically described seven thousand dead bodies "heaped" along a seven-hundred-yard front. Socialists used such vivid descriptions to encourage working-class opposition to war: "The workers of one country are misled to believing that they have some advantage in slaying the workers of another country," SPA leader Eugene Debs contended in the *Northwest Worker*. "War is Murder in Uniform," Debs later declared. "It is hell," the great agitator continued, "and the profit-mongers for whom it exists . . . are devilish."[10]

During the period of Australian preparedness before August 1914, socialists and IWW members dominated among the oppositional elements, as John Barrett acknowledges in his definitive history of "boy conscription" between 1911 and 1915.[11] After the Labor government's 1 January 1911 introduction of military training for males aged between twelve and twenty-six, the IWW Clubs issued a pamphlet that urged workers to refuse to fight "fellow workers of other lands" and to understand that "there are only two nations in the world—the working class nation, one despite race, creed, or color; and the capitalist nation, one in greed of gain, lust of exploitation, and unity of purpose to keep the working nation in subjection." Instead of patriotism, the Wobblies recommended "class hatred" and the international union of all workers, the IWW.[12] The social revolution required thoroughgoing industrial solidarity, so the IWW Clubs opposed all forms of divisiveness among workers, including craft unionism, "national prejudices," and "race hatred."[13]

The IWW Clubs had been established in Australia by the Socialist Labor Party (SLP) beginning in 1907. The SLP members were followers of American socialist Daniel De Leon, leader of the Detroit IWW, and placed equal emphasis on industrial unionism and socialist party organizing. Although the nonpolitical Chicago IWW, which was founded in Adelaide in 1911, became Australia's dominant IWW faction after its establishment and especially after 1914, IWW ideas were first brought to Australia by the earlier IWW Clubs and the SLP, which founded them. The SLP's weekly newspaper, *The People*, emphasized that the enemy was at home, not abroad. National prejudices and racial hatreds were "fostered by the ruling class and its emissaries" to keep workers of each nation "ready at command to fly at and tear one another's throats with the ferocity of wild beasts."[14] The SLP highlighted the Labor Party's sordid role in the process: "In defense of its infamous act of introducing child-conscription into Australia," Labor painted a lurid picture of a brown Australia "to get the working class of Australia shackled to Conscription and militarism."[15] The 1912 SLP Conference's anticonscription resolution ended, "The workers of the world, being a wage-slave class with economic interests in common, have no quarrel with each other, and urge upon the workers to organise upon the basis of the preamble of the I.W.W. and the S.L.P., for the complete overthrow of capitalism and the establishment of a universal republic."[16]

The other major socialist formation, the Australian Socialist Party (ASP), played a prominent role in encouraging boys to refuse to register. Like the SLP, the ASP supported the Second International's resolution for a general strike in the event of imminent war so that "the threat of industrial war [would] force the capitalists to refrain from military war."[17] In March 1912, ASP leader Harry Holland was one of the first parents convicted for failing to register his son for military training. Holland's pamphlet, *The Crime of Conscription*, published by the ASP, counseled all working-class boys to refuse drill: "We Socialists are no patriots!"[18] The only socialists who demurred were some members of the Victorian Socialist Party, close to the Labor government. Their prevarication on the issue of boy conscription prompted antimilitarist members of the Victorian party to form a Melbourne branch of the ASP in 1912. When the Victorian Socialist Party attempted to reunite with the ASP in 1913, the ASP refused on the grounds that the Victorian party supported Labor and many of Labor's members supported militarism, thereby discrediting the socialist movement.[19] A similar split occurred in Western Australia around September 1912, with the new Perth ASP arguing the older Western Australian Socialist Party was "a barrier to the progress of scientific socialism" because "they appear to believe that a Citizen Army has nothing to do with militarism. They support the Labour Party's Conscription Act."[20]

The Crime of Conscription promised that the ASP would urge a general strike to prevent Australia from marching armed forces against the workers of any country.[21] The party was unable to do so when the guns of August 1914 sounded, but the ASP remained confident that its socialist comrades in Europe were organizing a general strike to hamper warmongers.[22] The Australian socialists discounted the first information in mid-September that European socialists had done nothing to prevent the war, declaring such reports lies of the "yellow" press, and expressed confidence that "against war and militarism the Socialist party throughout the world is as solid as a rock."[23] The SLP likewise believed that the Second International was mobilizing to prevent war: "Alone, the Socialist, whether of German, French, British, Austrian, or Russian origin, sets his face against nationalities. . . . [N]o one country is so superior to any other country as to justify the sacrifice of a single life in its defence."[24] Although thousands of workers and many socialist party activists indeed mobilized to oppose the war, socialist deputies in Germany, Austria, and France voted for war credits, effectively putting an end to the Second International.[25]

When the truth was revealed, the ASP argued that alleged socialists who voted for war credits were no more socialists than Labor politicians.[26] "'The working man has no country,' said the authors of the Communist Manifesto, but the Socialists of Europe have been indulging in a lot of revisionism lately."[27] The SLP was likewise aghast to discover that European socialists had allowed "false sentiments" to govern their thoughts and actions.[28] In early 1915, *The People* concluded that the Second International had failed to prevent war because it was not organized along industrial unionist lines, resulting in an organization that could not enforce the general strike.[29] The collapse of the Second International proved the validity of Detroit IWW methods: ballots rather than bullets, industrial organization rather than military mobilization of the working class.[30]

However, the Chicago IWW led Australian antiwar agitation from the moment hostilities commenced.[31] In contrast, Melvyn Dubofsky argues, the American IWW "did nothing directly to interfere with the American war effort."[32] Other scholars of the American IWW broadly concur with this assessment, noting that the IWW even withdrew its antiwar pamphlets from distribution after deciding that antiwar activity would distract from organizing at the point of production and would invite government repression.[33] And indeed, the SPA faced government wrath as it continued its principled opposition to warfare in general and to US involvement in the Great War. According to Eric Foner, the SPA's opposition to the war "laid the party open to the massive repression" and despite some remarkable electoral successes as late as 1917 ultimately caused its demise.[34]

President Wilson's call for war came on 2 April 1917, and the formal resolution passed both houses of Congress on 6 April despite the continued objections of prominent statesmen such as William Jennings Bryan and Robert La Follette. The SPA quickly lodged formal protest. On 7 April, it held an emergency convention in St. Louis, where about two hundred delegates descended on the Planters Hotel as "the war clouds grew thicker and thicker." The attendees adopted a "united, decisive, and determined position on the question of war" that expressed the party's explicit antiwar commitment and reinforced objections to looming conscription and strike restrictions. Delegates drafted a pamphlet, *Proclamation and War Program*, and locals in many states arranged for distribution campaigns.[35]

As in Australia's prewar intrasocialist disputes over the Labor government's boy conscription, the St. Louis meeting revealed American socialists were not completely united on militarist matters, though opposition to both conscription and the war predominated. Socialist activist Kate Richards O'Hare chaired the new War and Militarism Committee, which listened to the delegates' varied positions. The hearings, with Washington State's Kate Sadler seated on the committee, indicated that a clear majority unabashedly opposed the war and hoped to continue their vocal resistance. Of the three formal opinions submitted to the committee, the first and most popular voiced clear opposition to capitalist wars and conscription. Three delegates offered a more moderate position that almost entirely reiterated the majority opinion but also upheld the right of socialists to mute their disagreements in public. Finally, a small but not insignificant minority resolved to support the war and make the sacrifices the nation needed. When the delegates came to vote on the matter, the convention excluded the middle position for its similarity to the majority one. During national balloting, socialists ultimately supported by a nearly three-to-one margin, opposition to the war.[36]

Though the St. Louis resolution opposing the war offered the appearance of agreement, the debates revealed the complex divisions that the war engendered within leftist American politics. According to World War I historians H. C. Peterson and Gilbert Fite, the war issue threatened to "split the Socialist party wide open." Throughout 1917, several popular and vocal socialist intellectuals criticized the SPA's antiwar position as "treasonous" and supported the American war effort. Some of them, including John Spargo, Charles Edward Russell, and Upton Sinclair, formally defected from the party. Their departure encouraged others in their belief that the party was factionalized between pro- and antiwar socialists. For example, the *Co-Operative News*, an Everett, Washington, publication, ran an article, "Socialism and the War," that observed how "the Socialists of America have split into two factions. It is one of the most remarkable political phenomenon [*sic*] of our history that at [a] time when the Socialistic movement of many years seemed nearest fruition, the Socialist[s] should fall out among themselves." According to David Shannon, "an overwhelming majority of Socialist Party members were strongly opposed to the war and were committed to agitation against it." In speeches, demonstrations and propaganda, the country's socialists voiced their objections to warfare in general and the Great War in particular. This majority position was expressed in 1917 by Adolph Germer, the SPA's national secretary, when he encouraged his comrades to "keep up the war on war. Don't relax one moment in your agitation."[37]

Though Australian socialists in both the ASP and SLP were also solidly antiwar, the IWW spearheaded left-wing opposition to Australia's participation. The principles and tactics of revolutionary industrial unionism provided an explicit and developed basis for IWW internationalism. Moreover, the ASP and the SLP were embarrassed by European socialist parties' support for war credits, further raising the profile of the IWW, which was untainted by the Second International's disgrace. Because the United States had not yet become involved in the war, the behavior of European socialists at that historic moment was less harmful to the morale and authority of American socialists than it was to their Australian counterparts; by the time the United States entered the conflict, new European socialist forces had somewhat restored the international socialist movement's antiwar credentials.

The Australian IWW was mindful of the dangers that had prompted American IWW circumspection about antiwar activity but threw itself wholeheartedly into antiwar campaigning. Perhaps such actions required less bravery than similar actions in the United States. Australia's IWW was protected by a strong union movement that was wary about the war from the outset. The American IWW's fears that antiwar activity would distract from industrial organization certainly did not hold in Australia. Instead, antiwar agitation increased the Australian IWW's opportunities to organize at the point of production, because such activities won support among workers inclined to be critical of the senseless slaughter and angered by inequalities of sacrifice on the home front. The IWW was therefore able to use this wartime moment to grow in size and influence.

On 7 August 1914, the Saturday night following the outbreak of war, IWW antiwar speakers in Bathurst Street in Sydney were heckled by "patriotic interrupters," and much argument ensued. The following day, the IWW organized an antiwar demonstration at the Domain, a popular outdoor venue in Sydney, at which orators denounced the war under an IWW banner that asked, "War! What for?"[38] On 10 August 1914, underneath a gruesome depiction of war, the front page of *Direct Action* answered that question: "For the workers and their dependents: death, starvation, poverty and untold misery. For the capitalist class: gold, stained with the blood of millions, riotous luxury, banquets of jubilation over the graves of their dupes and slaves. War is hell! Send the capitalists to hell and war is impossible."[39]

The following Sunday, the IWW Domain meeting drew an exceptional crowd whose members offered "ringing cheers" against the war and bought eight hundred copies of *Direct Action*. Detective Nicholas Moore visited IWW headquarters and asked J. B. King to promise that the Wobblies would stop criticizing the war; King demurred.[40] Instead, the next issue of *Direct Action* declared on its front page: "LET THOSE WHO OWN AUSTRALIA DO THE FIGHTING. Put the wealthiest in the front ranks; the middle class next; follow these with politicians, lawyers, sky pilots and judges. Answer the declaration of war with the call for a GENERAL STRIKE. . . . Don't be fooled by jingoism: The workers have no quarrel with Austria, Germany or Japan. The workers in those countries are as ruthlessly robbed and exploited as the workers of Australia."[41]

The IWW's distinctively insulting idiom railed against "patriotic boneheads" and "Mr Blocks" who boycotted "enemy aliens" in the workplace as well as the "mugs" who donned "the uniform of slavery and wholesale murder, and when the big war drum beats rush to the aid of a master class to slaughter their foreign class-brothers."[42] Mr. Simple, the cartoon character lampooned in *Direct Action*, was the type to go to war, devoid of class-consciousness and lacking insight into the nature of capitalism and imperialism. On the other side of the class ledger, "the whole horde of capitalist flunkeys" would sacrifice the last man and the last shilling "so long as he was not the last man and the shilling was not his own." "Let these cowardly wind-bags stop bleating and howling for blood."[43]

Direct Action emphasized the class-based inequality not just of sacrifices at the front but also of privations imposed at home. Bosses, the IWW pointed out, used the increasing unemployment in the early years of the war to attack wage levels and working conditions, forcing workers to work harder for less money. Landlords evicted the wives and children of men who had joined the army and even of those killed at the front. Wage workers lost their jobs as government finance was directed toward the war effort. Employers profiteered by providing the Australian government with goods for the army that were grossly underweight or woefully inadequate. The IWW argued that apart from the obvious opportunities for making vast profits, the war was useful to the capitalist class as a means of dividing workers and checking their rising aspirations.[44]

A "recruiting poster" that started appearing on Sydney buildings in July 1915 offered the ultimate IWW commentary on the hypocrisy of the war-mongers:

> TO ARMS!!
> Capitalists, Parsons, Politicians,
> Landlords, Newspaper Editors, and
> Other Stay-at-home Patriots.
> YOUR COUNTRY NEEDS YOU IN
> THE TRENCHES!
> WORKERS
> FOLLOW YOUR MASTERS!![45]

In December 1915 talented young *Direct Action* cartoonist Syd Nicholls vividly depicted the contrast in wartime experience between that of the worker who died at the front and the capitalist who prospered at home.[46]

Nearly seventy years later, activist Fred Coombe described the IWW as giving public voice to private feelings, "the thoughts in people's minds they couldn't articulate but the old Wobblies could."[47] Sydney IWW speakers—Donald Grant, Tom Barker, Tom Glynn, J. B. King, Charlie Reeve, Peter Larkin, and Jock Wilson—were "unrivalled in their agitational vigour," according to Norman Jeffery, alerting people to facts about the war obscured or repressed by the authorities. In Western Australia, too, Monty Miller, Mick Sawtell, and other Wobblies "exhibited courage and steadfastness with their anti-militarist views and critical attitude to the War." Ted Moyle, one of the central figures in the antiwar movement in South Australia, claimed that the IWW in Adelaide "faced up to the hostility of the soldiers and the 'patriots' practically on its own" as it "gave to its audiences what it considered to be the plain unvarnished Truth of having been wage-slaves they were now to become cannon-fodder in the interests of the same master class." In Queensland, IWW agitators regaled the crowds with antiwar propaganda. When Prime Minister Billy Hughes addressed a lunchtime meeting from the post office steps in Brisbane, Wobblies decided to "count the bastard out"; by the time they reached ten, the crowd had joined in so loudly that Hughes could no longer continue.[48]

In Australia, unlike the United States, the question of conscription was put to the people in referenda on 28 October 1916 and 20 December 1917 and was defeated both times. These referenda provided opponents of conscription with invaluable opportunities to explain their reasoning. Peter Rushton observed that the IWW was thus transformed from an organization on the labor movement periphery "into the most provocative and vocal, if not the most important, organ of anti-conscription."[49] Ted Moyle considers the conscription issue "food to the I.W.W.," giving it "life and movement" and "elbowroom to agitate" because it was on "the front line of a great & popular mass struggle."[50] Left-wing activist Ernie Lane recalled that the IWW played a prominent and uncompromising part in the anticonscription campaign: "Unlike the official Labour movement, the I.W.W. with rare courage and reckless of all consequences denounced and exposed the true causes of the war as a deadly clash of interests of conflicting imperial capitalist groups."[51]

The IWW carefully distinguished its extreme antiwar position from the more muted philosophy of most organizations with which it cooperated in the anticonscription movement, describing them as "pure and simple antis" who were "unscientific and illogical since they uphold the capitalistic system." The IWW "not only opposes conscription, but it attacks militarism in all its forms."[52]

It was not simply that IWW antimilitarist propaganda was more extreme than anticonscription rhetoric; so also were the means by which it intended to contest any introduction of conscription. As early as 1 October 1915, Wobbly leaders urged workers to answer the threat of conscription with a general strike: "A Conscription Act should be the signal for industrial revolt and insurrection." Be prepared, the organization advised workers, "to stop every industry and every wheel in Australia, and tell these unscrupulous vampires that if they want blood a little may be shed at home." According to V. G. Childe, the organization's rhetoric produced the impression that it was a formidable and desperate body that would resist to the utmost any attempt to impose compulsory service.[53]

Yet the IWW also made two distinctive points in its arguments specifically against conscription. Like radical antiwar activists elsewhere who argued that military conscription was the opening wedge for conscription of labor more generally, the Wobblies stressed that conscription would be used to discipline the workforce. In Australia in particular, the IWW also emphasized that as a fundamental matter of principle, opposition to conscription must not include pandering to racial fears about colored laborers who might replace white laborers who went to the front.

The ASP and SLP followed the IWW's lead. An editorial in *The People* announced, "Australia is in danger. At least the working class of Australia is in danger. The conscription conspiracy is raising its head and gathering all its force to shackle the workers with the chains of compulsory militarism."[54] In a lengthy November 1916 article, the ASP denounced the anticonscription elements of the Labor Party for using such a racial idea as the White Australia policy in the campaign, particularly at a time when efforts should be made to rid the world of national animosities.[55] The socialist contribution to the anticonscription movement was less dramatic than that of the IWW but was nonetheless significant. Indeed, the most famous anticonscription poem , "The Blood Vote," is attributed to W. R. Winspear, who served as the ASP's treasurer between 1912 and 1916 and often edited the *International Socialist*.[56]

In Australia the issue of conscription was to an extent separate from the matter of the war itself, as Robin Archer emphasizes elsewhere in this volume. It was possible, as many in the labor movement did, to support the war effort but vehemently oppose conscription. In the United States, war involvement and conscription were intertwined from the outset, with the government passing the draft law to introduce conscription on 18 May 1917, shortly after the US entry into the war.

Conscription emerged as a key component of the American preparedness campaign. Its advocates argued that Ralph Waldo Emerson's assertion that "our culture must, therefore, not omit the arming of men" implied the need for a draft. In line with contemporary progressive ideas of social reform, General Leonard Wood and others also thought that "military discipline would develop citizens morally, physically, and politically." Indeed, supporters said, military service and conscription would bring swift Americanization and even "yank the hyphen out of America," thereby offering distinct societal advantages. The *Chicago Tribune* even maintained that service would "reduce the criminal rate [and] produce a higher type of manhood, and level class distinction."[57]

The threat of conscription posed by preparedness strengthened opposition. At the center of labor's and the Left's objections to war were arguments against forced military service. A broad coalition of reform voices from labor, women's groups, and religious groups viewed preparedness with mistrust, sensing that the idea represented a menacing and overreaching government. Alexander Berkman (who famously committed what he called "the first terrorist act in American history" by attempting to assassinate Henry Clay Frick) ran a radical anarchist paper in San Francisco, *The Blast*. In one issue, Berkman urged those eligible for conscription not to register with the government: "The war shouters and their prostitute press, bent on snaring you into the army, tell you that registration has nothing to do with conscription. They lie. Without registration, conscription is impossible. . . . To register is to acknowledge the right of the Government to conscript." New York's *Sun* reprinted his pleas and observed that the comments "may interest the government," hinting that this type of disloyalty would not be tolerated.[58] Leftist critiques of the draft mounted by socialists and other radicals did not resonate with the American people. Nationally, according to Peterson and Fite, Americans did not generate a massive outpouring of opposition to conscription; instead, "the vast majority" of citizens "accepted conscription in rather calm resignation," believing it an obligatory and patriotic duty to support and raise an army.[59]

The debate over conscription that divided Australian society did not occur with such intensity in the United States. American involvement was relatively short, whereas war-weariness became serious in Australia. Americans did not receive the opportunity to vote on the issue, whereas the referenda in Australia encouraged polarization. Those who waged working-class war against warfare also galvanized the campaign against conscription, and the fight against compulsion was strengthened by the existence of a broader battle against militarism. By acting as a radical flank, the syndicalists and socialists who opposed patriotism in principle and waged war against all wars helped the anticonscription movement emerge as the comparatively moderate and reasonable compromise position that could attract majority support.[60] Like the IWW, the SLP and ASP opposed the war itself and Australia's participation in it, not just conscription, but in Australia, the IWW made the most noise about its antimilitarism and therefore had the most influence on the anticonscription cause. And the IWW subsequently paid the heaviest price.

In the United States, the socialists, outspoken against the war, felt the rebuke of the state most strongly and suffered the most. The US government sought to repress leftist and "disloyal" speech even before April 1917. During early 1916, *Labor World* cited seven attacks in ninety days on the "liberty of the working class press." Authorities arrested Margaret Sanger for "misuse of the mails," and the arrests of Elizabeth Gurley Flynn and Emma Goldman quickly followed. The government crackdown on those who opposed preparedness included suppression of three papers: *Revolt*, *The Alarm*, and a spring 1916 issue of Berkman's

Blast. For Berkman, this marked "an era of commercial imperialism backed by the bayonets of 'preparedness.'"[61]

With the US entry in the war, David Shannon argues that "a new problem confronted American Socialists" and radicals. Most socialist activity now involved antiwar agitation and dodging persecution for "disloyalty"[62] Though socialists had previously been targeted for government harassment, it escalated from name-calling and accusations to arrests and indictments. Minnesota politicians Jacob Bentall and James Peterson, for example, spent years in prison as a consequence of their anticonscription and antiwar actions. When Scott Nearing published an antiwar pamphlet, *The Great Madness,* indictments soon followed. All across the country, opposition to war provoked quick reactions from authorities.[63]

To empower the state in its repression of antiwar agitation, the federal Espionage Act (June 1917), Trading with the Enemy Act (October 1917), and the Sedition Act (May 1918) restricted speech and expression. By mid-1917, post offices regularly refused to distribute the *International Socialist Review* and *Appeal to Reason.* Later in the year authorities blacklisted approximately sixty papers nationally. National SPA leaders Victor Berger, J. Lewis Engdahl, Irwin St. John Tucker, William F. Krause, and Adolph Germer faced indictments. In June 1918 Eugene Debs delivered a three-hour antiwar speech in Canton, Ohio, telling listeners that they were slaves and "cannon fodder." Authorities convicted Debs under the Espionage Act, and he received a ten-year sentence.[64]

American antiwar socialists were also the main victims of the hysteria such legislation encouraged. In contrast, the IWW threat was of a broader industrial nature and was contained primarily by privatized retribution—beatings, lynchings, intimidation, and torturings by employers and loyalists. Corporations profiting and even profiteering from the war used wartime exigencies to justify thuggish brutality against Wobblies, who were proving effective in improving wages and conditions. This campaign of terror was backed up considerably by "criminal syndicalism" legislation enacted in twenty states and two territories between 1917 and 1920.[65] This legislation was unusually far-reaching in that it did not simply cover the actual commission of acts of violence against life, property, and government but made criminal the advocacy of doctrines that could be construed as supporting violent change to the existing economic and political order.[66] Federal troops were also used against IWW industrial activists in lumber and other strikes, but without legal sanction. War Department authorizations circumvented 1878 legislation that prevented federal law officers from using US troops, facilitating arrests on the pretext of protecting wartime production. Sheriffs could deny habeas corpus to arrested strikers on the grounds that they were being held by "military power."[67]

In these years during and immediately after American involvement in the war, being part of the nation's Left or in any way associated with "radicalism" had disastrous consequences for individuals. Undeterred, Debs again ran for president in 1920—from his jail cell. Antiradicalism reared its head again when Congress twice refused Wisconsin's Berger his rightful seat in the House of Representatives, and in 1920 the New York State Assembly unseated five socialists.[68] Though the war in Europe had ended, the 1919–21 Red Scare meant that US radicals remained under siege.

In Australia, however, the IWW rather than the lower-profile socialists most dramatically felt the iron heel of repression, not just as a consequence of their industrial militancy but also because of their leading role in antiwar activity.[69] In another contrast to the United States, this repression was carried out by federal and state governments run by IWW opponents within the labor movement. The IWW's antiwar agitation had encouraged the fragmentation of the labor movement into a left-leaning anticonscription majority and right-wing minority that favored conscription. Much earlier, the forces at the disposal of Hughes's national Labor government worked closely with those of William Arthur Holman's Labor government in New South Wales to meet the IWW's challenge.

Hughes, according to contemporary observers, "had felt the I.W.W. influence creeping into this party" and "was enraged at it."[70] In October 1916, Holman lamented that IWW members had "succeeded in gaining a good many important posts in the Labour world" and had "a controlling effect quite out of proportion to their numbers on the guidance of union policy."[71] IWW antiwar activism provided easy pretexts for state repression. The Hughes and Holman governments utilized the paraphernalia of patriotism to cast the IWW as an enemy agent and thus contest the organization's radical economic and social ideas, which were becoming increasingly influential within the labor movement.

For the poster prejudicial to recruiting, Barker was fined fifty pounds and given a two-hundred-pound bond or six months imprisonment with hard labor if he failed to comply with the War Precautions Act. Broken Hill miners responded by refusing to hear Holman on his propaganda tour, forcing him to stay on his train and return to Adelaide.[72] In March 1916, Barker was again convicted for publishing Nicholls's cartoon and was fined one hundred pounds; when Barker refused to pay, he was sent to jail on 4 May 1916.[73] Mat Hade's contemporary pamphlet claims that "the prosecution of Barker made known to everyone that the organisation was in existence. And from then on, it received a tremendous advertisement, and went ahead enormously."[74]

In October 1916, Holman and Hughes argued that the members of the IWW were violent saboteurs whose influence among workers should be confronted by the "true" representatives of the labor movement.[75] After a series of charges against and convictions of Wobblies, Sydney police arrested twelve additional Wobblies and charged that they did "feloniously and wickedly compass, imagine, invent, devise or intend to levy war against the King within the State of New South Wales." Specifically, police alleged that the activists were guilty of treason-felony for plotting arson against Sydney businesses.[76]

Humiliated by the defeat of the first conscription referendum on 28 October 1916, Hughes complained the following month that the IWW was "largely responsible for the present attitude of organised labor, industrially and politically, towards the war."[77] When the parliamentary Labor Party effectively expelled Hughes on 14 November, he and twenty-three supporters (more than one-third of Labor's sixty-five MPs) formed the National Labor Party; it ultimately became the Nationalist Party after it absorbed conservative members of the opposition Liberal Party in February 1917. Hughes's new "Win-the-War" government sought to win from Labor those voters who opposed conscription but not necessarily the war.[78] In the interim, the IWW was to be punished not just for its antipatriotism per se but for its radicalizing influence on the broader labor movement.

On 1 December, on the evidence of informants and witnesses anxious to avoid prosecution and of police testimony that contained many inconsistencies, a jury found the Sydney Twelve guilty. They received prison sentences ranging from five to fifteen years.[79] Labor organizations believed that, as the Newcastle Industrial Council in the important coal mining and industrial region north of Sydney put it, the Twelve were the "victims of one of the foulest conspiracies and frames-up known in history."[80] A few weeks later, Hughes's National Labor government enacted the Unlawful Associations Bill, which was akin to American criminal syndicalism legislation. Introducing the measure in December 1916, Hughes declared, "I say deliberately that [the IWW] holds a dagger at the heart of society, and we should be recreant to the social order if we did not accept the challenge it holds out to us. As it seeks to destroy us, we must in self defence destroy it." Passed on 19 December, the act provided that any member of the IWW could be imprisoned for six months.[81] In the next few months, 103 Wobblies were imprisoned, usually for terms of six months with hard labor, and many more lost their jobs. Jock Wilson's deportation resulted from an anticonscription speech in the Domain in which he declared, "I am not going to the war to have Broken Hill lead pumped into me by the Germans."[82] Wilson was one of the twelve foreign-born Wobblies deported; at the same time, American authorities, aided by the US Army, were shipping some American Wobblies to Australia.[83] They probably passed each other on the Pacific Ocean. In 1919, a Sydney newspaper noted that the IWW had been more effectively repressed in Australia than in the United States.[84] The organization had suffered severe punishment for endangering the existing order and Australia's participation in the Great War.

* * *

On both sides of the Pacific, those who sought to keep the working class out of the trenches suffered greatly for their principles. In the United States, nothing was gained while much was lost as the antiradical backlash exacted a high price, political and otherwise. American socialists, despite considerable maneuvering, could stop neither the war nor antiradicalism. While most socialists agreed on opposition to the war, Shannon argues, "they did not know what to do to stop the bloodshed. . . . [T]here was little they could do." Social critics and antiwar advocates of the period realized that the war was out of their control. As author and social critic Randolph Bourne recognized, "The war will go on whether it is popular or not."[85] The same held true in Australia, but the antiwar movement there at least succeeded in ensuring that military conscription did not compel workers to lay down their lives in a pointless war. This victory was facilitated by the fact that it was possible in Australia to separate the issue of conscription from opposition to the war. Indeed, the radical flank impact of the antiwar campaign on the anticonscription cause depended on the emergence of a distinct "pure and simple" anticonscription campaign, perceived by most Australians as the voice of reason amid patriotic hysteria on the one hand and militant proletarian antipatriotism on the other. In the United States, because conscription was imposed so quickly after the declaration of war and was not put to the people in referenda, opponents of conscription had little time or opportunity to mobilize separately from the broader antimilitarist movement.

Working-class antimilitarism before and during the Great War was an internationalist and international movement. Like many social movements then and since, it transcended national boundaries. Its adherents shared beliefs and values that bound them together around the world. Fundamental to the ideas they shared was the notion that workers should be loyal to their class rather than to their nation. Yet antimilitarists could not escape their nations. The circumstances of the countries in which they propounded their views provided the parameters that shaped the antimilitarist campaigns they conducted. In the United States, antiwar activists operated in a country with a relatively weak labor movement but an immensely powerful military-industrial complex that was anxious to be freed from the prevailing isolationist moorings. The socialists who led the US antiwar movement were truly beleaguered and might have suffered even more if US involvement had occurred earlier. In Australia, by contrast, the labor movement was precocious industrially and politically, with high union densities and a Labor Party regularly forming federal and state governments (though the wartime socialist and labor influence was greater at municipal level in the United States than in Australia, as Shelton Stromquist reveals in this volume). Precisely because Australian workers had experienced Labor governments and found them wanting, the most militant workers responded to the IWW critique not just of warfare but also of the Labor Party, sharpening the left-right polarization regarding the issue of conscription. Ultimately, Australian workers who opposed warfare, led to a large extent by the IWW, were repressed by the right wing of the labor movement—in government. As the public statements of Hughes and Holman and the actions of their governments indicate, this conservative minority resented syndicalist influence within the labor movement just as much as it feared antimilitarism and wanted revenge for the defeat of conscription, which would have forced Australian workers to join volunteers in the trenches.

Notes

1. Robin Archer, "Stopping War and Stopping Conscription: Australian Labour's Response to World War I in Comparative Perspective," *Labour History* 106 (2014): 62.

2. Douglas Newton, "At the Birth of Anzac: Labor, Andrew Fisher, and Australia's Offer of an Expeditionary Force to Britain in 1914," *Labour History* 106 (2014): 19–20, 25, 30.

3. Quoted in Brian McKinlay, *The ALP: A Short History of the Australian Labor Party* (Melbourne: Drummond, 1981), 39.

4. Harry Von Tilzer, "Don't Take My Darling Boy Away!" sheet music (New York: Broadway Music, 1915), available at http://library.duke.edu/digitalcollections/hasm_a6074/.

5. David R. Woodward, *Trial by Friendship: Anglo-American Relations, 1917–1918* (Lexington: University Press of Kentucky, 1993), 7; *Pearson's Magazine*, February 1915.

6. *Los Angeles Herald*, 12 June 1916.

7. Ibid.; Robert H. Zieger, *America's Great War: World War I and the American Experience* (Lanham, Md.: Rowman and Littlefield, 2000), 34. See also Norman Angell, *The Dangers of Half-Preparedness: A Plea for a Declaration of American Policy* (New York: Putnam's, 1916); *New York Times*, 15 June, 3 February 1916.

8. *San Francisco Chronicle*, 22 July 1916.

9. *International Socialist Review*, November 1914, 309.

10. *Northwest Worker*, 5 August 1915, 20 January, 1 June 1916.

11. John Barrett, *Falling In: Australians and "Boy Conscription," 1911–1915* (Sydney: Hale and Iremonger, 1979), 87–94.

12. IWW Clubs, *Anti-Militarism: An Appeal from the I.W.W. Clubs to the Australian Working Class* (Sydney: State Executive of the IWW Clubs, 1911).

13. IWW Club National Executive, *The Two Wars* (Sydney: IWW Club, n.d.), 1–31.

14. *The People*, 13 September 1913.

15. Ibid., 15 February 1913.

16. Ibid., 13 April 1912.

17. *International Socialist*, 24 June 1911. Founded in 1889, the Second International was the worldwide federation of socialist parties that replaced the First International, which Marx had founded in 1864 to promote international working-class solidarity.

18. H. E. Holland, *The Crime of Conscription* (Sydney: ASP, 1912), 13–15.

19. *International Socialist*, 20 December 1913.

20. Ibid., 28 December 1912.

21. Holland, *Crime of Conscription*, 13–15.

22. *International Socialist*, 15, 22, 29 August 1914.

23. Ibid., 12 September 1914.

24. *The People*, 27 August 1914.

25. See Andrew G. Bonnell, "The Great Catastrophe: 1914 and the End of the Second International," *Queensland Journal of Labour History* 19 (2014): 19–29.

26. *International Socialist*, 15 January 1916. See also *International Socialist*, 14 November, 14 October 1916.

27. Ibid., 14 October 1916.

28. *The People*, 7 January 1915.

29. Ibid., 18 February 1915.

30. Ibid., 4 March 1915.

31. *Direct Action*, 10 August 1914.

32. Melvin Dubofsky, "Dissent: History of American Radicalism," in *Dissent: Explorations in the History of American Radicalism*, ed. A. E. Young (De Kalb: Northern Illinois University Press, 1968), 202. See also Verity Burgmann, "Antipodean Peculiarities: Comparing the Australian IWW with the American," *Labor History* 40 (1999): 387–89.

33. Patrick Renshaw, *The Wobblies* (New York: Doubleday, 1967), 206–7; Thorstein Veblen, "Farm Labor and the I.W.W.," in *Essays in Our Changing World Order* (New York: Viking, 1954), 329; Joseph Robert Conlin, *Bread and Roses Too: Studies of the Wobblies* (Westport, Conn.: Greenwood, 1969), 80; Philip Taft, "The Federal Trials of the IWW," *Labor History* 3 (1962): 59, 71–73.

34. Eric Foner, "Why Is There No Socialism in the United States?," *History Workshop* 17 (1984): 72.

35. H. C. Peterson and Gilbert Fite, *Opponents of War, 1917–1918* (Seattle: University of Washington Press, 1957), 4–5, 8. This was the SPA's sixth national convention. Delegates from Washington, Idaho, and Montana all sat on committees. See *Northwest Worker* (Everett, Wash.), 5, 12 April, 10 May 1917; David Kennedy, *Over Here: The First World War and American Society* (New York: Oxford University Press, 1980), 26; David Shannon, *The Socialist Party of America: A History* (Chicago: Quadrangle, 1955), 93–94.

36. Shannon, *Socialist Party*, 95, 97.

37. Peterson and Fite, *Opponents of War*, 10; Shannon, *Socialist Party*, 99, 101–4; Kennedy, *Over Here*, 27; *The American Socialists and the War*, 1917, MSS 1513, Box 18, Folder

12, Oregon Historical Society; *Co-Operative News*, 18 April 1918; *Socialist Party Bulletin*, March 1917, Socialist Party of America Papers, Duke University, Reel 130.

38. Australian Peace Alliance File, Merrifield Collection, La Trobe Library; *Direct Action*, 22 August 1914; NSW Police Department, Special Bundles, re. IWW, Box 7/5543, State Archives of New South Wales.

39. *Direct Action*, 10 August 1914.

40. Australian Peace Alliance File, Merrifield Collection, La Trobe Library; L. C. Jauncey, *The Story of Conscription in Australia* (1935; Melbourne: Macmillan, 1968), 105; *Direct Action*, 22 August 1914; NSW Police Department, Special Bundles, re. IWW, Box 7/5543, State Archives of New South Wales.

41. *Direct Action*, 22 August 1914.

42. Ibid., 1 January, 15 May 1915; see also 1 May 1915, 1 August 1915.

43. Ibid., 15 August, 15 July 1915.

44. Ibid., 15 February, 16 October, 15 April, 25 December, 15 May, 15 June 1915, 22 August 1914, 1 April 1916.

45. Ibid., 1 October 1915.

46. Ibid., 4 December 1915.

47. Ibid., 15 February 1915, 24 June 1916; Fred Coombe, interview by Verity Burgmann, 15 May 1984.

48. Norman Jeffery, "The Labour Movement," 6, unpublished manuscript in possession of Verity Burgmann; Ted Moyle to Alan Finger, 10 August 1945, Ted Moyle, notebook no. 1, both in possession of Jim Moss, transcribed by Verity Burgmann; Ray Evans, *Loyalty and Disloyalty: Social Conflict on the Queensland Homefront, 1914–18* (Sydney: Allen and Unwin, 1987), 75; Dick Surplus, interview by Jim Beatson, 1972, recording in possession of Verity Burgmann.

49. Peter Rushton, "The Industrial Workers of the World in Sydney, 1913–1917" (master's thesis, University of Sydney, 1969), 207–8, 435.

50. Ted Moyle, notebook no.1, in possession of Jim Moss, transcribed by Verity Burgmann.

51. E. H. Lane, *Dawn to Dusk: Reminiscences of a Rebel* (Brisbane: Brooks, 1939), 174.

52. *Direct Action*, 28 October 1916.

53. Ibid., 1 October 1915, 6 May 1916; see also 9 October 1915, 1 July 1916; V. G. Childe, *How Labour Governs* (1923; Melbourne: Melbourne University Press, 1964), 146.

54. *The People*, July 1916.

55. *International Socialist*, 18 November 1916.

56. Verity Burgmann, "The Mightier Pen: William Robert Winspear," in *Rebels and Radicals*, ed. Eric Fry (Sydney: Allen and Unwin, 1983), 175–76.

57. Nancy Gentile Ford, *The Great War and America: Civil-Military Relations during World War I* (Westport, Conn.: Praeger, 2008), 8–9; Zieger, *America's Great War*, 34. See also Kennedy, *Over Here*.

58. *New York Sun*, 3 June 1917; Paul Avrich and Karen Avrich, *Sasha and Emma: The Anarchist Odyssey of Alexander Berkman and Emma Goldman* (Cambridge: Harvard University Press, 2012), 253.

59. Zieger, *America's Great War*, 34; Peterson and Fite, *Opponents of War*, 23.

60. For an elaboration of this argument, see Verity Burgmann, "Syndicalist and Socialist Anti-Militarism 1911–18: How the Radical Flank Helped Defeat Conscription," in *Fighting against War: Peace Activism in the Twentieth Century*, ed. Phillip Deery and Julie Kimber (Melbourne: Leftbank, 2015), 56–78.

61. *Labor World* (Duluth, Minn.), 22 April 1916.

62. Shannon, *Socialist Party*, 80.

63. Peterson and Fite, *Opponents of War*, 184; Clemens P. Work, *Darkest before Dawn: Sedition and Free Speech in the American West* (Albuquerque: University of New Mexico Press, 2005), 49; Shannon, *Socialist Party*, 87, 98; Kennedy, *Over Here*, 26.

64. *International Socialist Review*, November 1914, March 1915; "Platform of the Socialist Party of Washington, 1912," Ephemera, Washington State Historical Society; Ronald Schaffer, *America in the Great War* (New York: Oxford University Press, 1994), 13–15; *Co-Operative News*, 22 November 1917; Daniel Bell, *Marxian Socialism in the United States* (Ithaca: Cornell University Press, 1996), 105.

65. E. F. Dowell, *A History of Criminal Syndicalism Legislation in the United States* (New York: Da Capo, 1969), 21; Dubofsky, "Dissent," 202–3; R. E. Ficken, "The Wobbly Horrors: Pacific Northwest Lumbermen and the Industrial Workers of the World, 1917–1918," *Labor History* 24 (1983): 325–41; R. C. Sims, "Idaho's Criminal Syndicalism Act: One State's Response to Radical Labor," *Labor History* 15 (1974): 511–12.

66. Dowell, *History*, 46, 144–45; Sims, "Idaho's Criminal Syndicalism Act," 513; Dubofsky, "Dissent," 203.

67. Fred Thompson, *The I.W.W.: Its First Fifty Years (1905–1955)* (Chicago: IWW, 1955), 112, 116–17. On the role of military authorities in repression of IWW, see also Alfred W. McCoy, *Policing America's Empire: The United States, the Philippines, and the Rise of the Surveillance State* (Madison: University of Wisconsin Press, 2009); Peterson and Fite, *Opponents of War*; William Preston Jr., *Aliens and Dissenters: Federal Suppression of Radicals, 1903–1933* (New York: Harper and Row, 1966); Philip Taft, "The Bisbee Deportation," *Labor History* 13 (1972): 3–40.

68. Jeffrey A. Johnson, *They Are All Red Out Here: Socialist Politics in the Pacific Northwest, 1895–1925* (Norman: University of Oklahoma Press, 2008), 151.

69. For more detailed studies, see Verity Burgmann, "The Iron Heel: The Suppression of the IWW during World War 1," in *What Rough Beast? The State and Social Order in Australian History*, ed. Sydney Labour History Group (Sydney: Allen and Unwin, 1982), 171–91; Verity Burgmann, *Revolutionary Industrial Unionism: The Industrial Workers of the World in Australia* (Melbourne: Cambridge University Press, 1995), 181–245.

70. M. L. Hutchinson and W. Andrade, *Billy Hughes and His Critics* (Melbourne: Progressive and Economic Association, 1918), 8.

71. *Argus*, 12 October 1916.

72. *Direct Action*, 1 October 1915; Ian Turner, *Sydney's Burning* (Melbourne: Heinemann, 1967), 16; D. Grant, F. J. Morgan, N. Rancie, J. B. King, Barker Defence Committee, MS3516, IWW Correspondence, National Library of Australia; E. C. Fry, ed., *Tom Barker and the I.W.W.* (Canberra: ASSLH, 1965), 23, 25.

73. *Direct Action*, 4 December 1915, 29 July 1916; Turner, *Sydney's Burning*, 18–19.

74. M. J. Hade, *Justice Raped: Exposure of the I.W.W. Frame Up* (Sydney: McCristal, 1920), 3; Fry, *Tom Barker*, 28; *Direct Action*, 12 August 1916.

75. *Direct Action*, 21 October 1916.

76. NSW Police Department, Special Bundles, re. IWW, Box 7/5588, State Archives of New South Wales; P. J. Rushton, "The Trial of the Sydney Twelve: The Original Charge," *Labour History* 25 (1973): 56; Turner, *Sydney's Burning*, 35–36.

77. Jauncey, *Story of Conscription*, 223.

78. McKinlay, *ALP*, 46–48.

79. Kevin Seggie, "The Role of the Police Force in New South Wales and Its Relation to the Government, 1900–1939" (PhD diss., Macquarie University, 1987), 205, 180; *Argus*, 4 December 1916; H. E. Boote, *The Case of Grant: Fifteen Years for Fifteen Words* (Sydney: Worker Print, 1918), 8.

80. *Toiler*, 20 August 1920.

81. *Commonwealth Parliamentary Debates*, vol. 80, 18 December 1916, 10100, 10111, 19 December 1916, 10158, 10178–79.

82. Quoted in Alf Wilson, "All for the Cause," 79, unpublished manuscript in possession of Verity Burgmann.

83. Frank Cain, "The Industrial Workers of the World: Aspects of Its Suppression in Australia, 1916–1919," *Labour History* 42 (1982), 57–58; Ted Moyle, notebook 2, in possession of Jim Moss, transcribed by Verity Burgmann; Francis Shor, "Masculine Power and Virile Syndicalism: A Gendered Analysis of the IWW in Australia," *Labour History* 63 (1992): 98.

84. *Truth*, 29 June 1919.

85. Shannon, *Socialist Party*, 85; Randolph Bourne, *War and the Intellectuals, 1915–1919*, ed. Carl Resek (New York: Harper and Row, 1964), 41.

Domestic "Dogs of War" Unleashed

The Comparative Fates of Municipal Labor and Socialist Politics in the United States and Australia during the Great War

SHELTON STROMQUIST

The Great War weighed heavily on the lives of ordinary workers and their families. The issues of daily life—work, food, housing, and access to essential municipal services as well as the space for political expression and dissent—posed new challenges during wartime. Historians have lavished considerable attention on the geopolitics of the war and the role of nation-states in mobilizing their citizens as combatants or as workers. But this chapter shifts the focus to compare the impact of the Great War on the domestic politics of cities and their governance in Australia and the United States. How did the demands of war influence the political fortunes of social democrats in municipalities in both countries?[1] To what extent did municipal socialists' prewar gains survive wartime conditions on the home front? And how did the wartime experience in municipalities reshape the political landscape for labor and socialist parties in the postwar period?

Although local labor and socialist parties in a number of countries were torn between their internationalist principles and the nationalist pressures of wartime, they managed to carve out political space during wartime that enabled them to address the very real material hardships that workers faced.[2] Their wartime experiences provide a fascinating counterpoint to the generally prowar postures adopted by their national parties and many of their parliamentary leaders.

Much of the historiography of labor and socialist political development in the nineteenth and twentieth centuries bypasses the city as a political space. As Canadian political scientist Warren Magnusson has demonstrated, since the eighteenth century, political theorists, too, have made state sovereignty the focus of analysis and neglected local (and municipal) arenas. As new and in many ways limited forms of representative democratic government evolved, the city and its government took on a specific if subordinate role. The municipality, in his view, forms "an enclosure for popular politics" that renders its politics "safe for the state, the market, and other forms of government."[3]

The war directly affected the circumstances of everyday life in cities—the cost of living and daily bread, the disruptions of households and family life, the search for affordable housing, and women's employment opportunities or the provision of support for women and children temporarily or permanently without a traditional male breadwinner. In theory, the institutions of local government provided the first line of relief, and, indeed, social democrats in a number of countries had made significant inroads in this political arena before the war.[4] City councils, poor relief agencies, and school boards remained sites of contestation over the provision of public services. As wartime economic grievances mounted, citizens gathered themselves to protest conditions on the home front. Issues relating to the legitimate use of public space and the enforcement of wartime measures restricting speech and publication of opposing views also pressed to the fore. Conditions varied from one country—indeed, one city—to another. The extent of limits on the municipal franchise or even the suspension of local elections for the duration of the war (as happened in Britain) shaped local events and the forms of protest adopted, as did the nature and extent of hardship. To varying degrees, the war imposed common stresses and strains on municipalities and their working-class citizens across the countries at war.[5]

Before the outbreak of war, US socialist and labor parties had established a more robust foothold in municipal politics than was the case in Australia, not least because of a more unrestricted municipal franchise.[6] Socialist gains in local officeholding and the number of municipalities under their governance were more numerous in the United States between 1912 and 1914. But even as late as November 1917, well after US entry into the war, socialists' strength in municipalities was noteworthy.[7] Nevertheless, as James Weinstein has argued, the war massively disrupted and undermined that socialist progress in the United States. The Socialist Party of America took a principled stand against the war, as did the Australia's Socialist Party and Socialist Labor Party. In this respect, these parties were unique among socialist and labor parties of the affected countries. In the United States, socialists remained largely unified in that opposition and became a target of state and vigilante repression—mass arrests, violent suppression of meetings, and banned publications. This repression had the most decisive effects in municipalities where the socialists had established some strength before US entry into the war.[8]

Wartime Suppression of Dissent: Australia and the United States

Despite the fact that both Australia and the United States declared war on Germany and sent significant numbers of troops to fight in Europe, the two countries lay on the periphery of the Great War. Both experienced economic effects of the war but found their economies less adversely affected than did Europe's belligerents. Rising prices, especially for food, eroding real wages, spot unemployment, and housing shortages were generally less severe in Australia and the United States than in the other warring powers.[9] And, the economic stimulus of war production generated relatively tight labor markets, soaring profits, and a significant degree of economic concentration in both countries. At the municipal level the political momentum of prewar progressive, labor, and socialist parties was largely stifled. However, wartime economic hardships did produce some counter mobilization among progressive forces especially at the local level.[10]

In Australia, opposition to the war (or at least to conscription) produced a profound split in the Labor Party, the effects of which were felt more strongly in some states than others. But Laborites faced less outright repression of their opposing views than did socialists in the United States or than the syndicalist Industrial Workers of the World (IWW) in both countries. A Labor Party government at the federal level, while deeply and aggressively committed to promoting Australian participation in the war, nonetheless set limits on the extent of repression that might be directed at an opposition comprised very largely of the party's constituents. Labor's threat to block conscription legislation pushed by its own prime minister forced the government to seek to implement a draft through referenda, a decision that ultimately called forth a broad-based countermobilization.[11] And at least in some states—most obviously Queensland—the Labor government's outright opposition to conscription further encouraged popular mobilization against the conscription referenda.[12] In some respects, then, the broader anticonscriptionist movement in Australia provided cover for principled opposition to the war itself by the small but highly vocal IWW, the Socialist Party, and a growing segment of the labor movement.[13] At the same time, Australian Wobblies lent the muscle and energy that gave momentum to the anticonscription movement.[14] In the United States, no such cover materialized. The explicitly antiwar socialists and the Wobblies found themselves exposed and vulnerable to extreme repression and frequently violent retribution.[15]

Although the Labor Party remained a minority presence in most Australian local governments, its elected council members could still push forward a municipal agenda, which became a widely recognized if not fully implemented program. The adoption of further franchise reform in the postwar period—nearly universal municipal adult suffrage in many states—enabled local Labor parties to move quickly in some cities to become politically competitive around a well-recognized program of municipal socialism, although the limited powers of municipalities continued to restrict the scope of local-government initiative.[16]

The pattern differed in the United States, where wartime and postwar repression, including the active collaboration of the American Federation of Labor, the suffocating postwar Red Scare, immigration restrictions, and renewed open-shop campaigns, drove socialists and labor activists into retreat. In addition, intensifying factionalism within the Socialist Party of America effectively hamstrung any serious postwar effort to reestablish socialists' prewar municipal strength. And the retreat in the municipalities significantly eroded the party's strength overall.[17] One of the key questions is why governmental authorities and local voluntarist groups in the United States responded more harshly to wartime opposition than did their counterparts in Australia. It is instructive to examine comparatively the distinctive ways in which the suppression of wartime dissent played out in municipalities in the two countries.

Viewed through the prism of the local, the special character and intensity of state and voluntarist wartime repression of US opponents of the conflict becomes especially evident. Local and state agents (both private and public) did much of the dirty work sanctioned by the federal government under the Espionage and Sedition Acts. Operating in alignment with the US Justice Department and under the ideological umbrella of the Committee on Public Information, voluntarist agents of the American Protective League—typically including the "upper social, economic and political crust of each community"—carried out (illegal) arrests and detentions, wiretapped and opened mail of radicals and war opponents, and committed acts of "random terror."[18] In support of this effort, the *New York Times* editorialized, "These IWW agitators are in effect, and perhaps in fact, agents of Germany. The Federal Authorities should make short work of these treasonable conspirators against the United States."[19] For all of the disruptive impact of Postmaster General Albert S. Burleson's order banning socialist and opposition publications from the mails and of the work of local postmasters, whom Christopher Capazzola calls "the bottom-up state builders of the Espionage Act," the local suppression of dissent and the violence of attacks on local socialists and members of the IWW, the breaking-up of meetings, and the destruction of Socialist Party offices stand out most clearly.[20]

Such suppression of the Left in the United States did not have an exact counterpart in Australia. Verity Burgmann has noted that "the Australian IWW did not endure to the same extent the privatized retribution inflicted upon their American fellow workers: the beatings, the lynchings, the intimidation and torturings by individual loyalists." Unlike their American counterparts, Australian Wobblies' victimization came largely through the agency of state governments controlled by the more conservative Labor Party.[21] Under the War Precautions Act and the Trading with the Enemy Act, adopted with little opposition during the early months of the war, the government acquired the tools to allow it to censor publications and the mails. Prosecutions were fairly rare, let alone imprisonment for violations of the acts or for deeds that "advocate[d] or encourage[d] disloyalty to the British Empire or the cause of the Empire during the war." The campaigns against the 1916 and 1917 conscription referenda were conducted with little interference from the censor.[22] Popular actions against German immigrants, especially after the massive loss of life in Gallipoli, ultimately precipitated the internment of a total of 6,739 Germans and other "alien enemies" who were reservists in their countries of origin or of military age.[23]

Most victimized were members of the IWW, who, like their counterparts in the United States, were regarded with hostility by other segments of the labor movement and faced direct threats of imprisonment and harassment from employers and state authorities. The governing Labor parties in most states and at the federal level saw in the IWW's outspoken opposition to the war an opportunity to isolate and ultimately eliminate the organization and its most militant organizers.[24]

We must seek, then, a deeper understanding of the comparative severity of local repression in the United States than traditional accounts have provided. The class dynamics within specific communities may be essential to explaining the virulence of repression and the overlap between anti-immigrant and antiradical agitation. In addition, the artificial isolation of the war years from the period immediately before the war inhibits our understanding of the deeper patterns at work after war erupted.

Impact of Labor Conflict: Prewar and Wartime

The context of class war is ultimately critical to understanding the intensification of wartime repression in the United States, most notably in the West and Midwest. As important as wartime conditions were for understanding the attacks on socialists and syndicalists, class warfare and socialists' increasing prewar success at the local level played the pivotal role.

The "laborers' revolt" reached a crescendo in the United States just before the outbreak of the war in Europe, providing renewed incentive for local chambers of commerce and other business institutions, together with their political allies, to battle radical unions and their socialist cohorts. Those battles spilled into the preparedness period as labor markets tightened and employers sought to stem the unions' advances, particularly among unskilled immigrant workers and use the war emergency to stifle militant unionism.[25]

Wartime economic conditions precipitated a renewed, broad increase in US labor conflict—among East Pittsburgh machinists, Bridgeport munitions workers, Chicago packinghouse workers, and Colorado and West Virginia coal miners—that provides the context for the intensification of local and state repression of labor and its radical allies once the United States entered the war.[26] In addition, many of the most vigorously prosecuted cases against socialists and syndicalists did not come to trial until after the war, suggesting that deeper issues and polarities were involved than simply opposition to conscription and the war. The reemergence of a vigorous postwar open-shop campaign in midwestern industrial towns such as the socialist stronghold of Dayton cannot be separated from the local successes of employers and their allies in attacking their socialist and labor adversaries over their "disloyalty" during the war. Targeted for disloyalty and thus stripped of many allies, socialists and labor militants struggled to maintain their influence.

Levels of strike activity in the United States rose more sharply and involved more workers in a wider swath of industries than was the case in Australia, although that country experienced a notable escalation of workers' strikes in 1916–17.[27] Australia had not seen a surge in prewar strike activity comparable to the United States. The existence of a federal arbitration board and state wage boards channeled many conflicts into a process of formal dispute resolution that had no counterpart in the freewheeling US industrial relations "system."[28] A significantly larger share of the Australian labor force was unionized (32.8 percent in 1914) and subject to trade union discipline than in the United States (11.5 percent in 1914). This meant that Australia had fewer industrial disputes and that they were less bitter, less protracted, and marked by significantly lower levels of violence.[29] A surge of Australian patriotic fervor also discouraged conflict. In the United States, the war's initial impact was more modulated as a consequence of the delayed US entry.[30] Nevertheless, both countries witnessed a rising level of strike activity in 1916 and 1917. In the United States a tightening labor market fueled a sharp rise in strikes that embraced broad sectors of the industrial labor force and aligned the "control" struggles of skilled workers with the economic grievances of unskilled laborers. As David Montgomery has noted, "In each year of American participation more than a million workers struck, more, that is, than had ever struck in any year before 1915."[31]

In Australia, the rise in strike activity was initially concentrated in mining, but the Great Railway Strike of 1917, which ended in abject defeat, saw railway workers in New South Wales and in Queensland initiate general strikes that for a time included significant numbers of waterfront workers, coal miners, slaughterers, engineers, and tramway workers.[32] The 1917 collapse of the general strike in Australia resulted in a significant retreat from previous levels of industrial conflict over the last year of the war. However, the growth of trade union opposition to conscription, allied with segments of the Labor Party, produced a shift in strategy toward political mobilization. In the United States, strike activity continued at historically high levels through 1922, when massive defeats among railway shop workers, packinghouse workers, and miners led to a collapse in trade union membership and, except in limited sectors, the virtual disappearance of broader organization among industrial workers. By comparison, the labor movement in Australia came out of the war strengthened, with a growing segment of workers now committed to industrial organization.[33]

Prewar Municipal Labor Politics

Comparison of prewar labor and socialist politics in the municipalities of the United States and Australia suggests differences that had a bearing on levels of wartime repression and postwar labor and socialist political trajectories. The US socialist movement made impressive advances before the war, particularly in municipal arenas. As many as 180 US cities elected socialist administrations between 1911 and 1920, most before the United States declared war in 1917. In addition to the best-known example, Milwaukee, other cities in which socialists held power included Schenectady, New York; Reading, Pennsylvania; Flint, Michigan; Hamilton, Ohio; Minneapolis; Davenport, Iowa; Bridgeport, Connecticut; and New Castle, Indiana. In Ohio, 29 cities elected socialist administrations during this decade. According to Richard Judd, the Socialist Party of America estimated that in 1911 alone, 1,141 socialists won local and state offices in thirty-six states and 324 municipalities, and those numbers increased significantly over the next few years.[34] This widespread political mobilization posed a growing threat to local governing elites.

In Australia, the electoral data are fragmentary but suggest a more limited engagement by the Labor Party and socialists with municipal politics before the war. In New South Wales in the early 1890s, Labor Party candidates won scattered victories in MacDonaldtown (1893), Petersham (1895), Sydney City (1893, 1894), and most dramatically in the silver mining town of Broken Hill following a major strike defeat. After council election victories in 1896 and 1898, Labor won control of the Broken Hill city government in 1900 and remained in power for years to come.[35] The pace of Labor's municipal activity in New South Wales picked up considerably in the years just prior to 1910: Labor governments were elected in the working-class suburbs of Auburn (1908) and Redfern (1908) in addition to Broken Hill. Lithgow elected a labor-controlled council that held office from 1911 to 1919; Liverpool joined the ranks in 1911, and Dubbo followed three years later. At least 102 Labor candidates sought office in municipalities across the state in 1910, and in Sydney itself, Labor won 5 of the 26 seats on the city council in 1912; three years later, Labor took 11 seats as well as the mayor's office.[36]

Beyond New South Wales, Labor's efforts were constrained by relatively restricted rules for the municipal franchise and the smothering effects of a liberalism that battled for labor's loyalty. Nonetheless, in the industrial suburbs of Melbourne, the Political Labour Council won eight council seats in 1901. In the working-class suburb of Richmond, Labor augmented its two seats with two more. In 1905, the Council fielded seventeen council candidates in Melbourne municipalities, with four winning election. However, by 1914, Labor had majorities in only two municipalities, Port Melbourne and Richmond.[37] Labor also had a limited prewar presence in the Brisbane City Council and a few other Queensland municipalities.

One factor that may account for the varied responses of local authorities in the United States and Australia to the crises imposed by the Great War may have been the history and structure of local political governance itself. Australian states historically restricted local government activities to a limited set of functions pertaining to "services to property," such as street and footpath repair and garbage collection, although in some states—most notably, Queensland and Victoria—local governments fought to expand their responsibilities to include regulation of public health, housing, leisure facilities, and urban transit. But since municipal government was largely funded by property taxes, when city councils sought to expand services they faced what Martin Painter has called taxpayers' "hip pocket nerve."[38] In the most powerful states, like New South Wales, state government retained full control over police, education, public welfare, and public transportation, and virtually all funding for local government came through state and federal grants.[39] Nevertheless, the Labor Party eventually turned its attention to Sydney and offered a program intended to "capture the city and implement [Labor] policies."[40]

Despite the limited powers of local government, city councils remained potentially the most accessible point of democratic influence. Under some circumstances, councils became a vehicle for protesting and seeking redress for economic circumstances that were intolerable; councils could also be a site for the defense of the right to exercise free speech in public space, a function that was significant during wartime.

In the United States during the long colonial era, relatively isolated cities incubated traditions of self-government that nurtured a strong tradition of local control. Despite the commitment to localism that grew out of the American Revolution, the US Constitution was silent on the powers of local government and implicitly privileged the states.[41] The contested status of cities as corporations remained central to state-local government relations throughout the nineteenth century and beyond.[42] As legislatively chartered entities, municipal corporations were both instruments of states' governing authority and defenders of property rights. US Supreme Court decisions in the early to mid-nineteenth century decisively shifted the locus of governmental authority from cities to states. As the legal scholar Gerald Frug has written, "The subordination of cities to the state turned the political world as it then existed upside down." This shift of authority from city to state represented in part a response to changing urban demographics and the growing concentration of immigrant working classes in cities.[43] But Judge John Dillon's 1868 enunciation of what came to be known as Dillon's Rule most firmly and categorically subordinated cities to state authority: "Municipal Corporations owe their origin to, and derive their powers and rights wholly from the legislature. It breathes into them the breath of life, without which they cannot exist. As it creates, so it may destroy. [Cities] are so to phrase it, mere tenants at will of the legislature."[44] Dillon's theory became the ruling basis for subsequent court decisions and state political practice, though challenges to the rule arose in the early twentieth century.[45]

Progressive Era struggles over what came to be understood as "home rule" reflected the political demand for a more expanded definition of municipal rights. And within that space, urban reformers and socialists in some states moved to claim broader governing authority over municipal life and well-being.[46] In so doing, they reanimated elites' fears about losing their property.

In Australia, with governing power concentrated at state and federal levels, where the Labor Party had greater strength, repressive actions against war opponents were more muted than in the United States, where local authorities generally had more direct control over the public means of repression—local police forces. The local context of this class warfare in the United States is critical for understanding the nature and extent of wartime repression. The agents of that repression were first and foremost local businessmen and elites, for whom the suppression of labor militancy and rolling back the movement to municipalize city services flowed naturally into repression of war opponents. Indeed, the war provided elites with a convenient opportunity to mobilize a broader public against their long-standing labor and socialist (as well as syndicalist) foes.

Wartime Local Politics in Australia and the United States

A comparison of municipalities in wartime reveals both the limits and possibilities of labor and socialist activity. The Labor Party presence and activity in Sydney and Redfern; Footscray, Fitzroy, and Richmond in Melbourne and Brisbane; and Broken Hill, New South Wales, may be compared to similar activity in the Ohio "socialist" towns of Dayton and Hamilton as well as the cities of Cleveland, Milwaukee, and New York.[47]

AUSTRALIAN MUNICIPALITIES IN WARTIME

In prewar Australia, Broken Hill stood as the grand exception, although some Melbourne municipalities and Redfern in Sydney demonstrated significant Labor Party presence in local bodies.[48] Wartime intensified economic grievances, which continued to be aired in municipal bodies. But in many municipalities, the party's minority status meant that Labor council members could do little more than petition for municipalization of services, fight a rearguard battle on behalf of municipal employees' wages and working conditions, and demand unrestricted access to public space—town halls and parks—for use in anticonscription agitation.[49] Some Labor Party branches, such as the Leichhardt Political Labour League (Sydney) and the Essendon Political Labour Council (Melbourne) persistently petitioned their city councils to relieve distress brought on by the rising cost of living and to meet the needs of the unemployed, protect free speech, oppose conscription, and deal fairly with municipal employees.[50] In those municipalities where Labor's representation was stronger, such as Redfern (Sydney) and Richmond (Melbourne), Labor council members made significant headway in defending municipal laborers' rights, promoting the use of public space for anticonscription agitation, and providing relief to the unemployed. These elected officials improved the conditions and representation of municipal workers and challenged restrictions on what municipalities could do and on the limits of the municipal franchise.[51] Labor candidates for councils in a variety of municipalities during the war did not limit their program to these issues but challenged the limited powers granted by states to municipalities and demanded a much more expansive range of municipal activity. Running in Northcote (Melbourne) in July 1916, Angus McDonell argued for municipal trading (municipal ownership), day labor rather than private contracting, and municipal baths and markets. Labor candidates for Municipal Council in Sydney in December 1918 announced that "Labor is pledged to achieve" an ambitious program of municipalization "when the citizens by their votes give it the necessary power."[52]

With postwar changes in the municipal franchise and the renewed strength of Labor as a consequence of its grassroots wartime opposition to conscription, the Labor Party made significant gains at the municipal level despite the structural limitations of municipal governance. The postwar advances in Queensland and Brisbane were particularly noteworthy. Inroads also occurred in Sydney and in a large number of other municipalities in New South Wales.[53]

US MUNICIPALITIES IN WARTIME

Wartime initially enabled US socialists to build significantly on their prewar municipal successes by becoming the standard-bearers for opposition to direct US involvement in the Great War. However, the party's adoption of a strong antiwar platform at the special St. Louis Convention shortly after the declaration of war put it in the government's crosshairs and precipitated both government and vigilante action to suppress socialists' publications and public presence. Still, the electoral fruits of November 1917 initially looked promising. Socialists saw significant gains over their 1915–16 municipal vote, especially in those cities of the East and Midwest where they had established strength as early as 1911–12—New York City, Schenectady, Buffalo, Chicago, Minneapolis, Milwaukee, and others in Ohio and Indiana.[54]

Dayton and Hamilton, Ohio, as well as Cleveland and Milwaukee suggest the range of opportunities and barriers socialists faced. Hamilton's socialists had won control of local government in 1911 with the election of a city council majority, and in 1913 they elected the mayor and retained control of the council. Although defeated by a Democratic-Republican fusion ticket in 1915, socialists maintained a voice in city council throughout the war years, including 1917, when they garnered more than 40 percent of the vote despite again facing a fusion ticket. Their success rested on the maintenance of a ward-based system of representation.[55] Between 1916 and 1926, a mobilized working-class electorate defeated repeated attempts to "reform" the city charter and adopt comprehensive at-large representation and a city manager administration for municipal affairs.[56] Hamilton's voters also defeated wartime and postwar attempts by business elites to privatize municipal electric and natural gas utilities. Although the local socialist branch tacitly supported the party's antiwar position, its focus on municipal issues and its voice in city governance may have limited the virulence of the repression its members faced.

Unlike Hamilton, the city of Dayton adopted a new charter in 1913, after a flood devastated the Miami River Valley. The charter established a city manager form of local government with a small city council elected on an at-large basis. The Chamber of Commerce, which was closely identified with the city's open-shop tradition, promoted a "businessman's" government spearheaded by a "Citizens Committee but deliberately stayed in the background while strongly supporting the new charter. Democrats and socialists opposed charter reform, denouncing it "as a scheme of the business interests to gain perpetual control of the [local] government," an autocratic approach that would "destroy democracy."[57]

The November 1913 city council elections confirmed business leaders' dominance. Dayton socialists would have to wait four more years to mount a serious challenge for the at-large city council seats. The party's formidable 1917 campaign occurred in the context of rising wartime prices and a renewed push for municipally owned utilities. In a three-way primary race, the socialists came out on top by nearly nine thousand votes. With the election framed as pitting the people versus the business interests, the socialists seemed likely to win control of the council even under an at-large system. But a Democratic-Republic fusion ticket in the general election turned the tables, and the socialists were defeated for all of the at-large seats.[58] The most careful, if still biased, studies of charter reform acknowledge the socialists' defeat resulted from massive spending by "business interests" and the opposition's ability to bring the socialists' antiwar position into play.[59] Although the socialists received 8,659 more votes in the general election than in the primary, they were swamped by the "nonpartisan" fusion candidates, losing by roughly 12,500 votes.[60]

With the working class effectively denied representation in Dayton in 1917 despite winning more than 43 percent of the vote, the Socialist Party's antiwar position and its lack of direct influence in the new city council contributed to the party's more insular presence in the municipality. Full control of Dayton's municipal government enabled the business community to buttress the city's open-shop climate after the war and limit the development of a strong labor movement and the revival of a competitive municipal socialist program. Dayton's municipal socialists had found themselves exposed to charges of disloyalty as a consequence of the party's highly visible opposition to the war.

Cleveland had enjoyed a robust municipal reform tradition under the leadership of Tom Johnson, a Democrat and proponent of Henry George's single tax. Socialists found the programmatic ground cut from under them before the war and struggled to maintain a competitive political identity.[61] Wartime improved the socialists' position: in 1917, the party tripled its 1915 vote for mayor and elected two members to the city council and one member of the school board even though socialist mayoral candidate Charles Ruthenberg had been arrested for speaking against the war at a public meeting in June. The newly elected socialist council members then determined to "attend strictly to their civic duties" and avoid issues related to the war, but opponents on the council forced their hand with a prowar resolution. When they refused to back the measure, the socialists were permanently ejected from their council seats. As Judd has noted, a similar "unseating" occurred in Toledo for "disloyalty utterances," and members of Piqua's socialist local government were arrested for violating the Espionage Act.[62]

In some centers of socialist municipal strength, the party maintained its position despite the patriotic tide that washed across the country. In Hamilton, the socialists held onto a council presence and defeated charter reform despite fusion, and perhaps most notably, Milwaukee's socialists elected city attorney Daniel Hoan to successive terms as mayor between 1916 to 1920, even as their strength in city council eroded. The US Congress twice refused to seat Victor Berger, a prominent Milwaukee socialist and national leader of the party, despite his electoral victories, and in early 1919, he was sentenced to a twenty-year prison term for "conspiracy to violate the Espionage Act." (The US Supreme Court voted 6–3 to overturn his conviction on a technicality in 1921.) Like Berger, most socialist locals faced harassment and persecution that continued well beyond the conclusion of the war.[63]

Conclusion

Before the Great War, the lack of home rule and restrictions on the franchise severely limited municipal socialists' and Labor Party activists' access to power in both the United States and Australia; nevertheless, both countries witnessed some social democratic electoral successes in cities and partial implementation of a socialist reform agenda. The scale of those prewar advances was more impressive in the United States than in Australia. In the context of an intensifying class war on the US industrial front, employers and their political allies seized the opportunity of the outbreak of war in Europe, the expansion of war production in the United States, and a campaign for "preparedness" to move against the "new unionism" and its political allies in the socialist movement. The formal US entry into the war escalated this campaign to new levels. Municipal charter revisions and immigration restriction had constrained labor and socialist activism in municipalities. But the aggressive suppression of the Socialist Party by shutting down publications and meetings, arresting leaders, and encouraging physical attacks on immigrant and left-wing activists by local police and vigilantes was fundamentally a by-product of labor and socialist activists' opposition to the war. That opposition created openings for broader suppression that dramatically eroded the movement's prewar gains.

While suppression of wartime dissent had some parallels in Australia, it was neither as widespread nor as effective as in the United States. Because a Labor Party government orchestrated the campaign to suppress wartime dissent among its own party members both nationally and in some states, the extent of repression was inherently limited. Much of the effort focused on the relatively small IWW and the largely successful effort to isolate and destroy it as an agent of working-class mobilization. The fight over conscription further splintered the Labor governments' capacity to suppress dissent. With the formal split in the party, large segments of the labor movement and many Labor Party branches mobilized locally to oppose conscription in ways that reinvigorated local politics and Labor's municipal reform agenda. Critical to this development was postwar reform of the municipal franchise, which opened the door to wider working-class participation in local electoral activity.

The Left and the labor movements in the United States and Australia entered the postwar years on very different paths, profoundly shaped by the experience of the war and the shifts in local and national power. Socialists and the Labor Left in the United States entered a dark period of retrenchment, political persecution during the Red Scare, massive strike defeats in 1921–22, and a retreat from public influence for at least the next decade. In Australia, the Labor Party saw electoral gains in municipalities despite continuing structural impediments. The party's growth on the local level was fueled in part by the vitality of its grassroots mobilization against conscription and by the relative strength of the labor movement. While the 1920s proved turbulent and were marked by deep internal conflict within both the labor movement and the Labor Party, gains during wartime and in the immediate postwar period left Australia's organized working class vastly better positioned than their socialist and trade union counterparts in the United States to seize the opportunities of the next crisis, which arrived at the end of the decade with the onset of the Great Depression.

Notes

1. I use the term *social democrats* as a label for activists in labor and socialist parties who shared a fundamental commitment to the principles of democratic socialism in general and particularly municipal socialism.

2. This chapter is part of a larger book project examining the comparative history of municipal labor and socialist politics in seven countries—the United States, Australia, New Zealand, Germany, Austria, Sweden, and the United Kingdom—ca. 1890–1925.

3. Warren Magnusson, *The Search for Political Space: Globalization, Social Movements, and the Urban Political Experience* (Toronto: University of Toronto Press, 1996), 8, 10. See also Warren Magnusson and R. B. J. Walker, "Decentering the State: Political Theory and Canadian Political Economy," *Studies in Political Economy: A Socialist Review* 27 (1988): 37–71.

4. See Shelton Stromquist, "Municipal Socialism and the Contested Politics of Everyday Life, 1890–1920," in *Interventionen: Soziale und Kulturelle Entwicklungen durch Arbeiterbewegungen*, ed. David Mayer and Jürgen Mittag (Leipzig: Akademische Verlagsanstalt, 2013), 219–44.

5. Jay Winter and Jean-Louis Robert, eds., *Capital Cities at War: Paris, London, Berlin, 1914–1919* (Cambridge: Cambridge University Press, 1997). For Australia, see Max Solling and Peter Reynolds, *Leichardt: On the Margins of the City: A Social History of Leichardt and the Former Municipalities of Annandale, Balmain, and Glebe* (St. Leonards, N.S.W.: Allen and Unwin, 1997), 169–77; Janet McCalman, *Struggletown: Portrait of an Australian Working-Class Community, 1900–1965* (Ringwood, Vic.: Penguin, 1988), 89–119.

6. Some restrictions bearing on voter eligibility had been adopted in the United States, but in much of the North, voter participation in municipal as well as state and national elections remained relatively unrestricted. (The Jim Crow South was, of course, an altogether different story.) See Alexander Keyssar, *The Right to Vote: The Contested History of Democracy in the United States* (New York: Basic Books, 2000); Michael Perman, *The Struggle for Mastery: Disfranchisement in the South* (Chapel Hill: University of North Carolina Press, 2001).

7. Paul H. Douglas, "The Socialist Vote in the Municipal Elections of 1917," *National Municipal Review* 7 (1918): 131–39. For comparison of the Australian Labor Party's strength in municipalities before, during, and after the war, see Michael Hogan, "Municipal Labor in New South Wales," *Labour History* 72 (1997): 123–48.

8. James Weinstein, *The Decline of Socialism in America, 1912–1925* (New York: Vintage, 1967), 119–76. See also Richard A. Folk, "Socialist Party of Ohio—War and Free Speech," *Ohio History* 78 (1969): 104–15, 152–54; Richard W. Judd, *Socialist Cities: Municipal Politics and the Grassroots of American Socialism* (Albany: State University of New York Press, 1989), 161–84.

9. The argument for the war's lower impact on the Australian economy may be found in Marnie Haig-Muir, "The Economy at War," in *Australia's War, 1914–18*, ed. Joan Beaumont (St. Leonards, N.S.W.: Allen and Unwin, 1995), 93, 97, 105–6, 108–9, 115–20. For an overview of the war's economic impact in the United States, see David M. Kennedy, *Over Here: The First World War and American Society*, 2nd ed. (New York: Oxford University Press, 2004), 138–43.

10. Economic grievances bore home in municipalities in both Australia and the United States. See, for example, the eruption of agitation around unemployment in Broken Hill, New South Wales, reported in *Barrier Daily Truth*, 14, 15 May, 19, 22, 25 June 1915. For comparison in the United States, see reports on local socialist agitation in Dayton, Ohio, in John T. Walker, "The Dayton Socialists and World War I: Surviving the White Terror," in *Socialism in the Heartland: The Midwestern Experience, 1900–1925*, ed. Donald Critchlow (Notre Dame, Ind.: University of Notre Dame Press, 1986), 120. See also, for example, Local Dayton Socialist Party, Minute Books, 23 April 1915, 6 April 1917, Wright State University Archives.

11. See John Hirst, "Labor and the Great War," in *The Australian Century: Political Struggle in the Building of a Nation*, ed. Robert Manne (Melbourne: Text, 1999), 61–64. See also Joan Beaumont, "The Politics of a Divided Society," in *Australia's War*, ed. Beaumont, 48–52; Ian Turner, *Industrial Labour and Politics: The Dynamics of the Labour Movement in Eastern Australia 1900–1921* (Sydney: Hale and Iremonger, 1979), 97–121; J. M. Main, ed., *Conscription: The Australian Debate, 1901–1970* (Melbourne: Cassell Australia, 1970), 1–7, 31–107.

12. Raymond Evans, *A History of Queensland* (Cambridge: Cambridge University Press, 2007), 157–58; D. J. Murphy, "Queensland," in *Labor in Politics: The State Labor Parties in Australia, 1880–1920*, ed. Murphy (St. Lucia: University of Queensland Press, 1975), 200–204.

13. Verity Burgmann, *Revolutionary Industrial Unionism: The Industrial Workers of the World in Australia* (Cambridge: Cambridge University Press, 1995), 193–96.

14. Ibid., 198–201; Vere Gordon Childe, *How Labour Governs: A Study of Workers' Representation in Australia* (Melbourne: Melbourne University Press, 1923), 145–46.

15. The literature on the vigorous and sometimes violent suppression of dissent in the United States during World War I is enormous. See, for example, H. C. Peterson and Gilbert C. Fite, *Opponents of War, 1917–1918* (Seattle: University of Washington Press, 1957), 43–60, 157–80; William H. Thomas Jr., *Unsafe for Democracy: World War I and the U.S. Justice Department's Covert Campaign to Suppress Dissent* (Madison: University of Wisconsin Press, 2008), 89–109.

16. For general trends of increasing Labor Party success in postwar municipalities, see Hogan, "Municipal Labor," 128–29, 132–34. In Queensland, the story was quite different: see Gordon Greenwood and John Laverty, *Brisbane 1859–1959: A History of Local Government* (Brisbane: Ziegler, 1959), 296–303.

17. On the American Federation of Labor's wartime collaboration with the government, see Jennifer Luff, *Commonsense Anticommunism: Labor and Civil Liberties between*

the World Wars (Chapel Hill: University of North Carolina Press, 2012), 46–59. For strong evidence of the sharp declines in socialists' electoral success in municipalities between 1917 and 1919, see Weinstein, *Decline of Socialism*, 116–18. Postwar attempts to form local labor parties enjoyed limited success.

18. Robert Justin Goldstein, *Political Repression in Modern America from 1870 to 1976* (Urbana: University of Illinois Press, 2001), 110–15.

19. Peterson and Fite, *Opponents of War*, 50–68. Thomas, *Unsafe for Democracy*, , 89–109, 146–71, describes the patterns of local action against war dissenters that federal agents either fomented or failed to restrain. For the use of federal troops and agents to target striking workers deemed disloyal, see Goldstein, *Political Repression*, 107–21. For the massive roundups and detention of "slackers," see Christopher Cappazolla, *Uncle Sam Wants You: World War I and the Making of the Modern American Citizen* (New York: Oxford University Press, 2008), 41–53.

20. Cappazolla, *Uncle Sam Wants You*, 137–43, 153. Goldstein, *Political Repression*, 119–21, notes that the most aggressive and violent targeting of the Socialist Party came in the aftermath of its municipal victories at the polls in November 1917.

21. Burgmann, *Revolutionary Industrial Unionism*, 203–4. See also Verity Burgmann and Jeffrey A. Johnson, this volume. In Queensland, an atmosphere of intensifying labor conflict appears to have stirred into action private vigilantism to a greater degree than in other states, culminating in Brisbane's Red Flag Riots several months after the armistice. See Raymond Evans, *Loyalty and Disloyalty: Social Conflict on the Queensland Homefront, 1914–18* (Sydney: Allen and Unwin, 1987), 65–86; Raymond Evans, *The Red Flag Riots: A Study of Intolerance* (St. Lucia: University of Queensland Press, 1988).

22. Ernest Scott, *Australia during the War* (Sydney: Angus and Robertson, 1936), 53–54, 64, 69–71, 354.

23. Ibid., 108–14, 136–37.

24. Burgmann, *Revolutionary Industrial Unionism*, 206–28; Turner, *Industrial Labour and Politics*, 122–38.

25. For a discussion of the "laborers' revolt" and the events surrounding the US Commission on Industrial Relations's investigation into the "causes of industrial unrest," see Shelton Stromquist, *Reinventing "the People": The Progressive Movement, the Class Problem, and the Origins of Modern Liberalism* (Urbana: University of Illinois Press, 2006), 165–90. On employers' determination to use the war to undermine an expanding and militant labor movement, see Peterson and Fite, *Opponents of War*. See also Goldstein, *Political Repression*.

26. David Montgomery, "The 'New Unionism' and the Transformation of Workers' Consciousness in America, 1909–1922," *Journal of Social History* 7 (1974): 512–17; David Montgomery, *The Fall of the House of Labor: The Workplace, the State, and American Labor Activism, 1865–1925* (Cambridge: Cambridge University Press, 1987), 317–27, 332–56; Cecelia Bucki, *Bridgeport's Socialist New Deal, 1915–36* (Urbana: University of Illinois Press, 2001), 24–29; David A. Corbin, *Life, Work, and Rebellion in the Coal Fields: The Southern West Virginia Miners, 1880–1920* (Urbana: University of Illinois Press, 1981), 87–101; James

R. Barrett, *Work and Community in the Jungle: Chicago's Packinghouse Workers, 1894–1922* (Urbana: University of Illinois Press, 1987), 193, 200–202.

27. For data on strikes during the prewar and wartime periods, see *Historical Statistics of the United States*, pt. 1 (Washington, D.C.: US Government Printing Office, 1975), 179; *International Historical Statistics: Africa, Asia, Oceania* (Houndmills: Palgrave Macmillan, 2007), 138. For the broad outlines of strike activity in Australia between 1910 and 1920, see Malcolm Waters, *Strikes in Australia: A Sociological Analysis of Industrial Conflict* (Sydney: Allen and Unwin, 1982), 50–55. Less helpfully, see also Michael P. Jackson, "Strikes in Australia, USA, and the United Kingdom," in *Strikes* (Sussex: Wheatsheaf, 1987), 31–34, 38–39. Most influential has been the classic article by D. W. Oxnam, "Strikes in Australia," *Economic Record* 29 (1953): 73–89, but it gives very little attention to the strikes before and during the Great War. For the United States in the war years, see Montgomery, "New Unionism," 512–16. Less helpful is P. K. Edwards, *Strikes in the United States, 1881–1974* (New York: St. Martin's, 1981), 15–16.

28. Turner, *Industrial Labour and Politics*, 34–40. On the Victorian wage boards, see Charles Fahey and John Lack, "The Great Strike of 1917 in Victoria: Looking Fore and Aft, and from Below," *Labour History* 106 (2014): 81–88. See also Waters, *Strikes in Australia*, 109–10.

29. On the rate of unionization, see George Sayers Bain and Robert Price, *Profiles of Union Growth: A Comparative Statistical Portrait of Eight Countries* (Oxford: Blackwell, 1980), 88, 123. See also Waters, *Strikes in Australia*, 101.

30. On the immediate economic effects of the war for Australia, see Haig-Muir, "Economy at War," 97, 99, 106, 109. See also Turner, *Industrial Labour and Politics*, 69–73. On the economic effects of the war in the United States, see Kennedy, *Over Here*, 138–39, 258–62.

31. Montgomery, "New Unionism," 512–14.

32. Dan Cloward, "Crime and Punishment: The Great Strike in New South Wales, August to October 1917," in *Strikes: Studies in Twentieth Century Australian Social History*, ed. John Iremonger, John Merritt, and Graeme Osborne (Sydney: Angus and Robertson, 1973), 51–80, especially 56–57; Lucy Taksa, "Defence Not Defiance: Social Protest and the NSW General Strike of 1917," *Labour History* 60 (1991): 16–33. For the parallel strike in Queensland, see D. J. Murphy, "The North Queensland Railway Strike, 1917," in *The Big Strikes in Queensland, 1889–1965*, ed. Murphy (Brisbane: University of Queensland Press, 1983), 132–44.

33. Turner, *Industrial Labour and Politics*, 162–66, 178–81, 182–202; Montgomery, *Fall of the House of Labor*, 395–410.

34. Judd, *Socialist Cities*, 19; Weinstein, *Decline of Socialism*, 43–45, 93, 103–18.

35. Ray Markey, "The Emergence of the Labour Party at the Municipal Level in NSW, 1891–1900," *Australian Journal of Politics and History* 31 (1985): 410–12. See also George Dale, *The Industrial History of Broken Hill* (Melbourne: Fraser and Jenkinson, 1918).

36. Hogan, "Municipal Labor," 124–25, 128, 131–32. For a fuller account for Lithgow, see Greg Patmore, "Localism and Labour: Lithgow, 1869–1932," *Labour History* 78 (2000): 64; Greg Patmore, "Localism and Industrial Conflict: The 1911–12 Lithgow Ironworks Strike Revisited," *Labour and Industry* 10 (1999): 64–67, 70.

37. *Tocsin* (Melbourne), 29 August 1901, 32 July 1902; Fitzroy Branch, Political Labour Council, Minutes, June 14, 1905, Victoria State Library. See also Frank Bongiorno, *The People's Party: Victorian Labor and the Radical Tradition 1875–1914* (Melbourne: Melbourne University Press, 1996), 150.

38. Martin Painter, "Local Government," in *Politics in Australia*, ed. Rodney Smith and Lex Watson (Sydney: Allen and Unwin, 1989), 165–69. For a helpful summary of differences between the states, see M. A. Jones, *Local Government and the People: Challenges for the Eighties* (Melbourne: Hargreen, 1981), 34–41. See also G. H. Knibbs, *Local Government in Australia* (Melbourne: Mullett, 1919), especially 1–5.

39. The constitutional conventions of the 1890s failed to even mention the place of local government, which continued by default to receive "the leftovers" (Jones, *Local Government*, 42). See also R. K. Chapman and Michael Wood, *Australian Local Government: The Federal Dimension* (Sydney: Allen and Unwin, 1984), 30–33.

40. For the best account of Labor's efforts to win control of city government in Sydney between 1912 and 1925, see F. A. Larcombe, *The Advancement of Local Government in New South Wales, 1906 to the Present* (Sydney: Sydney University Press, 1978), 3:22–40.

41. Dale Krane, Platon N. Rigos, and Melvin B. Hill, *Home Rule in America: A Fifty-State Handbook* (Washington, D.C.: CQ Press, 2001), 8; Roscoe Martin, *The Cities in the Federal System* (New York: Atherton, 1965), 29 (quoted in Krane, Rigos, and Hill, *Home Rule*, 8).

42. For a less contested account of the legislative limitations on the power of cities, see Harold Lee McBain, *The Law and the Practice of Municipal Home Rule* (New York: Columbia University Press, 1916), 3–6.

43. Gerald E. Frug, *City Making: Building Communities without Building Walls* (Princeton: Princeton University Press, 1999), 43–44, 46.

44. *City of Clinton v. Cedar Rapids and Missouri River Railroad Company* (1868), quoted in Krane, Rigos, and Hill, *Home Rule*, 10.

45. See for example, Amasa Eaton, "The Right to Local Self-Government," *Harvard Law Review* (1900), quoted in Frug, *City Making*, 48.

46. Frug, *City Making*, 47–51. See also Krane, Rigos, and Hill, *Home Rule*, 10.

47. For general accounts of Australian local politics in wartime, see Hogan, "Municipal Labor"; Patmore, "Localism and Labour"; McCalman, *Struggletown*. For the US municipal campaigns, see Douglas, "Socialist Vote." For platforms in Dayton and Hamilton, see *Miami Valley Socialist*, October, November 1917; for Milwaukee, see Sally M. Miller, *Victor Berger and the Promise of Constructive Socialism, 1910–1920* (Westport, Conn.: Greenwood, 1973), 146, 197, 203–4; for platforms in other cities, see the *American Socialist*, October, November 1917.

48. Central Executive, Political Labour Council of Victoria, Minutes, 9 August, 5 September, 1 November 1902, 16 July, 13 August 1905, Victoria State Library; "Think Municipally," *Tocsin* (Melbourne), 31 August 1905. For Redfern, see, for example, *Sydney Morning Herald*, 3, 4 February 1908; Redfern City Council Minutes, 7, 13, 20 February, 25 June, 6 August, 3 September 1908, Sydney Municipal Archives; "What a Labor Municipal Council Has Done. . . ," *The Worker*, 19 January 1911.

49. In Brisbane, the fight to municipalize the hated Brisbane Tramway Company and to raise the "municipal log" (wage rates) for city employees continued unabated throughout the war: see "Report of the Mayor," Brisbane City Council Minutes, 10 February 1916, February 1917, John Oxley Library, Brisbane. For Melbourne municipalities, see Footscray Council Minutes, 9 October, 6 November 1915, Fitzroy Council Minutes, 16, 30 October 1916, 21 January, 18 February, 18 March 1918, Victoria State Archives. For a very helpful account of the contested wartime politics in Footscray, see John Lack, *A History of Footscray* (North Melbourne: Hargreen, 1991).

50. See Leichhardt Political Labour League Branch Minutes, 24 November 1915, 10 October 1916, 13 February, 12 September 1917, 26 June 1918, Mitchell State Library; Essendon Political Labour Council Minute Book, Victoria State Library. On the impact of the war in Leichardt, see Solling and Reynolds, *Leichardt.*

51. In Redfern, for example, Labor's city council members raised the wages of day laborers and won the use of the town hall for anticonscriptionist agitation. See Redfern City Council Minutes, 22 October 1914, 17 June, 12 August 1915, 5, 19 October 1916, Sydney Municipal Archives. And in Richmond, the Labor council members pushed an expansive agenda: see Richmond City Council Minutes, 27 April, 10, 24 May, 8 June, 5 July, 30 August, 6 December 1915, 8 May, 9, 23 October 1916, 19 November, 3 December 1917, Victoria State Archives. For a compelling account of wartime in Richmond, see McCalman, *Struggletown,* 89–105.

52. See "Angus McDonell, North Ward, City of Northcote, August 24, 1916" (Melbourne), "Fred W. Sear, South Yarra Ward, Prahran City Council, 18 July 1918" (Melbourne), "Labor's Manifesto, Sydney Municipal Elections, December 2, 1918" flyers, Australian Labor Party Leaflets, Mitchell State Library.

53. In Brisbane, despite some modest franchise changes, the Labor Party did not enjoy significant success until 1924: it then elected majorities in Brisbane, South Brisbane, Ithaca, and Coorparoo (Greenwood and Laverty, *Brisbane,* 302); in New South Wales, Labor won control in Forbes, Junee, Paddington, and Parkes (1920); Balmain, Lidcombe, Lithgow, Liverpool, Redfern, and Sydney (1922); Bourke, Canterbury, Erskineville, and Glebe (1925) (Hogan, "Municipal Labor," 125). On the continued success of the Australian Labor Party in Richmond well into the 1920s, see McCalman, *Struggletown,* 113–16.

54. Douglas, "Socialist Vote"; Weinstein, *Decline of Socialism,* 145–60; Morris Hillquit, *Loose Leaves from a Busy Life* (New York: Macmillan, 1934), 180–210; David Paul Nord, "Hothouse Socialism: Minneapolis, 1910–1925," in *Socialism in the Heartland: The Midwestern Experience, 1900–1925,* ed. Donald T. Critchlow (Notre Dame, Ind.: University of Notre Dame Press, 1986), 133–66; Sally Miller, "Casting a Wide Net: The Milwaukee Movement to 1920," in *Socialism in the Heartland,* ed. Critchlow, 18–45.

55. Socialists believed that ward-based representation insured working-class access to local government, see Samuel P. Hays, "The Politics of Municipal Reform in the Progressive Era," *Pacific Northwest Quarterly* 55 (1964): 165.

56. James Lehman, "The Socialist Party in Hamilton, Ohio" (master's thesis, Miami University, Ohio, 1964), 53–64, 104–10; Howard White, "City Manager Government in

Hamilton," in *City Manager Government in Seven Cities,* by Frederick C. Mosher, Arthur Harris, Howard White, John A. Vieg, Landrum Bolling, A. George Miller, David G. Monroe, and Harry O'Neal Wilson (Chicago: Public Administration Service, 1940), 183–85. For the pattern of prewar electoral success in Ohio and specifically in Hamilton, see Judd, *Socialist Cities,* 69–94.

57. Landrum Bolling, "City Manager Government in Dayton," in Mosher et al., *City Manager Government,* 268–70; Hays, "Politics of Municipal Reform," 164.

58. The Dayton Socialist Party conducted highly organized primary and general election campaigns that focused on local issues and a large influx of new members: see Dayton Socialist Party Minutes, 3, 17, 24 August, 28 September, 19 October, 9 November 1917, Wright State University Archives; Bolling, "City Manager Government," 265–73.

59. Chester E. Rightor, with Don C. Sowers and Walter Matscheck, *City Manager in Dayton: Four Years of Commission-Manager Government, 1914–1917, and Comparisons with Four Preceding Years under the Mayor-Council Plan, 1910–1913* (New York: Macmillan, 1919), 218–24 (quotation on 221). See also Bolling, "City Manager Government," 281–82. For an account by the socialists' leader in Dayton that emphasizes the renewal of fusion in 1917 not the antiwar posture of the party, see Joseph W. Sharts, *Biography of Dayton: An Economic Interpretation of Local History* (Dayton: Miami Valley Socialist Press, 1922), 118.

60. Rightor with Sowers and Matscheck, *City Manager in Dayton,* 221.

61. See Shelton Stromquist, "The Crucible of Class: Cleveland Politics and the Origins of Municipal Reform in the Progressive Era," *Journal of Urban History* 23 (1997): 192–220; Robert Emery Bionaz, "Streetcar City: Popular Politics and the Shaping of Urban Progressivism in Cleveland, 1880–1910" (PhD diss., University of Iowa, 2002).

62. Judd, *Socialist Cities,* 166–67; Folk, "Socialist Party of Ohio," 109; Douglas, "Socialist Vote," 136.

63. Miller, *Victor Berger,* 206–13. For the effects of the war and continuing persecution, see Weinstein, *Decline of Socialism,* 172, 232–33. At state levels, the radical Nonpartisan League in the northern Great Plains faced significant persecution over its ambiguous support for and criticism of the war effort: see, for example, Michael J. Lansing, *Insurgent Democracy: The Nonpartisan League in North American Politics* (Chicago: University of Chicago Press, 2015), 94–96, 204–5.

In Not a Few Respects, a Common History

Women, Wartime Lawmaking, and the Prosecution of Dissenters

DIANE KIRKBY

In the later years of her life, Australian labor activist and journalist Alice Henry (1857–1943) noted that Australia and the United States, having "a common ancestry, shared, in not a few respects, a common history."[1] That "common history" was evident during World War I, when both countries passed federal national security laws that for the first time extended "the criminal jurisdiction of the federal government over speech, press, and general dissent."[2] These new laws were a significant departure for nations that shared British ancestry and valued a tradition of freedom of speech.[3] They restricted the printing, publication, and dissemination of information about the war, with significant consequences for the daily work of journalists.[4] Both countries "removed certain forms of dissent from government protection" and brought increased surveillance of working journalists as well as antiwar activists and political radicals.[5] Those individuals for whom journalism was political and synonymous with antiwar activism now faced the threat of criminal prosecution.

This included people like Alice Henry, although she was not conspicuously an antiwar activist and never wrote specifically on the issue. During the war, she was living in Chicago, active in the woman suffrage movement, and editing the journal *Life and Labor* for the National Women's Trade Union League (NW-

TUL).[6] Many members of the NWTUL did become antiwar activists and therefore potentially subject to prosecution. Henry was well positioned to observe the meaning and impact of these national security measures, as intellectuals lamented that "never in the history of our country . . . has the meaning of free speech been the subject of such sharp controversy as to-day."[7] Another person affected by the change was American-born journalist Jennie Scott Griffiths (1875–1951), who lived and worked in Sydney during the war.[8] She was writing for the leftist press and editing the independently owned *Australian Woman's Weekly*, the forerunner of the commercially successful *Australian Home Budget*. Griffiths actively opposed the war and was placed under surveillance by the Australian authorities, although she escaped prosecution.[9]

These two women were career journalists, transnational in their identity and part of a wider international circle of labor activists, socialists, feminists, and peace advocates whose political views now put them at risk of violating national security measures. Their experiences represent something of the common history of Australia and the United States at a time when the criminalization of certain speech and forms of written expression and "unwarranted opinion, and association" posed an "ominous threat" to intellectuals and labor activists.[10] That legal history deserves more critical scrutiny from labor historians. In Australia, the passage of national security measures and the establishment of a censorship regime, was undertaken by a Labor government and marked the beginning of political surveillance.[11] Legal scholars have suggested that these laws form part of a tradition of suppression of political debate that is "always capable of resuscitation" and can be readily reinstated.[12] This chapter highlights the work of these World War I labor journalists, using the experience of women to show the intersections and divergences of national security measures in the legal suppression of dissent.

Contextualizing Australia's experience by reference to the United States is illuminating. It shows—as Shelton Stromquist and Verity Burgmann and Jeffrey A. Johnson argue elsewhere in this volume—the existence of commonalities in the way political radicals and antiwar activists were targeted by authorities in both nations. These commonalities emerged despite the strength of the Australian labor movement, the newness of Australian nationhood, and the conduct of the war by a Labor Party government. Differences in the historical scholarship of national experience are notable. US scholars have recognized links between the suppression of radicals and dissenters during the Great War and nationalist priorities, the extension of federal government powers, and the issues of civil liberties for other citizens during subsequent decades of peace.[13] US historians see the emergence of "a new type of repressive governmental action," a "startling new relationship" between government and citizens that affected the personal freedom of individuals.[14]

This perspective is notably lacking in Australian historical scholarship, which to date has conducted only limited examinations of the issue of free speech and censorship.[15] Apart from some earlier work on the legal prosecution of the Industrial Workers of the World (IWW), little attention has been paid to the implications of prosecuting labor activists under wartime national security laws.[16] While Australian historians, including labor historians, have exhaustively studied World War I as a national event, insufficient work has been done to set Australia's experience transnationally or comparatively.[17]

The Australian federal government rushed the War Precautions Act (no. 10 1914) through parliament as soon as the war broke out and as quickly as parliamentary procedure allowed.[18] The War Precautions Act covered all forms of written and illustrative material, including cartoons, pictures, and text depicting any military sites or the "gruesome effects of warfare" that was "likely to give offence to Allied or neutral nations."[19] Giving the governor-general power to confer power and duties to defend the commonwealth, in "an extraordinary and radical departure from customary legislation," the statute gave the federal government unprecedented and enormous new powers.[20]

One Australian historian has described the War Precautions Act as an "especially intrusive and partisan . . . extension of state power" that constituted a "response to the demands of military mobilisation."[21] Others, however, have portrayed the law as reflecting the excesses of a particularly authoritarian individual, former attorney general and wartime prime minister W. M. Hughes, who was willing "to subjugate the normal course of parliamentary and legal procedure to the winning of the war" and to carrying out his will.[22]

Yet a similar law, the Espionage Act, was passed in the United States after it joined the Allied war effort in April 1917. Many of the act's provisions covered matters of traditional espionage, such as interfering with shipping or exporting arms.[23] However, it also imposed restrictions on "anyone making false statements intended to interfere with the military" or "willfully obstructing" recruitment or enlistment. Title XII, Section 2 of the law made certain materials "nonmailable" and imposed harsh penalties, including long terms of imprisonment, on anyone trying to do so.[24] The US Congress did not grant President Woodrow Wilson the direct authority to censor that he had originally sought, but the postmaster general zealously used Title XII, Section 2 to prevent the distribution of printed matter opposing the war. This approach had consequences for the way the debate over the war could be conducted in public meetings, on podiums, and in the press.

In not all respects was this a common history. Unlike the United States, Australia was newly federated as a nation, with limited experience of military conflict and no previous experience in conducting a national war.[25] Australia had none of the "simmering of animosities" that were motivating the European nations to fight each other and "no experience of the restraints which war conditions imposed upon the liberty of the press."[26]

This was not true of the United States, which had experienced major war and the resulting tensions between civil liberties and wartime restraints that some have called the "necessities of war."[27] During the Civil War, President Abraham Lincoln had not often interfered with antiwar agitators, but he had suspended the writ of habeas corpus.[28] Litigation under the Espionage Act exemplified these tensions, and as had been the case sixty years earlier, the executive branch prevailed.[29] The US Supreme Court upheld the convictions of several people charged under the Espionage Act, most notably the Socialist Party's presidential candidate, Eugene Debs.[30]

Historian Raymond Evans has seen Australian law as more harshly applied than American law. Australian courts, however, did not jail dissenters for as long or punish them as severely as US courts did. The US law provided for harsher penalties and longer prison terms, and US courts imposed them. Between June 1917 and June 1921, more than two thousand people were prosecuted under the Espionage Act, with about half of them convicted.[31] Australia, by contrast, had a much smaller population, but saw thirty-five hundred prosecutions under the War Precautions Act, with about only a handful of them appealed to the High Court.[32] Few of these prosecutions were for offenses that might be regarded as military in nature, such as harboring an escaped prisoner of war; being on a wharf or dock or on board a ship without permission; forging or possessing unlawful documents; or sending letters or money to an enemy subject or country.

Most prosecutions involved relatively minor infringements. More than five hundred people were charged with offenses involving the sale of alcohol, selling food at excessive prices, or failing to furnish food census returns; selling badges or uniforms without proper authority; or trading under a changed name. In other words, the offenders were likely to be shopkeepers and small business owners. Several women (probably housewives) were charged with breaking restrictions on the use of coal gas and electricity. Two stewards on a ship, the *Sonoma* were charged with spreading reports likely to cause alarm: one was fined one hundred pounds and imprisoned for six months, while the other was discharged from the vessel.[33]

Many of the Australian national security prosecutions involved IWW members caught under the Unlawful Associations Act 1916 and reflected a "curious" definition of *national defense*.[34] The federal government had no power of criminal legislation, but the Unlawful Associations Act created a new crime—inciting, advocating, or encouraging the destruction of property and endangering life—that specifically identified the IWW.[35] A year later, the United States followed with its own raids against the IWW, events that reflect parallel timing but show no evidence of government collusion.[36] Both the United States and Australia targeted and deported IWW members, but they often simply went back and forth between the two countries.

Australian authorities prosecuted 89 Wobblies but nearly twice as many people who were working for the press.[37] Nearly all of the newspapers prosecuted were labor or left-wing periodicals, as laws ostensibly passed to control enemy agents were used as weapons against labor activists who criticized the Labor government's policy on the war. Some of the publications were local or rural, and some of those prosecuted had simply written letters to the editor. Henry Walsh, for example, was prosecuted writing to his local paper, the *Barmedman Banner*, on "Real Patriotism"; he was convicted and fined ten pounds. Unionist James Donaldson Michie was fined six pounds with costs of five guineas for publishing an article on "ANZAC Heroes and the Curse of Militarism" in the *Railways Union Gazette* on 20 January 1917.[38] Particularly targeted were radicals (the IWW and the editors of its paper, *Direct Action*), socialists (R. S. Ross, the editor of the *Socialist*), labor papers (the *Ballarat Daily Echo* and the *Labor Call*, which had its offices raided and material seized), and anticonscription organizations.

Several printers were prosecuted for publishing material not previously submitted to the censor. F. A. Holland, for example, was prosecuted several times for printing leaflets prejudicial to recruiting or for having banned material in his possession. Other journalists targeted included J. Ashton, publisher and printer of the *Labor Call*; H. J. Cunnington, publisher and printer of the *Queensland Leader*; and Fraser and Jenkinson, printers of pamphlets for the No Conscription Fellowship. Both the printer and the editor of the *Brisbane Daily Standard* were prosecuted. Authorities also charged staff at some mainstream papers, among them the editor of the *Sydney Mirror* and the proprietors of the *Perth Daily News*, who published without permission news allegedly of potential use to the enemy and news regarding military movements; however, the magistrate dismissed the case, and the High Court refused to hear an appeal.[39] Other papers whose editors were prosecuted included the *Truth*, *Advocate*, *Northern People*, and *Co-Operator*.[40]

Henry Boote, the editor of the *Australian Worker* and "probably the foremost Australia-wide publicist" against conscription, was prosecuted on four counts of publishing articles that had not previously been submitted to the censor.[41] He was found guilty and fined twenty-five pounds on each count, but charges that he had made statements likely to prejudice recruiting, most notably in an article, "The Lottery of Death," were dismissed. Still another charge—that he had falsely stated that there were six Australian divisions overseas—was withdrawn.[42] Tom Barker, the editor of the IWW's *Direct Action*, was charged with making statements likely to prejudice recruiting after he published a cartoon on 4 December 1915 alongside text that read, "Prime Minister Hughes has offered another 50000 men as a fresh sacrifice to the modern moloch. Politicians and their masters have always been generous with other people's lives." His initial fine of one hundred pounds plus costs was later reduced to twenty-five pounds.[43] Barker was also prosecuted for putting up posters, and he opted to go to jail rather than pay a fine after being convicted for publishing another cartoon.[44]

R. S. Ross, the editor of the *Socialist*, was prosecuted several times, the first of which for publishing a leaflet addressed "To Men Eligible for Military Service Who Object to Compulsion—Do You Want German Rule?" That case was dismissed, and another case regarding an article, "ANZACS Vote against Conscription," that appeared in the *Socialist* on 6 April 1917 was withdrawn.[45] In a third case, his appeal to the High Court was dismissed.[46] W. D. Barnett, editor of the *Barrier Daily Truth*, was charged with breaches of regulation 28 (likely to prejudice recruiting, causing disaffection to His Majesty, causing public alarm, prejudicing His Majesty's relations with foreign powers) for his October 1915 article, "The Gallipoli Adventure." The case was adjourned and subsequently withdrawn. Barnett faced additional charges related to a 1916 article on "The True Economic Position of the RSL," and his conviction brought a fine of fifty pounds. His appeal was dismissed and he was subsequently arrested and jailed until the fine was paid. He was prosecuted twice more in 1917. The first instance involved an article, "The Veiled First," deemed "likely to prejudice recruitment"; he was fined one hundred pounds and given nine months' imprisonment in default, though his appeal was upheld and his conviction quashed. The second time was for another article "likely to prejudice recruiting"; he was again fined one hundred pounds, but his appeal was again upheld and his conviction quashed.

These prosecutions amounted to constant harassment, interfering with the circulation of printed matter. By the end of 1917, even capital city newspaper editors were expressing alarm and anger about the heights political censorship had reached.[47] For their part, US journalists in the field in Europe refused to be restrained by military censorship.[48]

Suppressing political speech by opponents of the government seemed out of line with the modern nationalist rhetoric of fighting belligerent authoritarianism in Europe: it ran "contrary to modern decisions" and was "wholly out of accord with a common-sense view of the relations of state and citizen."[49] In the United States, liberals who were prepared to accept the Espionage Act as a whole were nevertheless alarmed by its censorship provisions, by its ambiguities, and by the way the law "disregarded traditional legal safeguards."[50] The 1918 Sedition Act subsequently amended the Espionage Act, adding nine more offenses.[51] The new law "prohibited language 'tending to incite, provoke and encourage resistance to the United States in said war'" and any "utterance, writing, printing [or] publication" that would interfere with the production of war materiel.[52] As a result, "thoughtful men and journals" began asking "how scores of citizens can be imprisoned . . . only for their disapproval of the war as irreligious, unwise, or unjust."[53]

Likewise, many unquestionably loyal Australian citizens found their country's national security measures to be "an assault . . . against one of the bulwarks of democracy."[54] Particularly when armed guards and their officers raided homes and offices to search for documents, "visions of military rule totally out of harmony with Australian traditions" were created. The censor also expressed this view, declaring censorship to be "an entirely novel experience in Australia" and adding that his job was complicated by the fact that it "ran counter to the very deeply rooted customs and prejudices of this country."[55] Disagreement with the government over the war had become a dangerous and subversive activity in both Australia and the United States. Australia, however, lacked the constitutional protection of freedom of speech contained in the First Amendment to the US Constitution, though that distinction mattered little in practice.

The differences between these national security provisions highlights the imperial (and arguably continuing colonial) relationship providing the framework for Australia's war effort. Differences in the US and Australian reasons for declaring war affected the nature of their respective national security laws. The United States came late to the battlefield, joining the fight only after President Woodrow Wilson convinced Congress that doing so was necessary. As Shelton Stromquist argues elsewhere in this volume, support for "preparedness" and for war in the United States came largely from the business sector. US loyalists who supported involvement in the war shared pro-British sympathies but to a lesser degree than did Australians, who felt a familial blood bond to the Crown, England and Empire. Patriotism and nationalism had slightly different connotations in Australia, which went to war immediately in 1914 on behalf of the British Empire to which it still belonged, and did so with bipartisan support.[56]

Even some Australian opponents of the war emphasized British imperial ties and cited them as grounds for opposition.

The War Precautions Act was modeled on the Defence of the Realm Act, passed by the British Parliament just a few weeks earlier than the bill Hughes, as attorney general, introduced into parliament.[57] Australia was fighting as part of an imperial force under British command.[58] Hughes's legislation sought to prevent the publication in British territory of news that might have a prejudicial effect on civilians or help the enemy.[59] These terms had been decided in the preceding decade and were implemented when war was declared.[60] Hughes was passionate about defending Australian democracy, very conscious of Australia's colonial status, and concerned that Australia should have its rightful place at the peace talks so that it could influence the outcome on matters that affected it in the wider Asia-Pacific.[61]

Australia's colonial status was further emphasized when the United States entered the war: Australians were then forbidden to publish any matter derogatory to or intended to weaken or minimize the terms of peace "laid down by the Prime Minister of Great Britain and the President of the United States"; later in the year, in the wake of the Russian Revolution, the restrictions were expanded to include anything that "commended the Bolshevik peace terms."[62] Portraying Germany as other than belligerent was also dangerous: In one case appealed to the High Court, Justice Isaacs found the defendant guilty under Regulation 28 on the grounds that his pamphlet "elevates Germany as a country seeking peace, without adding to the statement the only terms on which the enemy will at present have it."[63]

The war generated fierce opposition and deep and bitter ideological divisions in both the United States and Australia. Many who opposed the war did so as pacifists opposed to all forms of militarism—Quakers who had set up peace organizations in the early nineteenth century, other church and religious groups, and women who banded together in organizations in the first decade of the new century.[64] The start of war in Europe drew unprecedented numbers of American women in a myriad of organizations into the public sphere of war-related activities.[65] Before the end of August 1914, fifteen hundred women in mourning dress protested the war by marching silently down New York's Fifth Avenue to the beat of muffled drums.[66]

Others—internationalists, the IWW, labor activists, and socialists—opposed the war on ideological grounds, as a particular war run by and for capitalists and devouring the working class.[67] Their opposition, couched in terms of class struggle, made them susceptible to prosecution for writing and airing dissenting views. In the fervor and climate of war, when patriotic nationalism was the only acceptable public position, there was no space for internationalism; to be a socialist was automatically to be not only disloyal but also dangerous.[68] Before the war, political radicals had freedom to speak, although they faced constant police harassment and court injunctions. Now, with national defense taking priority, individual freedom of speech fell by the wayside and radicals suddenly became potential criminals. Many were imprisoned or deported, and still others found themselves in danger as a consequence of "an undeclared war on the Socialists for their stand against the war."[69]

Attacks on dissenters rapidly turned to vilifying German immigrants. Both Australia and the United States had resident populations of German and Austrian origin who suddenly became redefined as "enemy aliens." In the United States, a longtime fear that European immigrants were liable to bring anarchic and dangerous ideas evolved into a view of German Americans as the enemy within, hostile to the Anglo-Americans' support for Britain. The United States passed a 1917 act to restrict German immigration that was extended in 1918 to enable the easier deportation of aliens.[70] In Australia, the War Precautions Act was simply expanded to cover the prosecution of aliens. A significant number of prosecutions under the Australian national security regulations involved people who failed to register as aliens, failed to report to authorities, or traveled without passports.[71] Early in 1916, Australia's defense minister recommended that state authorities should "intern all Germans, whether naturalized or not, who were thought to be dangerous." War Precautions Regulations 55 and 56 formalized this recommendation and additionally authorized the internment of "natural-born British subjects of enemy descent who showed themselves disloyal."[72] Australians of German origin or descent were thus in a single stroke "transformed from citizens with full civil rights to outcasts who could be treated like criminals by the military authorities."[73] National security laws, however, removed the protections from aliens that criminals normally enjoyed, and Germans were interned in Australia in an action that legal scholars now argue contravened Australia's constitution.[74]

Although not German, both Alice Henry and Jennie Scott Griffiths were potentially "enemy aliens" because they were immigrants; neither woman was a citizen of the country in which she now lived. Henry had arrived in the United States in 1906, after twenty years as a journalist in Australia, and begun working to organize women into trade unions.[75] She joined the Socialist Party of America, and when war came, she wrote, "To all idealists of every shade of thought the catastrophe [of war] came as a stupefying blow."[76] In the United States, Henry was not subjected to censorship laws and was never in danger of prosecution, in large part because US authorities were reluctant to prosecute white middle-class women. Class and ethnic identity offered them protections that were not afforded to other protesters.[77]

Furthermore, Henry never wrote directly against the war or of government policy in the conduct of the war; rather, she opposed the militarism and jingoism that brought about the war. "Even in free England," she wrote, "militarism spells" harsh treatment for conscientious objectors. However, she left readers to draw their own conclusions about government policy.[78] According to her coeditor, Miles Franklin, a fellow Australian, her writing style could get past "even the Roaring Tories."[79] Her other concern was the use of hazardous chemicals in manufacturing and their effects on workers.

Before leaving Australia, Henry had opposed the dispatch of Australian colonial troops to fight in the Boer War, writing of the nationalist jingoism and materialist incentives (greed for land) that were driving enlistment.[80] Now, with war raging in Europe and Australia again fully involved on the side of empire, she returned to her opposition to warmongering, concentrating on the impact of war on workers' lives and livelihood. Anyone outside the warring countries could not realize the extent of suffering brought on by the war, she wrote, pointing out that US newspapers were not allowed to write about the subject "for fear of bringing on a panic." Henry focused on the meaning of the war for women, especially after Hungarian feminist Rosika Schwimmer toured the United States in 1914 to urge American women to oppose the war. Schwimmer had her greatest success in Chicago, among women of Henry's circle, who were outraged that women in war-torn countries were the first victims of conquering soldiers.[81] Henry believed that the internationalism of the women's peace movement would "bring us closer together" and that "European civilization was doomed to destruction."[82]

Among the most important new recruits to the peace movement were women settlement house residents and social workers.[83] Many of Henry's closest friends, such as Unitarian minister Anna Garlin Spencer; colleagues in the settlement houses, such as Jane Addams; and allies in the NWTUL, such as Rose Schneidermann, were now taking leadership roles, forming organizations for peace, speaking publicly, and marching against the war.[84] Though Henry wrote against militarism, she kept her concentration on the NWTUL's industrial feminist goals. She saw no purpose for women in "Europe's present turmoil" and no progress to be made toward reaching women's goals "by the blood being spilled." She was prepared to be optimistic about the world that would emerge "out of all this chaos," though the price was terrible: "a great deal of old timber will be burned by the war. Many old customs will disappear forever."[85]

On another occasion, Henry spoke of women in Europe taking up work normally done by men, "running street cars, handling the mail, tilling the fields, making munitions," and she emphasized the future dangers that would result if work and wages were not made independent of the sex of the worker: "Either women would be thrown out of work entirely, or the man's wages would be brought down so low that he would be unable to support his family."[86] After the United States had joined the conflict, she lamented the industrial dislocation associated with wartime mobilization and criticized the National American Woman Suffrage Association's policy of "extending care to one group of women wage-earners and ignore[ing] the rest."[87]

Henry's pacifism was consistent with the direction of the peace movement, which shifted left in both Australia and the United States as patriotism challenged the definition and meaning of pacifism.[88] Her old friends from the woman suffrage campaign in Melbourne were now members of the Women's Peace Army (WPA), which stood at the vanguard of militant opposition to the war and conscription there. The war gave rise to the Australian Peace Alliance, an umbrella group whose first chair was Vida Goldstein (1869–1949), a prominent feminist, the founder of the Women's Political Association, and a friend of Henry's.[89] The Alliance brought together various organizations that opposed the war, many of them attached to the labor movement, trade unions, or branches of the Australian Labor Party but also including church groups and organized women pacifists.[90] Goldstein was joined by experienced British suffragists Jenny Baines, Adela Pankhurst, and Cecilia John, who brought a militancy gained in the British suffrage struggle to the peace struggle.

The WPA was the radical arm of the peace movement, inspired by feminism, concerned with political change, and driven by the ideology of socialism to oppose this particular war as the outcome of capitalism and imperialism.[91] Jennie Scott Griffiths joined the WPA when branches were established in Sydney and subsequently in Brisbane. The WPA had developed a critique of society as both capitalist and patriarchal, holding that the root of war lay in the existing social and economic structure and that a militant approach was thus needed if women were to have any effect.[92] This viewpoint was consistent with Griffiths's belief that militarism should be opposed by feminist militancy. The WPA favored provocation, action, and opposition while the war was being waged, an approach that provoked Australian authorities and resulted in charges against several of the group's most prominent members.[93]

Where the US and Australian war policy differed most markedly was on the matter of conscription. Within a month of entering the war, the United States instituted conscription. In Australia, however, conscription was not attempted until more than two years into the war, at which point it became a national debate and the subject of two plebiscites, both of which failed. The application of national security regulations to interference with recruitment intensified along with the debate over conscription.

As war losses mounted and costs soared, the Hughes government complained that it was having difficulty meeting British demands for personnel and sustaining Australian forces as independent divisions. Enlistment rates declined, and the government turned to recruitment drives to bolster its troops. The reliance on voluntary enlistment meant that writings or speeches urging people to refuse to fight had particular power—the government had no means of compelling people to serve. Thus, national security regulations needed to prevent words from interfering with recruitment.

The Australian government focused particularly on suppressing opposition from organizations such as the IWW. In 1915, an amendment to the War Precautions Act proposed adding a regulation making it "an offence to utter or publish a statement 'likely to prejudice the recruiting, training, discipline or administration of any of His majesty's Forces.'"[94] When this amendment failed, the government attempted to introduce conscription, following the lead of Britain, Canada, and New Zealand and resulting in what has become known as "the most bitter struggle in the history of Australian politics."[95]

At Hughes's direction, the Australian military and police expanded their surveillance of anticonscriptionist, antirecruitment, pacifist, and generally leftist groups and organizations, among them the Quaker Society of Friends, the Australian Freedom League, the Australian Peace Alliance, the Irish National Association, Sinn Fein, the IWW; the Workers' Release and Defence League; the Women's Peace Army; the Labor College; the Free Speech Union; the Workers' Educational Association; industrial unionists; the Victorian Socialist Party; and members of the Labor Party. In fact, the government launched what amounted to "a vendetta against prominent Labor men."[96]

Most of those targeted for their political outspokenness against conscription were men. Among them were prominent labor lawyer Maurice Blackburn; academic archeologist and political theorist Vere Gordon Childe; Arthur Calwell, who later became minister for immigration and subsequently leader of the Australian Labor Party; and future Labor prime minister John Curtin, who was fined fifteen pounds plus costs of three pounds, six shillings for making a statement prejudicial to recruitment.[97] Curtin ran afoul of the law when he reportedly said, "Mr. Hughes says that if the referendum is not carried, conscription will be introduced in Australia and in that case if conscription is passed I deny their right to force conscription on us and the cause will be just as if we rebel and the worst form of rebellion is that forced on men of a free and democratic country. Rebellion in a despotic country is the necessary resolution of their difficulties." His fine was subsequently remitted on an undertaking given at the Governor-General's Conference in April 1918.[98] Other Labor members of Parliament and senators as well as the Queensland premier, Tom Ryan, were charged with "disloyalty or hostility to British Empire" or "making a false statement likely to affect the judgement of voters." Most of these cases were dismissed when they got to court, but they provide evidence of the differences within the Australian Labor Party and the amount of intraparty opposition engendered by Hughes's war policies.[99]

The state of war required women to play a more public role in connecting motherhood to citizenship. National security laws "operated within nationalist discourses that emphasized a close relationship between women's roles as mothers and their responsibilities" to reproduce nationalism and patriotism.[100] Australia differed from the United States, however, in that it had enfranchised women, and Australian women's voting power became paramount during the national plebiscites over conscription.

The propaganda from both sides of the conscription debates—"misleading, partial, irrational and vitriolic"—was a "barrage of indoctrination" largely directed at women.[101] Proponents as well as opponents of the draft appealed to women on emotional grounds, either as patriotic mothers willing to surrender of their husbands and sons to the nationalist cause or as wise mothers saving their sons from the folly of militarism. Simply saying "Women are mad to send their sons to war" earned one speaker prosecution under Regulation 28.[102]

Loyalist women who supported the war argued for conscription to support the soldiers who were already in the field, while the women who were most outspoken about women's rights before 1914 often went on to become active opponents of the war and ultimately conscription.[103] Nearly two-thirds of the almost half a million citizens who failed to vote in the plebiscites were women: despite their public patriotism, many women could not bring themselves to force their menfolk into battle.[104]

Jennie Scott Griffiths was a visible and vocal opponent of conscription. One flyer that she authored equated the New South Wales government under Premier William Arthur Holman with the German government, whose broken promise to guarantee Belgium's neutrality was a betrayal of trust that had provoked the British into war. She urged the voters of New South Wales to be similarly indignant and refuse to support conscription since "liars and traitors are always liars and traitors, whether German or British made."[105] Griffiths also made arguments of a more concrete practical nature, as in another flyer, "Here

Come the Married Men!"[106] She spoke out against the jingoism, the bands, the flags and "bombastic journalism and literature" intended to persuade men to fight.[107] She saw the war as driven by capitalist greed and militarism as masculinist politics for which women paid a heavy yet avoidable price.

As editor, Griffiths not only was vulnerable to prosecution for what she published in the *Australian Woman's Weekly* but also had to take care to avoid alienating nonpolitical readers. She informed readers of the *Weekly* about US women's peace activities and of British and European women who were working as nurses in the war effort.[108] When writing for political and labor publications, however, she took a much more vocal antiwar approach, specifically and directly criticizing government actions. She cited countries that had imposed conscription as examples of militarism and urged the "women of Australia" not to be fooled into backing conscription: "As your men have gone—as they believed—to crush militarism, and to protect you from its ravages, see that you prove yourselves worthy mates of the men of Gallipoli by protecting yourselves and your children from the same foe."[109]

Griffiths's anticonscription activism made her more vulnerable to prosecution than Henry was. Griffiths came under military surveillance, and her home was raided. She later claimed that her antiwar views resulted in the loss of her editorship of the *Australian Woman's Weekly*.[110] By war's end, she and her husband and their ten children had moved to Queensland, whose premier, Tom Ryan, had himself been prosecuted. His refusal to endorse the full powers of the War Precautions Act gave dissenting journalists and labor activists some safety. Her name appears in the Military Intelligence records as an associate of "various undesirables" such as IWW members, and she was connected to several other organizations targeted as threats to national security, including the Australian Peace Alliance, the Workers' Educational Association, the Women's Peace Army. She was a frequent contributor to the socialist press, occasionally wrote for the IWW's *Direct Action*, and sometimes edited the Woman's Page for the *Australian Worker*. She served as the interstate correspondent for the Melbourne-based *Socialist*, all of which ran afoul of the censor and the national security regulations.

Griffith consistently focused on the rights of women and the changes brought by war. "Women do not love war," she wrote in one article, because of its impact on their daily lives. "War has always smitten women more heavily than men. It takes away woman's chief source of livelihood: destroys the lives of both her strong men and her babies; and degrades her womanhood more than any other evil thing has power to do." She moved from this general opposition to war to a critique of "military-controlled countries" where force was idealized. There, the strong were favored and women—the weakest members of the nation—became "the bearers of children, and beasts of burden only." War endangered the lives of babies by making food scarce and made labor cheap by leaving only older, weaker workers who had no choice but to accept whatever wages were offered" "military control crushe[d] every semblance of freedom for the working people by whatever power it may be imposed."[111]

As an American married to a New Zealand businessman, Griffiths may well have had some protection from being prosecuted and deported. Other women anticonscriptionists faced charges for saying less. Western Australia's Lilian Foxcroft was convicted under Regulation 28 after she declared, "It is impossible to have Military Conscription without industrial conscription. More than half the people of Australia have already said they don't want conscription and if they try to impose something on us that we don't want they will hit trouble. Why should we send our men to the front? If the worst comes to the worst, we might as well die in Australia defending our liberties."[112]

Though only a small number of women actually faced charges in either United States or Australia, some of the highest-profile prosecutions in both countries involved women: Kate Richards O'Hare, Emma Goldman, and Mollie Dwyer in the United States and Adela Pankhurst, Cecilia John, Jennie Baines, and Alice Suter in Australia.[113] These women, as Kathleen Kennedy has argued, "challenged a wartime culture" that at its worst stripped citizens of their right to dissent from or disagree with those who governed them and "reduced women to their basest biological functions."[114] Although relatively few prosecutions occurred, wartime national security measures and state and local ordinances affected the daily lives of many more women—shopkeepers, publicans, teachers, birth control advocates, labor leaders, and suffragists. Political activism caused significant numbers of women to lose their jobs and livelihoods and to face violence and physical harassment.[115]

The US Espionage Act and the Australian War Precautions Act remained in force even after armed hostilities had ended, and "the most patently oppressive era of press censorship" did not come to a close until 1921.[116] The Australian national security regulations on deporting aliens remained in place until November 1920.[117] Australian activists continued to protest the War Precautions Act, an effort that culminated in Brisbane's 1919 Red Flag Riots, where Jennie Scott Griffiths was a featured speaker.[118]

Alice Henry saw "a common history" between Australia and the United States because of her own internationalism and antijingoist attitude toward militarism and warmongering. It is harder for historians to assess the validity of her judgment regarding the wider impact of the national security regulations, particularly on labor journalists. National security lawmaking in wartime Australia and the United States was driven by the perception of a "need to criminalize a variety of forms of protest and dissent" so that warfare could be contained by propaganda.[119] The new laws reflected the view that in a time of national emergency, federal government powers could and should override state government powers, freedom of speech and the press, and many other legal protections afforded ordinary citizens in peacetime. "Officials assumed 'emergency' discretion over . . . permissible nonconformity in people's attitudes and behavior."[120]

Historian Jay Winter has claimed that twentieth century wars presented problems that "severely tested" progressive socialist ideas.[121] Socialists' prewar concepts, social analysis, tactics, and strategies were "called into question by the experience of war." As the "common history" of Australia and the United States has shown, citizens who espoused socialist views found their democratic rights to dissent and to exercise freedom of speech and protest severely tested by nationalist responses to world war. National security laws subjected socialists to an unprecedented degree of harassment and prosecution. The IWW and some other organizations did not survive intact: although the IWW reemerged in the mid-1920s, many potential members had moved on to the Communist Party.[122] The Australian Labor Party split and lost control of the government. In the words of historian Barry Smith, the world war thus "served to wreck a great party and transform a government."[123] While the European countries that experienced "the actual ravages of battle" suffered "more devastating collapses of authority," the English-speaking allies also suffered consequences. Britain, Australia, and the United States entered the postwar period "bereft of the agreement about social aims and humane concern that makes progressive government possible."[124]

When Alice Henry returned to Australia for a visit in 1925 and ultimately to live in 1934, she lamented the loss of the progressive country she had left two decades earlier and regretted the now unrecognizable Labor Party.[125] The legacy of political surveillance, strengthened federal executive powers, and the practice of waging war by propaganda only strengthened over the ensuing century. She died during the dark days of World War II. Jennie Scott Griffiths, however, moved back to the United States in 1920 and lived to see the renewed suppression of left-wing dissenters during the Cold War. Observed leading Australian pacifist Eleanor Moore, "The spirit of the War Precautions Act never departed."[126]

Notes

1. Alice Henry, Memoirs, typescript, Mss. 1066, Alice Henry Papers, National Library of Australia.

2. William H. Rehnquist, *All the Laws but One: Civil Liberties during Wartime* (New York: Knopf, 1998), 173.

3. Enid Campbell and Harry Whitmore, *Freedom in Australia* (Sydney: Sydney University Press, 1966).

4. Rehnquist, *All the Laws*, 175, 178. See also Phillip Knightley, *The First Casualty: The War Correspondent as Hero, Propagandist, and Myth Maker from the Crimea to Vietnam* (New York: Harcourt, Brace, Jovanovich, 1975).

5. Paul L. Murphy, *World War I and the Origins of Civil Liberties in the United States* (New York: Norton, 1979), 52.

6. Diane Kirkby, *Alice Henry: The Power of Pen and Voice* (Cambridge: Cambridge University Press, 1991).

7. Zechariah Chafee, "Freedom of Speech in War Time," *Harvard Law Review* 32 (1919): 932.

8. Terry Irving, "Jennie Scott Griffiths (1875–1951)," in *Australian Dictionary of Biography*, vol. 16 (Carlton: Melbourne University Press, 2002); Joy Damousi, *Women Come Rally: Socialism, Communism, and Gender in Australia, 1890–1955* (Melbourne: Oxford University Press, 1994), 21–22.

9. Diane Kirkby, "Neither 'Militarism' nor 'Patriotic Motherhood': Gender, Law, and Citizenship in a Nation at War, Australia 1914–18," *law&history* 2 (2015): 177–201.

10. Murphy, *World War I*, 21

11. Frank Cain, *The Origins of Political Surveillance in Australia* (Sydney: Angus and Robertson, 1983), vii.

12. Simon Bronitt and James Stellios, "Sedition, Security, and Human Rights: 'Unbalanced' Law Reform in the War on Terror," *Melbourne University Law Review* 30 (2006): 926.

13. For a summary of the literature to 1980, see Murphy, *World War I*, 36, 16–25. See also William Preston Jr., *Aliens and Dissenters: Federal Suppression of Radicals, 1903–33*, 2nd ed. (Urbana: University of Illinois Press, 1994); William H. Thomas Jr., *Unsafe for Democracy: World War 1 and the U.S. Justice Department's Covert Campaign to Suppress Dissent* (Madison: University of Wisconsin Press, 2008).

14. Murphy, *World War I*, 36, 21. See also Brian Simpson, *In the Highest Degree Odious: Detention without Trial in Wartime Britain* (Oxford: Clarendon, 1992), 5.

15. Kevin Fewster, "The Operation of State Apparatuses in Times of Crisis: Censorship and Conscription, 1916," *War and Society* 3 (1985): 37–54; Kevin Fewster, "Expression and Suppression: Aspects of Military Censorship in Australia during the Great War" (PhD diss., University of New South Wales, 1981); Robert Pullan, *Guilty Secrets: Free Speech and Defamation in Australia* (Glebe: Pascal, 1994); Kerry McCallum and Peter Putnis, "Media Management in Wartime: The Impact of Censorship on Press-Government Relations in World War I Australia," *Media History* 14 (2008): 17–34; James Waghorne and Stuart

Macintyre, *Liberty: A History of Civil Liberties in Australia* (Sydney: University of New South Wales Press, 2011).

16. Verity Burgmann, "The Iron Heel: The Suppression of the IWW during World War 1," in *What Rough Beast? The State and Social Order in Australian History*, ed. Sydney Labour History Group (Sydney: Allen and Unwin, 1982), 171–91; Frank Cain, *The Wobblies at War: A History of the IWW and the Great War in Australia* (Melbourne: Spectrum, 1993).

17. A recent exception is Robin Archer, "Stopping War and Stopping Conscription: Australian Labour's Response to World War I in Comparative Perspective," *Labour History* 106 (2014): 43–67.

18. Ernest Scott, *Australia during the War*, vol. 9 of *Official History of Australia in the War of 1914–18*, ed. C. E. W. Bean (Sydney: Angus and Robertson, 1937), xx.

19. Ibid., 65.

20. Gerhardt Fischer, *Enemy Aliens: Internment and the Home Front Experience in Australia, 1914–20* (St. Lucia: University of Queensland Press, 1988), 65.

21. Joan Beaumont, ed., *Australia's War, 1914–18* (Sydney: Allen and Unwin, 1995).

22. F. B. Smith, *The Conscription Plebiscites in Australia, 1916–17*, 4th ed. (North Melbourne: Victorian Historical Association, 1974), 4; Stuart Macintyre, *1901–1942: The Succeeding Age* (Melbourne, Oxford University Press, 1986), 162.

23. Rehnquist, *All the Laws*, 173.

24. Espionage Act, Title XII, § 2, 65 Stat. 230 (1917). See Rehnquist, *All the Laws*, 173; Murphy, *World War I*, 79–80; Philip Glende, "Victor Berger's Dangerous Ideas: Censoring the Mail to Preserve National Security during World War I," *Essays in Economic and Business History* 26 (2008): 5–20.

25. Scott, *Australia during the War*, vi.

26. Ibid., 58.

27. Ibid.; Robert Menzies, "War Powers in the Constitution of the Commonwealth of Australia," *Columbia Law Review* 18 (1918): 11.

28. Donald Johnson, "Wilson, Burleson, and Censorship in the First World War," *Journal of Southern History* 28 (1962): 8; Rehnquist, *All the Laws*, 11–25, 182–83; Michael Brennan, review of William Rehnquist, *All the Laws but One*, *Marquette Law Review* 83 (1999): 221–36.

29. Rehnquist, *All the Laws*, 182. See also Brennan, review.

30. Rehnquist, *All the Laws*, 175–80; Ernest Freeland, *Democracy's Prisoner: Eugene V. Debs, the Great War, and the Right to Dissent* (Cambridge: Harvard University Press, 2008).

31. Rehnquist, *All the Laws*, 183.

32. See Return of Prosecutions under the War Precautions Act and Regulations, Including the Aliens Restriction Order, typescript, House of Representatives, Canberra, 1919.

33. Ibid.

34. Menzies, "War Powers," 7.

35. Ibid., 8.

36. For a discussion of the connections and interchange between Australian and US Wobblies, see Cain, *Wobblies at War*, 275–88; Raymond Evans, *The Red Flag Riots: A Study of Intolerance* (St. Lucia: University of Queensland Press, 1988), 43–44.

37. Return of Prosecutions; Evans, *Red Flag Riots*, 44, says that 120 Wobblies were incarcerated but provides no source for the information and does not indicate what charges they faced; it is quite possible that they were charged under other laws. See also Cain, *Wobblies at War*, 259–73.

38. Return of Prosecutions.

39. Ibid., cases 1086, 1087.

40. Ibid.

41. Frank Farrell, "Boote, Henry Ernest (1865–1949)," in *Australian Dictionary of Biography* vol. 7 (Carlton: Melbourne University Press, 1979).

42. Return of Prosecutions.

43. Ibid.

44. Cain, *Wobblies at War*, 230–35.

45. [Image 5585] Return of Prosecutions. See also Cain, *Wobblies at War*, 230–35.

46. *Ross v. Sickerdick* (1916) (HCA), available at http://www.austlii.edu.au/cgi-bin/sinodisp/au/cases/cth/HCA/1916/66.html?stem=0&synonyms=0&query=war%20precautions%20act.

47. Pullan, *Guilty Secrets*, 164.

48. Knightley, *First Casualty*, 110–12.

49. Chafee, "Freedom of Speech," 939.

50. Johnson, "Wilson, Burleson, and Censorship," 47, 48.

51. Rehnquist, *All the Laws*, 180; Chafee, "Freedom of Speech," 936.

52. Rehnquist, *All the Laws*, 181.

53. Chafee, "Freedom of Speech," 936.

54. Scott, *Australia during the War*, 58.

55. Quoted in ibid., 63.

56. Ibid., vii.

57. Simpson, *In the Highest Degree Odious.*

58. L. F. Fitzhardinge, *The Little Digger, 1914–52: William Morris Hughes: A Political Biography* (Sydney: Angus and Robertson, 1979), 2:114.

59. McCallum and Putnis, "Media Management in Wartime."

60. Ibid.

61. Macintyre, *1901–1942*, 178–82.

62. Scott, *Australia during the War*, 65.

63. *Sickerdick Informant v. Ashton* (HCA) 54, 25 CLR 506 (26 September 1918).

64. Ronald Marchand, *The American Peace Movement and Social Reform* (Princeton: Princeton University Press, 1972); Malcolm Saunders, *Quiet Dissenter: The Life and Thought of an Australian Pacifist: Eleanor May Moore, 1875–1949* (Canberra: Peace Research Centre, Research School of Pacific Studies, Australian National University, 1993).

65. Barbara Steinson, *American Women's Activism in World War I* (New York: Garland, 1982), i.

66. Marchand, *American Peace Movement,* 182; Steinson, *American Women's Activism,* 12.

67. See Freeland, *Democracy's Prisoner*; Verity Burgmann, *Revolutionary Industrial Unionism: The Industrial Workers of the World in Australia* (Cambridge: Cambridge University Press, 1995), 181–202.

68. Freeland, *Democracy's Prisoner,* 23.

69. Ibid., 22. See also James Weinstein, *The Decline of Socialism in America, 1912–1925* (New York: Monthly Review Press, 1967).

70. See John Higham, *Strangers in the Land: Patterns of American Nativism, 1860–1925* (New York: Atheneum, 1963) 202–3, 221.

71. Return of Prosecutions.

72. Raymond Evans, *Loyalty and Disloyalty: Social Conflict on the Queensland Homefront, 1914–18* (Sydney: Allen and Unwin, 1987), 57–58.

73. Fischer, *Enemy Aliens,* 66.

74. Peter McDermott, "Internment during the Great War—A Challenge to the Rule of Law," *University of New South Wales Law Journal* 28 (2005): 330.

75. Kirkby, *Alice Henry*. Henry did not become a US citizen until 1923, after she had retired from the NWTUL.

76. Alice Henry, *Trade Union Woman* (New York: Appleton, 1915), preface

77. Thomas, *Unsafe for Democracy*. See also Kathleen Kennedy, *Disloyal Mothers and Scurrilous Citizens: Women and Subversion during World War I* (Bloomington: Indiana University Press, 1999).

78. Alice Henry, "'Justice' Re-Enacted in England," *The Survey,* 8 July 1916, clipping in Henry Papers.

79. Quoted in Kirkby, *Alice Henry,* 119.

80. Ibid. 53

81. Steinson, *American Women's Activism,* 16, 19.

82. *Australian Worker,* 4 February 1915.

83. Steinson, *American Women's Activism,* 7.

84. Ibid., 23; Marchand, *American Peace Movement.*

85. "Sees Sweeping Changes Ahead for Women after the War," *Boston American,* July 1915, clipping in Henry Papers.

86. "Wage Problem a Big Issue after the War, Says Alice Henry," unidentified news clipping, 30 January 1917, in ibid.

87. Alice Henry, *Woman's Journal,* May 1917.

88. Charles Chatfield, "World War I and the Liberal Pacifist in the United States," *American Historical Review* 75 (1970): 1920; Marchand, *American Peace Movement,* 266; Saunders, *Quiet Dissenter,* 97; Steinson, *American Women's Activism,* 1.

89. Pat Gowland, "The Women's Peace Army," in *Women, Class, and History: Feminist Perspectives on Australia, 1788–1978,* ed. Elizabeth Windschuttle (Melbourne: Fontana/Collins, 1980), 217.

90. Saunders, *Quiet Dissenter*, 97.

91. Ibid.

92. D. Kruse and C. Sowerwine, "Feminism and Pacifism: 'Woman's Sphere' in Peace and War," in *Australian Women: New Feminist Perspectives*, ed. Norma Grieve and Ailsa Burns (Melbourne: Oxford University Press, 1986), 55.

93. Saunders, *Quiet Dissenter*, 89–90; Judith Smart, "The Right to Speak and the Right to Be Heard: The Popular Disruption of Conscription Meetings in Melbourne 1916," *Australian Historical Studies* 23 (1989): 203–19.

94. Cain, *Wobblies at War*, 229.

95. F. B. Smith, *Conscription Plebiscites*, 10.

96. Cain, *Origins*, 63.

97. Susan Blackburn Abeyasekere, "Maurice McCrae Blackburn (1880–1944)," in *Australian Dictionary of Biography*, vol. 7; Jim Allen, "Vere Gordon Childe (1892–1957)," in *Australian Dictionary of Biography*, vol. 7; Graham Freudenberg, "Arthur Augustus Calwell (1896–1973)," in *Australian Dictionary of Biography*, vol. 13 (Carlton: Melbourne University Press, 1993).

98. Return of Prosecutions, case 1054.

99. Return of Prosecutions.

100. Kennedy, *Disloyal Mothers*, 2. See also Steinson, *American Women's Activism*, 1, 4–5.

101. Evans, *Loyalty and Disloyalty*, 88.

102. Return of Prosecutions.

103. See, for example, F. Violette Smith, "A Mother's View," *Sydney Morning Herald*, 21 October 1916.

104. F. B. Smith, *Conscription Plebiscites*, 13.

105. Jennie Scott Griffiths, "Another Scrap of Paper," flyer, Anti-Conscription League of Australasia, Sydney, [1917], Riley and Ephemera Collection, State Library of Victoria, available at http://handle.slv.vic.gov.au/10381/157803.

106. Jennie Scott Griffiths, "Here Come the Married Men!," flyer, in *Literary Cuttings*, 104, Mss. 1071, Jennie Scott Griffiths Papers, National Library of Australia.

107. *Australian Woman's Weekly*, 12 September 1914.

108. "American Women's Call for Peace," *Australian Woman's Weekly*, 9 October 1915; "Women at the Fighting Line," *Australian Woman's Weekly*, 16 October 1915; "Jane Addams Pleads for Peace," *Australian Woman's Weekly*, 12 August 1916.

109. Jennie Scott Griffiths, "Women of Australia," unidentified flyer, in *Literary Cuttings*, 104.

110. Jennie Scott Griffiths, Memoirs, Griffiths Papers.

111. "Women and Conscription," *Australian Worker*, 5 October 1916, clipping in *Literary Cuttings*, 103.

112. Return of Prosecutions, case 1053.

113. Kennedy, *Disloyal Mothers*. See also Kirkby, "Neither 'Militarism' nor 'Patriotic Motherhood.'"

114. Kennedy, *Disloyal Mothers*, 112.

115. Ibid., 111. See also Joy Damousi, "Socialist Women and Gendered Space: Anti-Conscription and Anti-War Campaigns, 1914–18," *Labour History* 60 (1991): 1–15.

116. Johnson, "Wilson, Burleson, and Censorship," 58.

117. Cain, *Wobblies at War*, 285.

118. Evans, *Red Flag Riots*, 116.

119. Murphy, *World War I*, 52.

120. Ibid. See also Menzies, "War Powers."

121. Jay Winter, *Socialism and the Challenge of War: Ideas and Politics in Britain, 1911–18* (New York: Routledge, 1974), 1.

122. Cain, *Origins*, 198.

123. F. B. Smith, *Conscription Plebiscites*, 14.

124. Ibid.

125. Alice Henry to Alice Thatcher Post, 14 February 1934, quoted in Kirkby, *Alice Henry*, 213.

126. Quoted in Saunders, *Quiet Dissenter*, 319.

PART 2

Varieties of Labor Coercion

From Whips to Wages

From Coercive to Incentive-Driven Labor

JENNIE JEPPESEN

Colonial America and early Australia have a common history, as Diane Kirkby shows elsewhere in this volume. This history includes their unfree convict populations. Many scholars have treated transportation of convicts to Virginia between 1614 and 1778 and to Australia between 1788 and 1853 as two halves of a whole—as if Australia simply represented a continuation of the older American system. And indeed, on the surface, the two look similar. Virginia convicts were purchased by a planter, held on a plantation, and labored for the master's profit, while New South Wales convicts were assigned to a settler, often on a farm, and worked for the master's profit.[1] However, the surface is where the similarities end. The government retained property rights over convict labor in Australia, leading to regulation of convict living standards, work hours, usage, and punishment; limited or nonenforced controls existed for convicts in Virginia, where masters held property rights over labor.[2]

Virginia colonists almost universally justified coercion and punishment to force work patterns in pursuit of profit, and this inequality was most evident between masters and servants.[3] In contrast, New South Wales employers relied on incentives and rewards. This chapter argues that private control in Virginia allowed abuse, while government oversight (both home and colonial) in Australia limited punishment and improved access to freedom. The change in type of control caused a modification in strategy to force unwilling convicts to work—from coercion toward incentives. As Marjorie A. Jerrard and Patrick

O'Leary demonstrate in their chapter in this volume, stronger regulatory environments meant a need for a different approach to workers, whether convict or free.

Method of Labor Assignment

The earliest days of both colonies set the stage for later practices. Virginia began as a private enterprise geared toward profit, not settlement. While charters granted for settlement in the Americas provided for governance according to strict instructions given by the Crown, they also contained extensive immunities as a means to attract private capital.[4] Thus, Virginia colonists were not incorporated as organic parts of the English body politic, and virtual autonomy was gained through powers of self-government. Local colonial assemblies developed a great deal of power.[5] Although charters were subsequently revoked, assemblies retained their power, and when the Crown sought to maximize profit by curtailing earlier privileges and later attempted to assert direct Crown control of colonies, local resistance was strong.[6] This resistance included all attempts at regulation of labor laws.

Tobacco and the increasing demand for the labor resources it required determined the culture around work. Tobacco colonies, including Virginia, were among the most repressive: as Christopher Tomlins has written, —"Excesses defined and established the terms of mastery," with physical force and denial of food, clothing, and shelter used to control servants purchased on the open market as commodities.[7] Virginia, begun as a profit venture with all lands 'belonging' to the Virginia Company, had no private lands or wages available to motivate workers, and coercion thus was most commonly used to force labor for the company's benefit. This practice of coercion continued into the royal era, with laws of servitude acting to protect the expectations of food and lodging for volunteer servants to induce them to emigrate while retaining harshness to force them to work upon arrival.[8] While the brutal repression of the lower classes had a long tradition in England, in Virginia, this repression went to unprecedented lengths against both servants and nonservants.[9]

Unlike the American colonies, the colonization of Australia *was* directly funded by the Crown.[10] The difference between the two colonial systems was not the desire for imperial control but the ability to impose it. Politicians in London felt certain that assemblies would not arise because a convict settlement fell under military rather than civil control.[11] Unlike other earlier British colonies, New South Wales had no advisory council appointed, and power was totally vested in the governor.[12] While the distance from London always meant that the governors on the ground in Australia had as much on-the-spot autocratic initiative as earlier governors in Virginia, increased Crown control was reflected in local practices.[13] The two colonies thus were settled at different stages on a continuum of tightening imperial control, which was difficult to enforce as a result of distance, and large elements of self-sufficiency gave rise to local laws and practices.

Unlike other colonies, where settlers needed labor, New South Wales began with a plentiful labor supply. The colonial government used convict labor to clear land and establish houses and farms, and all of this effort occurred for public (rather than personal) benefit. Colonists in Australia were far from the source of their labor supply, and with no other labor forms of labor available, policies emerged to ensure good treatment to maximize convicts' laboring abilities. However, having the government maintain and employ all convicts was expensive—government bore the risk of the enterprise. As settlers arrived, this cost was shifted away from government by assigning convicts to labor on the farms of individuals who then bore the costs of food and clothing. While assignment began in a rather ad hoc manner at the local level rather than on instructions from England, John Thomas Bigge advocated expanding the assignment of convicts to free settlers as a means to save the home government money.[14] This assignment system in New South Wales and Van Diemen's Land offers the strongest parallels between the Australian and Virginian methods of labor assignment. Nevertheless, while the convict labor was assigned in Australia, the property rights were not.[15] Retention of the property rights meant that stronger regulatory practices were in place, limiting coercion.

Punishment and Coercion

With private control, most of the punishment for violation of rules in Virginia fell into the hands of masters, on the homestead, in private, and with almost no regulatory checks. Although masters' domination was not absolute, they had the power to threaten dependents, restrict movement, and traumatize workers.[16] In 1682, the home government instructed Governor Lord Culpepper to "endeavour to pass laws to restrain inhuman severity towards white servants or black slaves."[17] Such instructions strongly suggest that the colony's harshness attracted notice in England.[18] A 1666 Virginia law had banned the private burial of servants, a response to the many servants killed by masters during "correction."[19] In fact, this law stated that the suspicion that the master was responsible for death was "justified" when a private burial took place, showing that this kind of violent death at the hands of an owner was neither unknown nor uncommon.

In 1663, a female servant was beaten to death and servants of Richard Preston were whipped for asking for more food.[20] Richard Proctor's servant was beaten so badly that she was black and raw, and it was reported that if the surgeon did not tend to her, she "must needs perishe."[21] Nevertheless, Proctor was not reprimanded. Servants had the legal right to complain to the court about abusive masters, however it would take three such complaints from the same servant before any serious action was taken.[22] A month after Richard Baker's master was accused of conducting the "unchristian burial" of a servant maid, the master faced a second complaint of "bad usage" this time from Richard Baker; nevertheless, in spite of his master's violent history, Baker remained in his master's service though he was directed to "see [Baker] well cloathed."[23] Henry Smith was charged by his servants with abuse and rape and produced overwhelming evidence to support their claims. In spite of this, the servants were ordered back into Smith's service and ordered to serve double time.[24] Even in cases where masters were reprimanded, servants were returned to the same masters and thus faced further abuse as punishment for complaining.

Ads for runaway Virginia servants provide some insight into the punishments they faced at their masters' hands. According to C. Ashley Ellefson, "The authority that the master held over his servants and slaves bred in him an arrogance and a brutality."[25] Descriptions often included evidence of recent whippings, while other runaways had their ears cropped, had lost eyes or toes, or were chained or bound. For example, convict servant Hannah Boyer ran away with a chain and horse lock on her leg.[26]

Even death of a servant was rarely punished. When two young men died soon after being whipped with a stick, their masters were acquitted of any wrongdoing on the grounds that the servants "deserved" beating for absconding; the subsequent death was deemed an unfortunate result but the servants' own fault.[27] Alice Sandord was killed by "divers blows" from her master, Pope Alvery, who received no punishment.[28] Francis Leaven and Sean Hodgikins tortured their servant, putting lighted matches between his fingers.[29] Other masters similarly tried for abusing or killing servants were pardoned by proclamation, or the accuser was forced to apologize.[30] These cases are simply a sampling of the many abuse cases that ended in servants' deaths.[31] Corporal punishment was common in Virginia because masters had fewer institutional checks on their behavior.[32] Private ownership thus meant that little protection was available to convicts against abuse in spite of the rights they supposedly had in court.

There is perhaps room for the assumption, then, that under the assignment system in New South Wales there would have been similar abuses at the hands of the settlers toward convicts as occurred in Virginia. However government retention of property rights meant that officials had discretion to remove convicts from an employer, reallocate them, or replace them. This public control imposed limitations on the treatment of convicts. Punishment occurred by the order of a magistrate, rather than at the employers' discretion, thus curtailing Australian employers' ability to abuse their convict servants.

Employers had nearly unlimited power to send servants to the magistrates to be flogged for minor offenses, but before punishment was imposed, convicts had the chance to tell their side of the story in court.[33] At the same time, settlers hesitated to bring suits against servants because doing so might result in the loss of their labor, with no guarantee of replacement. For instance, the matron of the Female Factory was instructed not to consider applications for servants from employers who had a history of repeatedly taking to court convicts assigned to them.[34] As such, settlers might have been hesitant to take convicts to the court for minor infractions.[35]

While Virginia masters had the right to flog, Australian employers did not.[36] In 1838, Tasmanian governor George Arthur stated that a convict's employer "cannot apply corporal punishment by his own hand, or his own orders."[37] Even magistrates could not punish their own assigned convicts.[38] Employers were keenly watched and brought to account if they mistreated assigned convict servants, who could—and did—charge employers with assault.[39] In addition, employers were prohibited from withholding food—the colonial government mandated rations.[40] Abusive employers could lose servants and, unlike in Virginia, could be fined or jailed; those known to be cruel might have requests for convicts ignored.[41] In a two-year period beginning in March 1829, sixty-one convicts were removed from fifty-three employers as punishment for such abuses as refusing to supply food and clothing and engaging women convicts in prostitution.[42] The Australian restrictions meant that convict employers had less control over punishment than either American owners or English masters. Thus, the private control in Virginia enabled abuse, while the public control in Australia regulated punishment.

While coercion was not absent in Australia (just as incentive was not wholly absent in Virginia), it was tempered by the government's involvement. Some settlers argued that these checks weakened employers' authority over assigned servants.[43] Settler James Mudie, for example, begrudged government power over employers and argued that convicts needed "a sufficient degree of subjection to the will and powers of their immediate masters" rather than to the government "to enable them to be coerced to the performance of labour."[44] Other settlers complained that the "vast expense and trouble" of taking convicts to magistrates for punishment was worse than the twenty-five lashes the convicts received.[45] In 1822, during his testimony to the Bigge Commission investigation of transportation effectiveness aimed at reducing costs to the home government, convict superintendent William Hutchinson declared that "the idea of a sale would create a great deal of mischief. The constraint of government is, in my opinion, much preferred to that of individuals."[46]

The Australian colony did not lack brutality: the greatest coercion was the threat of being sent to a secondary punishment site, such as Port Arthur, Port Macquarie, or Moreton Bay.[47] In some respects, the chain gangs played a similar role to the "'nigger breakers' in the antebellum [US] South."[48] For women, there was the threat of the dark cells inside the Female Factories.[49] Fear of punishment and hope of reward were powerful motivators, but the fear of losing rewards was especially effective: as wool pioneer John MacArthur argued, "There are many ways of punishing them before taking them to the magistrate . . . by stopping their indulgences (tea, sugar, tobacco) in the first instance."[50] Governors in both Australia and Virginia strongly believed in giving convicts "something to lose."[51] The change from Virginia to Australia is that in Virginia, coercion was the foremost way to ensure labor, while in Australia incentive was the dominant force.

An interesting parallel existed within Australia that mirrored the Virginia situation. The Van Diemen's Land Company held the property rights over the labor of the convicts and indentured servants it employed.[52] Historian Jennifer Duxbury has shown that servants held by the company faced more brutality than was generally the case in Australia (51 percent of the company's servants were flogged, versus 11 percent for the colony as a whole). In addition, they were more likely to have their rights violated and less likely to have access to the court, and company employees did not receive wages.[53] This singular example supports my argument that the private or public control influenced the coercion or incentive faced by the convict.

The Role of the Court

Brandon Paul Righi has shown that in cases in which servants successfully petitioned against their masters in York County, Virginia, in the mid-eighteenth century, they prevailed on contractual violations; any other case would fail in court.[54] In contrast, Christine Daniels has written that 100 percent of colonial-era claims of ill usage in Maryland were resolved in the servants' favor.[55] However, Becky Showmaker argues that Daniels's claim "is proven inaccurate and oversimplified from the records."[56] My research supports Righi's and Showmaker's findings: despite the appearances of legal protection for servants in the American colonies, these laws were rarely enforced.

Although Virginia's servants had right to complain, even proven abuse often was not enough to free them from their masters, as in Richard Baker's case. Faced with this seemingly insurmountable court system, many Virginia convicts chose instead to run away; when caught, they subsequently faced longer sentences—as much as twice as long.[57] Baker, for example, had attempted to run away from his master in the same year as the abuse case, probably as a consequence of the same sort of abuse that he alleged in court.[58] Elizabeth Hasellton ran away because she was tied to a post and whipped; when she was captured and returned to her master, he beat her again and subsequently tried to retain her for a longer sentence.[59] Recaptured runaways were forced to serve double the time to 'repay' the time of their absence. In Australia however, convicts who complained about their employer could be removed and reassigned to another. Even a convict who ran away due to ill-usage (real or imagined) could be reassigned to a new employer after punishment.

Australian servants also ran away, but the government rather than individual settlers placed ads seeking absconders.[60] The difference is in the fact that a convict who ran in Australia was often placed back into the system when caught (the Factory for women and barracks or chain gang for men) and then reassigned elsewhere.[61] Unlike in Virginia, where a replacement required purchasing another laborer, at a cost of between nine and twenty-four pounds, in Australia the government freely gave the replacement.[62] In some instances, convicts ran from employers they found harsh or difficult, or where they felt hard done (justly or unjustly).[63] An American convict who ran for the same reason would be returned to the same master, and risked further abuses, and served an additional sentence. Thus, the involvement of government control over the convict labor, as a contrast to the private owner control, meant that a convict in Australia had a means other than the court to escape abuse.

Incentives

The Australian government's control of convicts did not just limit abuse but also established convict labor regulations. In the earliest days of the colony, Governor Arthur Phillip set working hours as five o'clock in the morning to three o'clock in the afternoon so that convicts would still have time to raise vegetables and other food supplies later in the day.[64] While this was in reaction to the starvation risk in the first few years, this government-mandated workday remained the regulation for the entire convict period. While hours fluctuated often in the early years based on food stores and starvation risk, they were only adjusted by a governor's order, not in accordance with an individual settler's needs.[65] Thus, public control meant set work hours and convicts could and did refuse to work outside of these hours unless they were provided with incentives to do so.

For men in Port Arthur, work hours fluctuated based on the month.[66] In the female factories, work hours were longer in summer than in winter.[67] All employers, even those outside the punishment sites, had to follow the prescribed work schedule or risk losing convicts. However, women assigned to private settlers were not governed by the mandatory work hours and were supposed to be available at all times, a reflection of the English cultural norm that women in domestic service were expected to be at their employers' beck and call around the clock.[68] During the assignment era, convicts would not work outside of these hours without a wage or other incentive. Employers attempting to force work outside hours faced refusal with no means at their disposal to force the convict—because punishment was limited to magisterial order. Virginia convicts, in contrast, were meant to work at the master's whim, with no regulation of working hours as there was in Australia.

During Lachlan Macquarie's governorship, road gangs responded to attempts to increase their working hours with work slowdowns.[69] In other instances, convicts worked slowly when they did not like their employers.[70] Another form of protest was refusing to accept food that was considered inferior or insufficient.[71] In addition, unlike in the Virginia convict labor market, Australian convicts who engaged in this sort of resistance could not simply be punished or sold on to the next employer; they might be taken to magistrates, reassigned, or sent to a punishment site, but more often the employer would negotiate, perhaps by offering extra incentives such as tea or tobacco. This evidence of the convict's power to negotiate their working situation was the basis of the incentive-driven labor that arises directly out of limits placed on punishment by public control.

There is little evidence of any kind of negotiations or incentives for Virginia convicts where the convict bargained from a position of power. Some servants could petition for incentives such as permission to get married—but in exchange agreeing to serve additional time.[72] Generally the Virginia master's interest was to exact as much work as possible, to maximize the profit from convicts' labor for the purchase price. This meant long work hours, dirty and dangerous labor, and little chance for self-work or betterment. While Australian settlers had similar interests in getting the most out of their convict labor, government limitations on working hours meant that convicts could work for themselves or others outside of assigned times, giving them a chance to earn a wage for the future. Between 1816 and 1823, Australian settlers had to pay their convicts a daily wage as well as their food ration.[73] These wages were meant to ensure that convicts would survive "off the stores" when freed from service. Australian employers who wanted convicts to be available for the employers work at all times had to pay an additional ten pounds per annum, but convicts had the right to refuse and work for themselves instead.[74] All evidence for any type of convict refusal to work in Virginia led to heavy reprisals, including abuse and extra time on their sentence. Australian overtime regulation was eventually converted to a flat ten pounds sterling a year for all convicts.

John MacArthur paid above the ten pounds minimum to his convicts because, as Dyster summarizes, "people might work in their employer's interest if they were paid better than the norm."[75] While wages were set by the government at modest rates, many employers paid above it, or with payments on the side, to secure the best convicts.[76] Other employers offered better food or allowed convicts to build their own quarters.[77] Wages often were banked on behalf of the convict so that they would accrue interest.[78] In some cases, convicts undertook work without written agreements and subsequently sued for unpaid wages. Though these claims usually failed in court as a result of lack of evidence, they show that convicts expected to be paid for working on their own time. Wages for women in Australia are less clear—some scholarship states that women were never awarded wages, even during assignment, while other studies argue that women earned slightly smaller wages than men did.[79] Others note that those in the first class in the Factory were paid per article created in excess of their quota (with part of the payment banked on their behalf and part given to them directly); however, any money they possessed on arrival at the Factory was confiscated.[80]

Some Australian employers protested the requirement that they pay wages. One farmer named Oxley testified that small farmers could not afford the ten-pound yearly wage, and D'Arcy Wentworth similarly testified that he was against any wage for the convict's free time.[81] Governor Thomas Brisbane abolished the working wage in 1823, in keeping with the view of authorities in both Australia and London that it constituted an inappropriate reward for people being punished. Nevertheless, many employers continued to pay wages as a means of motivating convicts to work toward employers purposes.[82] Wages meant that convicts in Australia had a greater deal of freedom over their lives while still under sentence than did Virginia convicts. They could spend and fall into debt or not as they wished.[83]

In Virginia, however, servants who completed their time received only a small amount of food. There is some conflicting evidence as to whether convicts or servants received wages. In a report prepared in the 1660s, Sir John Kelyng, instructed justices, "That such prisoners as are Reprieved with intent to be transported, be not sent away as perpetual Slaves, but upon Indentures betwixt them and particular Masters, to serve in our English Plantations for seven years, and three last years thereof, to have wages, that they may have a Stock when their Time is expired."[84] Nevertheless, evidence for convicts receiving a direct wage is slim, and it seems that if it was occurring, it was skilled workers who had the best chance of receiving one.[85] One indentured servant noted in 1664 that despite promises of high wages made in England, servants were paid "not one fartheing."[86] Moreover, all of these examples involve indentured servants, not convicts, and there is no concrete evidence to date that indicates that convicts in the American colonies received wages.

However, a few references indicate that American convicts might have received money of some kind. In 1751 Governor William Gooch of Virginia stated, "It is certainly no good policy to furnish convicts with money which they seldom use to good purposes," although this could have been in response to debates on Freedom Dues.[87] In another instance, the High Court ordered "no wadge to be given," suggesting that wages might have been paid in other cases.[88] However, another reference suggests that any wages to be paid should go to the master, not the servants—"which money is due to me, being his master."[89] Frederick Schmidt argues that servants were given money as tips, some brought money from England, and that some earned it on their own time, noting that runaway notices sometimes say that convicts had money on them.[90] However he does not offer any documentation other than the runaway advertisements to prove his theory, and evidence is slim for convicts actually receiving money. In all likelihood, convicts received wages haphazardly at best, and then only if they were skilled, and I argue that if it occurred their chance to capitalize on it would be much smaller than that of the Australian convict. After freedom, Virginia convicts lapsed back into poverty and reindentured themselves simply to survive.[91]

In Virginia slaves (and by extension possibly some convicts) occasionally were allowed a plot of land on which to grow food and were permitted to sell their produce (as long as it differed from that grown on the plantation).[92] This was more common where task work held sway, which was not Virginia.[93] Some slaves (and possibly convicts) also received "holidays"—usually Christmas—although it was rarely a time for leisure. Slave owner John Hammond wrote in his diary, "Holiday for the Negros who fenced in their gardens. Lazy devils they did nothing after 12 o'clock."[94] This shift from nonwage work in Virginia to time that was paid in Australia is an example of the shift from coercive labor to incentive labor.

Because Australian convicts received wages and earned after-hours income, they could rent their own accommodations in town.[95] Major George Druitt described a muster of new convict arrivals in Sydney finding their own lodging between 1810 and 1819.[96] Governor Ralph Darling wrote to Lord Bathurst that "the well conducted have always been allowed to sleep out of barracks . . . and maintain their families. . . . This system has prevailed so long that it could not without some risk and injury to the town and the inhabitants be put a stop to."[97] This unprecedented freedom was unheard of in Virginia, and there is no evidence that any Virginia convicts lived away from their masters, let alone on such a regular basis.

Freedom

Freedom was another incentive often used to motivate good behavior from convicts in Australia. Under the ticket of leave system, a convict received an initial ticket after a set period of service.[98] Ticket holders were allowed to work for themselves though technically still under sentence. Misbehavior, however, would result in the loss of this freedom. The holding out of the ticket of leave and the conditional pardon for good behavior was an appeal to the self-interest of the convict, and was popular among governors.[99] The next step after the ticket of leave was one of three certificates. The first, a conditional pardon, involved the suspension of the rest of a convict's sentence on the condition that he or she remain in Australia. This too was used as a powerful incentive. Governor Macquarie, for example, used the promise of a conditional pardon to motivate men to build a road through the Blue Mountains in just six months.[100] The other was a "certificate of freedom," which was given to those who had completed the length of their sentence. The final step on this freedom ladder was the full pardons, which technically could be bestowed only by the king or queen, had all the rights of free citizens. Such incentives appealed to convict self-interest and were popular among governors, in large part because they could serve as both carrot and stick: they could be dangled to encourage good behavior or withheld or withdrawn for misdeeds.[101] This program is another significant divergence from American practices that can be attributed to government regulations. While these Australian government-regulated practices granted freedom at a predetermined time, Virginia masters often tried to retain their servants as long as possible, often beyond the initial length of their sentences.[102] Given the high demand for labor in the colony, Virginia "masters were anxious to hold on to their bound laborers. Desperate and jealous masters meant more restrictive and overbearing environments for servants.[103] Despite Australia's labor shortage, public control curbed employers' ability to restrict workers.

One exception to the private/public dichotomy involved the fact that wealthy Virginia convicts could buy their own time as soon as they arrived and thus never serve as laborers. This was never an option in Australia. Convicts buying out their time in Virginia effectively ceased being convicts, although if they had returned to England, they would have been tried for returning early. These buyouts were merely exiles.

Conclusion

Through the eighteenth-century Enlightenment and nineteenth-century romanticism, ideas about original sin and innate depravity were shifting to a greater focus on the reformation of the individual rather than punishment of the body. At the same time, however, corruption was believed to easily fasten upon the soul.[104] Despite these ideological changes, indentured servants in America were treated the same between 1775 and 1789 as they had been before the revolution.[105] This suggests that the better treatment that Australian convicts received had more to do with the form of control than with the arrival of Enlightened ideas, although those ideas certainly had some influence. The fact that convicts held privately by the Van Diemen's Land Company were more heavily coerced than those who fell under Australian government control supports this argument.

Prison reform was also shifting in the period between the end of transportation to America and beginning of transportation to Australia. Italian scholar Cesare Beccaria, a prominent voice in legal reform, questioned how legal arbitrariness could be overlooked in an Enlightened age.[106] However, Beccaria's arguments initially had little impact on British court systems and did not become endorsed in the civil code of Europe until Napoleon's reign in the nineteenth century.[107] In the British Isles, Beccaria's proposals were at first seen as contradictory to common law and were not adopted there. Prison reformers William Eden (1771) and John Howard (1777) also encountered resistance from the ruling classes, and not until 1808 was Eden's proposal to reduce the number of crimes carrying the death penalty adopted.[108]

British penal reformers did not record their first successes until after the First Fleet embarked for Australia. Thomas Paine's *The Rights of Man*, an influential harbinger of humanitarianism, was not published until 1789. Jeremy Bentham did not publish his Panopticon plans until 1791. Robert Peel did not establish the British police force until 1829. Thus, these reforms did not affect the type of society that developed in Australia. While Michel Foucault sees a shift away from corporal punishment and toward a greater focus on rehabilitation between 1750 and 1820, that shift was motivated not by a concern for the welfare of prisoners but by a desire to make power operate more efficiently.[109] My study shows that convicts in a strong state-controlled system were less coerced than those in the private system. The fact that penal reformers were initially unsuccessful in their campaigns meant that most reforms were not in place prior to the embarkation of the First Fleet and did not impact the type of society that developed in Australia.

The differential treatment of convicts under public control in colonial Australia and private control in colonial Virginia created a pattern that is still evident in union negotiations today. By looking at Virginia and Australia comparatively we can see that, although profit from unfree labor was a motivator in both systems, the involvement of public control significantly changed the impact it had on the convicts themselves.[110]

Notes

1. Convicts and indentured servants were conflated in practice and law in Virginia, and it is nearly impossible to separate them in the evidence. See Jennie Jeppesen, "Searching for the Hidden Convict in Virginia's Servant Laws," *ANZLH E-Journal* 2013 (December 2013), available at http://www.austlii.edu.au/au/journals/ANZLawHisteJl/2013/2.html. To prevent confusion, I refer to those who used convict labor in Virginia as *master* or *planter*, while those in Australia are *employer* or *settler*.

2. Geo I C II 1717 (The Transportation Act).

3. David K. O'Rourke, *How America's First Settlers Invented Chattel Slavery* (New York: Lang, 2004), 6, 20.

4. George Louis Beer, *The Origins of the British Colonial System, 1578–1660* (Gloucester, Mass.: Smith, 1959), 297–98, 304.

5. George Louis Beer, *British Colonial Policy, 1754–1765* (New York: Macmillan, 1907), 2.

6. Beer, *Origins*, 304; P. J. Marshall, "Empire and Authority in the Later Eighteenth Century," *Journal of Imperial and Commonwealth History* 15 (1987): 110; Henry Lindsay Hall, *The Colonial Office: A History* (New York: Longmans, Green, 1937), 9; Hugh Edward Egerton, *A Short History of British Colonial Policy* (London: Methuen, 1897), 2; P. J. Marshall, introduction to *The Oxford History of the British Empire*, ed. William Roger Louis et al. (Oxford: Oxford University Press, 1998), 2:9; P. J. Marshall, "Britain without America—A Second Empire?," in *Oxford History*, ed. Louis et al., 587.

7. Christopher Tomlins, *Freedom Bound: Law, Labor, and Civic Identity in Colonizing English America, 1580–1865* (Cambridge: Cambridge University Press, 2010), 263; Terri L. Snyder, *Brabbling Women: Disorderly Speech and the Law in Early Virginia* (Ithaca: Cornell University Press, 2003), 89, 95. Douglas Greenberg, "Crime, Law Enforcement, and Social Control in Colonial America," *American Journal of Legal History* 26 (1982): 302.

8. William Edward Nelson, *The Common Law in Colonial America* (New York: Oxford University Press, 2008), 41; Sigmund Diamond, "From Organization to Society: Virginia in the Seventeenth Century," *American Journal of Sociology* 63 (1958): 465.

9. David Thomas Konig, "Dale's Laws and the Non–Common Law Origins of Criminal Justice in Virginia," *American Journal of Legal History* 26 (1982): 368, 369.

10. The First Fleet was funded by the King's Civil List. Georgia was the only other colony partially funded by the Crown and was also focused on the clearing of jails. Data provided by Dan Byrnes, June 2014; Alan Atkinson, "The Primitive Origins of Parliament," *The Push from the Bush* 24 (1987): 55.

11. T. O. Lloyd, *Empire: The History of the British Empire* (London: Hambledon and London, 2001), 60–61.

12. Marshall, "Britain without America," 589.

13. F. M. Bladen, ed., *Historical Records of New South Wales* (hereafter *HRNSW*), vol. 1, pt. 2 (Mona Vale, N.S.W.: Lansdown Slattery, 1978), 85–91.

14. John Thomas Bigge, *Report of the Commissioner of Inquiry into the State of the Colony of New South Wales* (London: n.p., 1822). Molesworth estimated the cost of punishing a convict under assignment was £71, while those not under assignment would cost £145. See James Edward Gillespie, "The Transportation of English Convicts after 1783," *Journal of the American Institute of Criminal Law and Criminology* 13 (1922): 365; *HRNSW*, 3:95; Henry Dundas to Governor Phillip, 10 January 1792, in *HRNSW*, vol. 1, pt. 2, p. 585; Phillip to Nepean, 17 June 1790, in *HRNSW*, vol. 1, pt. 2, p. 349; Duke of Portland to Governor Hunter, August 1796, in *New South Wales General Standing Orders: Selected from the General Orders Issued by Former Governors, from the 16th of February, 1791 to the 6th of September, 1800* (Sydney: Government Press, 1802) (hereafter *NSW Orders*), a341079, Mitchell Library, Sydney, Reference 449244; "all descriptions acquired by the labour of the convicts shall be considered as a public stock" (Governor Hunter's Orders, 1 July 1794, in *HRNSW*, 2:229); Phillip to Lord Sydney, 12 February 1790, in *HRNSW*, vol. 1, pt. 2, p. 300; Additional Instructions to Phillip, 20 August 1789, in *HRNSW*, vol. 1, pt. 2, p. 258; *NSW Orders*, secs. a341031, a341034, a341075, a341100; *HRNSW*, 2:232; Kristine McCabe, "Assignment of Female Convicts on the Hunter River, 1831–1840," *Australian Historical Studies* 29 (1999): 302.

15. 24 Geo. 3 c. 56 1784, "Convicts Being the Servants of the Crown," in *New South Wales General Standing Orders, 1802–1806*, State Library of New South Wales, Digital order no:Album ID: 852765, sec. a341078, 11 June 1810, http://archival.sl.nsw.gov.au/Details/archive/110341407. In 1817, a ruling stated that the employer had a "property in the service" of a convict (J. Beckett to H. Goulbourne, 25 March 1817, in Frederick Watson, ed., *Historical Records of Australia* [hereafter *HRA*] [Sydney: Library Committee of the Commonwealth Parliament, 1914], 9:383). However, Chief Justice Forbes wrote that this was out of date with current practice, and Murray wrote to Darling that "convicts labour should be regarded not as the property of a settler, but as an indulgence" (S. G. Foster, "Convict Assignment in New South Wales in the 1830s," *The Push from the Bush* 15 [1983]: 60, 78).

16. Snyder, *Brabbling Women,* 89.

17. Instructions to Lord Culpepper, Governor of Virginia, 27 January 1682, in *Calendar of State Papers, Colonial* (London: Longmans, H.M.S.O., 1860).

18. Richard Brandon Morris, *Government and Labor in Early America* (New York: Harper Torchbooks, 1965), 482, 483–500.

19. William Waller Hening, *Statutes at Large: Being a Collection of All the Laws of Virginia, from the First Session of the Legislature in the Year 1619* (Richmond: Pleasants, 1810), 2:53; Becky Showmaker, "'Corrected above Measure': Indentured Servants and Domestic Abuse in Maryland, 1650–1700" (master's thesis, University Missouri at Columbia, 2009), chap. 3.

20. Provincial Court, 31 March 1663, 8–10, S551, Maryland State Archives; Charles Hamrick and Virginia Hamrick, eds., *Northumberland County, Virginia, Court Order Book, 1699–1713* (Athens, Ga.: Iberian, 1999), 318.

21. Konig, "Dale's Laws," 372.

22. Convicts were barred from testimony after 1748, after which convicts did not have this right to complain of abuse. See Hening, *Statutes at Large,* 5:537–546; Hugh F. Rankin, *Criminal Trial Proceedings in the General Court of Colonial Virginia* (Williamsburg: Colonial Williamsburg, 1965); Allison Madar, "A People Between: Servitude in Colonial Virginia, 1700–1783" (PhD diss., Rice University, 2013). Even after repeated complaints, one Maryland servant was not freed until she was whipped with a rope end in front of the judge (Debra Meyers, *Common Whores, Vertuous Women, and Loveing Wives: Free Will Christian Women in Colonial Maryland* [Bloomington: Indiana University Press, 2003], 160–61).

23. Hamrick and Hamrick, *Northumberland County,* 287.

24. Terri Snyder, "To Seeke for Justice: Gender, Servitude, and Household Governance in the Early Modern Chesapeake," in *Early Modern Virginia: Reconsidering the Old Dominion,* ed. Douglas Bradburn and John C. Coombs (Charlottesville: University of Virginia Press, 2011), 135; Terri Snyder, "As If There Was Not a Master or Woman in the Land: Gender, Dependency, and Household Violence, 1646–1720," in *Over the Threshold: Intimate Violence in Early America,* ed. Christine Daniels and Michael V. Kennedy (New York: Routledge, 1999), 229.

25. *Pennsylvania Gazette,* 27 August 1747, 3; C. Ashley Ellefson, "The Private Punishment of Servants and Slaves in Eighteenth Century Maryland" (2010), 23, available at http://aomol.net/megafile/msa/speccol/sc2900/sc2908/000001/000822/pdf/am822.pdf.

26. Michael V. Kennedy has shown that over the decade leading up to Revolution, the whipping of servants increased by 213 percent, those reported with missing digits grew by 91 percent, and those beaten or bruised and scarred increased by 254 percent ("The Consequences of Cruelty: The Escalation of Servant and Slave Abuse, 1750–1780," *Essays in Economic and Business History* 22 [2004]: 127). See also Teresa Foster, "A Shameful and Unblessed Thing: Convict Bondwomen in Eighteenth Century Maryland," in *Order and Civility in the Early Modern Chesapeake,* ed. Debra Meyers and Melanie Perreault (Lanham, Md.: Lexington, 2014), 155–72.

27. Horn, *Adapting to a New World*, 270.

28. Debbie Hooper, *Abstracts of Chancery Court Records of Maryland, 1669–1782* (Westminster, Md.: Heritage, 2008), 2. At some point, Pope Alvery was also convicted of manslaughter in a different case but subsequently was acquitted with the benefit of clergy (something like a pardon) (Horn, *Adapting to a New World*, 355).

29. Abbot Emerson Smith, "AE Smith Research Notes," fol. 19.

30. Ibid., fol. 20; Ellefson, "Private Punishment."

31. Ellefson, "Private Punishment," 22; Horn, *Adapting to a New World*, 355; Abbot Emerson Smith, "AE Smith Research Notes," fol. 19.

32. David Eltis, Frank D. Lewis, and Kenneth Lee Sokoloff, eds., *Slavery in the Development of the Americas* (Cambridge: Cambridge University Press, 2004), 296.

33. Richard Davis, "William Smith O'Brien and Tasmanian Convict Workers," in *Beyond Convict Workers*, ed. Barrie Dyster (Sydney: Department of Economic History, University of New South Wales, 1996), 59; McCabe, "Assignment of Female Convicts," 296–97.

34. Babette Smith, *A Cargo of Women: Susannah Watson and the Convicts of the Princess Royal* (Dural, N.S.W.: Rosenberg, 2005), 44. Female Factory was a barracks, maternity ward, punishment site, and hiring yard combination for women. See Tony Rayner. *Female Factory, Female Convicts: The Story of the More Than 13,000 Women Exiled from Britain to Van Diemen's Land* (Dover, Tas.: Experance, 2004).

35. Employers would be more willing to take an unskilled convict to court than a skilled one, as skilled were harder to get.

36. John Hirst, *Convict Society and Its Enemies: A History of Early New South Wales* (Sydney: Allen and Unwin, 1983), 58. According to Hirst, this difference resulted from the legal attaint status of convicts versus other servants. However, convicts in America held the same attaint status as those in Australia, so I attribute the difference not to their attaint status but to the method of control. English common law provided that masters could flog workers on the spot, so the Australian restrictions meant that convict employers had less control over punishment than either American owners or English masters (John Braithwaite, "Crime in a Convict Republic," *Modern Law Review* 64 [2001]: 20).

37. *NSW Orders*, secs. a3341056, a341111. The Van Diemen's Land Company attempted to subvert this regulation by only allowing the in-house magistrate to order punishment. See Paula-Jane Byrne, *Criminal Law and Colonial Subject: New South Wales, 1810–1830* (Cambridge: Cambridge University Press, 1993); Miriam Dixson, *The Real Matilda: Woman and Identity in Australia, 1788–1975* (Ringwood: Penguin Australia, 1976), 116; *Report from the Select Committee of the House of Commons on Transportation* (London: Hooper, 1838).

38. Forbes to Bourke, 10 January 1834, in *HRA*, 9:332.

39. Stefan Petrow, "Policing in a Penal Colony: Governor Arthur's Police System in Van Diemen's Land, 1826–1836," *Law and History Review* 18 (2000): 365; S. G. Foster, "Convict Assignment," 66.

40. Michael Cannon, *Who's Master? Who's Man?* (Melbourne: Nelson, 1971), 52; Alan Atkinson, "Master and Servant at Camden Park, 1838, from the Estate Papers," *The Push from the Bush* 6 (1980): 43.

41. *NSW Orders*, sec. a341111; Robert Hughes, *The Fatal Shore: A History of the Transportation of Convicts to Australia, 1787–1868* (London: Random House, 2003), 307, 303; S. G. Foster, "Convict Assignment," 66.

42. S. G. Foster, "Convict Assignment," 61.

43. Petrow, "Policing in a Penal Colony," 386; S. G. Foster, "Convict Assignment," 60.

44. James Mudie, *The Felonry of New South Wales: Being a Faithful Picture of the Real Romance of Life in Botany Bay: With Anecdotes of Botany Bay Society and a Plan of Sydney*, ed. Walter Stone (Melbourne: Lansdowne, 1964), 2.

45. "Elisha on the Murrumbirdgee to His Excellency Sir George Gipps, Sydney Herald 19 October 1838," *The Push from the Bush* 15 (1983): 31.

46. Evidence of William Hutchinson, in Bigge, *Inquiry*, appendix.

47. Braithwaite, "Crime in a Convict Republic," 19. Hamish Maxwell-Stewart has suggested that the use of the lash, stocks, leg irons, and the like may have been less frequent than some historians have implied (*Reckoning with Convict Workers in Van Diemen's Land* [London: Sir Robert Menzies Centre for Australian Studies, 1990], 13). It also should be noted that some accounts of brutality are fabricated ("A Charists View," *The Push from the Bush* 13 [1982]: 7).

48. Hamish Maxwell-Stewart, "'Like Poor Galley Slaves': Slavery and Convict Transportation," in *Legacies of Slavery: Comparative Perspectives*, ed. Maria Suzette Fernandes Dias (Newcastle: Cambridge Scholars, 2007), 55.

49. Laurel Heath, "A Safe and Salutary Discipline: The Dark Cells at the Parramatta Female Factory, 1838," *The Push from the Bush* 9 (1981): 20–27.

50. Atkinson, "Master and Servant," 56.

51. Braithwaite, "Crime in a Convict Republic," 21.

52. Jennifer Duxbury, "Conflict and Discipline: The VDL Company," *The Push from the Bush* 25 (1987): 38.

53. Ibid., 39, 45; Jennifer Duxbury, *Colonial Servitude: Indentured and Assigned Servants of the Van Diemen's Land Company, 1825–41* (Clayton, Vic.: Monash Publications in History, Department of History, Monash University, 1989).

54. Brandon Paul Righi, "The Right of Petition: Cases of Indentured Servants and Society in Colonial Virginia, 1698–1746" (master's thesis, College of William and Mary, 2010).

55. Christine Daniels, "Liberty to Complaine: Servant Petitions in Maryland, 1652–1797," in *The Many Legalities of Early America*, ed. Christopher L. Tomlins and Bruce H. Mann (Chapel Hill: University of North Carolina Press, 2001), 219–49; Christine Daniels, "'Without Any Limitation of Time': Debt Servitude in Colonial America," *Labor History* 36 (1995): 232–50.

56. Showmaker, "'Corrected above Measure,'" 13. See also Snyder, *Brabbling Women*, 97; Snyder, "As If There Was Not a Master," 228.

57. Between 1763 and 1774, one of every forty servants ran. See Kennedy, "Consequences of Cruelty," 134: "Within the cycle of violence, servants and slaves were less pliable as regimes increased and punishment became more severe. As employers pressed for more,

bound laborers were more liable to try and remove themselves. As more workers fled, masters exerted more controls and increased punishments and as a result, more workers ran."

58. Hamrick and Hamrick, *Northumberland County*, 260.

59. Daniels, "Liberty to Complaine," 236.

60. James Mudie complained that the governor used the "soft and gentle name absentees" rather than *runaways* (*Felonry*, xiv).

61. Joy Damousi, *Depraved and Disorderly: Female Convicts, Sexuality, and Gender in Colonial Australia* (Cambridge: Cambridge University Press, 1997).

62. Farley Grubb, "The Transatlantic Market for British Convict Labor," *Journal of Economic History* 60 (March 2000): 94–122; Matthew Ridley to Duncan Campbell, 25 June, 19 May 1773, Ridley to Sonneville and Noble, 25 June 1773, all in Ridley Papers, Ms. N-797, Massachusetts Historical Society; Harry Piper to Dixon and Littledale, 28 June 1768, Harry Piper, "Items Relating to Alexandria, Va.," MSS 2981-a, vol. 1, Albert and Shirley Small Special Collections Library, University of Virginia; "Agreement to Serve," Section MF 204B, Box 1, John D. Rockefeller Jr. Library, Special Collections, Colonial Williamsburg; John Hook to David Ross, John Hook Records, 1763–1809, Business Records Collection, Library of Virginia; Frederick Hall Schmidt, "British Convict Servant Labor in Colonial Virginia" (PhD diss., College of William and Mary, 1976); *Virginia Gazette*, 3 March 1768, 8 March 1770, 28 March, 10 October 1771; James Cheston and Samuel Galloway Collection, 1681–1920, pt. 11, Maryland State Archives.

63. Babette Smith, *Cargo of Women*, 41.

64. Stephen Nicholas, "The Convict Labour Market," in *Convict Workers: Reinterpreting Australia's Past*, ed. Nicholas (Cambridge: Cambridge University Press, 1988), 128; Hughes, *Fatal Shore*, 99; Bruce Kercher, "Resistance to Law under Autocracy," *Modern Law Review* 60 (1997): 783.

65. *NSW Orders*.

66. Ian Brand, *Port Arthur, 1830–1877* (West Moonah, Tas.: Jason, 1975), 31.

67. Annette Salt, *These Outcast Women: The Parramatta Female Factory, 1821–1848* (Sydney: Hale and Iremonger, 1984), 78.

68. As a result, they had no free time to earn extra money. See Paula-Jane Byrne, "Women and the Criminal Law: Sydney, 1810–21," *The Push from the Bush* 21 (1985): 5. Ann Jackson was taken to court in 1828 for refusing to attend to her mistress at ten o'clock at night (David Philips and Susanne Elizabeth Davies, eds., *A Nation of Rogues? Crime, Law and Punishment in Colonial Australia* [Carlton, Vic.: Melbourne University Press, 1994], 16).

69. W. M. Robbins, "The Supervision of Convict Gangs in New South Wales, 1788–1830," *Australian Economic History Review* 44 (2004): 97.

70. Braithwaite, "Crime in a Convict Republic," 22.

71. Hirst, *Convict Society and Its Enemies*, 48.

72. Northumberland Order Book, 1749–53, 373, Northumberland Order Book 1753–56, 262, 346, both in MF51, Library of Virginia. Or they could apply for clothes (Washington

Preston Haynie, *Records of Indentured Servants and Certificates for Land, Northumberland County, Virginia, 1650–1795* [Bowie, Md.: Heritage, 1996], 11).

73. Governor Hunter, 10 March 1797, *NSW Orders*, sec. a341024; Barrie Dyster, "Why New South Wales Did Not Become Devil's Island (or Siberia)," in *Beyond Convict Workers*, ed. Dyster, 86.

74. Dyster, "Why New South Wales," 85.

75. Barrie Dyster, *Servant and Master: Building and Running the Grand Houses of Sydney, 1788–1850* (Kensington, N.S.W.: New South Wales University Press, 1989), 164.

76. Braithwaite, "Crime in a Convict Republic," 27.

77. Cannon, *Who's Master?*, 53.

78. W. D. Forsyth, *Governor Arthur's Convict System: Van Diemen's Land, 1824–36: A Study in Colonization*, 2nd ed. (Sydney: Sydney University Press, 1970), 50; Bruce Kercher, *An Unruly Child: A History of Law in Australia* (St. Leonards, N.S.W.: Allen and Unwin, 1995), 36.

79. Lucy Frost, ed., *Convict Lives at the Launceston Female Factory* (Hobart.: Convict Women's Press, 2013), 18; Damousi, *Depraved and Disorderly*, 67.

80. Salt, *These Outcast Women*, 72, 74, 76. Women in the Factory were sorted into three classes: first class was those waiting assignment; second was those who were waiting to give birth or who had just finished punishment; third was those being punished. See Lucy Frost, *Convict Lives: Women at Cascades Female Factory*, 2nd ed. (Hobart: Convict Women's Press, 2012); Salt, *These Outcast Women.*

81. John Ritchie, *Punishment and Profit: The Reports of Commissioner John Bigge on the Colonies of New South Wales and Van Diemen's Land, 1822–1823* (Melbourne: Heinemann, 1970), 126, 130.

82. Dyster, "Why New South Wales," 88. Some scholars have argued that wages were paid during the probation system to "distinguish it from the slavery assignment"; however, this simplifies the fact that convicts under assignment were paid wages (David Meredith and Deborah Oxley, "Contracting Convicts: The Convict Labour Market in Van Diemen's Land, 1840–1857," *Australian Economic History Review* 45 [2005]: 45).

83. Kercher, "Resistance to Law," 784. In fact, in 1798 under Governor John Hunter, convicts employed on public works who had fallen into debt could not be detained in jail (4 October 1798, *NSW Orders*, sec. a341028).

84. Sir John Kelyng, *A Report of Divers Cases in Pleas of the Crown, Adjudged and Determined; in the Reign of the Late King Charles II* (London: Cleave, 1708), 7.

85. Emmanuel Downing to John Winthrop Jr., 1644, Winthrop Papers, vol. 36, Colonial Massachusetts Historical Society; Robert Carter to Fairfax Harrison, 15 September 1729, Fairfax Harrison Papers, vol. 65 H25, Special Collections Research Center, Swem Library, College of William and Mary; Loose Indenture at London Guildhall, 25 October 1736, quoted in Abbot Emerson Smith, "AE Smith Research Notes," fol. 27; Righi, "Right of Petition," 28.

86. Matthew C. Pursell, "Changing Conceptions of Servitude in the British Atlantic, 1640–1780" (PhD diss., Brown University, 2005), 283.

87. William Gooch, Official Correspondence of William Gooch, 1681–1751, TR 16, John D. Rockefeller Jr. Library, Special Collections, Colonial Williamsburg. Freedom dues were paid to servants at the end of their service—usually some corn, a suit of clothes, and a small bit of money, though cash was rarely given (James Curtis Ballagh, *White Servitude in the Colony of Virginia: A Study of the System of Indentured Labor in the American Colonies* [Baltimore: Johns Hopkins Press, 1895]).

88. High Court Admiralty, Mic/636, Public Records Office, London

89. Thomas Lechford Letterbook, 27 June 1638–29 July 1641, 58–59, Mss. Folio vol. 50, American Antiquarian Society; Abbot Emerson Smith, "AE Smith Research Notes," fol. 7.

90. Frederick Hall Schmidt, "British Convict Servant Labor in Colonial Virginia" (PhD diss., College of William and Mary, 1976), 210, 222; *Virginia Gazette*, 9 March 1739.

91. A. Roger Ekirch, "Exiles in the Promised Land: Convict Labourers and the 18th Century Chesapeake," n.d., Maryland State Archives. The *Pennsylvania Gazette*, 20 August 1747, stated that one runaway man had a discharge from the man whom "he served his first time with" (Edith Miriam Ziegler, *Harlots, Hussies, and Poor Unfortunate Women: Crime, Transportation, and the Servitude of Female Convicts, 1718–1783* [Tuscaloosa: University of Alabama Press, 2014], 133).

92. This practice is far more common later in the antebellum period, though there are small pockets of it prior.

93. In the South Carolina Low Country, rice and cotton were the dominant crops. Virginia's tobacco farms used gang labor. See Robin Blackburn, *The American Crucible: Slavery, Emancipation, and Human Rights* (London: Verso, 2011), 306; Robert William Fogel and Stanley L. Engerman, eds., *Without Consent or Contract: The Rise and Fall of American Slavery* (New York: Norton, 1992), 192; Peter Kolchin, "Introduction: Variations of Slavery in the Atlantic World," *William and Mary Quarterly* 59 (2002): 551; David Brown, *Race in the American South: From Slavery to Civil Rights* (Edinburgh: Edinburgh University Press, 2007), 46.

94. 12 May 1832, quoted in Kenneth M. Stampp, *The Peculiar Institution: Negro Slavery in the American South* (London: Eyre and Spottiswoode, 1964), 84. Hammond was writing fifty years after the end of convict transportation, and the fact that slaves had gardens at this time cannot be considered proof that slaves also had gardens during the convict period.

95. Dyster, "Why New South Wales," 87.

96. Major Druitt quoted in Byrne, *Criminal Law and Colonial Subject*, 21.

97. Darling to Bathurst, 1 March 1827, in *HRA*, 13:136–37.

98. General Order, 10 May 1799: "Such as may appear to have been sent for here for life need not despair of being again in due time the master of their own labors, as ever man knows that a decent, industrious and obedient conduct has frequently in this colony recommended many to public favour" (*HRNSW*, 3:671; Governor Hunter to Duke of Portland, 1 May 1799, in *HRNSW*, 3:666; *NSW Orders*, secs. a341126, a341169).

99. *NSW Orders*, secs. a341062, a341085; Petrow, "Policing in a Penal Colony," 360, 365.

100. Hughes, *Fatal Shore*, 299.

101. *NSW Orders*, secs. a341062, a341085; Petrow, "Policing in a Penal Colony," 360, 365.

102. Jennie Jeppesen, "'To Serve Longer According to Law': The Chattel-Like Status of Convict Servants in Virginia," in *Order and Civility*, ed. Meyers and Perreault, 193–206.

103. Righi, "Right of Petition," 16.

104. James D. Rice, "Laying Claim to Elizabeth Shoemaker: Family Violence in Baltimore's Waterfront, 1808–1812," in *Over the Threshold*, ed. Daniels and Kennedy, 191.

105. William Miller, "The Effects of the American Revolution on Indentured Servitude," *Pennsylvania History* 7 (1940): 132, 136–39.

106. Cesare Beccaria, *An Essay on Crimes and Punishments* (Edinburgh: Donaldson, 1778).

107. Alastair Davidson, *The Invisible State: The Formation of the Australian State, 1788–1901* (Cambridge: Cambridge University Press, 1991), 6.

108. Ibid., 10, 14, 16–17.

109. Michel Foucault, *Discipline and Punish: The Birth of the Prison* (New York: Pantheon, 1977); Davidson, *Invisible State*, 13.

110. Lois Davey, Margaret Macpherson, and F. W. Clements, "The Hungry Years: 1788–1792: A Chapter in the History of the Australian and His Diet," *Historical Studies: Australia and New Zealand* 3 (1945): 192; Edmund S. Morgan, *American Slavery, American Freedom* (New York: Norton, 2003).

Union-Avoidance Strategies in the Meat Industry in Australia and the United States

MARJORIE A. JERRARD
PATRICK O'LEARY

Like its American counterpart, the Australian meat industry has poor working conditions and low pay and is not known for cordial relations between management and trade unions. Since the beginning of the 1980s, some Australian companies have deliberately chosen strategies that would enable them to avoid the industry trade union, the Australasian Meat Industry Employees' Union (AMIEU). In the United States, companies had previously developed strategies to avoid dealing with the United Food and Commercial Workers (UFCW), which represents meatpacking workers. The strategies for restricting or avoiding trade union influence have included shifting plant locations, using alternative workforces, manipulating the regulatory environment, and developing alternative labor relations practices. However, industry employers also make strategic decisions that are not driven by the union's presence but that nevertheless weaken the union's influence.

This chapter illustrates these strategies with case studies and vignettes, highlighting the convergence between Australian and American practices. Drawing on John Logan's[1] research and other union-avoidance literature, the chapter examines contextual factors in the two countries to explain similarities and differences, including the influence of neoliberalism and business principles on employer strategies, and outcomes of employment policies centered on migrants and race.[2]

Literature on Union-Avoidance Strategies

In the United States, law firms that specialized in union avoidance work with consultants rather than with management.[3] The consultants, in turn, then help management implement the law firms' suggestions. In Australia, however, management prefers to work directly with law firms but will also bring in consultants. In the United States, consultants' representatives manufacture dissent and division within the workplace, blaming the union for the hostile environment, and management warns employees that they must choose between the union and their jobs.[4] The consultants may also advise management to engage in illegal actions to counter the union, including targeting union members for dismissal, because the penalties for such actions are not severe. American consultants plan and orchestrate every aspect of management-initiated industrial action, beginning with a demand for "drastic cuts in existing wages, benefits or working conditions"; the union cannot agree to the demand without losing its members.[5] However, "only in the United States do employers, policy makers and (to a lesser extent) the general public consider the activities of union avoidance experts a legitimate part of mainstream industrial relations."[6]

In the United States, the use and threatened use of permanent replacement workers during industrial unrest has been an employer weapon since before the 1930s, although the widespread use of a large-scale immigrant workforce was a key focus of Upton Sinclair's *The Jungle* (1905), indicating that this tactic was well entrenched in Chicago by the turn of the twentieth century.[7] This strategy was not unique to the meat industry: for example, after the 1892 Homestead steel mill strike in Pennsylvania, around 75 percent of striking workers never got their jobs back. In contrast, the replacement of a unionized workforce after a plant closure did not become an accepted employer strategy in the Australian meat industry until the 1980s.

Lawrence Richards has explored American attitudes toward organized labor in the 1970s and 1980s. His case studies have found a strong worker predisposition to vote against trade unions in the workplace.[8] While he did not study meatpacking, his findings reflect the situation in parts of this industry; for example, at the Montfort abattoir, in Greeley, Colorado, management bypassed the UFCW by negotiating illegally with the National Maritime Union, then closing the plant and rehiring a nonunion workforce, whose members were subsequently encouraged to vote against coverage by the UFCW. For more than a decade prior to 1993, the abattoir was nonunionized; at that point, the UFCW finally won its appeal before the National Labor Relations Board, which found discrimination against union members and ordered the rehiring of workers terminated at the time of the plant's initial closure. The union then won the certification election.[9]

Rae Cooper and Greg Patmore have identified Australian employers' key antiunion employer tactics, including "the dismissal and harassment of union activists and members; relocation of operations; antiunion publicity campaigns in the workplace and community; the use of a range of sophisticated human resources management techniques to quell the desire for unionization; and a range of union 'substitution' activities such as employee involvement schemes and the promotion of in-house unions" as well as surveillance of union members and activists.[10] The Australian meat industry adopted many of these tactics during the 1990s, reflecting decollectivist strategies that David Peetz has identified: delaying or refusing to negotiate with a union, restricting or refusing entry to union organizers, restricting or preventing union delegates from undertaking their delegate duties, locking out the workforce, using legal action against the union and its members, and violence against union members.[11] Other strategies included threats of plant closure and layoffs, threats to dismiss employees who joined the union, and antiunion messages to the workforce.[12] The strategies focused on employment practices initiated at the workplace, the relational behaviors of management toward trade unions, and the informational behaviors of management.

The Labor Relations Regulatory Environment

In both countries, management's ability to use these strategies has been facilitated by the labor relations regulatory environment. Both the United States and Australia are liberal market economies in which employment protections have steadily weakened as a consequence of political ideology, employer demands, and increased industry competition. State regulation of employment matters and the labor market has shrunk, while regulation of trade union activities has increased. The US Labor Management Relations Act of 1947 (the Taft-Hartley Act), which amended the National Labor Relations Act of 1935 (the Wagner Act), was a response to business demands for increased government controls on trade union activity. The Wagner Act focused on "protecting commerce" while granting most workers the right to organize collectively and to strike. However, the Taft-Hartley Act limited trade union activity, specifying a multistep organizing process for union certification and a secret ballot to determine whether employees want union certification, a process that gives employers opportunities to discourage employees from voting for union representation. This certification process, the adoption of the business unionism model, and the lack of protection for trade union activities make the American labor relations system unique. While this labor relations regulatory framework appears out of date, the Labor Management Relations Act experienced somewhat of a renaissance beginning in the 1980s, and after 1996, the Australian labor relations regulatory framework began to move toward the American model.

Australia's passage of the Workplace Relations Act of 1996 and subsequent amendments, particularly the Workplace Relations Amendment (Work Choices) Act of 2005, resulted in the individualization of the employment relationship by diminishing collective bargaining and action and giving employers the opportunity unilaterally to reduce conditions and wages. Australia, however, retained a safety net that offers employees some protection against employer actions. In addition, Australia retains a tribunal to make decisions on employment-related matters and specialist courts; in the United States, such matters are treated like any other judicial matter. Despite the differences between the two countries, Australian employers have taken the opportunity provided by legislative change to adopt some strategies used by their American counterparts.

An Overview of the Meat Industry

In the United States, the red meat industry is divided into two subcategories, meatpacking, which is the slaughtering and processing of animals for meat, and meat processing, which takes in the basic materials produced from meatpacking and manufactures further processed products. In Australia, by contrast, the industry is referred to as the "meat processing industry" or the "meat processing and exporting industry" and covers all work done in an abattoir from the slaughtering of the animals through the packaging of the meat, including the manufacture of small goods.

Work in the industry in both countries is performed in temperature extremes and remains dirty, low-skilled, dangerous, and repetitive. The pace of slaughtering and boning is controlled by the chain system of disassembly, and the work involves physical risk factors, such as high work speeds, vigorous use of knives, and high grip forces for cutting. The industry is plagued by musculoskeletal disorders, accidents, and work stress.

In the early twentieth century, the American meat industry was dominated by five large companies: Armour, Swift, Morris, Wilson, and Cudahy. Over time, ownership changed hands, and by the 1980s, foreign companies such as the Japanese-owned Nippon Meat Packers had a presence on US soil. However, foreign ownership remained limited until a Brazilian company, JBS SA, took over Swift in 2007 and Smithfield in 2008, becoming the largest American meatpacker and processor. The industry remains dominated by a small number of companies: JBS; Tyson Foods, which purchased Iowa Beef Processors (IBP) in 2001; Cargill Meat Solutions; and the National Beef Packing Corporation. The American industry saw plant rationalization and closures as abattoirs were relocated from capital cities to rural and regional areas such as Austin, Minnesota, and Ottumwa, Iowa, that had demonstrated success in the industry.[13] The industry is now concentrated in Minnesota, Iowa, South Dakota, Michigan, Nebraska, Kansas, Illinois, Wisconsin, Colorado, Indiana, and Texas, many of which are not union strongholds, and wages and conditions have declined.[14] However deurbanization of the industry has also occurred within these states, affecting cities such as Kansas City, Omaha, Waterloo, and Minneapolis/St. Paul.

Ownership of the Australian industry remains split between the largely foreign-owned beef export industry and the Australian-owned domestic and export beef- and lamb-processing industry. Australian-based pastoralists initially owned and developed the country's industry. British ownership was introduced at the beginning of the twentieth century, when Borthwick and Vestey moved into the industry. American-owned Swift followed. The other main company was Australian-owned William Angliss. The foreign-owned companies operated for six to seven decades before withdrawing, briefly returning export ownership to Australian control. During the 1980s, Japanese interests began investing in the industry. In the 1990s, the American-owned ConAgra Holdings (Australia), a subsidiary of the ConAgra group, which, in turn, was acquired by Swift, became the parent company of Australia Meat Holdings (AMH). During the 1990s, AMH, the Australian-owned Consolidated Meat Group, and Japanese-owned Nippon Meat Packers dominated the industry, alongside domestic companies including G & K O'Connor and Teys Bros (now Teys Australia). The largest player in Australian meat processing is now the Brazilian-owned JBS Australia, a division of JBS, which acquired AMH's operations in 2007 after taking over the American-owned Swift. Nippon Meat Packers remains influential, and in 2002, Teys entered a joint venture with Consolidated Meat, taking over the latter's operations. Teys has entered a partnership with Cargill, a privately owned

American company, and now operates six abattoirs across Australia's eastern seaboard. The industry in both countries remains oligopolistic, with ownership and market share concentrated in a few major companies.

Relocating Plants and Alternative Workforces in the United States

Beginning in the mid-twentieth century, two trade unions—the United Packinghouse Workers of America and the Amalgamated Meat Cutters Union—negotiated working conditions in the meat industry, and from the 1930s to the 1970s, pay and conditions improved considerably, with meatpacking workers receiving higher wages than other manufacturing workers.[15] From 1946 until the early 1980s, industry pattern agreements dominated the American industry. In Australia, too, between the late 1940s and the 1980s, the industry was heavily unionized, and meat workers were among the highest-paid blue-collar workers, with industry contracts setting standard wages and conditions and the AMIEU, especially in Victoria, negotiating even higher wage increases. The restructuring of the American industry began in the 1960s, when large slaughter plants were relocated to rural areas in the Midwest and South, away from urban centers and union influence. The rise of the trucking industry also gave greater flexibility to plant location.

As Roger Horowitz has explained, in 1967, IBP introduced boxed beef, a new production and shipping process involving disassembling carcasses into vacuum-packed retail-sized portions. Boxed beef allowed IBP to restructure the labor process into a disassembly line, where each worker stands in the same place and makes the same simple cut thousands of times a shift. Butchers were largely replaced by meat cutters, who were paid less than the pattern wages across the industry. IBP also demanded a nonunion workforce, a strategy that was strengthened when the company acquired competitor meatpackers in bankruptcy, such as Wilson Foods, and reopened them with nonunionized workforces. IBP fought union demands during a series of strikes, including the Dakota City Strike in 1977, and closed or sold unionized plants in Iowa while opening new nonunion plants in Amarillo, Texas, and Emporia, Kansas.[16]

Charles Craypo has identified the changes at IBP, including the company-specific wages below the industry standard, as a reason for the collapse of the national collective bargaining structure in the American meat industry during the 1980s.[17] However, Jeffrey Keefe and Mathias Bolton have argued that other factors converged to move employers away from the industry pattern agreement system, which had provided long-term stability and relatively high wages for workers. These factors included new industry entrants such as IBP, MBPXL (formerly Missouri Beef and later Excel), Dubuque, and Land o'Lakes, which replaced the original five meatpackers by 1980, and further changes that concentrated ownership among IBP, ConAgra, and Cargill. Keefe and Bolton have also noted a reduction in American red meat consumption, with increasing competition from poultry, a shift to a neoliberal philosophy that saw an increase in employer militancy and control, and a simultaneous loss of union bargaining power in an industry struggling to retain market share, closing plants, and shedding jobs.[18] The decline in union power, accompanied by a decrease in meatpacking union militancy and identity (the United Packinghouse Workers of America and the Amalgamated Meat Cutters Union merged in 1968, and in 1979 they combined with the Retail Clerks International Union to form the UFCW), also appears to have diminished worker control over the pace of work and resulted in major declines in working conditions as the UFCW adopted a model of business unionism.

Consolidation of industry ownership between 1974 and 1997 saw larger companies buying out smaller competitors, closing plants and either reopening them with a nonunionized workforce or opening new larger slaughterhouses in rural areas. These rural areas often had dwindling populations as a consequence of the closure of other established manufacturers but had the advantage of rail and road links to enable transportation of livestock and meat products. Underemployed people remaining in these rural areas offered the beginnings of a workforce ready to move into meatpacking jobs, including women.[19] Where there was a labor shortage, companies could bring in labor, often African Americans from other states or migrants directly from Latin American countries, especially Mexico, and Asian countries.

In less than three decades, the red meat, poultry, and hog slaughtering industries transitioned to a predominantly migrant workforce, with extremely high labor turnover.[20] Migrant workers were unfamiliar with American labor law and lacked personal resources and community ties in their new towns. The UFCW had difficulty unionizing such workers, who often lacked a culture or understanding of unionism as well as English-language skills. Moreover, because many of these workers were transient, they had little incentive to think in terms of long-term socioeconomic advancement through unionization. Rural areas also lay outside of urban union strongholds. Employers can take advantage of undocumented migrant workers, offering substandard treatment because they cannot complain about poor working conditions and low wages. People smugglers brought undocumented workers into the United States, with some evidence showing that organized crime has participated in this effort.[21]

Undocumented workers provide employers with an increased competitive advantage, a benefit that increased even further with the labor intensity of the production process.[22] The success of this hiring strategy requires that three conditions be met. First, employers must know or be able to make an educated guess that a worker is undocumented. Given that large numbers of these workers come from Spanish-speaking Latin American countries and have limited English-language skills and relatively little education, employers can make hiring decisions with relative confidence. Second, employers must assume that the undocumented worker has limited employment opportunities and thus will accept a low-paying job with poor conditions without official complaint. Third, employers must assume that the expected benefit from employing an undocumented workforce exceeds the expected costs of breaking the law. Employers in nonborder states have a relatively small chance of facing investigations and fines, and for large employers with considerable market share, fines impose only minimal hardships. Dell Champlin and Eric Hake have argued that "hiring unauthorized workers who are already inside the United States is not regarded as a serious violation of immigration law. Moreover, employers who do so face no risk of sanctions, since the law only requires that documents presented not be 'obviously fraudulent.'"[23]

In Australia, negative publicity can cause meat industry employers to change strategies to avoid further media attention. For American meatpacking companies, however, employer reputation is not important, and even companies accused of employing and mistreating undocumented workers do not face public relations consequences. For example, on 12 December 2006, in the biggest immigration raid in US history, Swift meatpacking facilities in Hyrum, Utah; Greeley, Colorado; Marshalltown, Iowa; Grand Island, Nebraska; Cactus, Texas; and Worthington, Minnesota, were raided by US Immigration and Customs Enforcement officials, who detained about 10 percent of the company's workforce—1,282 undocumented immigrants from Mexico, Guatemala, Honduras, El Salvador, Peru, Laos, Sudan, and Ethiopia. The company did not face criminal penalties but did change its hiring practices. Management utilized a recruitment firm to assist in identifying and removing undocumented workers from the workforce and to find suitable alternatives among political refugees from Burma and various African countries who had been living elsewhere in the United States. These most recent refugees allowed Swift—part of Con-Agra and then bought by JBS in 2007—and other meatpackers to offer conditions unacceptable to American-born workers but with slightly higher wages than were paid to undocumented workers.[24]

Industrial Strategies in the United States: All Tied Up with a Migrant Workforce?

With the majority of American meatpacking industry ownership still in the hands of a small number of companies, a push toward standardization of mechanized production processes and reduced demand for skilled workers meant that power shifted to employers. Employers could control union elections—waste time, delay elections, refuse to negotiate, threaten workers who wanted to join, and distribute antiunion propaganda, all of which Logan has identified as common strategies among American employers.[25] Employers could push the UFCW to engage in concession bargaining, a tactic Logan and Peetz have identified as weakening trade unions.[26] While concession bargaining could keep an established plant open for slightly longer, it was not a successful long-term strategy, and urban slaughterhouses closed anyway, with new plants reopening in rural areas with nonunionized workforces. Throughout the 1980s and 1990s, the pattern of closures, reopenings, and then usually permanent closures and relocations appeared across the industry. William Whittaker and Charles Craypo have concluded that the strategy was both common and effective in deunionizing the workforce.[27]

In this context, Ronald Reagan's first administration (1981–85) emboldened employer antiunionism through direct intervention in the air traffic controllers' dispute, intervention in state agencies, and legislative reforms to corporate power, particularly with regard to hiring and firing. Reagan's smashing of the air traffic controllers' strike in 1981 was an important turning point, but his appointment of strongly pro-employer officials to the National Labor Relations Board had more enduring consequences for collective industrial relations. By invoking the law that striking government employees forfeit their jobs, Reagan's action gave weight to the legal right of private employers to use their discretion when hiring and discharging workers. This activism was motivated by the prevailing neoliberal assumptions concerning the individual, freed from the constraints of collectivist regulation and state intervention.[28] The Reagan initiatives emboldened American employers, including those in meat processing, to attempt to decollectivize their workplaces and to rely on alternative workforces if necessary.

IBP had pioneered plant closures and relocations to states with union-discouraging right-to-work laws. IBP also pioneered staffing and wage flexibility as a cost-minimization strategy. Underpinning employer flexibility strategies is job segmentation within the slaughtering and disassembly process: the jobs with the worst conditions, lowest pay, and highest levels of repetitive strain injuries remain the province of women workers and migrant workers, particularly the undocumented.[29] The poor pay and conditions promote a transient workforce because labor turnover is high. According to Whittaker, this approach suits employers' needs, since they do not want to invest in a workforce or run the risk of a permanent workforce becoming organized and protesting dismal pay and conditions. Further, high turnover enables employers to avoid such additional costs of a permanent workforce as medical insurance, annual bonuses, and paid annual leave. Employers also avoid costs associated with injury by terminating the employment of any workers who show signs of debility or slow the pace.[30] Given the speed of the disassembly chain, injuries and accidents are common, and the meatpacking industry is the most dangerous job in manufacturing and food processing in the United States.[31]

These strategies have spread to other employers, particularly across the rural Midwest and South, and have created significant community problems in these areas. For example, in Marshalltown, Iowa, where Swift implemented an immigrant-based antiunion strategy, high labor turnover has created major social dislocation.[32] In Garden City, Kansas, that social dislocation has had major implications for the educational system.[33] The widespread increase in migrant labor has transformed the industry and communities, not always in positive ways.

The Move to an Alternative Workforce in Australia

Teys employed 2,300 people in the mid-2000s. After Work Choices passed in 2005, Teys management at the Naracoorte abattoir, South Australia, attempted to force workers onto individual Australian Workplace Agreements (AWAs) by locking out members of the AMIEU who refused to sign AWAs reducing their pay and conditions.[34] Migrant workers, including two hundred experienced meat workers from Brazil, were brought in to work at the South Australian plant on temporary visas to weaken the union presence while filling skill gaps. However, the choice of Brazilian workers did not contribute to decollectivism because many of them were familiar with trade unions and joined the AMIEU.

Teys used a similar strategy at its Rockhampton, Queensland, plant but brought in foreign workers from the Ukraine, China, and Vietnam to fill a "skills shortage, especially in the boning room."[35] These migrant workers were actually employed by a labor hire company, AWX, rather than Teys and were paid two dollars less an hour than permanent Teys employees, resulting in a two-tiered workforce that disadvantaged the foreign workers. In 2013, following negative local publicity and AMIEU pressure, the company agreed to give the foreign workers the same benefits as permanent employees, and the foreign workers received extra pay for overtime and work on public holidays, shift allowances, and other benefits that they had not previously received.[36]

Teys eventually developed an internal and integrated approach to finding foreign workers that bypassed external agents. This strategy allowed Teys to move from the one-year visas offered to the original Brazilian workers to four-year visas at both the Naracoorte and Rockhampton abattoirs, providing the company with a stable and skilled workforce.

G & K O'Connor (Pakenham, Victoria) had pioneered the use of migrant and refugee workers after a nine-month lockout of AMIEU members in 1999.[37] The company subsequently extended its migrant worker recruitment to supply the majority of its permanent workforce. Evidence from the United States showed that migrant workers in the meat industry were difficult to unionize and that the employment of such workers could serve as an effective union-avoidance strategy.[38] This new workforce was akin to the permanent replacement workforces used by American employers in a range of industries and reflected a pattern common to the Australian industry: after seasonal closures, employers would hire different workers to weaken the union's influence. The company sought to avoid having any long-term employees. Both G & K O'Connor and Teys offered support services to assist the foreign workers as they settled into their new communities, including education and training in the English language and in safety procedures. Such services were complemented by training for Teys managers and supervisors in cultural transition, expatriate performance coaching, and interpersonal and leadership skills. In contrast, American companies have provided no such support services for workers or managers, meaning that the use of migrant workers has strained local schools, health care facilities, and legal services.

Both Australian companies benefited from state and federal government recognition of their training programs for migrant and refugee workers as well as financial support for hiring trainees. However, for Teys, the strategy did not avoid the union: the AMIEU responded by distributing multilingual recruitment materials to potential members. The union also appointed a Brazilian migrant worker to serve as an organizer, focusing on the needs of migrant meat workers with limited English-language skills.

These international recruitment programs were influenced by a range of interrelated factors such as the high Australian dollar, which negatively affected meat exports and consequently resulted in the downsizing of the workforce beginning in mid-2009. Teys stopped hiring new migrant workers and attempted to retain as many of its previous workers as possible. Hiring restarted in 2012, when beef demand increased and targeted refugees.

Other companies that used migrant workers on slaughterers' visas beginning in 2006 included AMH and the Nippon Group in Queensland and at least seven other abattoirs in eastern Australia and South Australia. However, there was doubt about whether these companies were employing the visa workers as slaughterers or in other capacities such as boning and slicing that were not covered by the visas to reduce labor costs.

Between December 2005 and January 2006, T & R Pastoral abattoir, in Murray Bridge, South Australia, imported two hundred temporary Chinese workers instead of hiring local workers although the region was dominated by high unemployment. T & R sought to reduce the labor costs associated with a local unionized workforce—the area's unemployed were unwilling to work for the low wages and in the poor conditions that the Chinese workers accepted. By the mid-2000s, other companies followed suit, including Luturn, Wagstaff, Pyramid Hill, Kilcoy Pastoral, and Western Exporters. The temporary workforces for the majority of these companies were found through migrant recruitment agencies in Australia and abroad that charged the workers fees to find jobs in Australia. This fee was deducted from the workers' wages, a practice that was and remains illegal in some Australian states. While some Australian meat processors definitely abuse the migrant visa program, they lack the opportunity to use large numbers of undocumented migrants in the same way that some American employers do.[39]

New Strategic Initiatives by Australian Employers

In the mid-1990s, the Australian Federal Coalition Government sought "to create one of the industrialized world's most favorable environments for decollectivist strategies through a combination of legislative and administrative arrangements."[40] The Workplace Relations Act provided employers with two forms of nonunion agreements, AWAs and collective nonunion agreements, as well as unionized agreements. A company could also terminate an enterprise agreement and return to the industry award, usually to reduce wage costs under the enterprise agreement.[41] Employers frequently implemented seasonal plant closures and then reopened the abattoir with standardized conditions and lower wages and with a workforce that excluded union activists. Such tactics undermined the job security of the remaining unionized employees and thus furthered decollectivization.

G & K O'Connor used a multipronged approach to union avoidance, first refusing to negotiate with the AMIEU for a new collective agreement and then locking out its unionized workforce and using a law firm specializing in union avoidance and industrial dispute litigation (an approach that echoed American employers' use of law firms). G & K O'Connor then hired a replacement workforce made up largely of migrant workers and refugees employed as trainees on AWAs. Finally, a specialist consultant advised management about surveillance, victimization, and intimidation of the abattoir's thirty remaining union members and delegates. The targeting of union members could be interpreted as part of the consultant's role to assist management and supervisors in engaging in unlawful tactics without facing fines. This company in this case followed the American approach, opening negotiations with an offer that cut existing wages and changed working conditions; accepting the offer would cause members to become dissatisfied and leave the union, leaving it with no choice but to refuse the offer and support members during industrial action.[42]

A three-and-a-half month lockout also took place at Conroy's Port Pirie Abattoir in South Australia to force workers to sign AWAs that introduced major changes to work practices, including removing the tally system that enabled workers to control their pace of work. Labor hire employees from an agency replaced the locked-out workers. In 2000, Peerless Holding locked out its unionized workers at its Laverton rendering plant in Victoria to force them to sign individual AWAs that introduced rotating shifts and reduced weekly and holiday pay rates. Labor hire replacements kept the plant operational during the lockout period. These companies' approach reflected American-style management-initiated industrial action aimed at weakening the union's position while blaming the union for the hostile environment.[43]

In 2002, the South Grafton Abattoir in New South Wales offered 121 unionized meat workers individual AWAs at lower pay than the union-negotiated collective enterprise agreement and state meat industry award, which theoretically set minimum wages and conditions. When the New South Wales Industrial Commission terminated these individual AWAs, the employer then attempted to remove union activists and members from its workforce via the traditional temporary plant closure and rehiring strategy. The company alleged that a livestock shortage forced the closure, meaning that the workers could be dismissed without the normal severance payments and not rehired. Ongoing delays over bargaining for a new labor agreement were combined with management attacks on AMIEU officials.[44] Once again, the Australian company took the American approach of refusing to bargain and then slowing down the bargaining process while creating a hostile environment, blaming the union, and targeting union members and delegates.[45] The company deliberately attacked the AMIEU, making "unfortunate vituperative" comments about the union and its officials.[46] The company ultimately lost the case, with the court ruling that it had discriminated against the union members.[47]

In 2003, Blue Ribbon, located in Launceston, Tasmania, attempted to force employees to become independent contractors and thus shift costs from the company to individual workers. Blue Ribbon used a labor hire company, Newemploy, to employ its workforce, but the court found that these contracting arrangements were "not genuine independent contractor arrangements" but "a sham, designed for the purpose of defeating the jurisdiction of [the] Commission." In addition, according to the court, Newemploy had been created as part "of an overall business plan to cushion Blue Ribbon from the consequences of the employment practices at the meatworks."[48]

The 2005 WorkChoices legislation opened the way for new management advisory and consultancy services to provide employers with solutions for labor relations issues by using independent contractors and labor hire agencies, promoting the benefits of a temporary workforce over a permanent one. Unlike their American counterparts, the Australian public and to a lesser extent policymakers do not consider union-avoidance consultants a legitimate part of mainstream labor relations. WorkChoices encouraged Australian employers to utilize individual agreements to bypass trade unions and weakened the legal protections for employees, allowing jobs to be terminated and alternative lower-paid jobs offered. Meat industry employers were among the first to adopt this strategy. In early 2006, the small New South Wales Cowra abattoir sought to reduce its workforce of twenty-nine to twenty by taking advantage of an exemption available under the act. The company announced that unionized employees were receiving five weeks' notice of termination but that twenty employees would be rehired on individual AWAs offering lower pay. While the strategy was legitimate under the act, management did not proceed with its plans, probably as a consequence of negative media coverage.[49]

Conclusions

Employers in both the American and Australian meat industries sought to deunionize their workforces to lower labor costs and increase flexibility. Such efforts by American employers have had more success than those by their Australian counterparts, primarily as a result of differences in labor relations regulations.

Australian employers used tactics drawn from America, such as consultants and antiunion law firms and temporary or replacement workforces that included at least some migrants and refugees. The Australian employers also relied on more traditional strategies, using the legal framework and the tribunal system to avoid union-negotiated agreements. However, Australian workers have been protected by legal requirements regarding minimum wages and conditions for all employees except migrants on temporary visas (the loophole that Teys exploited) and trainees (as G & K O'Connor did). In the United States, by contrast, employers have access to both legitimate and undocumented migrant workforces, increasing employers' wage flexibility and resulting in extremely poor and dangerous working conditions. The US workforce therefore experiences high turnover, while Australia's workforce, including the temporary migrant visa holders and trainees, is more stable, with workers seeking regular employment and regular accommodation.

The fact that some companies have operated on both sides of the Pacific at various times—for example, ConAgra in the 1990s–2000s and more recently JBS—does not guarantee the Australian employers any greater success in the deunionization strategy: the Australian labor relations regulatory system still protects trade union rights and workers' wages and employment conditions, whereas since the Taft-Hartley Act was passed, the American state has provided little protection for workers' rights to unionize and take collective action.

In both Australia and the United States, the meat industry retains negative characteristics; where trade unions are active, these features are more likely to be addressed or workers compensated with higher wages. Unionization thus adds to production costs and thus conflicts with the basic management principle of keeping costs as low as possible. However, *as possible* raises questions about the ethics of unsafe working conditions as well as about the safety of meat produced for human consumption, and public disapproval may alter the relationships among companies, their workers, and their unions.

Notes

We thank Gordon Stewart of Central Queensland University and the editors of this volume for their advice on this chapter.

1. See John Logan, "Consultants, Lawyers, and the 'Union Free' Movement in the USA since the 1970s," *Industrial Relations Journal* 33 (2002): 197–214; John Logan, "The Union Avoidance Industry in the United States," *British Journal of Industrial Relations* 44 (2006): 651–75; Patrick O'Leary and Peter Sheldon, *Employer Power and Weakness* (Ballarat, Vic.: VURRN Press, 2012); Dell Champlin and Eric Hake, "Immigration as Industrial Strategy in American Meatpacking," *Review of Political Economy* 18 (2006): 49–70; Stefanie Toh

and Michael Quinlan, "Safeguarding the Global Contingent Workforce? Guestworkers in Australia," *International Journal of Manpower* 30 (2009): 453–71; Rick Halpern and Roger Horowitz, *Meatpackers* (New York: Twayne, 1996).

2. Logan, "Consultants, Lawyers," 208.

3. Ibid., 204.

4. Ibid., 211.

5. Logan, "Union Avoidance Industry," 654–55.

6. Upton Sinclair, *The Jungle* (1905; New York: Heritage, 1965).

7. Jack Beatty, *Age of Betrayal: The Triumph of Money in America, 1865–1900* (New York: Knopf, 2007).

8. Lawrence Richards, *Union-Free America* (Urbana: University of Illinois Press, 2008).

9. Charles Craypo, "Meatpacking: Industry Restructuring and Union Decline," in *Contemporary Collective Bargaining in the Private Sector*, ed. Paula B. Voos (Madison, Wis.: Industrial Relations Research Association, 1994), 83–84.

10. Rae Cooper and Greg Patmore, "Private Detectives, Blacklists, and Company Unions: Anti-Union Employer Strategy and Australian Labour History," *Labour History* 97 (2009): 4.

11. David Peetz, "Decollectivist Strategies in Oceania," *Relations Industrielles/Industrial Relations* 57 (2002): 252–81.

12. Ibid.

13. Michael Broadway, "Meatpacking and Its Social and Economic Consequences for Garden City, Kansas in the 1980s," *Urban Anthropology and Studies of Cultural Systems and World Economic Development* 19 (1990): 321–44.

14. Champlin and Hake, "Immigration as Industrial Strategy."

15. Craypo, "Meatpacking."

16. Roger Horowitz, "The Decline of Unionism in America's Meatpacking Industry," *Social Policy* 32 (2002): 32–37.

17. Craypo, "Meatpacking."

18. . Jeffrey Keefe and Mathias Bolton, *When Chickens Devoured Cows: Union Rebuilding in the Meat and Poultry Industry* (2013), 9–10, available at https://www.researchgate.net/profile/Jeffrey_Keefe/publication/292966997_When_Chickens_Devoured_Cows/links/56b27f5108aed7ba3fede8fc.pdf.

19. Deborah Fink, *Cutting into the Meatpacking Line* (Chapel Hill: University of North Carolina Press, 1998).

20. Champlin and Hake, "Immigration as Industrial Strategy"; Mark A. Grey, "Marshalltown, Iowa, and the Struggle for Community in a Global Age," in *Communities and Capital*, ed. Thomas Collins and John Wingard (Athens: University of Georgia Press, 2000), 87–100.

21. Champlin and Hake, "Immigration as Industrial Strategy," 65.

22. J. David Brown, Julie L. Hotchkiss, and Myriam Quispe-Agnoli, "Does Employing Undocumented Workers Give Firms a Competitive Advantage?," *Journal of Regional Science* 53 (2013): 158–70.

23. Champlin and Hake, "Immigration as Industrial Strategy," 65.

24. Jerry Kammer, *The 2006 Swift Raids: Assessing the Impact of Immigration Enforcement Actions at Six Facilities* (2009), available at https://cis.org/2006-Swift-Raids.

25. Logan, "Union Avoidance Industry."

26. Logan, "Consultants, Lawyers"; Peetz, "Decollectivist Strategies."

27. William Whittaker, *Labor Practices in the Meat Packing and Poultry Processing Industry* (2005), available at http://nationalaglawcenter.org/wp-content/uploads/assets/crs/RL33002.pdf; Charles Craypo, "Strike and Relocation in Meatpacking," in *Grand Designs*, ed. Charles Craypo and Bruce Nissen (Ithaca: Cornell University Press, 1993), 201–2.

28. Henry S. Farber and Bruce Western, "Ronald Reagan and the Politics of Declining Union Organization," *British Journal of Industrial Relations* 40 (2002): 385–401.

29. Fink, *Cutting*; Brown, Hotchkiss, and Quispe-Agnoli, "Does Employing Undocumented Workers?"

30. Whittaker, *Labor Practices*, 35.

31. Rachelle Adams, Rebecca Beals, Rebecca Gonzales, Benjamin Graham, Jillian Husman, Lauren Lineweber, Veronica Messa, Norm Pflanz, Angel Rivera, Gloria Sarmiento, Nicholas Swiercek, Amy Swoboda, and Darcy Tromanhauser, *"The Speed Kills You": The Voice of Nebraska's Meatpacking Workers* (Lincoln: Nebraska Appleseed Center for Law in the Public Interest, 2009).

32. Grey, "Marshalltown, Iowa."

33. Michael Broadway, "Meatpacking and the Transformation of Rural Communities: A Comparison of Brooks, Alberta and Garden City, Kansas," *Rural Sociology* 72 (2007): 560–82.

34. AWAs are loosely equivalent to individual contracts in the United States.

35. "Teys Beefs Up Its Workers," *Morning Bulletin*, 22 May 2006.

36. "Meatworks Gives Equal Rights to Rockhampton Refugees," *Morning Bulletin*, 6 December 2012.

37. Marjorie Jerrard, "The G & K O'Connor Lockout (1999) and Its Aftermath: A Case Study of a Union Avoidance Campaign in the Australian Meat Processing Industry," *Labour History* 109 (2015): 131–48.

38. Champlin and Hake, "Immigration as Industrial Strategy."

39. Heather Ewart, "Meat Industry Accused of Exploiting Foreign Workers," *7:30 Report* (ABC), 31 July 2006; Brown, Hotchkiss, and Quispe-Agnoli, "Does Employing Undocumented Workers?"

40. Peetz, "Decollectivist Strategies," 257.

41. An Australian collective nonunion agreement is roughly equivalent to a nonunion contract in the United States, while an enterprise agreement approximates a union contract at the company or plant level. An industry award is quite peculiar to Australia but might very loosely translate in a US context as an industry-based contract.

42. Logan, "Consultants, Lawyers," 208.

43. Ibid.

44. *McIlwain v. Ramsey Packaging Pty. Ltd.* (2006) FCA 282 (30 June 2006).

45. Logan, "Consultants, Lawyers," 208.

46. *McIlwain v. Ramsey Packaging Pty. Ltd.*, paragraph 129.

47. Ibid., paragraph 12.

48. *Australasian Meat Industry Employees Union, Tasmania Branch v. Newemploy Pty. Ltd.*, T10797 of 2003 (1 October 2003).

49. "Cowra Abattoir Did Not Act Unlawfully, OWS Finds," *Workplace Express*, 7 July 2006, available at http://www:workplaceexpress.com.au/n106_news_print.php?selkey_31920; "Cowra Abattoir Back-Track Due to Media Attention Not the OWS, Says ALP," *Workplace Express*, 4 April 2006, available at http://www:workplaceexpress.com.au/n106_news_print.php?selkey_31384.

PART 3

Ethnicity and Class Identity: The Irish Diaspora in Australia and the United States

Catholic Irish Australia and the Labor Movement

Race in Australia and Nationalism in Ireland, 1880s–1920s

ELIZABETH MALCOLM
DIANNE HALL

There were many similarities between the Irish Australian and Irish American experiences during the nineteenth and early twentieth centuries , but within these broad similarities there was also a world of difference. The Irish who immigrated to Australia and the United States were mainly Catholic and working class, and in both countries many became involved in the labor movement. Historians of Catholic Irish Australia and of the Australian Labor Party (ALP) have long recognized the close links between the two, but these links were often problematic. The problems they generated were different from those existing within the Irish American labor relationship.[1] This chapter draws on newspapers to explore the links between Catholic Irish Australia and labor by examining race and Irish nationalism, two issues of deep concern to both groups between the 1880s and the 1920s.

The chapter begins by sketching key characteristics of the Irish Australian community, especially compared to the Irish American community. It then examines attitudes toward "colored" immigration and the White Australia policy as expressed by the Catholic community, its church, and its press up to 1901. Finally, the chapter considers how the labor press reported violent events in Ireland between 1914 and 1922. Given that Catholic Irish Australians were sometimes subjected to racial vilification, how did they view efforts to exclude "colored" people from Australia, and how did labor, which generally supported the British Empire, view attempts by Irish nationalists first to loosen and then, after 1916, to break the political union between Ireland and Britain? The protracted labor split of the 1950s, which occurred in different ways in different states and created divisions both within and between organized labor and the Australian Catholic community, has attracted considerable scholarly attention.[2] However, this chapter aims to interrogate some of the complex fissures apparent in the relationship long before the 1950s.

Irish Catholic Immigration to Australia and the United States

Irish immigration to Australia during the late eighteenth and nineteenth centuries had features that were unique, setting it apart from immigration to other major destination countries. Most obviously, the first Irish to arrive in Australia were convicts. Between 1788 and 1868, nearly forty-eight thousand Irish-born convicts, including around nine thousand women, were transported to Australia, accounting for roughly 25 percent of all convicts transported.[3] In addition, from at least the 1830s, large numbers of free settlers, again including many women, also began to make the long voyage from Ireland to Australia. These immigrants, like those going to the United States, were mainly young, single Catholics from rural areas, and they often came as part of extended networks or chains of family and friends. The voyage was not only long but also expensive, which meant that those intending to go to Australia usually needed access to more resources than those immigrating to Britain or the United States. This gave rise to another characteristic feature of Irish immigration to Australia: many free settlers had the cost of their passages subsidized by relatives and sponsors or by various government and private assistance schemes.[4]

Although the period of Irish assisted immigration and free settlement included the years of the Great Famine in the late 1840s and early 1850s, far fewer famine refugees reached Australia than the United States, likely because they lacked the financial and perhaps physical resources for such a long and arduous journey. However, the impact of the famine is evident in a jump in the proportion of Irish convicts, transported to Australia, many for property crimes.[5] Among the nearly 20,900 convicts reaching Australia in 1846–53, 45 percent of women and 33 percent of men were Irish-born.[6] In addition, in 1848–50 the colonies received 4,100 "famine orphans"—destitute teenage girls confined in

Irish workhouses who were shipped to Australia by the British government.[7] Irish Australia did not exhibit the intense bitterness of famine memory that came to characterize Irish America but was by no means totally immune from the trauma suffered by famine survivors.[8] Irish free immigration continued at substantial levels during the gold-rush years of the 1850s as well as during the early 1860s, late 1870s, and early 1880s—all periods of economic hardship in Ireland. Nevertheless, the Irish making the costly voyage to Australia still tended to have access to more resources than those crossing the Atlantic. By the 1890s, however, the major waves of free Irish immigration to colonial Australia were over.[9]

Whereas the number of Irish immigrants to Australia was certainly dwarfed by those leaving Ireland for the United States or Britain, the Irish and their descendants formed a larger portion of the Australian settler population. We cannot be certain of the size of the first Irish Australian generations as censuses did not record Irish ancestry. Historians have consequently used the number of Catholics as a proxy for those of Irish descent. This calculation should be reasonably accurate, however, because relatively small numbers of non-Irish Catholics arrived in Australia before 1945. On this basis, it appears that by the beginning of the twentieth century, nearly one-quarter of all non-indigenous Australians had a family background that was both Irish and Catholic.[10]

These descendants of Irish Catholic immigrants joined the descendants of overwhelmingly Protestant English, Scottish, and Welsh immigrants to form the vast majority of Australia's settler population, with only limited continental European migration until after the Second World War.[11] Australia's demographic profile therefore stood in marked contrast to that of the United States, which experienced successive waves of European arrivals during the late nineteenth and early twentieth centuries.[12] Australia's situation of large numbers of Irish and Catholics in colonies that were otherwise strongly British and Protestant, led inevitably to ethnic, sectarian, and political tensions with the Irish often accused of disloyalty to the British Crown and Empire, along with many other failings.[13]

Catholic Irish Australia and the Labor Movement, 1880s–1914

Irish-born immigrants spread widely throughout the Australian colonies. Yet, at the same time, clusters of Irish emerged in certain rural areas, in some country towns, and in the working-class inner suburbs of cities like Melbourne, Sydney, and Brisbane, where they lived close to the factories, workshops, railways, and docks that offered employment to many of the men.[14] Irish Catholic women in Australia, as in the United States, often worked in factories, but they also made up a significant proportion of the domestic servant labor force.[15]

Again like the United States, Irish Catholic men were at first disproportionately represented among unskilled workers and thus did not play a major role in Australia's early craft unions.[16] But as mass trade unionism developed, especially beginning in the 1880s, these men and increasingly their sons were drawn into the labor movement in all the colonies; indeed, many rose to leadership positions in both the unions and the emerging labor parties.[17] Unlike the United States, however, the role and impact of the Irish in Australian trade unionism has been little studied. Irish women as well as men were prominent in the American union movement. In Australia, again little research has been done, but it appears that the same may well have been the case. In a study of the entries for female trade union leaders in the *Australian Dictionary of Biography*, Raelene Frances has found that among the pre-1939 cohort at least 58 percent had Irish Australian family backgrounds—mostly Catholic. She speculates that education by nuns and an "Irish legacy" might have encouraged in these women a "willingness to be oppositional, to stand out, to be outspoken."[18]

By the 1890s, broad support in principle for organized labor was apparent in both the Catholic Church and the Catholic press. Sometimes reservations were expressed concerning the use of strikes, but even these were by no means always ruled out. During the 1890 maritime strike, the Irish-born cardinal archbishop of Sydney, Patrick Moran, spoke out strongly in support of striking seamen and wharf laborers.[19] In 1911, he went even further, alarming some leading Irish members of the American hierarchy by supporting a referendum proposed by a federal Labor government to nationalize monopolies. At least two senior American archbishops wrote to Moran in search of assurances that the Australian church was not in "alliance" with socialists.[20] Some modern historians have also queried Moran's tactics: Patrick O'Farrell, the leading historian of the Irish in Australia, attacked Moran for aligning Catholics too closely with the ALP and thereby reducing them to the "confines of political party" and leaving them "bivouacked on the outskirts of a hostile civilisation."[21]

Whereas in the United States from the mid-nineteenth century Irish Catholic immigrants had gradually made themselves a powerful force within the Democratic Party, in Australia by the end of the century Catholics had turned to the labor movement to represent their economic as well as political interests.[22] Despite his strictures regarding Moran and despite Rome's rejection of socialism, O'Farrell nevertheless concedes that this trend was probably a "natural drift": "Catholics were not only being pulled towards Labor by their self-interest as workers, but pushed towards it by the anti-Catholicism of non-Labor."[23] While there may well have been such a "natural" push-pull process in operation, there were still tensions within the Labor Party between Catholics and Protestants.[24] Conservatism in Australia, conversely, was overwhelmingly Protestant and British and thus fundamentally hostile to most things Catholic and Irish. Even upwardly mobile Catholic Irish Australians generally found themselves barred from the strongholds of conservatism, though Protestant Irish Australian were admitted.[25] Conservative hostility manifested itself in various ways. From the 1870s onward, it was widely apparent in opposition to the restoration of state funding for Australian Catholic schools, while, from the 1880s, it also took the form of opposition to proposals for Irish home rule. Such hostility was of course not lost on the Catholic press, with Melbourne's *Tribune* claiming in 1907 that conservative strategies were "driving Catholics and Laborites into one corner."[26]

Yet as Moran's experience demonstrated, Catholic involvement in a class-based movement and party, especially one that in theory espoused socialism, created problems for those whose church regarded left-wing political ideologies like socialism as atheistic and thus anathema. Matters were further complicated by the fact that the Labor Party, despite repeated promises, failed to address an issue that the Catholic Church saw as absolutely crucial: state aid to church schools. Therefore, although a strong bond had been forged by the Catholic Irish Australian community and its church with organized labor between 1880 and 1914, it was by no means a comfortable relationship but rather was characterized by tension and frustration centered on a range of religious, political, ethnic, and educational issues.

To what extent these tensions and frustrations affected how Irish Australians voted in elections has never been thoroughly investigated. But it is no doubt significant that when, especially during 1911–23, the church made strenuous efforts to get Catholics to vote for candidates in favor of state aid, regardless of their party affiliation, it largely failed.[27] This suggests that working-class Catholic Australians were less concerned about education than was their church and that the state aid issue did not significantly damage their loyalty to the Labor Party. The Sydney *Freeman's Journal* put the matter bluntly in 1915 when it said that although Catholics might be disappointed by the ALP's failure to endorse state aid, the truth was that "as a whole their claims have received more sympathy and support [from the Labor Party] than from any other political body in the country."[28] In other words, Catholics really could not afford to bite the hand that fed them, even if some among them, notably their clerical leaders, believed that it did not feed them enough. As regards state aid at least, for most Catholic Irish Australians, class allegiance would appear to have trumped religious or cultural identity.

Australia's Catholic Church and Catholic community were not always in agreement regarding relations with organized labor, and on occasion, large gaps opened up between the imperatives of the hierarchy and the views of the laity. As a consequence, understanding the level of church control is necessary when reading the Catholic press to determine to what extent the papers reflected the views of the priests or of the people.[29]

Although in Sydney the lay-controlled *Freeman's Journal* and church-controlled *Catholic Press* waxed and waned in their support for the nascent ALP, both joined with Cardinal Moran in enthusiastically endorsing Federation.[30] Moran's long episcopacy (1884–1911) marked the decisive shift from a largely Irish-born Catholic community to an overwhelmingly Australian-born one, and Moran actively sought to reflect this transition. In 1897, for instance, he took the unusual step of standing as a candidate for the Federal Convention, thus sparking sectarian outrage from many Protestants and even annoying labor leaders. His candidacy failed, but he did attract a sizable vote.[31] The strong support offered by Catholic Irish Australians and by most of their church and press for Federation signaled their embrace of a developing Australian identity. This identity offered them a weapon with which they could, to some extent at least, deflect accusations of disloyalty to Britain and the empire by arguing that they were simply putting Australia's interests first. Moran in particular used this weapon creatively during debates over the White Australia policy.[32]

Irish Australians in a White Australia

Restricting "colored" migration was a major and controversial political issue in colonial Australia from the 1850s onward, made more pressing by the economic problems of the 1890s. Initially sparked by fear of the Chinese, the issue expanded to include indentured Pacific-island workers, known as Kanakas, and later the Japanese.[33] Although at first there had been considerable disagreement over restrictions, by 1901 dissent had become muted or relegated to radical groups, and a general consensus had emerged strongly favoring not just restrictions on non-white immigration, but in fact a complete ban.[34]

Unlike the United States, the question of how far an Irish Catholic background was a factor influencing individuals' reactions to race and to immigration restriction has never been thoroughly examined in Australia. Some Catholics certainly opposed restrictions on "colored" immigrants. Lawyer and politician William Bede Dalley, the son of Irish convict parents, fought against an 1881 New South Wales bill aimed at denying basic civil rights to the Chinese.[35] Bernard O'Dowd, poet and editor of the Melbourne *Tocsin*, voiced concerns over the undemocratic nature of immigration restriction and in 1912 made clear that he considered "colour . . . one of the least important distinctions between man and man."[36] Galway-born Tom Glynn wrote articles against racial discrimination when he edited the Sydney-based *Direct Action*, which was published by the Industrial Workers of the World (IWW).[37] The main influences on the socialist opposition to White Australia appear to have come from the American IWW and also from elements within the British labor movement.[38] This opposition therefore does not seem to have had Irish roots. But there has been little serious study of what influence Irish socialists like Michael Davitt, who made an extensive speaking tour of Australia in 1895 and was a regular contributor to Australian Catholic newspapers, or James Connolly, an IWW supporter whose writings were popular in Australia, had on the country's labor movement.[39] In the absence of such study, no definitive conclusions are possible.

More can be said, however, regarding White Australia and the Irish-led Catholic Church. Cardinal Moran, at least during his early years in Australia, when he was eager to use the country as a base for a Catholic mission to China, spoke publicly in favor of Chinese immigration. During an interview with a journalist in Adelaide in 1888, he said he thought it "arbitrary and unchristian" of the colonies to prohibit Chinese immigrants from landing. Moran's advocacy of Chinese immigration provoked a storm of criticism, with the Sydney *Bulletin* in particular labeling him the "Chow's patron" and ridiculing him in several striking cartoons that raised the specter of Irish-Chinese miscegenation.[40] After this hostile reaction, Moran appears to have become less willing to speak publicly about immigration.

When the 1901 Immigration Restriction Bill was being debated in the new federal parliament, it received strong support from the Catholic Church and press, but the rationale behind this support was far from straightforward. Moran and the *Catholic Press* in particular pursued an outspoken nationalist line, trying to turn the issue into one involving Australia's rights versus Britain's "despotic policies." In response to British opposition to an outright ban on "colored" immigrants, the Australian government proposed a dictation test in a European language that intending immigrants would be required to pass. In October 1901, Moran reacted to the British stance by "denouncing" such interference in Australian affairs and comparing it to the sort of British actions that had driven the American colonies into rebellion more than a century earlier.[41]

Such bellicose rhetoric seems a far cry from the sentiments Moran had expressed in 1888. But at that time, he had been speaking as one of the leaders of a church with a worldwide evangelical mission, whereas by 1901 he was talking more like an Australian nationalist with a decidedly anti-British bias. It is doubtless significant that in 1901 his attacks were directed against the British government and those Australian politicians who, as the *Catholic Press* put it, had "kowtowed" to the British. Moran did not directly assail Asian immigrants themselves, probably because he had not totally abandoned his hopes of spearheading a Catholic mission to China.[42] But in the years since 1888, he had obviously recognized the strength of Irish Australian working-class feeling against "colored" immigration.[43] In fact, throughout 1901, many letters to Catholic newspapers and reports of meetings of Catholic clubs and societies indicated widespread support for a White Australia policy. The Catholic press editorialized in favor of White Australia on various grounds, including racial difference, the need to ensure social harmony, and the threat of competition from cheap labor. Moran clearly felt obliged to cater to such sentiment even if it posed a threat to his evangelical ambitions.[44] The *Catholic Press* certainly supported severe restrictions on "colored" immigration but simultaneously it took a nationalist line, arguing strongly for an independent Australian defense force and foreign policy, so that Australians could defend themselves without a slavish reliance on the Royal Navy or having to sacrifice their strategic interests to those of Britain.[45]

During these debates, the question of race and the Irish was also raised on occasion: Were the Irish who had settled Australia a different race from their fellow British settlers, or were both groups essentially the same—that is, both "white"? The racialization of the Irish is another issue that has attracted much scholarly attention in the United States but thus far little in Australia.[46] In 1903 Scottish-born federal MP George Reid, formerly premier of New South Wales, floated the notion that the Irish could be barred from Australia under the new immigration dictation test.[47] This suggestion attracted a sharp rebuke from the Sydney *Freeman's Journal*, which pointed out that as the Irish were not "colored immigrants," they could not be subjected to the test.[48] Cardinal Moran, by embracing an Australian identity during the immigration debates, was clearly attempting to supersede the old Irish-British divide and the racial arguments that had long surrounded it and to posit a new and united people, "white" Australians.

The Labor Press and Irish Nationalism, 1914–1922

The Labor Party faced the difficult task of accommodating support for Irish demands for greater political autonomy within a framework of empire loyalty.[49] This situation differed substantially from that prevailing in the United States, where Irish republicans had weathered the Know-Nothing movement and assaults on Irish groups such as the Molly Maguires and Clan na Gael and emerged to enjoy greater license to attack Britain and its policies toward Ireland.[50] In Australia the Catholic press was more constrained by the ties of empire than was its American counterpart, but unlike the Australian labor press, Catholic papers did feel able on occasion to indulge in outbursts of Irish nationalism and Anglophobia.[51]

Between the 1880s and the First World War, significant support for Irish home rule developed among the Catholic Irish Australian community, but there was also vociferous opposition in some quarters, especially among empire loyalists, fundamentalist Protestants, and of course the Orange Order.[52] Under home rule, Ireland would remain part of the United Kingdom, as it had been since 1801, but would elect MPs to sit in a Dublin parliament responsible for managing local affairs throughout the whole island.[53] As the Westminster parliament debated the third Irish Home Rule Bill during 1913–14, Ulster unionist opponents of home rule, led by Sir Edward Carson, and Irish nationalist supporters, led by John Redmond, established militias that began training and illegally importing arms, mainly from Germany. Many feared that Ireland was on the brink of civil war and that when home rule became law—as seemed inevitable sometime in late 1914—the country was likely to descend into bloody sectarian conflict.[54]

Whereas the Australian labor movement was generally sympathetic to Irish home rule, it did have problems with Irish nationalism, especially when republicans advocated rebellion against British rule and the establishment of an independent Irish state. Labor Party members of the Australian federal parliament had voted solidly for resolutions in favor of Irish home rule in 1905 and 1914, but these motions were carefully worded to emphasize that home rule was calculated to strengthen rather than weaken the British Empire.[55] Most ALP and trade union leaders, many of whom were of Irish birth or descent, were in agreement with most Australian conservatives in not wanting to see an end to the political union between Ireland and Britain. They feared that separation would undermine the United Kingdom and by extension the empire, with an independent Ireland potentially coming under German influence. However, unlike most conservatives, labor did advocate a degree of self-government for Ireland, seeing in home rule a potential solution to the country's endemic political unrest and hopefully its notorious poverty.

During 1914, Melbourne's *Labor Call* printed a number of articles about the progress of the Home Rule Bill at Westminster and the growth of militias in Ireland, with many of these pieces attacking Ulster and English unionism as hostile to Irish working-class interests rather than actually supporting Irish nationalism.[56] But as the Ulster crisis deepened during June and July 1914, the

IWW's *Direct Action*, unlike most other labor newspapers, had nothing at all to say about the matter. Later articles, however, made its attitude very plain. Some of *Direct Action*'s main contributors had been born in Ireland, among them Tom Glynn and Peter Larkin, brother of Irish trade union leaders Jim Larkin and Delia Larkin.[57] In an article published in May 1916, in the wake of Dublin's Easter Rising, Glynn lumped "Carsonites" and "Redmondites" together as "class enemies" of Irish workers.[58] The IWW was scornful of home rule. Like much of the labor press, *Direct Action* applied a class rather than a nationalist analysis to the Irish situation: according to this reading of events, unionists and home rulers were in fact both on the same side—against the working class.

In trying to explain to their readers the motives behind the Easter Rising in Dublin during the last week of April 1916, Australian labor newspapers continued to apply, in varying degrees the class analysis developed in the context of the 1914 Ulster crisis. Yet the rising had been staged in support of an Irish republic totally independent of the United Kingdom, not of a home-rule Ireland that would remain within the United Kingdom. Moreover, the rebels had secretly negotiated German support and struck while Britain and Australia were in the midst of a hard-fought war with Germany.[59] This made a sympathetic analysis much more difficult for a labor press that essentially favored Crown and empire, even if radical papers were already seriously questioning the war's rationale.[60]

Efforts to understand exactly what had occurred in Ireland were not helped by wartime censorship.[61] But, as early as 4 May, the editor of Sydney's antiwar *Australian Worker*, Henry Boote, produced a powerful and perceptive commentary on the Easter Rising just as the executions of its leaders were beginning and before news of them had reached Australia. Boote, who grew up in Liverpool, an English city with a large Irish immigrant population, began forcefully, "I am sorry for the Sinn Feiners [Irish republicans]. I do not loathe them. I pity them." According to him, they had been "corrupted" by the violent tenor of the times. But as well as the madness of the current war, Boote also identified the roots of the rebellion in the extraordinarily lenient treatment accorded the Ulster unionists in 1914, whose leader Carson now sat in the British cabinet. To Boote's mind, by thwarting Irish democracy over the issue of home rule, the British government and the Ulster unionists were ultimately responsible for the rising.[62]

After details of the fifteen executions became known, and especially the news that James Connolly had been shot although wounded, comparisons with the treatment of the Ulster unionist rebels became much angrier. The socialist Connolly was a particular hero in the eyes of the IWW as, while in the United States during 1903–7, he had joined the organization soon after its establishment in

1905 and acted as an effective propagandist and recruiter for it among Irish and Italian workers in New York City.[63] For *Direct Action*, his execution in 1916 was on a par with "German atrocities."[64] Contributors to other labor papers were also familiar with Connolly and his writings, and his participation in the rising was a major factor that encouraged the labor press's class reading of the event. The *Worker* pointed out that although the words *Sinn Féin* meant "Ourselves Alone," thus suggesting a nationalist agenda, "Connolly, one of the leaders, was a big-brained, big-hearted Internationalist." This led the paper to suspect the rising was actually an "industrial revolt, with Socialism as its objective." Like *Direct Action*, the *Worker* continued to highlight Connolly's role, claiming in late June that he, a "well-known Socialist," was "at the head of affairs," while Patrick Pearse was described as merely his "associate" and a "man of letters."[65]

Even when more information became available, the Australian labor press seemed reluctant to abandon its initial reading of the rising as a socialist revolt led by James Connolly. But in this it was quite mistaken, for the rising had been largely organized by anti-British Fenians, who were reliant for success on Irish American money and German-supplied arms. The rising's leaders were determined to break all links with Britain and its empire and to establish an Irish republic. Moreover, most of them were middle-class intellectuals and devout Catholics who, despite Connolly's belated presence among them, harbored little if any sympathy for socialism.[66]

Guerrilla war broke out in Ireland in 1919, pitting the nationalist militia established in 1914, now calling itself the Irish Republican Army, against the Royal Irish Constabulary, reinforced from early 1920 by contingents of former British soldiers known as the Black-and-Tans. The Australian labor press was once more confronted with the problem of Irish republicanism. Most papers did not want to see Ireland abandon the union with Britain and possibly also leave the empire, yet at the same time, their sympathies were largely on the side of the Irish insurgents. Given this dilemma, reporting was again, as in 1914 and 1916, highly selective.

Whereas the culpability of Tories and unionists had been emphasized in the past, during 1920 and 1921, blame was firmly fixed on the Black-and-Tans and also on the policies pursued by British prime minister David Lloyd George. The "atrocities" of the Tans were highlighted, while the aims of the Irish Republican Army, which entailed the breakup of the United Kingdom and Catholic nationalist rule of Protestant unionist Ulster, did not attract anywhere near as much attention. Headlines over stories about Black-and-Tan reprisal raids on Irish towns and cities capture the general tenor of labor press reporting: "White Terror in Ireland" and "Hell Let Loose in Ireland."[67] The Black-and-Tans were labeled "Lloyd George's Bashi-Bazouks," a Turkish term describing brutal and ill-disciplined troops or police.[68]

However, the labor press's Irish reporting also sounded a new and interesting note. The violence in Ireland was now portrayed against the backdrop of other postwar upheavals, especially in India, the Middle East, Russia, and parts of Europe. This reportage differed from that of 1914 and 1916, when Ireland was seen in narrow United Kingdom terms; after 1918, the Irish conflict was framed in the context of broader postwar struggles involving nationalism, socialism, and anticolonialism; some of these struggles even extended to Australia. This new note is evident in the reporting of the events of Bloody Sunday, 21 November 1920, when, in retaliation for the Irish Republican Army's shooting of twelve British army intelligence officers on the orders of Michael Collins, police and soldiers stormed Dublin's Croke Park football stadium during a game, firing indiscriminately on players and spectators, killing a further twelve people.[69] This incident was characterized by the Brisbane *Worker* in January 1921 as an "Irish Amritsar," referring to the Amritsar Massacre in the Punjab in April 1919, when a British general ordered his men to open fire on a large nationalist crowd, killing at least four hundred.[70] Parallels between Amritsar and Black-and-Tan reprisals in Ireland during 1920–21 were also made in the United States, in both Irish and Indian nationalist publications.[71]

But it was not only India to which the labor press turned in search of parallels to help its readers understand the conflict raging in Ireland during the early 1920s. The use of the terms *White Terror* and *White Guards* in headlines points to other common parallels drawn: with massacres committed by anticommunist, ultranationalist forces during the civil wars that had broken out in Russia (1917–23), Finland (1918), and Hungary (1919–21).[72] Comparisons were also made between the Irish and the Arabs, especially in terms of the revolt in Iraq (1920) against the imposition of a British mandate , during which the Royal Air Force was used to bomb and terrorize civilians.[73] In drawing such parallels, the labor press portrayed the Black-and-Tans as a bloodthirsty paramilitary force unleashed on the defenseless working-class inhabitants of Ireland by an unscrupulous Welsh leader, British prime minister Lloyd George, a leader rather in the mold of Australia's own Welsh prime minister. And indeed, comparisons with William Morris Hughes were explicitly made.

Such reporting certainly avoided the hazard of appearing too anti-British and blaming the British people as a whole for what was happening in Ireland, but at the same time it was intended to highlight for Australians that they, like the British, were governed by a prime minister who had shown himself very ready to adopt extreme measures to get what he wanted. At the beginning of

1921, the *Australian Worker* was calling the newly established federal police force "Hughes's 'Black and Tans.'" Reprisals "appear imminent," it claimed, and a "second Ireland" it believed was "possible" in Australia.[74] It was little wonder, then, that in 1922, after an Anglo-Irish treaty had been signed and Britain was seeking employment for thousands of disbanded Irish policemen, the labor press was adamant that none should be allowed into Australia, especially as it was feared that their ranks contained many former Black-and-Tans.[75] The Brisbane *Worker* insisted that the Tans had been "forged" by conservative politicians "for use against . . . workers," certainly in Ireland, probably in England, and possibly in Australia as well.[76]

Conclusion

During the late nineteenth century in both Australia and the United States, working-class Irish immigrants and their children involved themselves in the labor movement. Australian and American men and women of Irish Catholic descent figured prominently as activists and leaders in trade unions and in the ALP and the Democratic Party. Fear of job competition from cheap "colored" workers, combined with anxieties about their own racial status, led most Irish in both countries to strongly support immigration restriction. Yet while the similarities are striking, so, too, are the differences. It could be argued that in both political and religious terms, the situation of Irish Australians was more complex and problematic than that of Irish Americans. In certain respects, their situation was actually more like that of those Irish who had crossed the sea to Britain than like those who had crossed the ocean to the United States.[77] The Catholic Church in Australia, like the church in Britain, had to deal with the fact that the political party supported by the vast majority of its flock was dedicated, in principle at least, to socialism. Also like Britain, Australia was part of the British Empire, and imperial loyalty remained strong among Australians both before and after Federation in 1901.[78] By contrast, the United States took great pride in its rejection of British rule during the late eighteenth century and in its republican traditions. Thus, Irish Americans, many descendants of those driven out of Ireland by the Great Famine, felt freer to fund Irish nationalist causes, while from the 1850s onward, the United States provided a vital base for Irish republicanism. The situation of Irish Australians, however, was very different: Irish republicanism never won a major following in Australia, and support for even moderate Irish political reforms, like home rule, had to be tempered with frequent expressions of empire solidarity to win over politicians—even Labor politicians.[79]

Disentangling the threads of the relationship in Australia between organized labor, on the one hand, and the Catholic Irish Australian working class and its church, on the other, is a challenging task. This relationship can be characterized as an alliance, but it was by no means a straightforward or comfortable alliance. The Catholic press generally favored the White Australia policy, which clearly also enjoyed widespread support among the Irish Australian working class and among Labor politicians. Yet, at the same time, White Australia posed significant difficulties for the Catholic Church. Cardinal Moran strove to deflect criticism away from "colored" immigrants themselves and onto the British government, while ironically the church shared some of the imperial government's basic problems with White Australia. Like the British Empire, the Catholic Church was an expansionist, international organization, and to continue to proselytize in Asia, it could not afford to offend rising powers like Japan or populous ones like China. Moran sought to manage this dilemma by playing an Australian nationalist card in preference to a racist one in 1901, hoping thereby to placate the Australian Catholic working class while at the same time not alienating the authorities in Japan and China and making Catholic missions to those countries even more difficult than they already were.

At the same time the Australian labor press, reflecting the views of the Catholic working class, fairly consistently supported a measure of self-government for Ireland. But this stance created problems, in particular after 1916, when Irish nationalism veered strongly in the direction of republicanism. The ALP and the mainstream labor press did not endorse republicanism, either for Ireland or for Australia, and neither did most of the Catholic hierarchy and laity. The labor press sought to manage this particular dilemma by imposing a class analysis on events in Ireland and using highly selective reporting to limit its attacks to particular groups and individuals. Thus it conveniently avoided a full-frontal assault on Britain and sidestepped some of the less palatable goals and methods of Irish republicanism.

If White Australia and Irish republicanism posed problems, there was in addition the perennial question of state aid to church schools. As far as the Catholic Church at least was concerned, this remained the most persistent problem for the Catholic-labor relationship. By 1919 the Australian Catholic Federation, a political lobbying group established with church support in 1911, had become so thoroughly disillusioned with the ALP that it set up its own political party, the Democratic Party, aimed to garner Catholic votes and elect candidates supportive of state aid. Although this initiative failed comprehensively, it was nonetheless a further sign of the continuing strains between the

Catholic Church and the Labor Party.[80] Thus, when a major split finally did occur during the early and mid-1950s and a far more successful Catholic party emerged, these developments need to be seen against the backdrop of decades of simmering tensions between the Catholic Church and community and organized labor. The issue of communism proved the final breaking point, but other issues like state aid, race, and nationalism had served to create significant strains in the alliance from its very outset.

Notes

Research for this article was funded by the Australian Research Council. The authors also thank Val Noone and Verity Burgmann for valuable advice and Lee Ann Monk for assistance with research.

1. For a comparative study, see Malcolm Campbell, *Ireland's New Worlds: Immigrants, Politics, and Society in the United States and Australia, 1815–1922* (Madison: University of Wisconsin Press, 2008).

2. See, for example, Brian Costar, Peter Love, and Paul Strangio, eds., *The Great Labor Schism: A Retrospective* (Melbourne: Scribe, 2005).

3. A. G. L. Shaw, *Convicts and the Colonies* (1966; Melbourne: Melbourne University Press, 1977), 148, 182–83; Deborah Oxley, *Convict Maids: The Forced Migration of Women to Australia* (Cambridge: Cambridge University Press, 1996), 67–72, 109–45.

4. R. E. Reid, *Farewell My Children: Irish Assisted Emigration to Australia, 1848–1870* (Sydney: Anchor Australia, 2011); Lindsay Proudfoot and Dianne Hall, "Points of Departure: Remittance Emigration from South-West Ulster to New South Wales in the Later Nineteenth Century," *International Review of Social History* 50 (2005): 341–78.

5. George Rudé, *Protest and Punishment: The Story of Social and Political Protesters Transported to Australia, 1788–1868* (Oxford: Clarendon, 1978), 31–40, 145.

6. Shaw, *Convicts and the Colonies*, 368.

7. Trevor McClaughlin, *Barefoot and Pregnant: Irish Famine Orphans in Australia* (Melbourne: Genealogical Society of Victoria, 1991).

8. J. S. Donnelly Jr., "The Construction of the Memory of the Famine in Ireland and the Irish Diaspora, 1850–1900," *Éire-Ireland* 31 (1996): 26–61.

9. David Fitzpatrick, *Oceans of Consolation: Personal Accounts of Irish Migration to Australia* (Ithaca: Cornell University Press, 1994), 11.

10. Wray Vamplew, ed., *Australians: Historical Statistics* (Sydney: Fairfax, Syme, and Weldon, 1987), 8, 11, 421–26.

11. For discussions of the small number of non-Irish Catholics in colonial Australia—mostly Italians, Germans, and English—see James Jupp, ed., *The Australian People*, 2nd ed. (Cambridge: Cambridge University Press, 2001), 300–303, 360–62, 486–95.

12. For relations between the Irish and newer US immigrant groups, see J. R. Barrett and D. R. Roediger, "The Irish and the 'Americanization' of the 'New Immigrants' in the Streets and the Churches of the Urban United States, 1900–1930," *Journal of American*

Ethnic History 24 (2005): 3–33; Kevin Kenny, *The American Irish: A History* (Harlow: Longman, 2000), 185–92.

13. M. M. Pawsey, *The Popish Plot: Culture Clashes in Victoria, 1860–1863* (Sydney: Studies in the Christian Movement, 1983); Keith Amos, *The Fenians in Australia, 1865–1880* (Sydney: University of New South Wales Press, 1988).

14. Chris McConville, *Croppies, Celts, and Catholics: The Irish in Australia* (Melbourne: Arnold Australia, 1987), 47–54, 85–89.

15. B. W. Higman, *Domestic Service in Australia* (Melbourne: Melbourne University Press, 2002), 62–64; Margaret Lynch-Brennan, *The Irish Bridget: Irish Immigrant Women in Domestic Service in America, 1840–1930* (Syracuse: Syracuse University Press, 2009).

16. D. N. Doyle, "The Irish and American Labour, 1880–1920," *Saothar* 1 (1975): 42–53; David Montgomery, "The Irish and the American Labor Movement," in *America and Ireland, 1776–1976: The American Identity and the Irish Connection*, ed. D. N. Doyle and O. D. Edwards (Westport, Conn.: Greenwood, 1980), 205–18; J. R. Barrett, *The Irish Way: Becoming American in the Multiethnic City* (New York: Penguin, 2012), 108–11.

17. For the employment experience of the Irish in the main cities, see Chris McConville, "Emigrant Irish and Suburban Catholics: Faith and Nation in Melbourne and Sydney, 1851–1933" (PhD diss., University of Melbourne, 1984), 147–201. For the Irish in the late-nineteenth-century labor movement, see Keith Pescod, "Irish Participation in Victoria's Union Movement, 1850–1900," *Australasian Journal of Irish Studies* 11 (2011): 7–27; Ross McMullin, *The Light on the Hill: The Australian Labor Party, 1891–1991* (Oxford: Oxford University Press, 1991), 19, 23, 29, 31, 35–36, 42, 44.

18. Raelene Frances, "Authentic Leaders: Women and Leadership in Australian Unions before World War II," *Labour History* 104 (2013): 11–13, 16–17; Barrett, *Irish Way*, 139–43.

19. Patrick Ford, *Cardinal Moran and the A.L.P.* (Melbourne: Melbourne University Press, 1966), 63–74.

20. A. E. Cahill, "Cardinal Moran's Politics," *Journal of Religious History* 15 (1989): 527–28; Philip Ayres, *Prince of the Church: Patrick Francis Moran, 1830–1911* (Melbourne: Miegunyah, 2007), 274–78.

21. Patrick O'Farrell, *The Catholic Church and Community in Australia: A History* (Melbourne: Nelson, 1977), 285, 296; Cahill, "Cardinal Moran's Politics," 529–31.

22. Kenny, *American Irish*, 82–83, 116–21; Reginald Byron, *Irish America* (Oxford: Clarendon, 1999), 165–67.

23. O'Farrell, *Catholic Church and Community*, 288.

24. *Tomahawk*, cited in *Freeman's Journal*, 21 November 1896.

25. Paul de Serville, *Pounds and Pedigrees: The Upper Class in Victoria, 1850–80* (Oxford: Oxford University Press, 1991), 26, 80, 190, 212–13, 367.

26. *Tribune*, 2 March 1907, cited in Frank Bongiorno, *The People's Party: Victorian Labor and the Radical Tradition, 1875–1914* (Melbourne: Melbourne University Press, 1996), 169.

27. Jeff Kildea, *Tearing the Fabric: Sectarianism in Australia, 1910 to 1925* (Sydney: Citadel, 2002), 208–11.

28. *Freeman's Journal*, 4 November 1915; Bongiorno, *People's Party*, 187.

29. Patrick Naughtin, "*The Melbourne Advocate*, 1868–1900: Bastion of Irish Nationalism in Colonial Victoria," in *Visual, Material, and Print Culture in Nineteenth-Century Ireland*, ed. Ciara Breathnach and Catherine Lawless (Dublin: Four Courts, 2010), 223–33.

30. A. E. Cahill, "Cardinal Moran and Australian Federation," *Australasian Catholic Record* 78 (2001): 3–15.

31. Ayres, *Prince of the Church*, 194–204; McMullin, *Light on the Hill*, 20.

32. Mark Hearn, "Containing 'Contamination': Cardinal Moran and *Fin de Siècle* Australian National Identity, 1888–1911," *Journal of Religious History* 34 (2010): 20–21.

33. Marilyn Lake and Henry Reynolds, *Drawing the Global Colour Line: White Men's Countries and the Question of Racial Equality* (Melbourne: Melbourne University Press, 2008), 15–45.

34. Andrew Markus, *Fear and Hatred: Purifying Australia and California, 1850–1901* (Sydney: Hale and Iremonger, 1979), 228.

35. Robert Lehane, *William Bede Dalley* (Canberra: Ginninderra, 2007), 210, 231–33, 370–72.

36. Frank Bongiorno, "Bernard O'Dowd's Socialism," *Labour History* 77 (1999): 97–116.

37. *People*, 11 December 1909; Verity Burgmann, "Racism, Socialism, and the Labour Movement, 1887–1917," *Labour History* 47 (1984): 50.

38. Burgmann, "Racism, Socialism," 54.

39. Carla King, "'I Am Doing Fairly Well in the Lecturing Line': Michael Davitt and Australia, 1895," *Australasian Journal of Irish Studies* 12 (2012): 23–46.

40. See, for example, Patricia Rolfe, *The Journalistic Javelin, 1880–1980: An Illustrated History of the Bulletin* (Sydney: Wildcat, 1979), 67.

41. *Catholic Press*, 5 October 1901.

42. Patrick Comerford and Richard O'Leary, "'Heroism and Zeal': Pioneers of Irish Christian Missions to China," in *China and the Irish*, ed. Jerusha McCormack (Dublin: New Island, 2009), 74–78.

43. C. A. Price, *The Great White Walls Are Built: Restrictive Immigration to North America and Australasia, 1836–1888* (Canberra: Australian National University Press, 1974), 261–63.

44. *Freeman's Journal*, 27 November 1897, 15 March 1902; *Catholic Press*, 28 September, 26 October 1901, 6 August 1903.

45. *Catholic Press*, 12 October 1901.

46. See, for example, Noel Ignatiev, *How the Irish Became White* (New York: Routledge, 2005). For an Australian study using cartoons as evidence, see Dianne Hall, "'Him Now White Man': Images of the Irish in Colonial Australia," *History Australia* 11 (2014): 167–95.

47. Gwenda Tavan, *The Long Slow Death of White Australia* (Melbourne: Scribe, 2005), 27–28.

48. *Freeman's Journal*, 28 November 1903.

49. For the difficult relationship between the ALP and empire after 1916, see Neville Kirk, "'Australians for Australia': The Right, the Labor Party, and Contested Loyalties to Nation and Empire in Australia, 1917 to the early 1930s," *Labour History* 91 (2006): 102–4.

50. Barrett, *Irish Way*, 243–48; Campbell, *Ireland's New Worlds*, 55–56, 164–65.

51. This was especially true in Melbourne after the arrival from Ireland in 1913 of Archbishop Daniel Mannix. See *Advocate,* 1 August 1914, 13 May 1916, 23 March 1918; James Griffin, *Daniel Mannix: Beyond the Myths* (Melbourne: Garratt, 2012), 198–217.

52. John Poynter, *Doubts and Certainties: A Life of Alexander Leeper* (Melbourne: Melbourne University Press, 1997), 364–70.

53. Alvin Jackson, *Home Rule: An Irish History, 1800–2000* (London: Phoenix, 2004), 126–31.

54. The classic account remains A. T. Q. Stewart, *The Ulster Crisis* (London: Faber and Faber, 1967).

55. Patrick O'Farrell, *The Irish in Australia* (Sydney: University of New South Wales Press, 1986), 241–42; *Advocate,* 4 July 1914.

56. *Labor Call,* 2 April, 7 May 1914.

57. P. J. Rushton, "Revolutionary Ideology of the I.W.W. in Australia," *Historical Studies* 15 (1972): 427; Ian Turner, *Sydney's Burning: An Australian Political Conspiracy,* rev. ed. (Sydney: Alpha, 1969), 30; *Direct Action,* 13 May, 30 September 1916.

58. *Direct Action,* 13 May, 22 July 1916.

59. See Charles Townshend, *Easter 1916: The Irish Rebellion* (London: Lane, 2005).

60. Mark Cryle, "'Natural Enemies': Anzac and the Left to 1919," in *Labour and the Great War: The Australian Working Class and the Making of Anzac,* ed. Frank Bongiorno, Raelene Frances, and Bruce Sates (Sydney: Australian Society for the Study of Labour History, 2014), 145–47.

61. *Worker,* 11 May 1916.

62. *Australian Worker,* 4 May 1916.

63. F. A. D'Arcy, "James Connolly (1868–1916)," in *Dictionary of Irish Biography,* ed. James Quinn and James Maguire (Cambridge: Cambridge University Press, 2009), 2:759; Barrett, *Irish Way,* 143–44.

64. *Direct Action,* 27 May 1916.

65. *Worker,* 11 May, 29 June 1916.

66. For a recent analysis of the rising's leaders, see R. F. Foster, *Vivid Faces: The Revolutionary Generation in Ireland, 1890–1923* (London: Lane, 2014).

67. *Worker,* 30 August 1920; *Australian Worker,* 2 December 1920.

68. *Australian Worker,* 9 December 1920.

69. Charles Townshend, *The Republic: The Fight for Irish Independence, 1918–1923* (London: Penguin, 2014), 201–10.

70. *Worker,* 6 January 1921.

71. Michael Silvestri, "'315 Million of India with Ireland to the Last': Irish and Indian Nationalists in North America," in *Ireland and India: Colonies, Culture, and Empire,* ed. Tadhg Foley and Maureen O'Connor (Dublin: Irish Academic, 2006), 249.

72. *Worker,* 30 September, 14 October 1920.

73. *Australian Worker,* 9 December 1920.

74. Ibid., 6 January 1921.

75. Ibid., 26 April 1922.

76. *Worker*, 7 April 1921.

77. D. M. MacRaild, "Crossing Migrant Frontiers: Comparative Reflections on Irish Migrants in Britain and the United States during the Nineteenth Century," in *The Great Famine and Beyond: Irish Migrants in Britain in the Nineteenth and Twentieth Centuries*, ed. MacRaild (Dublin: Irish Academic, 2000), 40–70.

78. Luke Trainor, *British Imperialism and Australian Nationalism: Manipulation, Conflict, and Compromise in the Late Nineteenth Century* (Cambridge: Cambridge University Press, 1994), 8–11.

79. O'Farrell, *Irish in Australia*, 62–69, 208–54.

80. Kildea, *Tearing the Fabric*, 204–13, 230–42.

Gatekeepers and "Americanizers"

Irish Americans and the Creation of a Multicultural Labor Movement in the United States, 1880s–1920s

JAMES R. BARRETT

In the heart of the nineteenth-century American industrial city, Irish workers created a defensive and somewhat belligerent culture shaped by their experiences in the Great Famine and in negotiating English colonial rule, their extreme poverty, the nativist and anti-Catholic prejudice they faced in the United States, and their lowly place in the nation's evolving racial hierarchy. Less predictable perhaps was the Irish success in establishing themselves in the labor movement by the early twentieth century, an achievement built on elaborate parish, neighborhood, and workplace networks.

This chapter focuses on migrants who arrived after the famine era, on American-born persons of Irish descent, and on their impact on working-class America. It also offers some reflections on similarities and differences with the experience of the Irish in Australia. By 1900, twice as many Irish people in the United States had been born there as had been born in Ireland, and that proportion continued to grow throughout the early twentieth century. Entrenched in workplaces and unions, Irish American workers developed attitudes and undertook actions that had enormous consequences as the American working-class population was continually remade through later waves of migration.

Irish Traditions and New Labor Strategies

As in Australia, US workers' decisions and actions often turned on issues of race and ethnicity, though as Elizabeth Malcolm and Dianne Hall note, the numbers and range of diversity and thus the significance of such social difference were much more striking in the United States.[1] The five million first- and second-generation Irish in the United States by 1890, along with large numbers of German and other Northern European immigrants, were joined by more than eighteen million "new immigrants," primarily from Eastern and Southeastern Europe, between 1890 and 1920.[2] During the World War I era and the 1920s, millions of African American and Mexican migrants arrived in North American cities, vastly complicating the process of working-class formation and placing the American Irish, more than their Australian counterparts, in the position of "gatekeepers" in terms of jobs and unions.[3] Their actions often marginalized immigrants, the unskilled, women, and people of color, tendencies that left an enduring mark on the US labor movement. This defensive response was shaped by Irish American workers' arrival in advance of the great twentieth-century migrations and the hostile reception that the Irish had experienced between the middle and end of the nineteenth century.

Yet a tradition of progressive labor activism helped to lay the foundation for a new multiethnic movement in the early twentieth century. Countless organizers and shop stewards, labor activists and union officers, rank-and-file workers and middle-class sympathizers reached out to immigrants and to migrants of color, especially during World War I, conveying a different sort of Americanism than the one the newcomers encountered in government, corporate, and settlement house programs. The Irish were particularly important in this process of Americanization of new immigrants; ignoring this side of the story risks misunderstanding both the mentality of the Irish American worker and the complexity of the situation facing newcomers as they negotiated the era's workplaces and social movements.[4] Even if we focus entirely on the question of their relationship to independent labor politics, the American Irish, usually considered quite conservative, might have more in common with the Australian Irish, who also had a somewhat ambivalent relationship to the Australian Labor Party. While labor politics never achieved the lasting acceptance in the United States that it found among the Irish in Australia, this progressive legacy suggests some connections between the two cases.

A nineteenth-century reform tradition fused Irish nationalism, land reform, and labor radicalism. Strategically and organizationally, American unions owed a great deal to Irish social movements. The Molly Maguires, a secret miners' group, bore direct links to Irish secret societies that acted in the interests of poor farmers and agricultural laborers by terrorizing landlords and their agents, and this kind of violence was common to early labor protests in various settings. The secrecy and rituals of the Knights of Labor, by far the largest and most important of the late-nineteenth-century labor reform organizations, were shaped by employers' hostility to the group and by American Masonic traditions, and the heavily Irish Catholic membership embraced the approach despite the church's denunciation of all secret societies. The labor boycott was adapted from strategies used during the land wars in the west of Ireland. The Land League and secret Clan na Gael organizations often overlapped in constituency with the Knights of Labor and other labor groups that carried these approaches to an ethnically diverse body of workers. As business unionism emerged as a national movement, both German and Jewish immigrants played critical roles, but the Irish tended to predominate. Both the labor reform and business union traditions remained vital to the Irish American community, and a series of movements in the World War I era suggested the promise of an interethnic, progressive labor movement in the context of global political transformation.[5]

Green, Black, and Yellow: Irish Americans and Racism

For most of the second half of the nineteenth century, the legacy of slavery and its tendency to create a racial binary led Irish Catholic workers to occupy what was at best an ambiguous and at worst degraded racial status. The social and often physical proximity of the Irish to African Americans as well as competition between the two groups in some labor markets fueled Irish claims to whiteness and led to frequent conflict.[6] Nothing as ambitious as the White Australia policy emerged in the United States, but the popular and official thinking behind the restrictive US immigration policy was comparable. The Irish were particularly important in pursuing restriction, most notably of the Chinese.

From the mid-nineteenth century on, Irish American class consciousness and organization became increasingly racialized. Irish Americans fraternized with both Chinese and African Americans in antebellum New York, where neighborhoods were mixed and intermarriage was not uncommon. This situation was transformed, however, by the Civil War years, as the Irish objected to the draft, which they identified closely with blacks, and the two groups competed more directly for jobs on the docks and elsewhere. The fact that many of the accusations leveled at the Chinese by the 1870s had recently been directed at the Irish seemed to make the Irish reaction all the more desperate. Radical economist Henry George, who attracted enormous Irish American support with his theories of a single tax and land redistribution, saw the Chinese as the main threat facing American workers in the industrial era. In the context of the 1873–77 depression, George "nationalized" the anti-Chinese movement, though its heart certainly remained concentrated among the West Coast Irish. As with other examples of Irish American racism, the anti-Chinese movement received its force precisely from the rhetoric of antimonopoly and class solidarity. Both became touchstones of the Workingmen's Party of California, the creation of Irish American activists. Perhaps because of the larger numbers involved and the direct competition for unskilled laboring positions, Irish American reaction to Chinese immigrants in the late nineteenth century was less ambiguous than that of the Australian Irish. This story of relations between the Irish and Chinese was part of a broader narrative that included an ongoing conflict with African Americans and more recent immigrants in many cities that resulted in riots throughout the late nineteenth and early twentieth centuries.[7] While the proportion of aboriginal people in Australia was significantly smaller than that of blacks in the United States, the statuses of the two groups and their relationships with the Irish and the labor movement might reveal some interesting parallels between the two societies.

Biddy's and Paddy's Jobs

By the late nineteenth century, the Irish were "scattered throughout the length and breadth of American industry," as historian David Montgomery has written. "They were everywhere and into everything."[8] As in Australia, early Irish immigrants to the United States settled into unskilled laboring positions. The slow, halting rise of the Irish meant that Irish women immigrants remained largely confined to domestic work and that Irish men were disproportionately concentrated in building construction, coal mining, waterfront work, and the metal trades: one in seven male Irish American workers and one in four Irish immigrants overall remained in unskilled labor positions. Members of a "lace curtain" class had made their way up through building contracting and other small businesses, yet two-thirds of the Irish American workforce remained blue-collar in 1900.[9] Whereas many Irish immigrants in Australia entered farming and agricultural work, the American Irish were overwhelmingly concentrated in cities and industrial settings. When Irish men rose out of manual work, it was often into lower-level management positions as foremen and straw bosses.

They directed ethnically mixed construction crews and steel mill and factory labor gangs throughout the country.

The quintessential work for most Irish immigrant women was domestic service, a carryover to some degree from their situation in Ireland, where domestics accounted for nearly half of the female labor force in 1881 and where domestic service remained the most common female occupation until 1911.[10] In the United States, at least 60 percent of Irish immigrant working women were domestic servants as late as 1900, at which point more than 40 percent of the nation's 320,000 servants were Irish-born. Even after the influx of "new immigrant" women from the end of the nineteenth century until the 1920s, Irish women still predominated, as it seems they did in Australia. Bridget or "Biddy," the great symbol of the American servant class, and her colorful Hibernian partner, "Paddy," the Irish laborer, became stock subjects for jokes, vaudeville routines, and cartoons.[11]

If Irish women often settled into unskilled work in the United States, however, they also valued education. By the late nineteenth century, their experience in the Irish national school system established by the British meant that most emigrants left Ireland literate and with a range of domestic skills. Thus, the Irish were among the most literate of turn-of-the-century immigrants—about 95 percent read and wrote English as of the 1890s.[12]

Frustrated with their own prospects, domestics and other Irish women often passed a hunger for education and upward mobility along to their younger sisters, daughters, and nieces. In 1900, more than 61 percent of Irish immigrant women worked as domestics or waitresses, but the proportion had fallen to only 16 percent in the second generation. This striking mobility suggests a different perspective on the old generalization about slow Irish mobility out of the working class. In the late nineteenth century, even most American-born Irish men were moving up, though often only into skilled manual work. Perhaps through a combination of the savings of domestic servants and laborers, deep resentment at past discrimination, and striking ambition, Irish American women entered the professions, particularly teaching and nursing, in disproportionate numbers. In Chicago, only 16 percent of second-generation Irish men entered white-collar jobs, but for women, that proportion topped 25 percent. National figures were comparable. Had Irish Australian women achieved this level of upward mobility by the early twentieth century, and if so, how did this accomplishment relate to their activity in the labor movement? In the United States, given the sorts of occupations Irish American women entered, such mobility meant even more influence on later immigrants and others than Irish men exercised. By the early twentieth century, more than 20 percent of New

York and Boston public schoolteachers were the children of Irish immigrants. In Chicago, the proportion exceeded one-third, while in San Francisco it was about half. By 1920 an estimated 70 percent of Chicago's teachers were Catholic, most of them second-generation Irish.[13]

In practice, this meant that the Americanization of many recent immigrant children came not through a WASP elite but rather through the efforts of Irish-descended lay teachers and nuns. Not enough is known about the lessons learned, but there is clear evidence of working-class values and activism among the young teachers. Once settled in urban schools, the women began to organize. In Chicago, San Francisco, New York, and elsewhere, they established the earliest teachers' unions, often building on family and neighborhood connections in Irish-dominated labor federations. Where they did not rise into the professions, Irish American women entered newer industries such as telephone and switchboard operations, where they again launched the earliest unions.[14] A comparable generation of women activists emerged in Australia, raising intriguing questions about reasons for the assertiveness of this generation of Irish women.

In contrast, many Irish men had risen little by the end of the nineteenth century. As late as 1890, 90 percent of Boston's male Irish workers remained manual laborers. There and in other large cities, many worked on the docks, as teamsters, or as construction laborers. These unskilled positions brought newer Irish immigrants into direct contact with other immigrant and black workers.[15]

Yet the Irish had distinct advantages within the blue-collar world. By the turn of the century, they could rely on their elaborate social networks to secure not only city employment but also jobs in construction and other parts of the private sector. In New York, the various county societies, reinvigorated by immigration during the Land Wars and agricultural crisis of the 1880s, facilitated employment. These societies persisted through the early twentieth century not only because of their popular dances and outings but also because they functioned as employment networks. Even Irish-speaking greenhorns from the island's rural west had access to their English-speaking predecessors through the church and a range of voluntary organizations. In New York, they were quickly "connected"; in Chicago, they soon had some "clout."[16] This extensive network of parish-based voluntary groups provided contacts even for newcomers: "Should your brother Paddy come to America," an immigrant wrote home in the early 1920s, "he can rely on his cousins to promote his interests in procuring work."[17]

Irish influence in the craft unions under the American Federation of Labor (AFL) assured their control of apprenticeship and hiring and thus a new generation of Irish American skilled workers. Community relations with the burgeoning strata of Irish building contractors and foremen often provided jobs for friends and relatives. In building construction, this meant a disproportionate number of Irish bricklayers, plumbers, stonecutters, and eventually electricians, structural ironworkers, and others. Not coincidentally, construction represented the most thickly organized and most strike-prone sector of the American economy at the turn of the century.[18] If building construction demanded a high degree of solidarity to maintain wages and standards in a highly fluid workforce, ethnic networks provided the basis for such solidarity. Elaborate work rules, strictly enforced through community ostracism of strikebreakers, reflected a mutualistic ethic and allowed some element of control in an extremely competitive industry.

Closing the Gate

This ethic of mutualism and the solidarity it sustained often extended only to the limits of the Irish community, however. Where Irish Americans were able to influence hiring, as on the New York docks, other workers were at a disadvantage. Where a "connected" Irishman got the job, a newcomer might be excluded. In the midst of the building boom in turn-of-the-century cities, newer migrants often encountered fierce resistance from entrenched Irishmen. Fights on construction sites could easily develop into full-scale riots because of the size and ethnic solidarities of the work crews and the surrounding neighborhoods. Strikes by one ethnic group against another were not unusual.[19]

The same dynamic applied on the docks. Rather than some cultural throwback, violent nineteenth-century conflicts between Irish laborers from different regional and county backgrounds usually represented struggles for control of work. It was a tactic the Irish soon employed on the docks and other job sites of New York, New Orleans, and other cities. Many of the nation's early nineteenth-century dockworkers were slaves and free people of color, especially in southern ports. In the wake of the Great Famine, Irish immigrants drove African Americans from one job niche after another in the seaports, transforming the waterfront into an overwhelmingly Irish space. Racialized job competition had become "a stark and dangerous reality" by the 1860s, excluding blacks from the docks in Albany, Boston, Buffalo, Chicago, Cleveland, and Detroit as well as in New York City. "In the Irish neighborhoods that adjoined the West Side waterfront . . . Irish-born and Irish American residents developed a sense of entitlement and fought . . . to defend the jobs they regarded as theirs against invasion by 'strangers.'"[20]

By the 1880s an estimated 90 percent of New York dockworkers were Irish or Irish American. Foremen had to number the many Pat Murphys and John Sullivans on a single dock to distinguish them from one another. Where blacks resisted, as they often did, Irish laborers might attack. Such conflict, together with the Irish support for the Democratic Party and reputation for resistance to abolition, fueled black resentment. The introduction of Italians or African Americans often brought work stoppages.[21]

At times, the logic of class reshaped that of race. In New Orleans, as it became clear that employers would continue pitting the heavily Irish white workers against blacks, the two groups devised a Jim Crow "biracial equilibrium" that also became characteristic of other southern ports. Spectacular interracial general strikes broke out in 1894 and again in 1907. In New York Harbor, the American Longshoremen's Union took as its motto "All men are brothers" and rejected distinctions based on race, color, or creed. In 1898–99 the union organized somewhere between thirteen thousand and twenty thousand men, mostly Irish but also Italians and other nationalities. The union's successor, the Longshoremen's Union Protective Association, with strong roots among both Irish and Italians, led an unsuccessful strike in 1907. In its wake, the International Longshoremen's Association gradually consolidated its strength in this and other ports. Though dominated by the Irish and often corrupt, the association faced the issues of race and ethnic conflict by chartering ethnically based locals and by carefully integrating a few blacks and Italians into lower-level leadership positions.[22]

The surplus of dock labor, however, often meant fierce competition for work, and connections could help in gaining employment. Thousands of would-be longshoremen thronged the waterfronts each morning for the "shape-up." The Irish often remained in their old neighborhoods to be close to this volatile market. Linked to global markets through the busy port of New York and surrounded by people from all over the world, Irish longshoremen could be peculiarly parochial in perspective, clinging to their inward-looking slum neighborhoods on Manhattan's West Side. Unlike their ubiquitous counterparts in London, who first embraced their class identity and soon assimilated into British neighborhoods, New York's Irish longshoremen "held on to a more ethnicized class identity" as late as the 1940s, "simply as a response to ethnic succession and the extraordinarily ethnic character of New York working-class life." In New York and elsewhere, sustaining a sense of Irishness facilitated the control of good jobs and union offices.[23] San Francisco dock leader Harry Bridges and his International Longshore Workers Union represented a more diverse population of dockers and a more progressive form of union representation on the West Coast, but here, too, Irish American activists loomed large. While there is certainly evidence in Australia of both Irish domination on the docks and anti-Irish sentiment, the Irish there appear to have assimilated more readily than in the United States. In the face of the massive early twentieth-century immigration, Irish American dockworkers reacted in similar ways to the introduction of blacks, Italians, Eastern Europeans, and other interlopers. When employers tried to introduce blacks or recent immigrants, often to reduce wages or as strikebreakers, riots ensued. The tactic usually failed, but it helps to explain persistent tension between the Irish and later groups.

Recent work has tended to diminish the significance of job competition in the development of Irish American racism, stressing instead the cultural and psychological dimensions of the problem and the benefits of being viewed as white. This work leaves little doubt that the development and reproduction of racism was a complex transformation of consciousness that operated at many levels, but the history of Irish/African American relations is littered with bloody conflicts over work and labor struggles. In these situations, a strong sense of class, shot through with ethnic chauvinism and enhanced by a desperate struggle for existence, lent a potent force to race prejudice.

For all these reasons, Irish Americans played an important role in the formation of an interracial working class. The danger was that Irish American prejudices would be conveyed to later ethnic groups. When E. Franklin Frazier interviewed black longshoremen in New York in the early twentieth century, they reported that Italian longshoremen showed "less racial antipathy" and were more likely to accept African Americans on the docks; however, the Italians also seemed to be "assimilating the prejudices of the white men, in order apparently to insure their own standing."[24]

This narrative overlooks the more progressive role Irish American women and men played in creating an interracial labor movement. Looking at two distinct traditions of Irish American labor helps illustrate both dimensions of this critical story.

Business Unionists

The Irish exercised greater influence on the American labor movement than any other ethnic group in the late nineteenth century and for much of the twentieth. Nearly half of the AFL's 110 national unions had Irish American presidents through the first decade of the twentieth century, even though the Irish represented only 10 percent of the nation's native-born population and only 3 percent of its immigrants.[25] No reliable study exists of the intermediate and lower levels of union activism, but the leadership of many city and state federations, union locals, and shop floor organizations appears to have been dominated by the Irish. In Boston in the 1920s, for example, nearly 90 percent of the city's 347 elected union officials were Irish Americans.[26] The typical early twentieth-century Irish American labor leader was the child of immigrants who had grown up in an industrial city or town, someone steeped not in traditional Irish culture but in urban American society.

Irish influence may well have been just as strong in the Australian labor movement but had a different nature. The character of the influence was mixed in both places, but most Australian Irish Catholics fell in line behind the Labor Party, while in the United States many opposed socialist influence in the AFL and the overwhelming majority supported the Democratic Party and moderate reform. Exclusive by definition, AFL craft unionism often turned to nativism, racism, and the exclusion of women and minorities from the workplace and the union. Irish activists generally supported AFL efforts at literacy tests and other strategies to restrict immigration, as did the Catholic Church well into the twentieth century.[27] The narrow equation of labor's cause with that of the Irish community lent it an internal strength by mobilizing the ethnic community behind strikes, but it also encouraged a parochial attitude toward outsiders. Jere Sullivan, the Irish-born business manager of the Hotel and Restaurant Employees Union, ignored thousands of immigrant waiters and organized the largely Irish bartenders. His advice to immigrants was blunt: "If you are an American at heart, speak our language. If you don't know it, learn it. If you don't like it, move!"[28] When the new immigrants launched huge strikes around the time of World War I, they often faced off against Irish policemen and Irish American business unionists who denounced them as volatile and dangerous.[29] The AFL craft unions came closest to what the radical Industrial Workers of World called "jobs trusts."

Rebels

Despite the frequent (and correct) observation that the great mass of Irish American workers held back from socialist movements, however, a significant Irish American radical tradition remains largely unexplored. Each of the major radical movements of this era—the Socialist Labor Party, Socialist Party, Industrial Workers of the World, and Communist Party—all counted Irish Americans among their leaders (for example, Joseph McConnell, James Larkin, James Connolly, Elizabeth Gurley Flynn, William Z. Foster, the Dunne Brothers, James Cannon, and Mother Mary Jones).[30] Particularly during the high tide of radical Irish nationalism between the 1880s and the 1920s, a close fit between labor reform and nationalist agitation is key to understanding both phenomena. The relevance of labor radicalism for Irish Americans is likely underestimated unless it is defined a bit more broadly than the Socialist Party.

A new generation of Irish American women activists led much of the early twentieth-century women's labor movement. Until New York's "Great Uprising" produced a generation of Jewish women activists, "virtually all the prominent activists in either the Knights of Labor or the AFL were Irish Americans." The assertiveness of many Irish women could make them transgressors of standard sexual roles and behavior within and beyond the Irish Catholic community. They also played a particularly strong role in the nationalist, labor, and revolutionary movements in Ireland and then in cities throughout the United States, as they did in Australia, and they provided a vital link between middle-class woman suffrage reformers and the great mass of immigrant working women.[31] And while many Irish American women activists fused fairly traditional Catholic attitudes about marriage and family with progressive views of working-class organization and politics, a tradition of "Rebel girls" such as Flynn and the birth control pioneer Margaret Sanger consciously broke with the church and embraced both revolutionary lifestyles and radical politics.

A generation of Irish American women activists deeply rooted in immigrant working-class communities greatly expanded the social range of these movements by creating alliances with working women from other ethnic communities.[32] In addition to more famous personalities such as Mother Jones, the group included thousands of local activists in cities throughout the United States. Early twentieth-century Chicago was a hotbed of women's unionism, and Irish American women were at the center of this organizing among scrubwomen, clerks, telephone and switchboard operators, and waitresses.[33]

Several characteristics stand out among these activists. Most were the children of immigrants, born and raised in industrial cities and towns, but they inherited from their immigrant parents a commitment to the labor movement and notions of social justice. The Knights of Labor and Henry George's radical economics were key to these ideals. Yet they were also charting their own course, cultivating links with both native-born middle-class reformers and the new immigrants pouring into American workplaces. Most of them were influenced by Catholicism but encountered tensions between their social and religious commitments.

Disproportionately well educated in English by the standards of other immigrant groups, Irish women's devotion to Catholic social teachings and to radical Irish nationalism encouraged them to take a role in the public sphere and in social reform movements. More important, perhaps, the strong Irish social networks in America's industrial cities and their physical and social proximity to impoverished immigrants from their own and other ethnic communities meant that Irish American women inclined toward public service as teachers or nurses; some also tended toward social activism.

Creating an Interethnic Labor Movement

The distance between radical and business union traditions can be overstated. By the World War I era, craft strategies based on the ability to control the flow of skilled labor in various trades were increasingly unworkable in many industries. Division of labor and mass production processes meant that employers relied increasingly on unskilled immigrant labor, especially in heavy industry and manufacturing. Here was a challenge more profound than the one facing Irish activists in Australia. The increasing ethnic and racial diversity in US factories, steel mills, and coal mines meant that unionization could never be an Irish affair. Mainstream organizers turned toward a broader vision of the labor movement, motivated by necessity if not by an inclusive ethic. Irish American activists—women organizers in the Women's Trade Union League and unions and progressive unionists in state and municipal federations—worked to integrate the newer immigrants into the movement. These exigencies and nineteenth-century traditions of labor reform and radical nationalism shaped a group of progressive unionists at the heart of the AFL.

The result was often a kind of Americanization from the bottom up that conveyed in distinctly working-class tones what it meant to be an American.[34] An immigrant worker's introduction to the American political and economic system was more likely to come via informal conversations at work, discussion and debate at union meetings, and union publications than via formal corporate and government Americanization programs. The Americanizers in this sense might be experienced workers from the immigrant's own community or any of the older workers from a range of other communities, but Irish Americans loomed particularly large in this process.

In the context of world war, revolution, and working-class militancy, some activists saw their wartime labor and nationalist movements as part of a transnational workers' mobilization. They could embrace an expansive political and social perspective that linked prospects for Irish liberation with the broadest issues of industrial and social reform and with the aspirations of peoples from other small nations.[35] Or, they could root their movement firmly in the defensive

Irish American community, develop strategies based on the two-party system, and accept leadership by the "lace curtain" elite.

At the municipal level, Irish American progressive traditions thrived within the mainstream of the AFL in the Chicago, Detroit, Minneapolis, and other city federations. For a moment, Chicago's labor movement seemed to promise a way in which the remarkably diverse American working-class population might come together as part of a transnational social movement. Born in County Westmeath in 1871, John Fitzpatrick embodied this promise. He arrived on Chicago's South Side in 1882 and went to work in the stockyards at the age of twelve. He immersed himself in the city's vibrant labor movement, married a schoolteacher, and settled into the heart of the Irish working-class community. Fitzpatrick remained president of the Chicago Federation of Labor (CFL) for most of his adult life (1899–1901 and 1906–46). Tall and powerfully built, he symbolized Chicago's aggressive labor movement, which he infused with a sense of idealism and purpose. In a city famous for rampant corruption, Fitzpatrick was a straight arrow. He gave up drink and shunned labor meetings in saloons. An ardent Irish nationalist, he demonstrated a deep respect for the city's other nationalities. A devout Catholic, he refused to countenance anti-Semitic or racist remarks. He investigated allegations of racial discrimination by employers and unions, appointed black organizers, and sought the support of the black community's religious leaders. Fitzpatrick worked with socialists and communists and backed women's suffrage and the organization of the city's women workers, including teachers.[36]

The late-nineteenth-century CFL was dominated by Irish labor bosses from the powerful and corrupt Building Trades Council. Comparable groups of Irish American labor bosses operated in New York and elsewhere. Aligned with old-line Democratic bosses, many of the federation's leaders put their energies into lining their own pockets. On the other end of the spectrum, Fitzpatrick and others not only offered honest leadership, aggressive organizing, and progressive labor politics but envisioned a multiethnic labor movement that embraced all the city's workers. This conflict between two distinct elements in the Irish American community represented a struggle for the future of the labor movement.

Fitzpatrick led a remarkable burst of organizing. When the men's clothing workers, dominated by Jews, Italians, and Poles, went on strike in 1910, Fitzpatrick coordinated relief efforts. During World War I, he put Irish American radical William Z. Foster in charge of a massive and remarkably successful organizing drive in the stockyards, bringing together black and white, native and immigrant, skilled and unskilled from more than forty distinct ethnic groups to create a powerful movement.[37] Fitzpatrick and Foster then moved on to the open-shop steel industry. Sweeping into the steel towns, organizers built the largest strike movement in the nation's history, bringing more than three hundred thousand largely unskilled immigrant workers out on strike in late 1919 and holding them out for months. Both movements were crushed in an employers' offensive and the Red Scare of 1919–22, but Fitzpatrick and Foster had demonstrated that unskilled immigrant workers could be organized.[38]

During the war, Fitzpatrick forged the CFL into an invigorating amalgam of industrial unionism, independent labor politics, and progressive internationalism. CFL organizers penetrated the various ethnic communities around the city, carrying a new language of Americanism that stressed ethnic and racial tolerance while demanding industrial as well as political democracy. Fitzpatrick emerged as a leading challenger of Samuel Gompers's conservative brand of business unionism. When Fitzpatrick became convinced that the labor movement could not get fair treatment from the city's mainstream press, he launched a spirited labor weekly, *New Majority*, that covered the CFL's industrial and political exploits.

Irish Americans and Independent Labor Politics

A major difference between Australia and the United States lies in the area of labor and socialist politics. The American Irish were deeply involved in labor reform movements of the late nineteenth century, including "workingmen's" slates in cities and towns across the country. As in Australia, such movements fused with Irish nationalist politics, notably in the Land League and Henry George's single-tax movement, both of which burgeoned during the "Great Upheaval" of the 1880s. And a minority of "rebels" pursued socialist politics. From World War I through the early 1920s, a major labor party movement emerged, modeled in part on the movement in England. One of the earliest efforts came in 1918 in Chicago, where activists launched the Cook County Labor Party with machine-style clubs in ethnic neighborhoods including the Black Belt. Fitzpatrick led the party's ticket as mayoral candidate, but the group also fielded male and female candidates for alderman from a dozen different ethnic groups, projected a "Chicago for the workers," and won considerable support for Irish independence at mass meetings in the city's ethnic neighborhoods. The movement spread throughout the country, often allied with radical farmer movements, but was hobbled by the Red Scare and by factional conflict and co-opted reform movements within the main parties.

Repeated efforts to form a US labor party ultimately failed, and the Irish played a major role in maintaining the sort of urban machines that represented a more conservative alternative. Even in Australia, the Irish were somewhat ambivalent toward labor and socialist politics, but they became a far more important element in the Australian Labor Party than they ever did in comparable movements in the United States.

Some of this distance from radicalism is explained by the remarkable success of the Irish within the AFL and their hostility to other ethnic groups with strong socialist influence, particularly Jews and Italians. Another part of the answer lies in the Irish success in building complex urban Democratic Party machines. Often featuring corruption and duplicity, they were a conservative influence in many respects. But the phenomenon of blue-collar progressivism—the machines' support for a wide range of social reforms and the often-close connections between city machines and the more conservative elements of the labor movement—meant that the machines were viewed as a legitimate solution to class problems. And they openly competed with socialists.

A second noticeable difference between the two societies lies in the antagonism between the American Catholic Church and the socialist movement. Again, this legacy is more complex in both the United States and Australia than is often recognized. Irish Catholics in the United States had a long tradition of support for social reform and activism—Father Edward McGlynn and the early "labor priests," neighborhood and parish support for strikes, the liberal encyclical *Rerum Novarum* (1891), and the *Bishops' Program for Social Reconstruction* (1919), which called for government pensions, unemployment insurance, and public housing as well as the right to organize and bargain collectively. Yet McGlynn was formally excommunicated for his political efforts and regained his status only after an aggressive movement in Irish American neighborhoods. Unlike their Australian counterparts, who were excluded from the Conservative Party, American Irish Catholics found a home in the Democratic Party. Clerics and lay Catholics tended to support the Democratic machines and organized opposition to the socialists within the AFL through the Militia of Christ for Social Justice. Whereas Cardinal Patrick Francis Moran flirted with the Australian Labor Party, the American hierarchy repeatedly condemned socialist efforts. The unusual level of Irish support for the American church enhanced such influence. Although some liberal bishops supported labor organization and reform, the United States had no counterpart to Moran who championed independent labor politics and radical Irish nationalism. Still, even American Irish Catholics grappled with issues of class inequality and the problems facing working-class families through a broad range of institutions and through their support of moderate social reform. In so doing, they offered an alternative to labor politics.

Irish Revolution and Irish American Nationalism

The fact that a more subdued, respectable form of Irish nationalism came to predominate in the United States should not blind us to efforts that promised to link the Irish cause to broader movements of colonial peoples throughout the world. As Malcolm and Hall note, if Irish domestic politics in the United States remained more conservative than those in Australia, the nationalist movement tended to be more radical.[39] Whereas the imperial connection moderated nationalist agitation in Australia, support for physical force flourished in American cities in the wake of the Easter Rebellion and the subsequent revolution.

After a long period of dormancy, the emergence of armed conflict in Ireland brought an explosion of nationalist sentiment. A narrower agitation linked to older groups such as Clan na Gael that were often led by the Irish American bourgeoisie was challenged by a popular movement that had links to labor and socialist organizations and was often led by working-class groups such as the Irish Progressive League. The connections among the various radical groups were close enough that government agents often referred to labor organizers, strike leaders, and socialist activists as well as Irish nationalist agitators as Sinn Feiners.

During and after World War I, the progressive element of the nationalist movement engaged more than ever with international anti-imperialist efforts. Irish revolutionaries traveled back and forth between Dublin and American cities to secure financial and logistical support for military action, Irish American activists (unsuccessfully) pushed the AFL to enforce a boycott of British goods, and when Irish revolutionary James Larkin was arrested during the 1919 Red Scare, Irish organizations launched a defense committee in conjunction with the Socialist Party and the emerging American Civil Liberties Union. But the focus was broader than Irish independence. Irish progressives linked a range of social and political movements with the ethnic nationalism sweeping through immigrant communities. Thus, demands for a workers' republic in Ireland and Polish or Indian independence often echoed from the same platform as demands for labor rights and support of the Russian and Mexican Revolutions.[40]

In August 1920, the normally parochial neighborhoods along Manhattan's West Side docks erupted in the largest political strike to date when Irish longshoremen ignored their conservative union leadership and walked off the job to support the hunger strike of Terrence MacSwiney, Sinn Fein lord mayor of Cork, and to protest the incarceration in England of Daniel Mannix, the anti-war, pro-labor Irish nationalist archbishop of Melbourne. Irish dockers were joined by African American and British sailors and dockworkers, creating what historian Bruce Nelson has called "a remarkably diverse line of march."[41]

Conclusion

Important differences exist between the Irish experiences in the United States and Australia—imperial connections and their effects on the character of Irish nationalism; racial and ethnic distinctions in working-class populations; the political behavior of the Catholic Church; and Irish resistance to socialism and labor politics. In both cases, however, the narrative is ambivalent. Despite the connections with England and the empire, Irish nationalism persisted in Australia, though it was not as militant as in the United States. Greater ethnic and racial diversity sparked more conflict in the United States, but some Irish emerged as gatekeepers and others as mentors and organizers among the newcomers. The American church tended to oppose socialist politics and fostered a more conservative labor movement; the Australian Church showed greater support, but tensions abounded. The American Irish became the cornerstones of conservative and often corrupt municipal and state political machines, while the Australian Irish emerged as the bedrock of the Australian Labor Party. But the American political machines often supported labor and social reforms, and although they never sustained their support for a national political organization comparable to the Australian Labor Party, some Irish Americans did support a variety of labor parties and reform organizations. Thus, the differences between the Australian and American Irish are vital, but the nuances in the narratives are important for reaching a fuller understanding of both groups.

Notes

Parts of this essay draw on James R. Barrett, *The Irish Way: Becoming American in the Multi-Ethnic City* (New York: Penguin, 2013), 105–55. For helpful suggestions, especially regarding US-Australian comparisons, I thank Shel Stromquist.

1. See Elizabeth Malcolm and Dianne Hall, this volume.

2. Kevin Kenny, *The American Irish: A History* (New York: Longman, 2000), 131–41; Roger Daniels, *Coming to America: A History of Immigration and Ethnicity in American Life* (New York: HarperCollins, 1990), 121–45.

3. See Bruce Nelson, *Divided We Stand: American Workers and the Struggle for Black Equality* (Princeton: Princeton University Press, 2001), xxxviii–xix.

4. James R. Barrett, "Americanization from the Bottom Up: Immigration and the Remaking of the Working Class in the United States, 1880–1930," *Journal of American History* 79 (1992): 996–1020.

5. Kevin Kenny, *Making Sense of the Molly Maguires* (New York: Oxford University Press, 1998), 13–22; Michael A. Gordon, "The Labor Boycott in New York City, 1880–1886," *Labor History* 16 (1975): 184–229; Leon Fink, *Workingmen's Democracy: The Knights of Labor and*

American Politics (Urbana: University of Illinois Press, 1983); Eric Foner, "Class, Ethnicity, and Radicalism in the Gilded Age: The Land League and Irish America," in *Politics and Ideology in the Age of the Civil War* (New York: Oxford University Press, 1980), 150–200; Bruce Nelson, "Irish Americans, Irish Nationalism, and the Social Question, 1916–1923," *boundary 2* (2004): 147–78.

6. David R. Roediger, *The Wages of Whiteness: Race and the Making of the American Working Class* (London: Verso, 1991); David R. Roediger, *Working toward Whiteness: How America's Immigrants Became White: The Strange Journey from Ellis Island to the Suburbs* (New York: Basic Books, 2005). On the racialized character of the Irish in British and American eyes, see also Bruce Nelson, *Irish Nationalists and the Making of the Irish Race* (Princeton: Princeton University Press, 2012).

7. Alexander Saxton, *The Indispensable Enemy Labor and the Anti-Chinese Movement in California* (Berkeley: University of California Press, 1971); Neil Larry Shumsky, *The Evolution of Political Protest and the Workingmen's Party of California* (Columbus: Ohio State University Press, 1991); Iver Bernstein, *The New York City Draft Riots: Their Significance in American Society and Politics in the Age of the Civil War* (New York: Oxford University Press, 1990); Barrett, *Irish Way*, 18–22, 31, 47–50, 117–20.

8. David Montgomery, "The Irish and the American Labor Movement," in *America and Ireland, 1776–1976: The American Identity and the Irish Connection*, ed. David Noel Doyle and Owen Dudley Edwards (Westport, Conn.: Greenwood, 1980), 205.

9. Barrett, *Irish Way*, 108–10, 112.

10. Maria Luddy, *Women and Philanthropy in Nineteenth-Century Ireland* (New York: Cambridge University Press, 1995), 11, 12; Mona Hearn, "Life for Domestic Servants in Dublin, 1880–1920," in *Women Surviving: Studies in Irish Women's History in the Nineteenth and Twentieth Centuries*, ed. Maria Luddy and Cliona Murphy (Dublin: Poolbeg, 1989), 148–79; Mona Hearn, *Below Stairs: Domestic Service Remembered in Dublin and Beyond, 1880–1922* (Dublin: Lilliput, 1993).

11. John R. McGivigan and Thomas J. Robertson, "The Irish American Worker in Transition, 1877–1914," in *The New York Irish*, ed. Ronald H. Bayor and Timothy J. Meagher (Baltimore: Johns Hopkins University Press, 1996), 311; Kerby A. Miller, David N. Doyle, and Patricia Kelleher, "'For Love and Liberty': Irish Women, Migration, and Domesticity in Ireland and America, 1815–1920," in *Irish Women and Irish Migration*, ed. Patrick O'Sullivan (Leicester: Leicester University Press, 1995), 54; Daniel E. Sutherland, *Americans and Their Servants: Domestic Service in the United States from 1800 to 1920* (Baton Rouge: Louisiana State University Press, 1981), 50–53.

12. Deirdre Magean, "Making Sense and Providing Structure: Irish American Women in the Parish Neighborhood," in *Peasant Maids, City Women: From the European Countryside to Urban America*, ed. Christiane Harzig (Ithaca: Cornell University Press, 1997), 239.

13. Janet Nolan, *Servants of the Poor: Teachers and Mobility in Ireland and America* (Notre Dame: Notre Dame University Press, 2004); Barrett, *Irish Way*, 129.

14. Nolan, *Servants of the Poor*; Marjorie Murphy, *Blackboard Unions: The AFT and the NEA, 1900–1980* (Ithaca: Cornell University Press, 1990).

15. Kerby A. Miller, *Emigrants and Exiles: Ireland and the Irish Exodus to North America* (New York: Oxford University Press, 1985), 499–500, 503; Sarah Deutsch, *Women and the City: Gender, Space, and Power in Boston, 1870–1940* (New York: Oxford University Press, 2000), 62; Thomas Kessner, *The Golden Door: Italian and Jewish Mobility in New York, 1880–1915* (New York: Oxford University Press, 1977), 48–56; Stephan Thernstrom, *The Other Bostonians: Poverty and Progress in the American Metropolis, 1880–1970* (Cambridge: Harvard University Press, 1973), 186; Seamus P. Metress, *The Irish American Experience: A Guide to the Literature* (Washington, D.C.: University Press of America, 1981), 16–42.

16. Barrett, *Irish Way*, 115–16.

17. Miller, *Emigrants and Exiles*, 500–501.

18. Dennis Clark, "The Irish Ethic and Spirit of Patronage," in *Self-Help in Urban America: Patterns of Minority Business Enterprise*, ed. Scott Cummings (Port Washington, N.Y.: Kennikat, 1980); Miller, *Emigrants and Exiles*, 500–501; Montgomery, "Irish and the American Labor Movement," 211.

19. "Irishmen Fight Italians," *New York Times*, 12 August 1900; *Chicago Tribune*, 25 September 1893; *Brooklyn Eagle*, 25 September 1893, 18 June 1894; Kessner, *Golden Door*, 57–58; *New York Times*, 27 March 1900, 24 November 1903, 18 May 1906. For comparable confrontations in Boston and other cities, see Dennis P. Ryan, *Beyond the Ballot Box: A Social History of the Boston Irish, 1845–1917* (Rutherford, N.J.: Fairleigh Dickinson University Press, 1983), 142–43; Edwin Fenton, *Immigrants and Unions, a Case Study, Italians and American Labor, 1870–1920* (New York: Arno, 1975).

20. Nelson, *Divided We Stand*, 16, 19, xli; James T. Fisher, *On the Irish Waterfront: The Crusader, the Movie, and the Soul of the Port of New York* (Ithaca: Cornell University Press, 2009), 2–3, 6. See also Eric Arnesen, *Waterfront Workers of New Orleans: Race, Class, and Politics, 1863–1923* (New York: Oxford University Press, 1991), 19–20.

21. Charles Barnes, The *Longshoremen* (New York: Survey Associates, 1915), 5, 61; Earl Niehaus, *The Irish in New Orleans, 1800–1860* (Baton Rouge: Louisiana State University Press, 1965), 49–53, 47.

22. Arnesen, *Waterfront Workers*; Nelson, *Divided We Stand*, 48–50, 59, 64–65; Barnes, *Longshoremen*, 121–28.

23. David Montgomery, *Fall of the House of Labor: The Workplace, the State, and American Labor Activism, 1865–1925* (New York: Cambridge University Press, 1987), 100; Nelson, *Divided We Stand*, 13–24. On defensive responses to outsiders in New York Harbor and other settings, see also Jeff Kisseloff, *You Must Remember This: An Oral History of Manhattan from the 1890s to World War II* (San Diego: Harcourt, Brace, Jovanovich, 1989), 488; Colin J. Davis, "The Elusive Irishman: Ethnicity and the Postwar World of New York City and London Dockers," in *Racializing Class, Classifying Race: Labour and Difference in Britain, the USA, and Africa*, ed. Peter Alexander and Rick Halpern (New York: St. Martin's, in association with St. Antony's College, Oxford, 2000), 94–95; Fisher, *On the Irish Waterfront*, 23–25. For a similar mentality in a very different setting, see David M. Emmons, *The Butte Irish: Class and Ethnicity in an American Mining Town, 1875–1925* (Urbana: University of Illinois Press, 1989).

24. E. Franklin Frazier, "The Negro Longshoremen" (1921), quoted in Cal Winslow, "On the Waterfront: Black, Italian, and Irish Longshoremen in the New York Harbor Strike of 1919," in *Protest and Survival: Essays for E. P. Thompson*, ed. John Rule and Robert Malcolmson (London: Merlin, 1993), 372.

25. Montgomery, "Irish and the Labor Movement," 206. See also Marc Karson, *American Labor Unions and Politics, 1900–1918* (Carbondale: Southern Illinois University Press, 1958).

26. Ryan, *Beyond the Ballot Box*, 147 n. 24.

27. Barrett, "Americanization," 1000–1002; Nick Salvatore, "Some Thoughts on Class and Citizenship," in *A l'Ombre de la Statue de la Liberté*, ed. Marianne Debouzy (Saint-Denis: Presses Universitaire de Vincennes, 1988), 215–30; Catherine Collomp, "Les Organizations Ouvrières et la Restriction de l'Immigration aux États-Unis à la Fin du Dix-Neuvième Siècle," in *A l'Ombre*, ed. Debouzy, 231–46; Gwendolyn Mink, *Old Labor and New Immigrants in American Political Development: Union, Party, and State, 1875–1920* (Ithaca: Cornell University Press, 1986), 228–35; A. T. Lane, "American Unions, Mass Immigration, and the Literacy Test," *Labor History* 25 (1984): 5–25; Roediger, *Working toward Whiteness*, 78–92.

28. Robert Asher, "Union Nativism and the Immigrant Response," *Labor History* 23 (1982): 334–35; Roediger, *Working toward Whiteness*, 81–82; Mink, *Old Labor and New Immigrants*.

29. David Montgomery, *Workers' Control in America: Studies in the History of Work, Technology, and Labor Struggles* (New York: Cambridge University Press, 1979), 91–112; David Montgomery, "Immigrants, Industrial Unions, and Social Reconstruction in the United States, 1916–1923," *Labour/Le Travail* 13 (1984): 101–14; Thomas Mackaman, *New Immigrants and the Radicalization of American Labor, 1914–1924* (Jefferson, N.C.: McFarland, 2017).

30. L. A. O'Donnell, *Irish Voice and Organized Labor: A Biographical Study* (Westport, Conn.: Greenwood, 1997), 117–41; James R. Barrett, *William Z. Foster and the Tragedy of American Radicalism* (Urbana: University of Illinois Press, 1999).

31. Agnes Nestor, *Woman's Labor Leader: An Autobiography* (Rockford, Ill.: Bellevue, 1954), 87–104; Nancy Schrom Dye, *As Equals and as Sisters: Feminism, the Labor Movement, and the Women's Trade Union League of New York* (Columbia: University of Missouri Press, 1980), 125; *New York Times*, 13 July, 30 June 1915; Deutsch, *Women and the City*, 222–28; Ryan, *Beyond the Ballot Box*, 51–52; Suellen Hoy, "The Irish Girls' Rising: Building the Women's Labor Movement in Progressive-Era Chicago," *Labor: Studies in Working Class History of the Americas* (2012) 9: 77–100.

32. Mary Kenney O'Sullivan, autobiography, in Papers of the Women's Trade Union League (microfilm); Margaret A. Haley, *Battleground: The Autobiography of Margaret A. Haley*, ed. Robert L. Reid (Urbana: University of Illinois Press, 1982); Nestor, *Woman's Labor Leader*; Nolan, *Servants of the Poor*, 69. On the connections between Irish women's organizing and the Women's Trade Union League in Chicago and New York, see Elizabeth Anne Payne, *Reform, Labor, and Feminism: Margaret Dreier Robins and the Women's Trade Union League* (Urbana: University of Illinois Press, 1988); Dye, *As Equals*.

33. See Dorothy Richardson, "Trade Unionists in Petticoats," *Leslie's Monthly Magazine*, March 1904, 489–500; Stephen Norwood, *Labor's Flaming Youth: Telephone Operators and Labor Militancy, 1878–1923* (Urbana: University of Illinois Press, 1990); Hoy, "Irish Girls' Rising."

34. Howard E. Wilson, *Mary McDowell, Neighbor* (Chicago: University of Chicago Press, 1928), 99. See also Ethelbert Stewart, *The Influence of Trade Unions on Immigrants* (Washington, D.C.: US Government Printing Office, 1905), reprinted in *The Making of America*, vol. 3, *Labor*, ed. Robert M. La Follette (1905; New York: Arno, 1969), 230; Peter Roberts, *The New Immigration: A Study of the Life of Southeastern Europeans in America* (New York: Macmillan, 1912), 195.

35. See Nelson, *Irish Nationalists*.

36. John Keiser, "John Fitzpatrick and Progressive Labor" (PhD diss., Northwestern University, 1965); David Brody, "John Fitzpatrick," in *Dictionary of American Biography*, supp. 4, ed. John A. Garraty (New York: Scribner, 1974), 279–80; O'Donnell, *Irish Voice*, 143–61; Barrett, *Irish Way*, 264–65.

37. James R. Barrett, *Work and Community in the Jungle: Chicago's Packinghouse Workers, 1894–1922* (Urbana: University of Illinois Press, 1987); Rick Halpern, *Down on the Killing Floor: Black and White Workers in Chicago's Packinghouses, 1904–54* (Urbana: University of Illinois Press, 1997).

38. David Brody, *Steelworkers in America: The Non-Union Era* (New York: Harper, 1970), 214–78; William Z. Foster, *The Great Steel Strike and Its Lessons* (New York: Huebsch, 1920); Barrett, *William Z. Foster*, 81–101.

39. See Malcolm and Hall, "Catholic Irish Australia and the Labor Movement".

40. Elizabeth McKillen, *Chicago Labor and the Quest for a Democratic Diplomacy, 1914–1924* (Ithaca: Cornell University Press, 1995), 140–46, 162, 214; Elizabeth McKillen, *Making the World Safe for Workers: Labor, the Left, and Wilsonian Internationalism* (Urbana: University of Illinois Press, 2014), 215–18; Elizabeth McKillen, "American Labor, the Irish Revolution, and the Campaign for a Boycott of British Goods, 1916–1924," *Radical History Review* 61 (1995): 35–61.

41. Nelson, *Irish Nationalists*, 226–29; Joe Doyle, "Striking for Ireland on the New York Docks," in *New York Irish*, ed. Bayor and Meagher, 357–73.

PART 4

Working-Class Collective Action and Labor Regulation

Causes of Railroad Labor Conflict

The Case of Queensland, Australia, and the Northern US Plains, 1880–1900

BRADLEY BOWDEN
PETA STEVENSON-CLARKE

Railroads played a seminal role in shaping Australian and US society during the nineteenth century's closing decades. In the Australian colonies, where railroads differed from most other New World societies in that they were state-owned monopolies, railroads connected agricultural and pastoral activities in the interior with national and international markets. In the American West, as Arthur Hadley recorded in 1885, privately owned railroads reached "out in all directions to collect grain for the great western markets."[1] By 1890, however, interest payments were consuming a disproportionate share of railroad revenue almost everywhere. As finances deteriorated, wage labor came under attack. In the United States, the 1894 Pullman Boycott represented the culmination of what Shelton Stromquist calls an "unprecedented" period of railroad labor conflict.[2] In this momentous struggle, adherence to the militant American Railway Union—whose strongest support was among semiskilled workers in the American West—was effectively destroyed, leaving only the conservative railroad brotherhoods as representatives of organized labor. Australian railroad workers also suffered. In Victoria, one politician observed in 1893 that "never before" had such a "revision" of staffing been imposed. By 1897, Victorian railway employment was down 39.6 percent from its 1890 peak.[3] In Queensland, wages dropped by as much as 30 percent in 1893.[4]

In the United States, there was an obvious culprit for the woes suffered by railway labor—competition. As Charles Adams Jr. concluded in 1870, railroad competition "disturbs every calculation, vitiates every result, puts a stop to all experiment, destroys all system."[5] More recently, Alfred D. Chandler Jr. famously observed that the "logic" of American railroad competition was "bankruptcy for all."[6] American labor historians have similarly argued that competition was integral to managerial behavior. In the American West, according to Stromquist, the "locational monopoly" of pioneering railroads provided workers only "fleeting" benefit, since with "increased competition managers came to perceive the wages accorded to scarce railroad labor as a burden."[7] By 1890, US western railroads were undoubtedly suffering a catastrophic fall in freight income relative to goods shipped, with one observer noting that the roads of Iowa, Minnesota, and Nebraska were "all alike unremunerative."[8] Statistics marshaled by Henry Poor in his annual series, *Manual of the Railroads of the United States,* supported this view. Grouping the states of the "Northwest" or "Northern Plains" (Minnesota, Iowa, Nebraska, Wyoming, Montana, and North and South Dakota) on the basis of railroad operations, Poor demonstrated that between 1882 and 1900, the gross revenue obtained for moving a ton of freight fell an average of 56.8 percent, to $1.74 (figure 1).

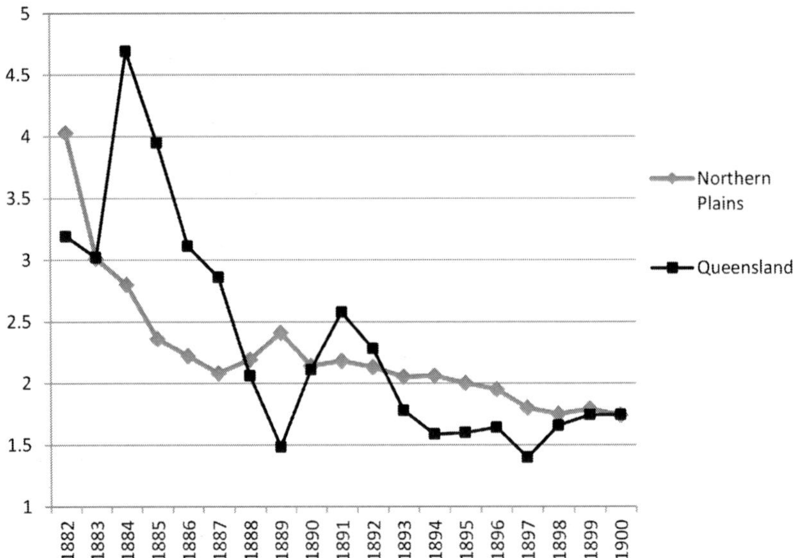

FIGURE 1. Gross Revenue per Ton of Freight, Northern Plains and Queensland, 1882–1900. *Source*: Henry Poor, *Manual of the Railroads of the United States* (1883–1901); *Queensland Votes and Proceedings* (1882–1901).

If the assumption that competition was the main factor in falling US freight income and managerial attacks on labor costs is correct, however, we would expect that regions where competition was largely absent would not have suffered such problems. But as figure 1 shows, per-ton agricultural freight income in Queensland, where state ownership restricted competition, followed a similar pattern.

Similarities between the Northern Plains and Queensland are also evident in labor relations. During the 1870s and especially the 1880s, railroads in both regions constructed networks disproportionately large relative to population. By 1890, Queensland, with a landmass 2.5 times greater than that of Texas, boasted 5.62 miles of road per thousand people. The Northern Plains claimed 5.48 miles per thousand. Both results were well above national norms—3.21 miles per thousand in Australia and 2.66 miles per thousand in the United States—and far in excess of the rate for the United Kingdom (0.5 miles per thousand).[9] In buoyant labor market circumstances, railroad workers in both regions were initially rewarded with superior working conditions. Queensland railroad employees were, as one railways' minister observed, "better paid than men working outside the Government service."[10] On the Northern Plains and other regions of the US West, railroad workers enjoyed consistently higher wages than did their brethren in either the East or the Midwest.[11] However, the years after 1890 witnessed changed managerial attitudes as labor costs were vigorously attacked.

How can we explain the similar trends in Queensland and the Northern Plains not only in per-ton income but also in managerial labor strategies, and how can those explanations inform a wider appreciation of the causes of industrial conflict? Competition was clearly not a common dominator, for while rivalries were intense in the Northern Plains, Queensland's railroads were a state-owned monopoly. One area where commonalities existed is the nature of their freight cargo and the associated exposure to falling agricultural prices, even in Queensland, where the railroads were originally built to serve the pastoral industry's needs. As early as 1890–91, Queensland's railroads hauled eleven times as much grain and other farm produce as wool. By 1900, tonnage of the former exceeded that for wool by a margin of more than thirty-four to one.[12] But wholesale corn prices fell in both the western United States and Queensland from approximately sixty cents per bushel in the early 1880s to around forty cents per bushel a decade later. Wheat prices fell by even bigger margins.[13] This dynamic, rather than competition, eventually drove managers in Queensland and the Northern Plains to attack labor costs.

Railroads and Patterns of Settlement

The intimate connections between growth in the grain trade and New World railroad expansion during the nineteenth century are well understood. To date, however, attention has focused on how falling freight rates produced increased farm output and declining grain prices, with C. Knick Harley concluding that the "radical reduction" in railroad rates was "the main influence on the movement of the frontier and the growth of trade."[14] Looking at Canada, Trevor Dick similarly notes that railroad mileage "and the amount of farmland bore a steady proportional relationship to one another . . . and that the prices of alternative crops (wheat, oats and barley) moved closely together."[15] However, if lower railroad rates produced lower grain prices, did lower grain prices also have a deflationary effect on railroad freight income?

The connection between railroad expansion and grain cultivation is particularly evident in the United States and Australia, where railroad expansion was as much about fulfilling a national ideal—premised on the settlement of small "homesteaders" (the American term) or "selectors" (the Australian equivalent)—as it was about economics. On the Northern Plains, the federal government funded much of the cost of railroad construction through loans and land grants. So bolstered, the region's railroads expanded exponentially. In 1860, the region boasted a mere 655 miles of road, all of it in Iowa. By 1900, more than half of the Northern Plains' 32,104 miles of track lay west of the Missouri River. As mileage increased, so, too, did population, which grew from 880,664 to 6.7 million between 1860 and 1901. A disproportionate number of these new residents were grain farmers, as the region's hard spring wheat attracted a global price premium. Between 1880 and 1891, regional wheat production grew by 135 percent, reaching 184.7 million bushels. Thereafter, output fluctuated violently, reflecting both price and climatic variations.[16]

Queensland's railroads initially serviced "sheep-lords" rather than farmers. Construction began in 1864 from Ipswich, a river port upstream from the capital, Brisbane, and proceeded due west in search of the largest flocks, which were located on the Darling Downs, a vast black-soil plateau only fifty miles from Ipswich. Pushing westward, the southern trunk system opened up ever more country, and by 1880, trunk lines also extended from Rockhampton and Townsville, servicing flocks in Central and North Queensland, respectively. So abetted, the number of sheep grew from 4.3 million in 1862 to a peak of 27.7 million in 1892.[17] Servicing the pastoral industry, however, required only modest mileage. A high-value commodity, wool could provide growers with a return even if it had to be hauled long distances to the nearest rail siding. In

1880, therefore, Queensland possessed only eight hundred miles of road. Thereafter, however, railroad policy was directed toward the fostering of agriculture. In 1888, the Railway Commissioners became legally obligated to work the railroads "as will best conduce . . . the promotion of [agricultural] settlement."[18] The growing gap between railroad policy and economics can be seen in the scale of railroad investment. Between 1886 and 1890, Queensland spent more on its railroads than on the pastoral sector, agriculture, mining, manufacturing, and nonresidential construction combined.[19] By 1890, despite a population of only 392,100, Queensland had 2,205 miles of road.[20]

Queensland's wheat industry was slow to get started because the colony's humidity made it unsuited for traditional wheat varieties. Farmers thus initially focused on sugar and corn. Sugar was concentrated in a number of coastal pockets and placed modest demands on the railways. Cane was typically transported by river punt, with refined product then shipped out by coastal steamers. Moreover, sugar prices declined by 50 percent between 1883 and 1889, leading sugar output to fall by 44.7 percent to 55,771 tons between 1890 and 1895.[21] Sugar's decline made the growing of maize or "Indian corn" the predominant farm activity, and output typically hovered between two and three million bushels between 1889 and 1898. Much of this crop was exported to southern Australian colonies, where little corn was grown, with most of the remainder destined for local animal fodder. By 1890, however, a number of factors fostered a belated surge in wheat growing: the development of varieties resistant to rust (a fungal disease), the imposition of a protective import duty of sixteen cents per bushel, and the extension of "agricultural lines" to the Darling Downs with its deep black soils. By 1900, 1.2 million bushels of wheat were being harvested each year, with virtually all of it transported by rail for milling in either Brisbane or the regional centers of Warwick and Toowoomba.[22]

Commodity Prices and Freight Income

Reliance on wheat and corn presented railroads with problems even when prices were high. Not only was grain growing seasonal, the low value of the harvested product also demanded a much more tightly meshed railroad network than was required for commodities such as wool and gold. Edgards Dunsdorfs calculated that Australian wheat (and corn) "could scarcely be grown even ten miles from a railway line" Otherwise the cost of animal-drawn road transportation would rapidly erode farm margins.[23] Even if we exclude the costs of hauling freight by road, estimates show that by 1895, Australian wheat farmers typically paid out 15 percent of the gross value of their crop in freight.[24] For the railroads and their workforce, the tightly meshed grid demanded by farmers provided mixed benefits. While grain filled many wagons, extensive mileage also resulted in high capital costs and rising working expenses.

The problems associated with servicing grain-producing regions were magnified during periods of low price.[25] US and Australian railroads were both instigators and victims of commodity price deflation as they facilitated increased global production. In the United States, Harley estimates that nearly 85 percent of the wheat crop in Minnesota and the Dakotas was being exported by the 1890s.[26] In Australia, Dunsdorfs estimates that after 1878, "the price in the world market became the key factor influencing the [wheat] industry."[27] Thorsten Veblen has identified 1882 as the tipping point, with the global wheat market shifting from undersupply to oversupply as an array of New World producers (Canada, Australia, Argentina, and South Africa) undercut US price dominance.[28] Unfortunately for farmers, global oversupply—from not only the United States, Canada, and Australia but also Ukraine, Argentina, India, and South Africa—produced a 41.5 percent decline in the London "Gazette price" between 1881 and 1901.[29] In local wholesale markets, prices fluctuated violently. In the western United States, the prime benchmark that recorded such fluctuations was the Chicago wholesale price; in Queensland, the Brisbane wholesale price served a similar function for both corn and wheat.

The correlation between per-ton freight income and grain prices in the Northern Plains is evident from a comparison between figure 2, which records the Chicago per-bushel price for corn and wheat between 1881 and 1901, and figure 1, which shows the per-ton freight income of the Northern Plains railroads. From an 1882 high point, both grain prices and per-ton freight income fell markedly before recovering between 1888 and 1891. When grain prices resumed their fall after 1891, they were joined by per-ton freight income. From a peak of $1.175 per bushel in 1882, wheat fell 51.5 percent to $0.57 per bushel in 1894 before staging a partial recovery. Corn, which always traded at lower prices than wheat, fared even worse, falling by 66 percent to $0.26 per bushel between 1882 and 1896. Commensurate with these price movements, the average cost of moving a ton of freight fell by 51.6 percent to $1.95 between 1882 and 1896.

Grain prices became a poorer predictor of per-ton income after the mid-1890s. Whereas the wheat price in 1900 was 24.6 percent above the low point of 1894 and corn was trading 46.2 percent above its 1896 low, freight income per ton continued its slide. In 1900, the average cost of transporting a ton of freight was $1.74, 10.8 percent lower than in 1896. The continued slide in per-ton income in the face of rising grain prices is particularly remarkable given the industry consolidation that occurred after the bankruptcies of 1893–97, which placed two-thirds of US

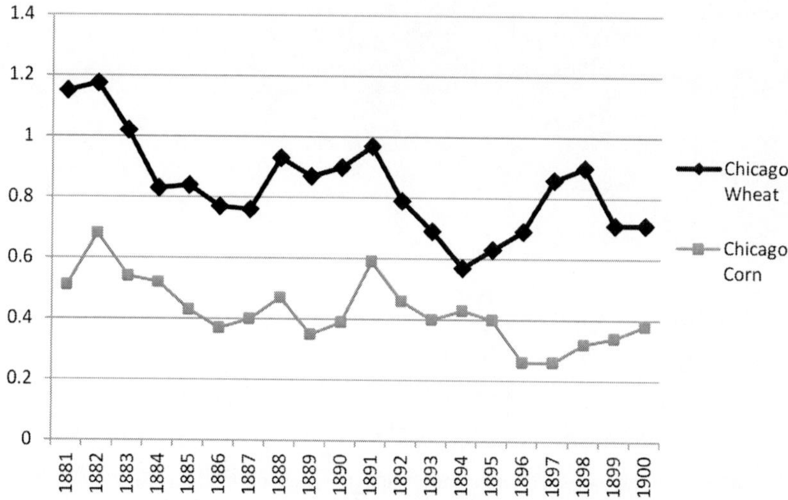

FIGURE 2. US Wholesale Wheat and Corn Prices, 1881–1900. *Note*: Calculated on the basis of Chicago wholesale prices. *Source*: Henry Wallace, *Agricultural Prices* (Des Moines, Iowa: Wallace, 1930), 118–19, 123–24.

mileage under the control of seven large systems.[30] One of the expectations of railroad expansion was that decreases in income per ton would be offset by increases in the volume and value of goods shipped. However, as figure 3 indicates, such expectations were largely unfulfilled prior to the mid-1890s. Even though the Northern Plains railroad mileage grew by 89.7 percent, to 23,421 miles, between 1886 and 1895, the value of the regional wheat crop remained largely static at approximately ten million dollars per year before declining sharply between 1891 and 1894.[31] Beginning in 1895, however, Northern Plains wheat farmers enjoyed better fortunes. In 1897, 1899, and above all 1898, the increased size and value of the crop meant that railroads could finally offset falling per-ton income through gains in total freight income.[32] After gross revenues fell by 21.3 percent to $62.9 million between 1892 and 1894, the Northern Plains railroads obtained gross receipts of $88.9 million in 1898, $94.8 million in 1899, and $106.7 million in 1900.[33] The fact that the boom in freight income continued into 1900 suggests increased farm purchasing power in the wake of a number of favorable seasons.

In Queensland, understanding the correlation between per-ton income and rural commodity prices requires examining trends not only in corn and wheat but also in wool. In essence, the finances of Queensland's railways reflected the ability of wool haulage to cross-subsidize the less remunerative transport of agricultural produce. This ability rested on three factors: the tonnage of wool

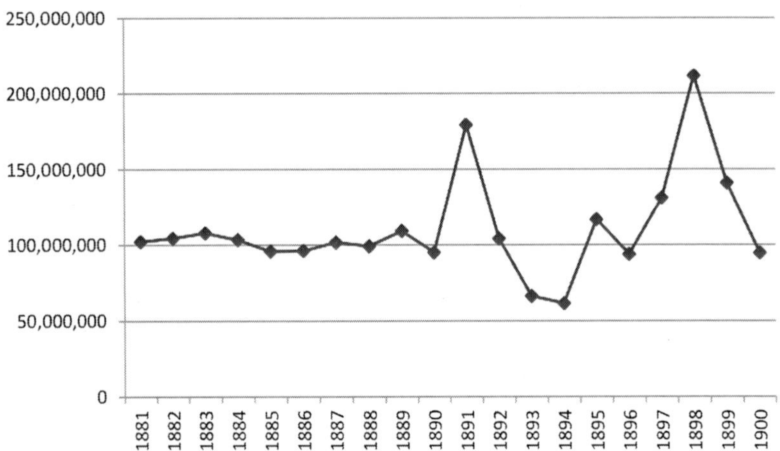

FIGURE 3. Gross Value of the Northern Plains Wheat Crop, 1881–1900. *Note*: Calculated on the basis of Chicago wholesale prices. *Source*: Henry Wallace, *Agricultural Prices* (Des Moines, Iowa: Wallace, 1930), 123–24.

moved and its price, the tonnage of agricultural produce moved and its price, and the relationship between wool and agricultural goods.

As figure 4 shows, until 1898–99 Queensland's railroads made more money from hauling wool than from hauling agricultural produce. Moreover, the eventual decline of wool receipts appears to have in large part been offset by rising income from agricultural products. But although the tonnage of agricultural business rose tenfold between 1883 and 1898–98, the value of this business grew by a more modest 490 percent.[34] In other words, the per-ton income from agricultural business dropped by half. The wool business, in turn, suffered three problems. First, the export price for a pound of wool fell by 40.7 percent to sixteen cents between 1881 and 1898. Second, the value of business steadily declined between 1890–91(when a record $20.7 million was obtained) and 1897–98. Finally, the industry's foundations were threatened by the Federation Drought (1892–1902), the worst in the national experience. As the sharp drop in railroad wool income illustrates, the drought's worst effects were felt in the century's final two years, when the number of sheep numbers fell from 17.5 million to 10 million.

Greater agricultural tonnage and declining wool income meant that the finances of Queensland's railways, like those of the Northern Plains, increasingly rested on income from shipping corn and wheat. Unlike the situation in the Northern Plains, however, Queensland's wheat initially enjoyed more favorable prices, in large part as a result of the sixteen-cent tariff imposed on imports. As figure 5 demonstrates, Queensland wheat rarely sold for less than one dollar per

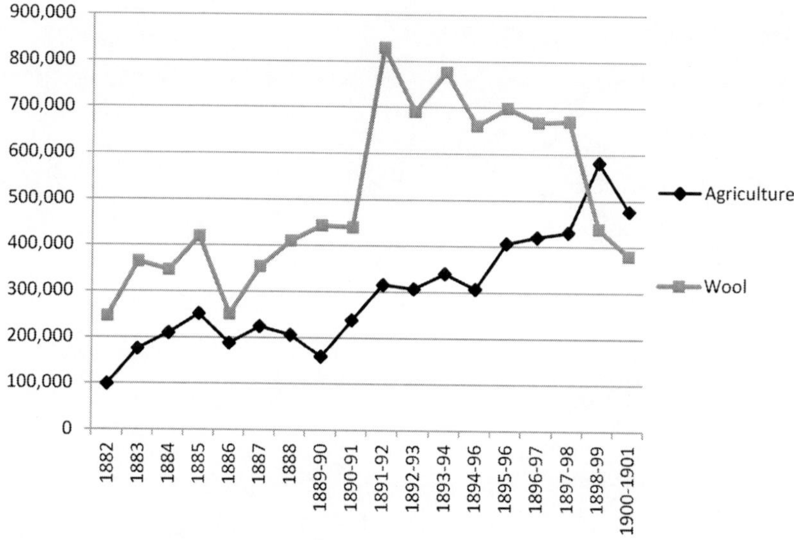

FIGURE 4. Queensland Railroad: Gross Revenue from Wool and Agricultural Produce, 1882–1901. *Source: Queensland Votes and Proceedings* (1882–1901).

bushel before 1890. However, wheat provided only modest financial benefits for the railroads since wheat growing did not become a substantial industry until after 1890. Further, wheat's expansion was associated with sharp price declines as more of the crop entered the export market, negating the import tariff's effects. By 1900 the Brisbane wheat price ($0.73 per bushel) differed little from the Chicago price ($0.71 per bushel), a 38.7 percent decline from the peak of $1.19 in 1891. Of greater significance were two other trends: marked fluctuations in per-bushel corn prices and a general stagnation in the value of the grain harvest after 1890. The first of these trends is evident in figure 5 as corn, more highly tradable outside Queensland's borders than wheat, was caught in the deflationary price spiral that characterized global grain markets. After fluctuating between $1.01 (1881) and $0.71 (1887), the corn price fell by 52.7 percent to $0.46 between 1889 and 1891. Thereafter it traded between $0.85 (1894, 1898, 1899) and $0.47 (1897).

The second adverse trend in agricultural business, the stagnation in the grain crop's value, can be seen in figure 6, which traces the changing value of Queensland's corn and wheat harvests. Only in 1895 and 1900 did the harvests' combined value exceed that obtained in 1890. In 1900, the combined value of Queensland's wool, corn, and wheat ($35.8 million) was still less than the value of 1890 output ($41.4 million).[35]

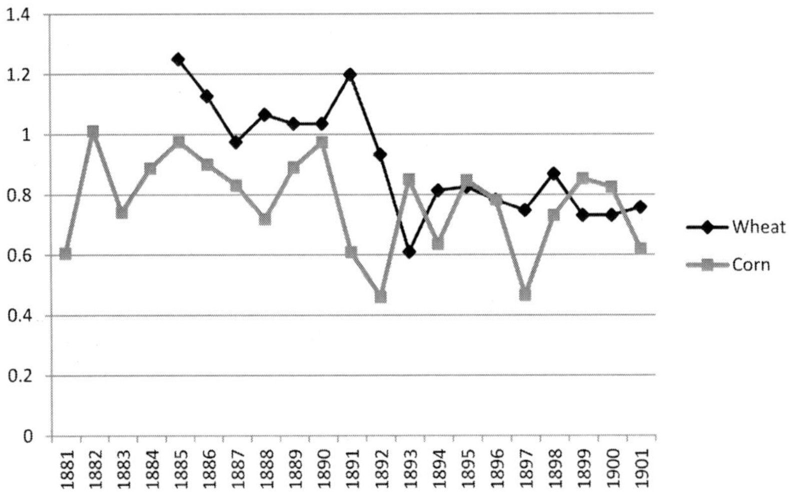

FIGURE 5. Queensland Wholesale Wheat and Corn Prices (in Brisbane), 1880–1901. *Note*: Primarily a corn producer in the 1880s, Queensland did not begin recording wheat prices and output until 1885. *Source*: *Queensland Parliamentary Debates*; *Queensland Votes and Proceedings* (1882-1901).

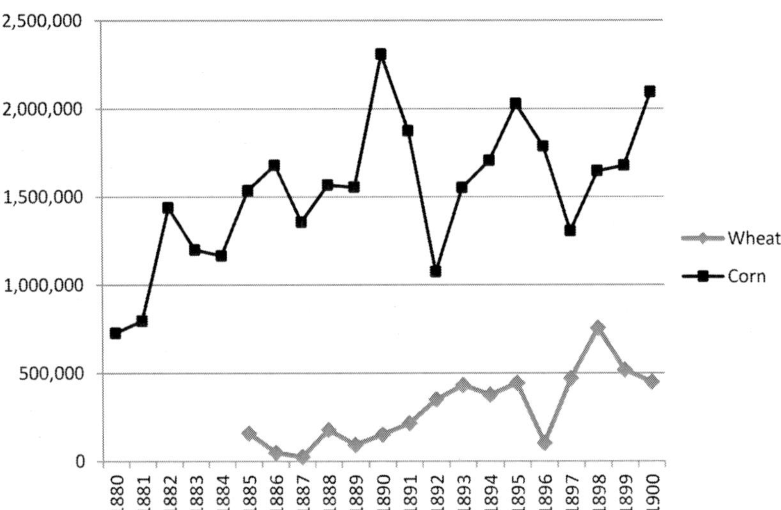

FIGURE 6. Gross Value of Queensland Corn and Wheat Crops, 1880–1900. *Source*: *Queensland Parliamentary Debates*; *Queensland Votes and Proceedings* (1882–1901).

Managerial Cost Cutting: A Doomed Labor Relations Response

Understanding why the labor relations strategies of the railroads of both the Northern Plains and Queensland were fundamentally misguided first requires understanding that their economic problems resulted primarily from high capital costs and declining per-ton revenues rather than from excessive operating costs. By 1890–91, interest payments were consuming 77 percent of net revenues on the Northern Plains and a staggering 161.7 percent of Queensland's net receipts. Despite cost-reduction policies in both regions, the situation had not substantially improved five years later, when interest payments absorbed 104.4 percent of the Northern Plains' net receipts and 157.3 percent of Queensland's net income.[36]

Why did cost-reduction strategies fail to remedy these financial problems, and why did employers continue to pursue labor policies that had so little effect? Employers in both regions mistook a symptom of their financial plight—rising working expense ratios—as its cause. Typically calculated by dividing operating expenses (including wages, repairs, and other variable expenses but excluding interest costs) by operating income, working expense ratios were viewed by investors as a prime measure of performance. As a rough rule of thumb, investors approved of working expense ratios below 60 percent and disapproved of ratios above 70 percent. Paradoxically, Northern Plains and Queensland railroads initially enjoyed favorable ratios because farmers and ranchers were willing to travel long distances to the limited number of railroad sidings. As late as 1883, therefore, working expense ratios remained well below those in urbanized areas. Whereas working expenses consumed 63.8 percent of US national railroad operating revenue, in the Northern Plains, such expenses accounted for only 57.3 percent. Queensland working expenses accounted for a mere 47.4 percent of gross operating revenues. The ensuing seven years, however, witnessed a marked deterioration as mileage rapidly expanded. In 1890, the percentage of revenues consumed by working expenses stood at 65.4 percent in the Northern Plains and at 72.8 percent in Queensland.[37] This deterioration stemmed primarily not from labor costs but from the inherent difficulties involved in servicing agricultural regions. To capture or bring into existence new agricultural business, the railroads needed more mileage, given that farms served by existing roads were unlikely to make significant additions. The need to construct more track increased both fixed and operating costs. Such circumstances differed markedly from those found in industrialized regions, where railroads could expect increased tonnage and value from existing roads as industrial output increased.

The failure of cost-reduction strategies is most evident on the Northern Plains, where gross revenues rose by 75.5 percent to $95.7 million between 1883 and 1890 but working expenses rose by 95 percent to $62.6 million and interest charges increased 142.8 percent to $25.5 million. Even though Northern Plains railroads cut labor costs severely after the Pullman Boycott, when the power of the militant American Railway Union was broken, with working expenses falling by 6.5 percent between 1890 and 1895 to $58.5 million, such gains were offset by an 8.2 percent decline in gross revenue (to $88 million) and a 20.8 percent increase in interest costs (to $30.8 million). Employers consequently failed to achieve desired improvements in working expense ratios, which in 1895 stood at 66.4 percent, a marginal deterioration from the 1890 ratio of 65.4 percent.[38]

Cost cutting produced superficially better results in Queensland, where working expense ratios fell from 72.8 percent in 1890–91 to 56.7 percent in 1895–96. However, such achievements are deceptive because the key measure of railroad performance was not the ratio between working expenses and gross operating revenues but rather the ratio between interest costs and net revenues. As figure 7 indicates, gains in terms of working expenses between 1890–91 and 1895–96 were achieved by keeping working expenses constant while increasing total revenue. However, increased revenue was only achieved by adding mileage and hence increasing interest costs. This vicious cycle worsened rather than improved the situation, with net income collapsing after 1898–99.

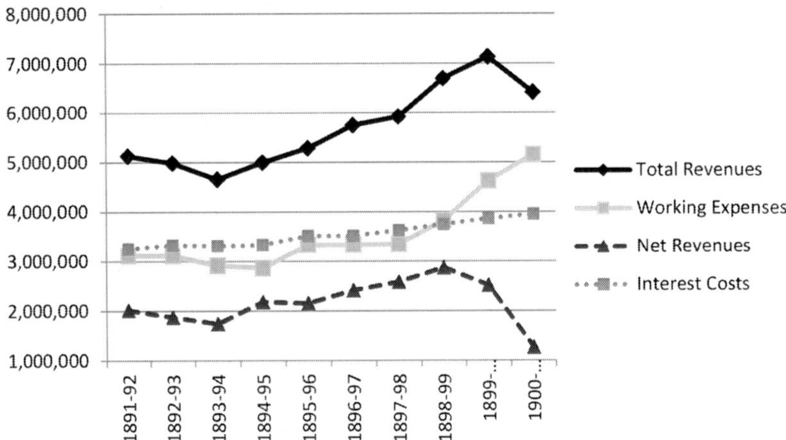

FIGURE 7. Queensland Railroad Finances, 1891–1901: Gross Revenue, Working Expenses, Net Revenue, and Interest Repayments. *Source*: *Queensland Votes and Proceedings* (1883–1902).

Not a Solution: Conflict with Organized Labor

If managerial cost cutting in Queensland and the Northern Plains only marginally improved a poor financial situation, the impact of these cuts on the workforce was far from modest. Queensland's parliament enacted wage cuts of between 15 and 30 percent for railroad workers in June 1893.[39] Cost cutting also led to less desirable working conditions. In 1900, Queensland's railway commissioner reported that reductions in expenditures meant that employees in the Ipswich workshops, the colony's largest, were "working under great disadvantage, as may be apparent to any casual visitor."[40] Similar outcomes were evident in the Northern Plains. As early as 1890 one St. Paul–based analyst observed that western railroad workers were suffering "many hardships" as "railroad companies . . . cut down expenses to conform to diminished earnings."[41]

The situation further worsened for US railroad workers following the employer victory in the most significant industrial dispute in US railroad history, the Pullman Boycott of 1894. Occurring amid a sharp deterioration in railroad operating conditions, this dispute reflected a fundamental shift in the railway labor market following the effective "closing of the frontier" after 1890. As railway expansion halted, the labor market became oversupplied, creating a logjam on the promotional ladder, which western railroad workers expected to ascend as a matter of course.[42] Turning to the militant American Railway Union, dissatisfied employees found themselves in conflict not only with management but also with the railroad brotherhoods that represented the skilled locomotive workforce, whose relatively privileged position within the job hierarchy could only be assured through managerial acquiescence. The head of the US Brotherhood of Locomotive Engineers declared in 1881 that the union had to use "every opportunity offered to maintain the peaceful and friendly relations now existing with our employers."[43] When the Pullman Boycott threatened managerial authority, the brotherhood expelled from its ranks those who chose to stop work. The other brotherhoods (the Brotherhood of Locomotive Firemen and the Brotherhood of Railroad Trainmen) took similar action.[44]

In Queensland, the Locomotive Engine-Drivers, Firemen, and Cleaners Association (LEFCA) differed from its US equivalents in uniting all locomotive crew operatives in a single union. Otherwise, it played a similar role, with LEFCA's secretary, James Wilkinson, advising its members in 1886 that there was not "anything of trade unionism about the association."[45] When members of the all-grades Queensland Railway Employees Association (QREA) engaged in a wildcat strike in support of striking shearers in 1891, LEFCA declared that any striker who was dismissed by management "shall forfeit all right of assistance."[46] Although Queensland management had initially regarded the QREA benignly, this view changed with the Queensland shearers' strike of February–July 1891. Fearful that QREA membership was encouraging sympathy for militant unionism within the railroad workforce, management turned on the QREA with a vengeance, directing staff to resign either from the QREA or from their jobs.[47] The subsequent wave of resignations affected junior as well as senior staff and effectively destroyed the union.

By the mid-1890s, management in both the Northern Plains and Queensland occupied a much stronger industrial position than had previously been the case. These gains did little, however, to remedy the railroads' financial problems, which stemmed from revenues rather than costs. In Queensland, as figure 7 indicates, net railroad revenue continued to fall well short of the amount required to meet annual interest obligations despite wage cuts of between 15 and 30 percent in early 1893. In the Northern Plains, the employer victory in the Pullman Boycott also failed to insulate the railroads from their financial woes. Between 1893 and 1897, the American West witnessed the largest wave of railroad bankruptcies in US history. Under court administration, railroads such as the Union Pacific and the Northern Pacific were recapitalized through the issuance of receiver bonds that gave new debt holders preference over their predecessors, wiping out a significant proportion of the accumulated railroad debt.[48] By 1900, therefore, the annual railroad interest bill of $25.7 million was 12.9 percent lower than it had been in 1895. Moreover, the marked increase in both the size and value of the wheat crop caused gross railroad revenue to rebound. Despite such improvements, however, the core business of the Northern Plains railroads, tied as it was to the farm sector, remained precarious. In 1900 average per-ton income was $1.74, 13 percent less than it had been in 1895 and 56.8 percent lower than the 1882 level.[49]

As figure 1 indicates, the situation in Queensland was even more catastrophic. In 1900, the $1.74 typically received for shifting one ton of freight represented a 62.9 percent fall from the 1882 peak. Such declines destroyed the financial assumptions on which railroad expansion was premised in Queensland and the Northern Plains and help to explain the managerial assaults on organized labor that occurred with increasing vigor after 1890. At the same time, those declines rendered managerial success in such assaults economically meaningless. Organized labor was not the source of management's financial woes.

Conclusion

Although these events took place more than a century ago, they have a contemporary resonance. Like many of today's companies, Queensland's and the Northern Plains' railroads existed as cogs in a production system that funneled primary commodities toward the world's industrialized regions. Consequently, the railroads fell victim to forces that they had helped to unleash. By contributing to increased commodity supply, these New World railroads helped drive down global prices. Although this decline added to general prosperity by making foodstuffs and textiles cheaper, it also undercut the per-ton value of the products that the railroads transported. This drop, rather than increased competition, as most previous studies have suggested, was the main cause of railroad financial woes in the Northern Plains. That falling global commodity prices constituted the main driver of events is evidenced by the marked similarity to the Queensland situation. In the two regions, wholesale corn and wheat prices significantly tracked per-ton freight income. The fact that the privately owned railroads on the Northern Plains were subject to intense competition while the state-owned network in Queensland experienced almost none made surprisingly little difference.

Railroad management also pursued markedly similar labor relations strategies in both regions. A key factor here was the closely woven network of road and sidings demanded by grain-growing regions. This network created demand for a considerable workforce, many members of which were compelled to congregate in regional rail hubs. Both outcomes created problems for management. A large amount of mileage relative to the (low) value of the business resulted in rising working expenses that undercut a railroad's capacity to repay the cost of capital. Attempts to improve a railroad's financial circumstance by attacking labor costs made management stronger industrially but did little to improve the railroad's finances.

Notes

1. Arthur Hadley, *Railroad Transportation* (New York: Putnam's, 1885), 85.

2. Shelton Stromquist, *A Generation of Boomers: The Pattern of Railroad Labor Conflict in Nineteenth-Century America* (Urbana: University of Illinois Press, 1987), 3.

3. *Victorian Parliament Debates* 69 (1893): 963; John Mathieson, "Annual Report of the Victorian Railway Commissioner, 1897–98," *Victorian Parliamentary Papers* 3 (1898): 1–15.

4. Robert Gray, "Annual Report of the Queensland Railway Commissioner, 1896–97," *Queensland Parliamentary Debates* 76 (1896): 1188.

5. Charles F. Adams Jr., "Railway Problems in 1869," *North American Review* 226 (1870): 132–34.

6. Alfred D. Chandler Jr., *The Visible Hand: The Managerial Revolution in American Business* (Cambridge: Belknap Press of Harvard University Press, 1977), 134.

7. Shelton Stromquist, "Enginemen and Shopmen: Technological Change and the Organization of Labor in an Era of Railroad Expansion," *Labor History* 24 (1983): 489. See also Herbert Gutman, "Trouble of the Railroads in 1873–74," *Labor History* 2 (1961): 215–35; Herbert Gutman, *Work, Culture, and Society in Industrializing America* (New York: Knopf, 1976); Richard Schneirov, Shelton Stromquist, and Nick Salvatore, eds., *The Pullman Strike and the Crisis of the 1890s* (Urbana: University of Illinois Press, 1991).

8. Harry Robinson, *Our Railroads: The Value and Earnings of the Railroads of the Western States* (St. Paul, Minn.: Northwestern Railroader, 1890), 23.

9. C. H. Knibbs, *Commonwealth of Australia Yearbook 1917* (Melbourne: Commonwealth Printer, 1918), 98, 634; US Department of Commerce and Labor, *Statistical Abstract of the United States, 1901* (Washington, D.C.: US Department of Commerce and Labor), table 106 (mileage), table 3 (population).

10. *Queensland Parliamentary Debates* 74 (1895): 1418.

11. Stromquist, *Generation of Boomers*, 280–82.

12. In 1900–1901, 841,367 tons of agricultural products were shipped, versus 24,525 tons of wool (John Gray, "Annual Report of Queensland's Railway Commissioners, 1900–1901," *Queensland Votes and Proceedings* 4 [1901]: 701).

13. Henry Wallace, *Agricultural Prices* (Des Moines, Iowa: Wallace, 1930), 118–19 (corn), 123–24 (wheat). For 1897–1901, Queensland statistics came from the Queensland Department of Agriculture's Annual Reports. Earlier years are drawn from either Ministerial statements in *Queensland Parliamentary Debates* or from Pugh's *Queensland Almanac*, available at http://www.textqueensland.com.au/pughs-almanac.

14. C. Knick Harley, "Transportation, the World Wheat Trade, and the Kuznets Cycle, 1850–1913," *Explorations in Economic History* 17 (1980): 229.

15. Trevor Dick, "Canadian Wheat Production and Trade, 1896–1930," *Explorations in Economic History*, 17 (1980): 278.

16. Calculated from US Department of Commerce and Labor, *Statistical Abstract*, table 98.

17. N. G. Butlin, *Investment in Australian Economic Development* (Canberra: Australian National University Press, 1972), 67; William Blakeney, "Report of the Registrar-General of Agriculture and Stock, 1893," *Queensland Votes and Proceedings* 3 (1893): 876.

18. *Queensland Parliamentary Debates* 55 (1888): 133.

19. G. J. R. Linge, *Industrial Awakening: A Geography of Australian Manufacturing, 1788 to 1890* (Canberra: Australian National University Press, 1979), 676–77.

20. Knibbs, *Commonwealth of Australia Yearbook*, 98, 634.

21. William Groom, "Report of the Royal Commission into the Sugar Industry of Queensland," *Queensland Votes and Proceedings* 4 (1889): 37–69.

22. D. H. Dalrymple, "Report of the Secretary of Agriculture, 1900–1901," *Queensland Votes and Proceedings* 4 (1901): 198.

23. Edgards Dunsdorfs, *The Australian Wheat-Growing Industry, 1788–1948* (Melbourne: Melbourne University Press, 1956), 164.

24. Roger Speight, "Testimony of the Former Victorian Railway Commissioner," in J. Casey, W. Cain, D. Whitley and C. Grant, "Report with Minutes of Evidence: Railway Inquiry Board into the Workings of the Victorian Railways," *Victorian Parliamentary Papers* 4 (1895): 301.

25. To ease comparisons of price trends, all prices in this chapter are given in historic US dollars. Although Australian prices were expressed in sterling (pounds, shillings, and pence) until 1966, few Australians today fully understand sterling. Conversions are undertaken separately for each year using the *Measuring Worth* website (https://measuringworth.com/).

26. Harley, "Transportation," 226, 232.

27. Dunsdorfs, *Australian Wheat-Growing Industry*, 166.

28. Thorsten Veblen, "The Price of Wheat since 1882," *Journal of Political Economy* 1 (1892): 82.

29. Dunsdorfs, *Australian Wheat-Growing Industry*, 115.

30. Chandler, *Visible Hand*, 174.

31. Henry Poor, *Manual of the Railroads of the United States, 1895* (New York: Poor, 1896), iii–iv.

32. These estimates are obtained by multiplying the bushels harvested by the prevailing Chicago price.

33. Henry Poor, *Manual of the Railroads of the United States, 1902* (New York: Poor, 1903), xiii.

34. Tonnage grew from 30,901 tons (1882) to 351,026 tons (1899), whereas the value of business increased from US$98,574 to US$581,492.

35. Calculated from Pugh, *Queensland Almanac*, 1881–1901.

36. Calculated from Poor, *Manual, 1902*, xv; Robert Gray, "Annual Report," 316.

37. Henry Poor, *Manual of the Railroads of the United States, 1891* (New York: Poor, 1892), xiv–xv; John Mathieson, "Annual Report of the Queensland Railway Commissioners, 1892–93," *Queensland Votes and Proceedings* 3 (1893): 758.

38. Henry Poor, *Manual of the Railroads of the United States, 1896* (New York: Poor, 1897), x–xix.

39. *Queensland Parliamentary Debates* 76 (1896): 1188.

40. John Gray, "Annual Report," 704.

41. Robinson, *Our Railroads*, 21.

42. Stromquist, *Generation of Boomers*, 201.

43. Ibid., 56.

44. Ibid., 51.

45. *Queensland Times*, 5 August 1886.

46. *Queensland Parliamentary Debates* 64 (1891): 376.

47. *Brisbane Worker,* 8 August 1891.

48. Chandler, *Visible Hand,* 173–74.

49. US Department of Commerce and Labor, *Statistical Abstract,* table 98; Poor, *Railroads of the United States, 1902,* xv.

Comparative Mutinies

Case Studies of Working-Class Agency in the 2nd Maine Volunteer Infantry Regiment, 1863, and the Australian Imperial Force, 1918

NATHAN WISE

In May–June, 1863, more than one hundred men of the 2nd Maine Volunteer Infantry Regiment, veterans of over two years of hard fighting throughout the eastern theater of the US Civil War, protested their treatment by military authorities. Fifty-five years later, in September 1918, several battalions of volunteers from the Australian Imperial Force (AIF) conducted a similar series of protests on the Western Front in World War I, also as a form of resistance to their treatment by military authorities. These were very different fighting forces in very different wars, but remarkable similarities exist in the causes of their actions, in the sentiments expressed by the soldiers, in the nonviolent nature of the action, and in the eventual resolution of the issues at the heart of the action. By exploring key similarities and differences between these two "mutinies of disbandment," this chapter asserts that both events were forms of nonviolent direct action carried out by groups of rank-and-file working-class men to express their opposition to the breaking up of their units and their attempted transfer to different units. Striking parallels exist in the motivations of protesters, their treatment by authorities, and the manner in which these actions were eventually resolved. In both cases, while their actions challenged the decisions made by military authorities and thus were a cause of concern for military elites, the men intended no direct challenge to either the structure of that authority or to the power it exercised within the military's operational environment. By contrasting these two events and treating the military as a social system, intricately linked to the values and norms of the civilian society from which it was formed, the chapter also contributes to the growing global history of military labor and identifies some of the common aspects of rank-and-file soldiers' approach toward and expectations regarding military service.

There is growing recognition around the world that within military forces of the past, soldiers, particularly the rank and file, approached their service as work. Service personnel often enlisted for the pay or for the long-term social or economic benefits they hoped would result from military service, and they thought of daily work within the military much as they conceived of daily work within the civilian world. Previous analyses have argued that during World War I, this approach toward military service included responses to complaints that utilized prewar understandings of industrial action and bargaining.[1] There are also increasing efforts to link these themes throughout different conflicts and to identify the similarities and differences in the nature of military labor in various times and places. Erik-Jan Zürcher's 2013 compilation, *Fighting for a Living*, brought together nineteen case studies of aspects of military labor around the world through five centuries of conflict.[2] This chapter adopts Zürcher's comparative approach.

The growing recognition of soldiers as workers enables this comparative approach to be increasingly applied to forms of military labor. Specifically, the chapter uses the analytical approach described by V. E. Bonnell to discern variations in "equivalent units" of military labor in two different military forces in two different eras.[3] US volunteer regiments and Australian battalions had between eight hundred and one thousand men at full strength, served in brigades comprising four units, and included volunteer recruits who approached military service as temporary citizen-soldiers. Closer analysis of these units can identify additional similarities in their enlistment patterns, composition, working cultures, and purpose within their broader military organizations, but such an analysis lies beyond the chapter's scope.

However, differences also existed between the units, which were formed in different nations, in different conflicts, with different motivations for conducting war. The events took place fifty-five years apart, and the societies and cultures from which the men involved in those events originated were very different. In Maine in the 1860s, labor was largely preindustrial, even less advanced than in other areas of the United States at the time and certainly less than Australia in the 1910s. C. Scontras has argued that much of the work within the state was hybrid, "one might farm and be part-time lumberman, or farm and fish, or farm and perhaps make a voyage to the West Indies or Grand Banks."[4] Even so, labor disturbances in Maine gradually increased during the 1840s and 1850s, largely in urban and relatively industrialized centers, and although large unions had not yet organized in the state, various forms of industrial action and protest were recorded there, with most incidents involving the issue of wages.[5] Thus, at the start of the US Civil War, workers in the state were conscious of the distinction between themselves and the upper classes, and many were familiar with (although not necessarily personally experienced in) the practice of protesting unfair working conditions.[6]

In contrast, the AIF was formed in an era where theories of scientific management were being applied to the highly industrialized workforce, where union membership was growing rapidly throughout the country, and where industrial action was a familiar response to unfair working conditions.[7] Despite these differences, the men who participated in the events of 1863 and 1918 clearly expressed a similar sense of justice within their military working environment and of their right to protest against injustices perpetrated by authorities.

While military historians have often described rebellious behavior in military environments as "mutinous," labor historians have recently sought to place such incidents within broader social and working frameworks and to see these incidents as protests or strikes against unsatisfactory working conditions. Such analyses of military labor have revealed that soldiers often identified military service as a form of work. As Zürcher argues, "Soldiers are not a separate category of people who sometimes fulfill the role of workers; they are workers."[8] Consequently, histories of military labor approach their analyses of the military environment much as they would any other civilian workforce.

Protests and small-scale mutinies were a relatively common occurrence during the American Civil War, primarily because regiments formed in 1861 and 1862 typically were built on the relatively informal state militia tradition (in contrast to the professional standards employed within the regular Federal forces of the same era). Those volunteers brought independent and egalitarian values to their regiment from civilian life. Democratic and egalitarian principles were further supported, for example, by the constitutionally prescribed practice of electing officers in the military during this early period of the war. Richard Miller has noted that within the Maine state militia, "Companies elected captains and lieutenants; these officers elected the regimental field officers; and field officers elected brigadier generals."[9] The practice carried over into the 2nd Maine during the Civil War, and R. H. Stanley and G. O. Hall report on several elections in Maine regiments.[10] Maine's military forces thus had a clear tradition of egalitarian, democratic, and independent expression. Having volunteered for military service, many men believed they deserved better treatment than that provided within the military environment, and protests and resistance to authority were common, particularly early in the war, before authorities sought to professionalize the volunteer forces. Protests were also common within the AIF during the First World War, but they took on a different nature. Men frequently complained about authorities and even resisted orders, but their actions were more careful and calculated. They tended to be more selective with the timing and the nature of their protests to avoid punishment.[11] Even so, large-scale protests did occur, some involving several thousand men, such as the Liverpool-Casula protest and riot, also known as the Battle of Sydney, which took place on 14 February 1916.

Background and Motivations

Both incidents took place several years into the conflict, after years of horrific and exhausting fighting. By May 1863, the war was going poorly for the Union. What had originally been expected to be a short and swift war against the southern rebels had turned into a long and protracted conflict that had forced the mobilization of many of the Union's people and much of its industrial resources. The men who volunteered in April 1861 never expected the war to last long and never fully anticipated the inhumane environment within which they would be ordered to work. Similarly, in September 1918, the men of the AIF were amazed that they were still being used to spearhead the Allied advance, and their exhaustion contributed to their decision to protest. In both cases, the seeds for these incidents were planted in the units' formation and recruitment.

The 2nd Maine Volunteer Infantry Regiment was created in April 1861, the first month of the US Civil War. The unit's members included some of the region's most eager and enthusiastic men. During this early phase of recruitment, provisions for the enlistment of soldiers were often rushed and ill conceived. As a result, recruits into the 2nd Maine signed several different types of enlistment papers. Some, particularly the earliest recruits, signed the existing ninety-day militia papers, binding them only to a short period of service. They, along with others who enlisted during the first few weeks, were required to sign an additional contract binding them to the two-year period of service authorized by the state legislature on 22 April 1861, in accordance with the service duration of the 2nd Maine. However, men who subsequently joined the unit were asked to sign three-year service papers. Consequently, a unit that was to serve for two years included some men who signed for ninety days, some who signed for two years, and some who signed for three years.[12]

The regiment quickly became recruits' new home and family. Indeed, James H. Mundy notes that unlike regiments formed later in the war, which increasingly drew recruits from multiple regions, the 2nd Maine was recruited from a relatively small geographical area, and some of the companies "were quite literally family. It was not unusual to have a father, a son and an uncle and cousin in the same outfit."[13] For the next few years, these men would spend just about every hour of every day with the other members of their regiment. Individual companies within the regiment further linked men with their home areas and/or associations: for example, Company B—Castine Light Infantry, Company D—Milo Artillery, and Company K—Old Town Company, were formed around particular localities near Bangor.[14]

As the war progressed and men became increasingly disillusioned and homesick, the motivation to continue fighting was increasingly tied to regimental pride and esprit de corps. This spirit was further strengthened by prewar connections such as links with friends, associations, and locales.[15] Men fought for their unit and their comrades much more than for their state, the nation, or individual motivations.[16] When the 2nd Maine was mustered out in 1863, at the completion of its two years of service, most of its men also were mustered out. However, the men who had signed three-year contracts were required to serve an additional twelve months with a different unit. Those men were outraged: the disbandment of the 2nd Maine removed much of their motivation to continue serving and working. In May–June 1863, that frustration reached the surface as the men utilized the strategy of withdrawing their labor.

Like the men from Penobscot County, Maine, the men of the AIF identified their battalions as their home and family. Those Australian battalions were typically raised within particular geographical areas (usually states), and men who enlisted together commonly served alongside one another. By September 1918, the men had clearly established their sense of home and social solidarity in the battalion, and their ties to the unit were particularly strong.

Also like the 2nd Maine, the AIF had a strong reputation for democratic and egalitarian values, which became core tenets of soldiers' common identities as "diggers."[17] Throughout the war, these characteristics were reflected in the behavior and actions of the AIF, particularly with regard to protests within the military.[18] By 1918, the members of the AIF had established a clear history of negotiating with their officers and protesting working conditions.

Losses due to combat and illness inevitably sapped these units of their strength, and reinforcements simply could not keep up with this decline. Thus, in February 1918, approval was given to disband one battalion in each Australian brigade, with those used to strengthen the remaining three battalions.

The process was intended to be carried out slowly, on a case-by-case basis, as deemed necessary.

Over the next seven months, only three battalions were disbanded, but in mid-August 1918, the disbandment of additional battalions was deemed a high priority. By September the strength of these Australian battalions had been heavily reduced. For example, C. E. W. Bean noted that in September 1918, the attacking battalions of the 4th Australian Division averaged "only 19 officers and 405 other ranks (including headquarters)."[19] Following a protest among many of its members, the 1st Battalion went into battle on 21 September 1918 with only 10 officers and 84 other ranks.[20]

The timing for these disbandments was difficult for other reasons. On 8 August 1918, the Allies commenced an offensive that shattered German defenses and began the final push back toward the German border. Australian battalions played a key role in this push, contributing to significant victories on the Western Front. For years they had waged a largely static and seemingly futile war of attrition over a bomb-scarred landscape, but by August 1918, the front lines had moved to environments hitherto untouched by war, with the Allies gaining substantial territory. Bean noted that "Australian battalions had never been so effective as in the last month when they were all far below strength."[21] Given these successes, many soldiers, including their commanding officers, saw no need to make radical changes. A deputation of officers from the 21st Battalion appealed to their commanding officers and raised a number of issues for clarification, one of which was "We are not now fighting with our backs to the wall. Excellent news is coming in from all fronts and prospects of peace are brighter than ever before. . . . Surely we, who are so few in numbers and have done so much, are not of such vital importance that we cannot be spared a little now that America's millions are arriving and peace is in sight."[22]

The resistance to the disbandment of these units in September 1918 can be contrasted with the uneventful disbandment of the 36th, 47th, and 52nd Infantry Battalions in April–May 1918. The 47th Battalion War Diary noted the "regret of all at having to leave a unit," but there is no evidence of any protest or vocal resistance to the disbandment.[23] These April–May disbandments were slightly more staggered than the eight disbandments that occurred in September, meaning that men from different units might not have been able to share their complaints and their planned responses. Furthermore, the strategic situation in April–May was dire, with Ludendorff's Spring Offensive under way and the Australians fighting desperately to halt the German advance. This was not a suitable time for resistance and mutiny within the army.

The Australian role in the military victories of 1918 contributed to a sense of skill and pride in the unit that gave troops confidence that they could use in industrial action within the military, with these attributes serving as "bargaining chips" in their favor.[24] Many men may have also felt that, after their extensive service on the front lines and especially their central role in halting the German offensive, the military owed them something. In addition, they may have also believed that their combat success had earned them a greater say in the management of affairs relating to their battalion. Furthermore, from August onwards, with the Allies holding the strategic advantage on the Western Front and the German army in retreat, the environment was ripe for protest and industrial action. General John Monash, commander of the Australian Corps, which comprised all five Australian infantry divisions, asked that the changes be postponed until the following year.[25] The request was rejected, but officials conceded that none of the original sixteen battalions would be reduced.

Following consultation with their brigadiers, divisional commanders selected eight battalions to disband in September and October 1918.[26] According to Bean, "To officers and men of these [disbanding] battalions, the blow was overwhelming. The step might be necessary—but why should *their battalion* be chosen?"[27] This question most concerned the men. They interpreted the order as an insult to their battalion and to their combat history and inferred that theirs was considered the worst-performing unit in their brigade. The 21st Battalion sent several soldiers to ask their commanding officer, "Why should the 21st Australian Infantry Battalion be disbanded?" The men then went on to defend their military performance and reputation, implying that other battalions were more deserving of disbandment: they had received "202 Decorations and Mentions [in dispatches] as against 199 of the 23rd Battalion." Moreover, they noted, "Our present weakness in strength is partly due to having to perform tasks which other Battalions in the Brigade failed to accomplish. As our weakness is due to the effective carrying out of our duties are we to be punished on this account?"[28]

As in the case of the 2nd Maine, the members of the AIF units would transfer to other battalions, separating them from their comrades and placing them in a new unit with complete strangers and with an unfamiliar set of traditions and cultures. The men from the 21st Battalion argued that the disbandment of their battalion would constitute "the greatest injustice . . . to the men who have gone before."[29] Similarly, the deputation of officers from the 21st Battalion suggested that the spirit of a battalion "means everything": "If the Battalion were disbanded the loss of morale would more than counteract the numerical gain of a few men."[30] Reports from other battalions also commented on the strong bonds that existed between men and on the importance of such bonds to good morale. This esprit de corps had sustained those men through the most difficult stages of the war, and the orders to disband threatened to unravel all that they had built. The clear message was that these men, both officers and other ranks, considered the battalion their home and their family, and the threat of losing that base culminated in the September 1918 protest.

The Nature of the Protests

By May 1863, the 2nd Maine had completed its two years of service, and the men who had signed two-year contracts were ordered to return to Maine, where they were welcomed home as heroes. Dignitaries provided an escort, church bells rang, buildings throughout Bangor were decked out in flags, and crowds cheered. The men who had signed three-year contracts, however, not only were sent to new units but were threatened by their brigade commander, Brigadier General James Barnes: half of the men would be transferred into the 3rd Massachusetts Battery, an artillery unit that was not even from their home state, and anyone who defied orders would be court-martialed.[31] Nonetheless, the men refused, withdrawing their labor. Military authorities deemed the protest a mutiny, and the men from the 2nd Maine were placed under arrest, denied rations, and forcibly marched to the 20th Maine under guard by men from the 118th Pennsylvania Volunteer Infantry Regiment. The commanding officer of the 20th Maine, Colonel Joshua Chamberlain, then played a key role in managing these men, understanding and resolving their issues, and ending their protest.

The mutinies of disbandment within the AIF followed similar patterns as news of the pending disbandments spread in mid-September. Men in the 37th Battalion learned of the possibility of disbandment on 14 September, and the unit's War Diary reported that "all ranks are very upset on hearing of the news of the possibility of the Battalion being disbanded."[32] A day later, according to the diary, "Men are still very upset at the possibility of the Battalion being disbanded."[33] The 21st Battalion received word that it was being disbanded on 20 September, with the unit's War Diary reporting that "this sudden and unexpected blow caused great dismay amongst all concerned."[34] Confirmation was received in the 37th Battalion on 18 September, and officers were advised that following parade on 23 September, they were to march out from their battalion and join other units. In all of these units, hearing the news led the men, including officers, to meet to discuss the disbandment.[35]

The advance notice gave the men in these units ample time to discuss disbandment and organize a response. The 21st Battalion War Diary reported on 24 September, one day ahead of the planned disbandment, that "it came to the knowledge of the C.O. that the men had decided to carry out all duites [*sic*] required of them with the one exception of falling in in marching order to proceed to another Unit."[36] Other units did not require much time to organize their response. The 54th Battalion War Diary reported that meetings were almost immediately held by the men to determine what action they would take.[37] Hector Brewer, a lieutenant serving in the 54th Battalion, provided an officer's perspective on the events: "The companies were paraded under their respective company commanders at 10 a.m. and the men told to move off to their respective battalions but not a man budged an inch. They refused to recognise any other Bn for themselves but the 54th."[38] Similar plans for protest were made and carried out throughout the other battalions ordered to disband. At the moment that the rank and file of those battalions were ordered to move to their new units, they universally refused. The 54th Battalion War Diary reported on 23 September, "In every Coy. The men refused to move to their new units, and stood on their Parade Grounds in silent protest against the order. . . . [I]t had become plain that neither an order or an appeal would bring any change in the situation."[39]

Because of the peculiar nature of their protest, the soldiers involved in the event felt uncertain about how to classify their actions. For example, Reynold Potter, serving in the 21st Battalion, wrote in his diary,

> I didn't know how much attached to the Battalion I was until ordered to report to another. I am glad to be able to say now, that, for the present at least, we are to remain of the 21st Batt. For one day we were officially in the 22nd but on that day we were all absentees. . . . [W]hen we should have reported to our respective new O.C's we refused to be disbanded; and remained and drilled under our Sergeant-Majors as a protest against the business.[40]

The responses among the battalions differed subtly but had several common factors. First, in response to the news, deputations from among the rank and file and sometimes from among officers met to discuss how to respond. In many cases, these deputations presented a case to their commanding officers, often with a set of alternative suggestions. When the men received the final order to march to their new units, they universally refused to obey that particular order. Bean noted that only the members of the 60th Battalion were convinced to cease their protest and obey the initial order, a phenomenon Bean attributed to "the unrivalled hold of Brig.-Genl. 'Pompey' Elliott on the loyalty of his men."[41]

Resolution

When the men from the 2nd Maine arrived in the camp of the 20th Maine, many had ceased their protest, but others were still refusing to serve. Colonel Chamberlain later recalled that he was ordered, "to take them into my regiment and 'make them do duty, or shoot them down the moment they refused'; these had been the very words of the Corps Commander in person."[42] Chamberlain had been in command of the 20th Maine for less than a week, and these men presented his first serious test as a regimental commander. Chamberlain began by riding to speak to Major General George Meade, commanding the Army of the Potomac, to request permission to deal with the protesters in his own way. With Meade's approval, Chamberlain dismissed the armed guard, fed the men, and began listening to their complaints. He responded empathetically, telling the protesters that he believed that they were right but that he had no option to send them home: his orders required him to absorb them into his ranks. Describing the situation to Maine's newly appointed governor, Abner Coburn, Chamberlain laid out the causes of the protest, expressed his sympathy for their cause, and conveyed his dissatisfaction at the men's treatment:

> The transfer of the "three years men" of the 2nd Maine has been so clumsily done, that the men were allowed to grow quite mutinous—left uncared for in their old camp after the 2nd had gone for several days & having time & provocation to work themselves up to such a pitch of mutiny. . . . You are aware, Governor, that promises were made to induce these men to enlist, which are not now kept, & I must say that I sympathize with them in their view of the case. Assured as they were that they would be mustered out with the 2nd, they cannot but feel that they are falsely dealt with in being retained & sent to duty in other Reg'ts.[43]

To further appease the 2nd Maine protesters and ensure their smooth transition into the 20th Maine, Chamberlain promoted one of their numbers, Andrew Tozier, to the position of color sergeant. Chamberlain also distributed the 2nd Maine men throughout the companies of the 20th Maine to "equalize companies, and particularly to break up the 'esprit de corps' of banded mutineers."[44] Chamberlain hoped to convey to the 2nd Maine men that although their old home, the 2nd Maine, was gone, they should embrace their new home among the men of the 20th.

Chamberlain's approach worked, and he reported that, "all but one or two had gone back manfully to duty, to become some of the best soldiers in the regiment."[45] Indeed, several former 2nd Maine men went on to receive commendations during their time with the 20th Maine, including Tozier, who received the Medal of Honor for his exploits during the Battle of Gettysburg. Some 2nd Maine men who moved to the 20th Maine, among them Frank Grindle, one of the leaders of the May–June protest, and John O'Connell, reenlisted at the end of their three-year terms.[46]

Like Chamberlain, AIF officers generally treated the September 1918 protesters with empathy and respect. By late September, the need to organize these battalions and get them back in the front lines was deemed more important than enforcing an administrative order, and the order to disband was temporarily delayed. Following a day of peaceful protest by the men of the 21st Battalion, the unit's War Diary reported that "for the present the disbandment would be in abeyance."[47] The 54th Battalion War Diary reported on 25 September, "a wire was received intimating the Battalion would be reformed temporarily on account of the impending movements of the 5th Australian Division."[48] For the moment at least, the rank and file had forced their officers to compromise.

Hector Brewer was initially critical of the protest but wrote gleefully in his diary on 27 September, "The boys have had a win though we are assured that is only a temporary arrangement. . . . [W]e are going into action as the 54th Bn. The good old 54th. Every body is delighted. The men are taking it very soberly though."[49] Similar compromises were reached in all other units except for the 60th Battalion. The order to disband would be delayed until October, and the units would go into battle one last time in the current structure, in their current battalions. This compromise seemed to satisfy all concerned, and aside from the obvious frustration felt by commanding officers and the sadness felt by the rank and file, no subsequent protests occurred. Officers clearly empathized with the men and appreciated the central cause for complaint: the breaking up of unit loyalty, identity, and esprit de corps. They sought to resolve the protest by specifically targeting those values and utilizing the otherwise high morale evident throughout those units during the military successes of late 1918.

As with the 2nd Maine's protest, resolution was reached via a caring, empathetic approach. Nevertheless, in both cases, the disbandments ultimately took place. But officers' caring approach meant that in both cases long-term protests largely failed to materialize. The 37th Battalion's War Diary entry for 11 October 1918 reported that the men "are very downhearted over the breaking up of the Battalion" but that they nonetheless moved out.[50] In 1863, only one man, Henry H. Moore, continued to refuse to serve; he was court martialed and sentenced to be shot, but President Abraham Lincoln commuted his sentence to hard labor. Even Moore's attitude eventually changed, and he was returned to the 20th Maine in April 1864 to serve out the remainder of his term. And as Bean noted, of the thousands of men who protested in 1918, "No man was punished for his part in the disbandment munity."[51]

Conclusion

These specific incidents were separated by vast amounts of time and space, but remarkable similarities exist in the motivations for protest, the nature of the protest, and in the way the protests were resolved. Moreover, these case studies demonstrate common elements in the expectations of military service, of military customs, and of military justice. In particular, these incidents reveal the shared struggle for agency and justice among the typically working-class members of the military's rank and file. These men believed they were entitled to contribute to the management of their lives. With those beliefs crushed by disbandment orders and a prevailing sense of injustice, both sets of men felt that they were entitled and justified to withdraw their labor, resist authority, and protest circumstances despite the military environment.

Both sets of men came from democratic and egalitarian-minded backgrounds. They valued their independence and their ability to contribute to the nature of their workplace environment and workplace conditions as well as within civil society.

These incidents reveal that soldiers were not always obedient servants and that they carried over their sense of workplace agency from civilian life into the new world of the military. Gerald F. Linderman has concluded that "the Civil War soldier, moving from peace to war but seldom severed from civilian influences, suffered little serious sense of discontinuity. . . . [H]e found little cause to doubt that he remained master of his own destiny."[52] And as J. G. Fuller has similarly argued in his analysis of British and dominion soldiers during the First World War, "The fact that there was a large degree of continuity in enthusiasms and attitudes from civilian to military life is significant not only in its effects but also in what it says about the nature of the war experience. It suggests that for many men the war was not quite the chasm, cutting across individual and collective experiences and sundering past from future, that it is sometimes depicted."[53] These incidents suggest that although these men enlisted to serve in the military, their sense of loyalty and purpose was not always tied to their original motivations or to the ideas of the state, nation, or military; rather, it could be tied to other motivating factors, such as comrades and the esprit de corps of a collective working body such as a regiment or battalion.

This analysis contributes to the growing body of research on social and labor histories of the military and assists in the development of the foundations for broader social and labor-focused investigations of military forces throughout the world. Service personnel must be seen as more than just obedient servants of the military. They develop in a civil world and accumulate dearly held social values. Characteristics and discernable patterns exist across the forms of military labor in different times and places, and these patterns help us to understand the nature of labor relations worldwide.[54]

Notes

1. N. Wise, "The Lost Labour Force: Working Class Approaches towards Military Service during the Great War," *Labour History* 93 (2007): 171–73, N. Wise, "'In Military Parlance I Suppose We Were Mutineers': Industrial Relations in the Australian Imperial Force during the Great War," *Labour History* 101 (2011): 161–76.

2. Erik-Jan Zürcher, ed., *Fighting for a Living: A Comparative History of Military Labour, 1500–2000* (Amsterdam: Amsterdam University Press, 2013).

3. V. E. Bonnell, "The Uses of Theory, Concepts, and Comparison in Historical Sociology," *Comparative Studies in Society and History* 22 (1980): 156–73.

4. C. Scontras, *Collective Efforts among Maine Workers: Beginnings and Foundations, 1820–1880* (Orono, Me.: Bureau of Labor Education, 1994), 1.

5. Ibid., 154–56.

6. Ibid., 9.

7. See L. Taksa, "'All a Matter of Timing': Managerial Innovation and Workplace Culture in the New South Wales Railways and Tramways prior to 1921," *Australian Historical Studies* 110 (1998):1–26.

8. Zürcher, *Fighting for a Living*, 12.

9. Richard. F. Miller, *States at War*, vol. 1, *A Reference Guide for Connecticut, Maine, Massachusetts, New Hampshire, Rhode Island, and Vermont in the Civil War* (Hanover, N.H.: University Press of New England, 2013), 154.

10. R. H. Stanley and G. O. Hall, *Eastern Maine and the Rebellion: Being an Account of the Principal Local Events in Eastern Maine during the War and Brief Histories of Eastern Maine Regiments* (Bangor, Me.: Stanley, 1887), 33, 210, 233.

11. See, for example, Wise, "'In Military Parlance'"; N. Wise, "Fighting a Different Enemy: Social Protests against Authority in the Australian Imperial Force during World War I," *International Review of Social History* 52 (2007): 225–41.

12. James H. Mundy, *Second to None: The Story of the 2d Maine Volunteers, "The Bangor Regiment"* (Scarborough, Me.: Harp, 1992), 5–6, 96–97.

13. Ibid., 75.

14. Stanley and Hall, *Eastern Maine and the Rebellion*, 33.

15. Joseph Allan Frank and George A. Reaves, "Emotional Responses to Combat," in *The Civil War Soldier: A Historical Reader*, ed. Michael Barton and Larry Logue (New York: New York University Press, 2002), 391–92.

16. Gerald F. Linderman, *Embattled Courage: The Experience of Combat in the American Civil War* (New York: Free Press, 1987), 252–53.

17. Graham Seal, *Inventing Anzac: The Digger and National Mythology* (St. Lucia: University of Queensland Press, 2004), 3.

18. Wise, "Fighting a Different Enemy"; Wise, "'In Military Parlance,'" 161–76; N. Wise, *Anzac Labour: Workplace Cultures in the Australian Imperial Force during the First World War* (Basingstoke: Palgrave Macmillan, 2014), 77–90.

19. C. E. W. Bean, *Official History of Australia in the War of 1914–1918*, vol. 6, *The Australian Imperial Force in France during the Allied Offensive, 1918* (Sydney: Angus and Robertson, 1941), 896.

20. 1st Battalion War Diary, September 1918, Australian War Memorial (hereafter AWM) 4, Class 23; 1st Infantry Brigade War Diary, September 1918, 135–37, AWM4, Class 23.

21. Bean, *Official History*, 6:936.

22. 21st Battalion War Diary, Appendix 19—Copy of Minutes of Deputation to G. O. C. Division, September 1918, AWM4, Class 23.

23. 47th Battalion War Diary, 25 May 1918, AWM4, Class 23.

24. Wise, "'In Military Parlance,'" 170; N. Wise, "Job Skill, Manliness, and Working Relationships in the Australian Imperial Force during World War I," *Labour History* 106 (2014): 99–122.

25. Bean, *Official History*, 6:936.

26. The units selected for disbandment included the 19th Infantry Battalion (5th Brigade), 21st Infantry Battalion (6th Brigade), 25th Infantry Battalion (7th Brigade), 29th Infantry Battalion (8th Brigade), 37th Infantry Battalion (10th Brigade), 42nd Infantry Battalion (11th Brigade), 54th Infantry Battalion (14th Brigade), 60th Infantry Battalion (15th Brigade). Battalions disbanded in April and May 1918 included the 36th Infantry Battalion (9th Brigade), 47th Infantry Battalion (12th Brigade), and 52nd Infantry Battalion (13th Brigade)].

27. Bean, *Official History*, 6:937.

28. 21st Battalion War Diary, Appendix 17—Copy of Minutes of Deputation to Brigadier, 20 September 1918, AWM4, Class 23.

29. Ibid.

30. 21st Battalion War Diary, Appendix 19—Copy of Minutes of [Officers'] Deputation to G. O. C. Division, September 1918, AWM4, Class 23.

31. Mundy, *Second to None*, 7.

32. 37th Battalion War Diary, 14 September 1918, AWM4, Class 23.

33. Ibid., 15 September 1918.

34. 21st Battalion War Diary, 20 September 1918, AWM4, Class 23.

35. Bean, *Official History*, 6:937.

36. Ibid., 24 September 1918.

37. 54th Battalion War Diary, 22 September 1918, AWM4, Class 23.

38. Hector Brewer, No. 820, Groom, diary, 24 September 1918, Mitchell Library, MSS 1300.

39. 54th Battalion War Diary, 23 September 1918, AWM4, Class 23.

40. Reynold Clive Potter, No. 6080, Carpenter, diary transcript (originally written in shorthand), ca. September 1918, 38–39, Mitchell Library, MSS 2944.

41. Bean, *Official History*, 6:939.

42. Joshua L. Chamberlain, "Through Blood and Fire at Gettysburg," *Hearst's Magazine*, January–June 1913, 899–900.

43. Joshua Chamberlain to Governor Coburn, 25 May 1863, in Chamberlain, *Through Blood and Fire: Selected Civil War Papers of Major General Joshua Chamberlain*, ed. Mark Nesbit (Mechanicsburg, Pa.: Stackpole, 1996), 59–60.

44. Ibid., 899–900.

45. Ibid.

46. Mundy, *Second to None*, 8–9.

47. 21st Battalion War Diary, 25 September 1918, AWM4, Class 23.

48. 54th Battalion War Diary, 25 September 1918, AWM4, Class 23.

49. Hector Brewer, No. 820, Groom, diary, 27 September 1918, Mitchell Library, MSS 1300.

50. 37th Battalion War Diary, 11 October 1918, AWM4, Class 23.

51. Bean, *Official History*, 6:935.

52. Linderman, *Embattled Courage*, 42.

53. J. G. Fuller, *Troop Morale and Popular Culture in the British and Dominion Armies* (Oxford: Clarendon, 1990), 154.

54. Zürcher, *Fighting for a Living*, 41.

PART 5

Economic Democracy and Working-Class Institutions

How to Build a Trade Union Oligarchy

Guidance from the United States and Australia, 1886–1970

SCOTT STEPHENSON

Beginning in the mid-nineteenth century, workers in both the United States and Australia overcame resistance from employers and governments and built extensive trade union movements. The extent to which the members controlled these unions, however, varied greatly within each country. This chapter investigates the US and Australian experiences of trade union oligarchy between 1886 and 1970, comparing two prominent unions that developed oligarchical tendencies, the United Automobile Workers (UAW) in the United States and the Australian Workers Union (AWU). Both of these unions were large and influential and have extensive historiographies, and they were arguably the most prominent examples of trade union oligarchy in their respective countries. Similarities and differences between the two nations affected these unions, and the comparison offers insight into the causal factors behind oligarchy. In particular, the chapter focuses on each country's dominant union type, union political affiliation, methods of industrial bargaining, civil rights movements, and anticommunism.

Both the United States and Australia were former British colonies with a federal system of government and the early introduction of suffrage for all white males.[1] But Australia more quickly developed "new unions" of unskilled workers, a successful Australian Labor Party (ALP), and a system of compulsory industrial arbitration in which industrial courts settled disputes through legally binding awards. The United States had a much larger population spread more evenly across its territory, a larger nonwhite population, a stronger civil rights movement, and a more influential anticommunist movement.

Union democracy means control of unions by the ordinary members. At the opposite end of the spectrum is trade union oligarchy, which is organizational domination by a small group of leaders. Most scholars acknowledge a strong tendency toward oligarchy within trade unions but argue that it can be overcome in some circumstances. Union oligarchy is easier to create than union democracy but still requires certain conditions to thrive, and these conditions were present in both the UAW and AWU though manifested in different ways.

The UAW was founded in 1935 as an industrial union based primarily in the Midwest. The AWU was founded in 1886 and based in rural Australia; it remained the country's largest and most influential union throughout the first half of the twentieth century. Originally a union of shearers, it grew to encompass a wide range of unskilled pastoral and construction laborers. The UAW was democratic in the 1930s but, as Matthew Mettler has demonstrated, by the 1950s had succumbed to oligarchical tendencies. The AWU, in contrast, was highly centralized from its founding and quickly became and remained an oligarchy.[2] Some of the characteristics of these unions came from factors unique to their organizations, industries, members, and leaders, while others came from the broader national contexts. Despite significant national variations, the experience of trade union oligarchy in the United States and Australia was more similar than it was different.

Democracy and Oligarchy within Trade Unions

The field of union governance has centered on arguments for and against Robert Michels's "iron law of oligarchy."[3] In 1911, Michels, a German sociologist, argued that all supposedly democratic organizations, including trade unions, would inevitably become oligarchies because members are incapable of controlling leaders, who will govern the organization to benefit themselves and entrench their positions.[4] Critics of Michels have acknowledged the propensity toward oligarchy that he identified but have argued that it can be overcome. Richard Hyman, for example, argues from a Marxist perspective that "countervailing tendencies" can offset the tendency toward oligarchy. These tendencies include membership pressure on the leaders from below and ideological support for democracy among the leaders themselves.[5] The consensus in the field is that trade unions have a strong inclination toward oligarchy but that it can be overcome in some circumstances.[6]

While different scholars have stressed different factors, the literature generally agrees that there are seven key requirements for union democracy. First, the rules must be formally democratic. Second, members must form a close-knit "occupational community" that creates a participatory culture.[7] Third, local autonomy facilitates participation and allows the development of local power bases, which provide opposition to the national leadership.[8] Fourth, rank-and-file decision making gives members power over key union decisions. Fifth, leaders tolerate internal organized opposition that facilitates electoral competition and accountability.[9] Sixth, equality of salary, status, skill and education between officials and members minimizes the gap in political skills and causes leaders to feel less pressure to maintain their positions through undemocratic means.[10] Seventh, free communication gives members access to information that allows informed participation and criticism of sitting officials and enables opposition groups to communicate with members.[11] These seven democratic requirements provide the framework for my comparison of the UAW and AWU.

The History of the UAW and AWU, 1886–1970

In the 1880s, many US unions rejected the industrial unionism of the Knights of Labor and founded the craft-unionist American Federation of Labor (AFL). Following the onset of the Great Depression in 1935, the left wing of the AFL broke away to form the Committee on Industrial Organization to promote industrial unionism, in which all workers in an industry joined a single union regardless of occupation. The industrial-unionist Congress of Industrial Organizations (CIO) rivaled the AFL until 1955, when the two organizations merged to form the AFL-CIO.

The UAW began in 1935 in Detroit and affiliated with the new CIO a year later. The autoworkers union was founded on militant, local shop-floor collective action and negotiation. During World War II, two coalitions competed for control. A center-left faction of New Deal progressives, communists, and other leftists led by UAW secretary-treasurer George Addes battled a broad center-right anticommunist faction led by Walter Reuther.[12] Reuther's victory in the union's 1946 presidential election marked the beginning of his increasing domination of the UAW and the union's slide into oligarchy.[13]

Immediately after the war, Reuther engaged in anticommunist red-baiting and expelled his opponents in the UAW and CIO. At the core of this conflict was a battle over trade union strategy. Reuther advocated top-down bureaucratic negotiation and cooperation with employers, while his opponents championed the union's traditional rank-and-file militancy.[14] By the late 1950s, the UAW was an industrial giant with more than 1.5 million members in 932 locals.[15] Reuther had imposed his top-down bureaucratic strategy on the union and cemented his control.[16] He led the UAW until he died in office in 1970.[17]

The AWU, Australia's dominant rural union, was founded by shearers in the southeastern state of Victoria in 1886 and quickly spread throughout the country, enrolling a wide variety of semiskilled and unskilled rural and construction workers.[18] By 1920, the AWU had become Australia's largest union, with more than one hundred thousand members divided into nine regional branches.[19] Although it expanded into many other areas and industries, a "bushworker ethos" continued to dominate the AWU.[20] The ideological heart of this ethos both reflected and helped to shape the wider national consensus regarding the "Australian Settlement"—chiefly, White Australia, compulsory arbitration, and tariff protection. Most AWU members and officials were conservative reformists, and many also occupied important positions within the ALP.

Opposing the conservative reformists within the AWU and the wider labor movement were militant reformists who promoted strikes and radicals who worked to overthrow capitalism. Militant and radical AWU members formed internal dissident groups in the 1920s before breaking away in 1930 to form the rival Pastoral Workers Industrial Union.[21] By the mid-1930s, most AWU members lived in Queensland in northeastern Australia. The AWU there had benefited from compulsory unionism and extensive public works. Queensland's branch secretary Clarrie Fallon used this massive membership to govern the union in an unofficial dictatorship until he died in office in 1950. Fallon's fellow Queenslander and protégé turned rival, Tom Dougherty, then ruthlessly dominated the union until he, too, died in office in 1972.[22]

Democratic Rules

The UAW rules contained several major democratic flaws. Most important, the members did not directly elect any of the international officials or staff. Members elected local delegates to the annual convention, which was the highest authority in the union. The convention delegates then elected the international officials and executive board, which was the highest authority between conventions.[23] Because sitting officials appointed most positions within the union, the UAW operated as a spoils system.[24]

The AWU rules were even less democratic. As in the UAW, the incumbent AWU officials appointed many positions in a patronage system.[25] The annual convention was the union's highest authority, and the executive council was the highest authority between conventions. Unlike the UAW, AWU members directly elected annual convention delegates, executive council representatives, and national officers.[26] However, these elections were undermined by a series of undemocratic rules that made it almost impossible to defeat the incumbents.

The AWU rules banned campaigning and canvassing in union elections.[27] This provision strongly favored incumbents, who were already well known to the members and used their positions to gain publicity in the union newspapers and other formal communications.[28] The rules also required the incumbent branch executive and executive council to approve rival electoral candidates' "ability" and "good behavior."[29] Citing fear of libel lawsuits, the executives provided no reasons for the rejection of rival candidates.[30]

Australian arbitration courts had the power to disallow union rules that were tyrannical or oppressive or that ran contrary to law.[31] However, this power offered only very limited legislative protection for union democracy, and several AWU members tried but failed to have the union's antidemocratic rules disallowed.[32] The United States had similarly minimal legislative protection of union democracy until the Landrum-Griffin Act of 1959. While the act was considered antiunion not only at the time but also by subsequent labor scholars, it did mandate democratic member rights such as freedom of speech and periodic election of officials by secret ballot. The ALP legislated similar requirements for Australian unions in the 1970s. Such laws provide valuable safeguards against the worst undemocratic abuses, but flourishing union democracy cannot be legislated and requires commitment from members and officials.

Occupational Community

The UAW initially possessed a strong occupational community. The union's leadership organized sports teams, dances, children's camps, food cooperatives, and women's auxiliaries.[33] But the occupational community declined rapidly during the 1950s as a result of the increase in assembly line work, the union's top-down bureaucratic contract bargaining, the closed shop, and the union's growing gender and racial divide.

In the 1930s, less than 20 percent of manual autoworkers worked on the assembly line. Militancy generally came from the non-assembly-line workers, who were more skilled, maintained strong group identification, and had greater levels of communication at work. However, postwar technological change caused steady increases in the proportion of workers on the assembly line and thus declines in group identification and communication.[34] Work became more boring and more individualized, and Reuther's institution of top-down national collective bargaining meant that workers had less power to combat these changes.[35]

In 1942 the UAW won the union shop, meaning all employees had to join the union and that the union had to accept them.[36] Conversely, closed shops mean that employers agree to hire only existing union members. Closed shops became illegal in 1947 under the federal Taft-Hartley legislation, while union shops remained legal.[37] The union shop guaranteed the UAW a large membership but also meant that many workers joined the UAW only because they had no choice. One local official complained that most members paid their dues simply "for the privilege of working," with "no understanding at all of the union and . . . probably a little mystified as to how they ever got into it."[38] This captive membership was less likely to participate in union affairs or demonstrate group solidarity.

Prior to World War I, the vast majority of autoworkers were white and male. During the war, however, thousands of African Americans from the South migrated to Detroit in search of work. Ford was the most welcoming company: its African American workforce increased from 50 individuals in 1916 to 8,459 by 1922.[39] During World War II, tens of thousands of additional African Americans and women entered the auto industry.[40] Official UAW policy promoted equal rights for all workers, but many white male members and their local leaders fought to maintain racial and gender exclusion and hierarchy.[41] Wildcat "hate strikes" by white UAW workers against blacks ensued. Atlanta UAW members joined the white supremacist Ku Klux Klan and Citizens' Councils, and in 1956 white UAW members at the Hayes Aircraft plant in Birmingham, Alabama, formed a new whites-only union.[42] Such incidents constituted part of a broader backlash against the civil rights movement.[43]

In the 1960s, the UAW's deep racial divisions became entangled in Democratic Party politics. As part of Democratic president Lyndon Johnson's War on Poverty, UAW leaders encouraged the government to reduce corporate power and shift economic relations to favor labor over capital. Instead, Johnson's administration took a much less radical approach and provided targeted assistance to disadvantaged social groups, especially African Americans. Many white UAW members came to oppose the War on Poverty, seeing it as a redistribution of labor's share of the economy away from white workers and toward black workers. African Americans, in turn, accused the UAW of trying to co-opt the black civil rights movement for its own political ends.[44]

Reuther's control of the UAW was oligarchic but not absolute. He had won control through a complicated set of allegiances, and maintaining those allegiances constrained him on some issues. Reuther was a strong advocate for civil rights but the backlash among white UAW members prevented him from pushing reform within the union as quickly as he would have liked.[45] The widespread racial hostility within the UAW caused many factories to divide into "a balkanized set of rival work groups" and destroyed solidarity and community among union members.[46]

Unlike the UAW, the AWU was not internally divided by race or gender. The union viewed nonwhites and women as a threat to wages and jobs and excluded them from membership.[47] But the AWU was divided in other ways. The semiskilled AWU shearers considered themselves working-class elites, or "bushworker Aristocrats." These shearers enjoyed a robust culture of mateship, but shearing at each station lasted for less than two months per year, so the seasonal and itinerant nature of the work undermined the formation of lasting occupational communities.[48] Furthermore, while the AWU had begun essentially as a shearers' craft union it quickly became a new union of mostly unskilled rural laborers. The shearers and AWU officials treated nonshearers as second-class members, and in the 1890s, only shearers could be convention delegates. The AWU's occupational community was thus deeply divided and hierarchical almost from the outset.

The AWU's transition into a general union was part of a late-nineteenth-century push in both Australia and the United States to organize unskilled workers from a variety of jobs and industries into new unions, distinct from conventional craft unions that organized one skilled profession. Australian craft union leaders largely supported new unionism, but their US counterparts did not.[49] By the 1890s new unions represented more than 60 percent of Australian unionists but less than 20 percent of their US counterparts.[50] There were periodic eruptions of general unionism in the United States, most notably the Knights of Labor in the 1880s, the American Railway Union and United Mine Workers of America in the 1890s, and the Industrial Workers of the World in the early twentieth century, but craft unionism and the AFL remained dominant until the formation of the CIO in 1935.

The diverse variety of unskilled, scattered, and often itinerant workers common among new unions usually prevented the formation of strong occupational communities and cultures of participatory democracy. By the early twentieth century, the AWU covered a multitude of jobs across a vast continent. Members worked in the pastoral industry as shearers, farmhands, rabbit trappers, sugarcane cutters and fruit pickers as well as in construction, mining, metals, factories, cooking, baking, hotels, clubs, restaurants, and more.[51] The AWU and other new unions also had far more difficulty than craft unions did in launching successful strikes because employers could easily replace unskilled workers, further dampening militancy and solidarity and making new unions more likely to pursue alternative tactics such as political action and compulsory arbitration.[52]

The early UAW members were not craft unionists, yet they still created strong occupational communities and militancy. As an industrial union, the UAW organized unskilled, semiskilled, and skilled workers. More important, unlike AWU members, most UAW members were not isolated or itinerant but lived and worked in large numbers in the same place for extended periods. This also reflected the fact that the AWU was a mostly rural union, while the UAW was mostly urban. Although rural workers were more likely to be isolated than urban workers in both Australia and the United States, this rural isolation was generally greater in Australia, which was almost as large as the United States but contained a fraction of the population. Moreover, most of Australia's people lived in the three east coast cities of Sydney, Melbourne, and Brisbane.

A minority of semiskilled and unskilled AWU workers did form strong occupational communities where a significant number of members worked and lived together. For example, AWU members in Port Kembla, New South Wales, worked primarily in smelting, metalwork, and fertilizer manufacture; lived in the surrounding area; and regularly attended mass AWU meetings.[53] They often staged strikes, even sympathy strikes, in defiance of the union's no-strike policy.[54] The Port Kembla AWU members were similar to UAW locals such as Ford 600, which retained a strong occupational community and militancy in defiance of their union's general oligarchical trend.[55]

Unlike the largely egalitarian foundational culture of the UAW, the AWU's founding culture contained strong hierarchical and aspirational elements. This AWU ethos was born in the shearing sheds in the 1890s and was promoted and sustained by the union's officials and newspapers. Even as late as the 1950s, almost all AWU leaders were former shearers.[56] Pastoral stations had a clear hierarchy that stretched down from the boss to the shearers to the laborers. Until the early twentieth century, most shearers were smallholders. Their sons, who aspired to become their own bosses, were shearing to make extra money toward that end. Many station hands and shed hands also hoped to climb the ladder by becoming shearers and/or landholders.[57] Shearers were paid per sheep, which facilitated competition, and a clear pecking order existed with the "gun" shearers at the top and the beginners at the bottom.[58] The aspirational, hierarchical culture of the shearing shed and pastoral station was perfectly suited to top-down oligarchical union leadership. Leaders took their position at the top of the existing hierarchy, with power to rival that of pastoralists.

Local Autonomy

Locals within the early UAW were highly autonomous.[59] In the 1930s, the UAW organized largely from the bottom up, with each work group electing a steward to negotiate with managers on its behalf. Stewards organized the wildcat strikes that won the union significant gains during the 1930s. But this adversarial local militancy also discouraged employers from recognizing and cooperating with the union. UAW leaders feared that when the labor market became more favorable toward employers, they might destroy the union.[60]

The national leadership drastically reduced local autonomy without significantly altering the union constitution, a process that culminated in Reuther's 1950 "Treaty of Detroit" contract with General Motors, which featured a no-strike pledge in exchange for improved wages and conditions.[61] Top-down organization and cooperation with employers had replaced local negotiation and collective action.[62] Local stewards and members who went on strike in breach of the national contract faced harsh discipline from employers and received no assistance from the union.[63]

The first major example of UAW abandonment of a striking local had occurred in April 1946, when the eighty-five hundred members of Local 248 went on strike at the Allis-Chalmers plant in West Allis, Wisconsin. Reuther and his anticommunist allies sought to undermine the militant communist leadership of Local 248 and negotiated a secret peace deal in which they accepted all of Allis-Chalmers's demands. Abandoned by their national union, the defeated members of Local 248 returned to work in March 1947. By the end of that year, Reuther had removed the Local 248 officials from office.[64]

In the AWU, the union's isolated and itinerant membership necessitated centralization from the outset. The federal annual convention and executive council enjoyed plenary power and total control over the branches.[65] The AWU was not formed through the combination of strong locals with decades of autonomous operation. Instead, it was an amalgamation of recently formed local shearers' unions organized from the top down.[66]

Australia's compulsory arbitration system caused further centralization. Access to the benefits of the federal arbitration court, which under Justice H. B. Higgins from 1907 to 1920 was more employee-friendly than most state arbitration courts, encouraged the AWU and other unions to federate, a process that usually meant a decrease in local autonomy. Arbitration judges also required unions to give their federal committees of management extensive powers to alter rules and impose levies.[67] This allowed unions to quickly and easily adopt court instructions but also undermined democracy and local autonomy by centralizing extensive power into the hands of a small group of federal officials.

In the UAW, top-down collective bargaining suffocated membership involvement and interest. As US scholars have observed more broadly, collective bargaining "tends to have an adverse effect on representative systems, as the professionalization and specialization needed to negotiate and implement collective bargains is likely to increase the size and power of unions' full-time staff at the expense of members being directly involved in decision-making."[68] Australia's arbitration system constituted an earlier and more extreme version of this phenomenon. Its courtroom operations involved no participation by ordinary members and discouraged membership interest and involvement.[69]

Arbitration judges altered jurisdictional boundaries to disadvantage militant unions and advantage conservative ones. In New South Wales, Judge Charles Heydon limited the jurisdiction of the militant Rockchoppers and Sewer Miners Union and weakened it to the point that it was forced to amalgamate with the AWU in 1917.[70] The threat of fines and deregistration by the arbitration courts for strikes also encouraged and legitimized union leaders' suppression of militancy among their members. This was similar to what occurred under the no-strike pledges in national UAW contracts. For these reasons, militant and radical unionists in the AWU campaigned against arbitration. Former AWU president Arthur Rae led a dissident Bushworkers Propaganda Group within the AWU in the 1920s that broke away in 1930 to form the rival Communist Party–aligned Pastoral Workers Industrial Union. The Pastoral Workers operated outside the arbitration system but peaked at just two thousand members and disbanded in 1936. The union was hampered by cooperation between the AWU and employer organizations; more significantly, however, it was too radical for most AWU members, who continued to support arbitration and oppose communism.[71] As Peter Clayworth shows, the New Zealand Federation of Labour similarly campaigned against compulsory arbitration and instead promoted direct action as a way to enable workers to have greater control.[72]

Rank-and-File Decision Making

UAW members had almost no direct decision-making capacity by 1950. In the 1930s, members enjoyed significant power over local disputes. But as authority centralized, the members lost that power, as their only input at the international level was to elect convention delegates.[73] AWU members, too, had minimal decision-making authority. The arbitration system's industry-wide awards undermined local workplace negotiation and prevented members from voting on employment contracts. Leaders also played on the aspirational and hierarchical elements of the union's ethos, arguing that leadership, not rank-and-file members, should make important union decisions. In 1926, national president John Barnes announced, "Each member of our organization must respond to discipline.... [T]hey will have to realize that when AWU decisions are made there is no questioning them."[74] Barnes and other officials clearly believed that the members supported such hierarchical organization.

The most fundamental decision that rank-and-file union members can make is whether to join and remain in the union. But arbitration greatly limited members' ability to leave the AWU even when they were unhappy with its management. The arbitration courts would recognize only one union in each area of employment, which meant that the first union in a field was very difficult to displace. Preference for unionists in arbitration awards and compulsory unionism in Queensland and some other jurisdictions forced many workers to join and remain in the AWU against their will.

In this way, compulsory arbitration resembled the UAW's union shop. In theory, US workers had the opportunity to choose a new union or no union at the expiration of each employment contract. But once a union won coverage of a group of workers, it had a great advantage in maintaining contractual exclusiveness. National Labor Relations Board decisions also made it very difficult for rival unions to displace existing unions.[75]

The union shop was and is a controversial issue in US labor relations. Such compulsory representation was the norm under the 1935 Wagner Act and National Labor Relations Board rulings. Taft-Hartley permitted states to pass "right-to-work" laws banning union shops, but only a minority of states in the South and West instituted such legislation, and it did not significantly affect the UAW.[76] Most labor activists argue that closed shops and union shops strengthen unions, but compulsory unionism can also undermine union democracy. In democratic unions, compulsory unionism may not diminish union democracy because unionists do not need to leave or threaten to leave the union to influence the leaders. In oligarchical unions like the UAW and AWU, however, one of the only ways that members could influence leaders was by leaving or threatening to do so, and compulsory unionism stripped them of this power.[77]

Organized Opposition

Between 1850 and 1970, most US unions banned internal groupings.[78] In the UAW in the 1940s, however, two major factions openly fought for control, resulting in membership engagement and close elections.[79] As Reuther cemented his control, his toleration for opposition declined, and he engaged in extensive red-baiting against his more militant opponents.

Reuther won the 1946 union election with the slogan, "Against outside Interference," a reference to his desire to eliminate communist influence in UAW locals. In 1947 he criticized the leaders of striking Local 248, saying that communists "should not be allowed to utilize our union and its members for the prosecution of their alien ideology." By the end of that year, he had shepherded a motion through the UAW convention requiring members of locals to sign affidavits that they were not communists.[80] As internal opposition died away, it was partly replaced by external opposition groups. The Communist Party, Socialist Workers Party, Association of Catholic Trade Unionists, Freemasons, and ethnic groups all frequently provided unsuccessful external opposition to the UAW leadership.[81]

Like many US unions but unlike the UAW, opposition groupings were forbidden within the AWU on the grounds that officials should be elected on their individual merit rather than as representatives of "divisive" intraunion groupings. The AWU banned opposition groups and expelled their members from the union.[82] Like their UAW counterparts, AWU officials red-baited their militant opponents, falsely and sensationally labeling dissidents as communists, foreigners, and traitors. In 1929, Henry Boote, editor of the AWU's newspaper, the *Australian Worker*, claimed that a rank-and-file reform movement had "resulted from efforts of an alien body in China [the Chinese Communist Party] to control the Labor movement in this country."[83] This propaganda played on the nationalist xenophobia and racism of the AWU ethos. Anything "foreign" was highly suspicious; anything Asian was inherently foul. Yet the AWU leaders' red-baiting had less success than the UAW's, partly because the anticommunist movement in Australia was not as strong.[84]

AWU officials faced external organized opposition similar to that encountered by the UAW leadership. This occurred primarily through the AWU's affiliation with the ALP. The militant New South Wales ALP faction's *Labor Daily* regularly attacked the AWU officials and described the union as having "had the misfortune to suffer from the blight of political bossism."[85] Affiliation also brought Labor Party disputes into the AWU. For example, the AWU's conflict with popular New South Wales Labor premier Jack Lang caused some pro-Lang AWU members to join opposition groupings within the union and eventually the Pastoral Workers Industrial Union.

External organized opposition could be highly damaging to the AWU leaders. In 1923 the AWU's most powerful and prominent leader in New South Wales, Jack Bailey, was expelled from the ALP. Despite a lack of conclusive evidence, his factional enemies found him guilty of conspiring to build ballot boxes with secret sliding panels to corrupt internal party elections.[86] Unlike the UAW leaders' external opponents, the AWU leaders' opponents could wield power over them within a separate organization to which both groups belonged.

Equality of Salary, Status, Skill, and Education

A large status gap existed between the well-paid UAW officials and ordinary members, and this gap widened as oligarchy became entrenched in the 1950s. The creation of the Leadership Studies Center deliberately extended the status, education, and skills gap between officials and members by professionalizing union officials into white-collar managers.[87]

A significant pay gap also existed between AWU members and officials. In 1939, the union's two highest-paid paid officials, the general secretary and the secretary of the giant Queensland Branch, each received one thousand pounds per annum, more than four times the lowest-paid full-time members.[88] As in the UAW, the pay gap increased as oligarchy became further entrenched. Both AWU officials and members had minimal formal education, but the officials developed crucial skills and education on the job, especially in relation to the arbitration system. AWU organizer Tom Dougherty, who went on to serve as the union's general secretary between 1944 and 1972, argued that an ordinary member took three years to become a "competent organiser" because of the "many and varied awards and matters affecting members."[89] Secretaries "had to prepare and present cases to the [arbitration] court" and developed skills similar to those of a lawyer.[90] Members' lack of understanding of the complicated arbitration system made them dependent on officials and removed the rank and file from the bargaining process. Again, this was similar to what happened in the UAW, where officials negotiated complicated national contracts that most members did not understand.

Affiliation with the ALP exacerbated the status gap between AWU members and leaders. Control of the AWU brought power within the ALP in the form of delegates and representatives on the party's governing bodies, and many AWU officials also became ALP politicians. Leaders gained further status and became more desperate to keep their union positions even if doing so meant resorting to undemocratic means. While most Australian unions were directly affiliated with the ALP, Taft-Hartley barred US unions from contributing membership dues to political parties or candidates.[91] Reuther had hoped to earn power within the Democratic Party through the UAW's ability to convince its members and other workers to vote for the party. However, new media such as television undermined Reuther's plans by allowing the party to appeal over his head to the members directly.[92]

Like their UAW counterparts, the AWU leaders professionalized themselves and deliberately distinguished themselves from the ordinary members, playing on the hierarchical and aspirational aspects of the union's culture. Photographs in union publications featured leaders in expensive suits, fraternizing with elites.[93] Dissident Ernest Lane referred disparagingly to the leadership group as "the AWU high priests." The officials built a pseudoreligious cult of leadership, making pilgrimages to the graves of former leaders and the hotel in Ballarat where the union had been founded. The death of a leading official commonly resulted in a call for donations to build a memorial in his honor.[94]

Free Communication

UAW leaders tightly controlled union communication. The president appointed the Education Department's director and the regional representatives who controlled the department, giving him enormous power.[95] By the early 1950s, Reuther also controlled the supervising executive board, further increasing his power.

UAW communication was easily the most advanced of any Australian or US union in this period. The Education Department produced a monthly union magazine, *Solidarity*, various other printed material, and the Detroit UAW *Eye Opener* radio and television programs. It also ran education courses and conventions for members and officials and organized social activities and community outreach.[96]

The Education Department used techniques from professional media and advertising to make its propaganda as stimulating and engaging as possible. It also employed advanced applied psychology and social science techniques to communicate with members and shape their opinions. The union conducted opinion polling of members and targeted propaganda at "opinion makers" within work groups.[97]

AWU officials also closely controlled communication within the union. The key sources of official AWU communication were its labor newspapers, most importantly the *Worker* in Queensland; the *Australian Worker* in New South Wales, Victoria, South Australia, and Tasmania; and the *Westralian Worker* in Western Australia. In contrast to the UAW's sophisticated propaganda techniques, the AWU leaders used the blunt tactics of censorship and suppression, an approach that succeeded because the union lacked the strong occupational community and democratic culture of the early UAW. The UAW leaders needed advanced techniques to control union communication to overturn the early UAW's strong occupational community and democratic culture.

Conclusion

Despite their differences in context and strategy, both the UAW and AWU became oligarchies. The fact that the AWU and other new unions were more common in Australia inhibited the formation of strong occupational communities and union democracy. But occupational communities in the United States were similarly eroded through the deskilling of jobs by employers, authoritarian leadership by union officials, and national collective bargaining as a consequence of the combined efforts of employers and union officials. The AWU's affiliation with the ALP had both positive and negative effects on union democracy. Compulsory arbitration devastated union democracy in the AWU in much the same way that national collective bargaining affected the UAW. The UAW was more racially divided than the AWU but the Australian union was more divided by occupation. Leaders in both the AWU and UAW engaged in extensive red-baiting against their militant opponents, but that approach garnered more success in the United States, where the anticommunist movement was stronger.

By the 1950s the UAW had abandoned its foundational militancy and become more like the AWU. Both unions tied themselves to a moderate, reformist political party and a system of peaceful industrial bargaining that did not involve ordinary members. Members of both unions merely paid their dues, voted for the ALP or Democratic Party, and left employment negotiations to the leadership. The leaders of the UAW and AWU had become a new elite, with more in common with employers than with the workers in their own unions, just as Michels predicted. These top-down tactics appeared to work well for the UAW and AWU as well as for many other US and Australian unions during the postwar boom but left them weak and unable to respond effectively to the challenges posed by deindustrialization. This weakness contributed to the dramatic decline of unionism in both countries since the 1970s.[98]

Notes

1. Robin Archer, *Why Is There No Labor Party in the United States?* (Princeton: Princeton University Press, 2007), 236.

2. Kay Stratton, "Union Democracy in the I.T.U.: Thirty Years Later," *Journal of Labor Research* 10 (1989): 119–34; Matthew Mettler, "Social Science and Solidarity: Psychology,

Organizational Reform, and Democracy in Walter Reuther's U.A.W." (PhD diss., University of Iowa, 2013); Mark Hearn and Harry Knowles, *One Big Union: A History of the Australian Workers' Union, 1886–1994* (Melbourne: Cambridge University Press, 1996), 136.

3. Margaret Levi, David Olson, Jon Agnone, and Devin Kelly, "Union Democracy Reexamined," *Politics and Society* 37 (2009): 205; Kim Voss, "Democratic Dilemmas: Union Democracy and Union Renewal," *Transfer: European Review of Labour Research* 16 (2010): 372.

4. Richard Hyman, *Marxism and the Sociology of Trade Unionism* (London: Pluto, 1971), 14; Robert Michels, *Political Parties: A Sociological Study of the Oligarchical Tendencies of Modern Democracy* (1911; Kitchener: Batoche, 2001), 30.

5. Hyman, *Marxism*, 29–32.

6. Voss, "Democratic Dilemmas," 372.

7. Seymour Martin Lipset, Martin Trow, and James Coleman, *Union Democracy: The Internal Politics of the International Typographical Union* (Glencoe, Ill.: Free Press, 1956), 415; Levi et al., "Union Democracy Reexamined," 207, 209.

8. Lipset, Trow, and Coleman, *Union Democracy*, 415; Levi et al., "Union Democracy Reexamined," 207, 209, 213.

9. Lipset, Trow, and Coleman, *Union Democracy*, 416.

10. Ibid., 415; Levi et al., "Union Democracy Reexamined," 209.

11. Lipset, Trow, and Coleman, *Union Democracy*, 416; Levi et al., "Union Democracy Reexamined," 207.

12. Nelson Lichtenstein, "Auto Worker Militancy and the Structure of Factory Life, 1937–1955," *Journal of American History* 67 (1980): 350.

13. Mettler, "Social Science and Solidarity," 107.

14. Ibid., 101.

15. William A. Faunce, "Delegate Attitudes toward the Convention in the U.A.W.," *Industrial and Labor Relations Review* 15 (1962): 464.

16. Mettler, "Social Science and Solidarity," 115.

17. Ibid., 102.

18. John Merritt, *The Making of the AWU* (Melbourne: Oxford University Press, 1986), 1, 98.

19. AWU Annual Convention Report, *Worker*, 5 February 1920.

20. Hearn and Knowles, *One Big Union*, 7.

21. Jim Hagan, *The History of the ACTU* (Melbourne: Longman Cheshire, 1981), 6–10.

22. Hearn and Knowles, *One Big Union*, 179.

23. Faunce, "Delegate Attitudes," 466.

24. Mettler, "Social Science and Solidarity," 112.

25. AWU Annual Convention Report, *Australian Worker*, 23 January 1924.

26. Rule 63, AWU Constitution and General Rules, 1909–10, AWU, E154/1–2, Noel Butlin Archives Centre, Australian Capital Territory.

27. Rule 66, AWU Constitution and General Rules, 1919–20, in ibid.

28. AWU Annual Convention Report, *Australian Worker*, 12 April 1917; AWU Annual Convention Report, *Australian Worker*, 14 June 1917.

29. AWU Annual Convention Report, *Australian Worker*, 25 February 1915; AWU Annual Convention Report, *Australian Worker*, 22 March 1917; Rule 55, AWU Constitution and General Rules, 1909–10, AWU, E154/1–2, Butlin Archives.

30. AWU Annual Convention Report, *Australian Worker*, 17 February 1937.

31. S58D, s58E *Commonwealth Conciliation and Arbitration Act* (1904).

32. "Federal Arbitration Court Decision in the O'Sullivan Case," *Australian Worker*, 8 June 1938.

33. Mettler, "Social Science and Solidarity," 114.

34. Lichtenstein, "Auto Worker Militancy," 336, 337, 352, 353.

35. Mettler, "Social Science and Solidarity," 279.

36. Lichtenstein, "Auto Worker Militancy," 341.

37. Lipset, Trow, and Coleman, *Union Democracy*, 18–23.

38. Ibid., 342.

39. David Lewis-Colman, *Race against Liberalism: Black Workers and the UAW in Detroit* (Urbana: University of Illinois Press, 2008), 5.

40. Lichtenstein, "Auto Worker Militancy," 341.

41. Elizabeth Fones-Wolf, "No Laughing Matter: The UAW and Gender Construction on Labor Radio in Fifties' America," *Labor* 8 (2011): 87.

42. Ibid.

43. Lewis-Colman, *Race against Liberalism*, 65.

44. Kevin Boyle, *The UAW and the Heyday of American Liberalism, 1945–1968* (Ithaca: Cornell University Press, 1996), 7.

45. Ibid., 6.

46. Lichtenstein, "Auto Worker Militancy," 347.

47. Mark Hearn, "Mates and Strangers: The Ethos of the Australian Workers Union," in *Australian Labour History Reconsidered*, ed. David Palmer, Ross Shanahan, and Martin Shanahan (Adelaide: Australian Humanities Press, 1999), 27.

48. Timothy Rory O'Malley, "Mateship and Money-Making: Shearing in Twentieth Century Australia" (PhD diss., University of Sydney, 2009), 13.

49. Archer, *Why Is There No Labor Party?*, 34; David Montgomery, "The 'New Unionism' and the Transformation of Workers' Consciousness in America, 1909–22," *Journal of Social History* 7 (1974): 509.

50. Archer, *Why Is There No Labor Party?*, 36, 237.

51. Hearn and Knowles, *One Big Union*, 147.

52. Archer, *Why Is There No Labor Party?*, 37, 39.

53. "A Port Kembla Grievance," *Illawarra Mercury*, 11 January 1924.

54. "Port Kembla," *South Coast Times and Wollongong Argus*, 22 July 1927; "AWU Members Locked Out," *Australian Worker*, 13 August 1924.

55. Judith Stepan-Norris, "The Making of Union Democracy," *Social Forces* 76 (1997): 475–510.

56. Hearn and Knowles, *One Big Union*, 7.

57. John Merritt, "Shearers, Mountain Stockmen, and the Australian Legend," *Journal of Australian Colonial History* 10 (2008): 59, 63.

58. Hearn and Knowles, *One Big Union*, 37.

59. Lipset, Trow, and Coleman, *Union Democracy*, 145.

60. Lichtenstein, "Auto Worker Militancy," 339.

61. Mettler, "Social Science and Solidarity," 102.

62. Ibid., 6–7.

63. Ibid., 147.

64. Stephen Meyer, *"Stalin over Wisconsin": The Making and Unmaking of Militant Unionism, 1900–1950* (New Brunswick, N.J.: Rutgers University Press, 1992), 194, 198.

65. Rule 6, General Rules and By-Laws of the Amalgamated Shearers Union of Australasia, 1890, 24430423, National Library of Australia, Australian Capital Territory.

66. Hearn and Knowles, *One Big Union*, 29.

67. AWU Annual Convention Report, *Australian Worker*, 17 February 1937; AWU Annual Convention Report, *Australian Worker*, 16 March 1938.

68. Voss, "Democratic Dilemmas," 374.

69. Ray Markey, "Trade Union Democracy and the Labor Party in N.S.W., 1880–1914," *Historical Studies* 22 (1986): 89.

70. Peter Sheldon, "System and Strategy: The Changing Face of Unionism among N.S.W. Construction Labourers," *Labour History* 65 (1993): 124, 129.

71. Harry Knowles, "Arthur Rae: A 'Napoleon' in Exile," *Labour History* 87 (2004): 103; Andrew Moore, "The Pastoral Workers' Industrial Union, 1930–37," *Labour History* 49 (1985): 74.

72. See Peter Clayworth, this volume.

73. Faunce, "Delegate Attitudes," 466.

74. AWU Annual Convention Report, *Australian Worker*, 25 February 1926.

75. Christopher Tomlins, *The State and the Unions* (Cambridge: Cambridge University Press, 1985), 322.

76. Devin Kelly and Jon Agnone, "I.L.W.U. Contract Negotiations: The Confluence of Politics, Economics, and Labor" (2010), available at https://depts.washington.edu/pcls/documents/research/AgnoneKelly_ILWUContract.pdf.

77. Clyde Cameron, introduction to Merritt, *Making of the AWU*, xiii; Angelo Panebianco, *Political Parties: Organisation and Power* (Cambridge: Cambridge University Press, 1988), 32, 41.

78. Lipset, Trow, and Coleman, *Union Democracy*, 238.

79. Mettler, "Social Science and Solidarity," 109.

80. Meyer, *"Stalin over Wisconsin,"* 11, 197.

81. Stepan-Norris, "Making of Union Democracy," 486–87.

82. "Bushworkers Propaganda Group," *Worker*, 12 March 1925.

83. AWU Annual Convention, *Australian Worker*, 6 February 1929.

84. Jennifer Luff, *Commonsense Anticommunism: Labor and Civil Liberties between the World Wars* (Chapel Hill: University of North Carolina Press, 2012); Randi Storch, *Red*

Chicago: American Communism at Its Grassroots, 1928–35 (Urbana: University of Illinois Press, 2008).

85. "'Bosses' and Alleged 'Moderation,'" *Labor Daily*, 15 July 1927.

86. Scott Stephenson, "'Ballot-Faking Crooks and a Tyrannical Executive': The Australian Workers Union Faction and the 1923 New South Wales Labor Party Annual Conference," *Labour History* 105 (2013): 93–111.

87. Mettler, "Social Science and Solidarity," 289.

88. "Hobart Conference of AWU," *Advertiser*, January 1937; "£1000 Year Salary for Mr Fallon," *Courier-Mail*, 24 January 1939.

89. AWU Annual Convention Report, *Australian Worker*, 23 March 1938.

90. Ibid., 16 March 1938.

91. Mettler, "Social Science and Solidarity," 218.

92. Ibid., 228.

93. Central Branch Annual Report, 31 May 1928, 31 May 1930, AWU, E154/41/1, Butlin Archives.

94. Ernest Henry Lane, *Dawn to Dusk: Reminiscences of a Rebel* (Brisbane: Brooks, 1939), 305.

95. Mettler, "Social Science and Solidarity," 110.

96. Ibid., 116, 113.

97. Ibid., 115.

98. Boyle, *UAW*, 2.

The Experience of Labor in the Age of Reform

Workers' Subjectivity, Welfare Legislation, and Liberal Hegemony in 1930s Australia and the United States

BENJAMIN HUF

Both Australia and the United States are often described as political societies characterized by their "liberal hegemony."[1] Historians in both countries have invoked this liberality to distinguish the "exceptional" political development of these former British colonial societies from the social democratic traditions of their European forebears. In America, this has classically taken the form of Louis Hartz's thesis of a historical "consensus" around "Lockean individualism." In Australia, it centers on a settlement involving a more state-interventionist but nonetheless individualist "Benthamite ideology."[2] The unique development of American and Australian social policy is often cited as one of the most striking expressions of this liberal exceptionalism. In America, according to these generalizations, a small government ethos and "weak" labor movement retarded the formation of the welfare-state until the 1930s, and even then these programs were minimal (or "liberal" or "market-oriented") in comparison to Europe.[3] In Australia, the pioneering wage legislation and arbitration system initiated by a liberal-paternalist state immediately after Federation in 1901 set its social policy development on a unique trajectory that comparative policy analyst Francis Castles has called "the wage-earners welfare-state." Here, according to this argument, social policy was determined by the maintenance of "fair" wages rather than redistribution as in Europe (and later America).[4]

Reconciling this notion of liberal hegemony with the political role and identity of the working class has long presented a recurring common problem for labor historians in both countries. In the early twentieth century, foreign observers were among the first to comment on what appeared to be the anomalous features of working-class politics in these modern liberal democracies. Werner Sombart famously asked, "Why is there no socialism in the United States?," and Albert Métin described the strange compound of social protection and the culture of individualism in the newly federated Australia as "socialism without doctrine." Such typologies would cast a long shadow over the labor historiography in both countries.[5] Following Sombart and Métin, successive generations of American and Australian labor historians attempted to explain these anomalies by deploying essentialist understandings of the "working class" that were usually informed by a shallow Marxism or European experience, that presumed a predetermined pattern of historical development, and that prescribed how workers and the labor movement ought to look and act. When measured against these standards, the Australian and US labor movements repeatedly appeared exceptional or problematic. From the 1960s, under the New Left and neo-Marxist reinterpretations of labor history, such theoretical commitments (or assumptions) led many observers repeatedly to lament the "failure" of the Australian and US working classes to realize their "true ends" or their "betrayal" by labor leaders.[6] Again, these readings were often explored in the history of the welfare state. A generation of labor historians came to see social security in the United States and arbitrated wages in Australia not as a triumph of working-class agitation, as it might have been in Europe, but as an expression of bourgeois or liberal-capitalist control, coercion, or consent.[7]

These interpretations have not held firm. Such approaches have been challenged over their reductive treatment of "class" and "class experience," which often led to a cynical account of the politics of the American and Australian working classes.[8] These critiques have ignited a process of intense revision over the past two decades in both countries. Following the pioneering work of Gareth Stedman Jones and Patrick Joyce in British labor studies and their appropriation of insights from the "linguistic turn" (but avoiding the same stifling epistemological debates), American and Australian labor historians have approached "class" far more critically and explored the ways working-class identities and experiences have been historically and contingently "constructed."[9] The focus has turned to various working-class language games and idioms, intellectual movements, narrative identity, intellectual biography, and labor's discursive relationship to gender and race.[10] The result has been a much more critical, fine-grained understanding of the ways in which unique working-class experiences have been produced in America and Australia, opening the possibility of evaluating what workers "did and did not want to accomplish," as Michael Kazin has argued, on their "own terms."[11]

Again utilizing welfare history as a site of inquiry, this chapter continues such reassessments of how labor historians might approach the "problem" of working-class politics in liberal political societies such as the United States and Australia. I compare American and Australian workers' responses to major passages of welfare reform in the 1930s: US president Franklin Roosevelt's Social Security Act (SSA) in 1935 and conservative Australian prime minister Joseph Lyons's commonwealth government's failed attempt to implement a National Health and Pensions Insurance scheme (NI) in 1938. Both of these schemes were to be funded by a contributory principle—a regressive payroll tax on employees and employers—that became contested ground. While European workers had become accustomed to such a principle since the late nineteenth century, prior to the Great Depression, federal policymakers in both Australia and the United States had continued to reject it. Consequently, working-class responses to these proposed contributory schemes, which entailed new social and political rights and responsibilities and challenged existing self-understandings, provide a fertile site to explore how workers understood and expressed their political identity.

This chapter makes a twofold contribution. First, a comparative approach provides added salience to the historicity and contingency of working-class self-understandings, experience, and agency. In so doing, it helps resist recourse to rigid Marxist models or European experience as a standard for interpreting working-class politics and highlights the mutability of working-class subjectivities even in relatively similar political societies such as the United States and Australia. A number of essays in this volume stress the transnational flow and adaptability of working-class ideas and organizational models between these two "liberal" political societies. In particular, Tom Goyens, Peter Clayworth, and Robert Cherny highlight what Clayworth describes as "how workers create international webs, transmitting their experiences and ideologies from one geographical and industrial context to another."[12] In contrast, this chapter emphasizes the difference and variety of working-class identities and experiences in the two countries despite their national similarities.

The second contribution, which forms this chapter's core argument, relates to the ways institutions (and acceptance or resistance to institutional change) help shape working-class self-understandings. Here, I deploy the concept of subjectification or subject formation as a means of exploring this historical process.[13] In a recent but cautious reflection on the impact of "discourse theory" on Australian labor history, Nick Dyrenfurth has rightly suggested that labor historians need to "reconnect" their analysis of the languages of labor with workers' practical (or "material") engagement with institutions (in his case, the ALP) in shaping class "consciousness." Discourses, Dyrenfurth argues, are mediated by the practices of and experiences with institutions, which "works out . . . the shared ontological sense of an imagined . . . national working class."[14] I take Dyrenfurth's point further, exploring the ways in which institutions contribute to this process of subject formation on a much smaller, everyday scale. Subjectivities—our various modes and practices of self-understanding—are constituted, challenged, and reinforced by a range of vocabularies, norms, practices, technologies, and institutions, creating a field of discursive practice that produces meaning and in turn gives meaning to experience. Institutional forms and their reform help disseminate and implant such self-understandings. In the case of the construction of working-class identities, even where labor is not central in reforming institutions (and, aside from American railroad workers, labor was in no way the creative force behind either the SSA or NI), workers are not passively molded in this process of subject formation. Indeed, while labor's political and industrial antagonists greatly influence the parameters of workers' experience, workers' negotiation of these parameters, such as institutional change, affirms or alters their mode of political self-understanding. As Nikolas Rose reminds us, subjects are always active participants in their own subjectification.[15]

Australian workers rejected the contributory principle because it violated an existing mode of political self-understanding—that is, their expectations about the role of government, assumptions about entitlements to an old-age pension, and ultimately their sense of an independent, self-contained political identity, which had been formed thirty years earlier with the institution of arbitrated wages. In America, the contributory principle of the SSA was far more agreeable to workers because no competing institutional architecture existed. Rather than a violation of workers' existing self-understanding, social security enabled American workers to embody a new sense of citizenship, just as Australian workers felt they were defending theirs by rejecting the same principle. These arguments were couched in seemingly liberal language: Australian workers talked of independence and entitlement, as did American workers, who began to conceive of themselves as consumer-citizens. But independence was not necessarily synonymous with liberal individualism or consenting to some mode of status quo. As Gary Gerstle has argued, American workers' adoption of the middle-class language of "Americanism" in the 1930s reflected their political empowerment and agency to appropriate mainstream idioms for their own ends.[16] Ultimately, in both cases, workers affirmed a conception of their working selfhood that became characteristic of the post–World War II decades—that of the white, male breadwinning "citizen wage-earner."[17]

The Social Security Act and National Insurance may seem like odd measures to compare. The former became the cornerstone of the American welfare state, while the latter was a failed experiment before the ALP implemented its enduring reforms in the 1940s. And, indeed, little links the two schemes transnationally. Although Lloyd Churchward has noted that the New Deal captured "considerable interest and even enthusiasm" in Australia (and Australian newspapers certainly watched its reforms closely), the SSA had no influence on the Australian plan, which was modeled on the British scheme and designed by a British bureaucrat.[18] American workers' general celebration of social security was not echoed in Australian workers' attitude toward NI. Considerable differences also existed between the two schemes. SSA was notable for its unemployment insurance and absence of health insurance; the inverse was true of NI. Despite these differences, their central, common feature—the contributory principle and workers' reaction to it—makes them rich for comparison. I first analyze American responses to the SSA and then contrast those responses with Australian workers' reactions to NI. These comparisons are only general and cannot account for the great regional differences in these respectively vast countries. I then conclude with some general remarks on the potential for further comparative research into the subjectivities of the US and Australian working classes.

American Workers and the Social Security Act

The Social Security Act of 1935 was not, as an earlier generation of historians has argued, a benevolent moment in the "Roosevelt Revolution" of the 1930s; rather, it was a solution to problems aggravated by competing business interests, complex labor relations, and diverse state regulations that had compounded on one another since the end of World War I.[19] After World War I, many employers instituted their own private welfare programs as what Colin Gordon describes as "a means of retaining skilled workers, moderating turnover, encouraging employee loyalty and discouraging unionization."[20] Employers saw this "welfare capitalism" as a relatively inexpensive means of gaining the material consent of workers. Yet by the mid-1920s, the costs of these programs were outstripping the benefits. Business began seeking ways to spread the burden among their competitors and advocated state pension and unemployment laws to enforce more standardized and equitable systems of welfare capitalism in their respective states. By the late 1920s, a patchwork of state laws loosely reflected business goals, creating political and economic problems for the state governments, which had come to business's rescue (particularly in the industrial Northeast and Midwest) and now bore the economic burden of scattered and uncoordinated laws.[21]

The Great Depression brought these fragmented problems into the spotlight of federal politics. The SSA was a solution to these diffuse and inconsistent attempts scattered across the northern United States to instigate some system of social welfare. At the core of this solution was a regressive tax system that meant employers and employees would pay an equal share toward the scheme. The question of compulsory contributions had plagued American policymakers, business, and organized labor for the better part of a quarter century. Yet by the time of the passing of the SSA, contributions had become almost a nonissue for the labor movement. Exploring the ways in which the SSA generally and contributions specifically reconstituted workers' political self-understanding first requires considering how organized labor, especially the American Federation of Labor (AFL), came to terms with the idea of contributory social insurance in the three decades preceding the SSA.

In the early twentieth century, craft unions, hoping to maintain the prerogative of craft autonomy they had enjoyed in the nineteenth century, remained suspicious of any state intervention. They sought self-protection and initiated programs of small-scale aged care relief at the local level. However, the standardization and homogenization of the labor process around the turn of the century undermined craft-union voluntarism. Changes in the mode of production created a rapidly increasing class of semi- and unskilled workers who could not fall back on the same craft tradition for social protection. The result was twofold. First, the nature of unions changed. Craft unions began to relax their admission rules to include a wider range of members. With expanded membership, unions, beginning with the Granite Cutters' International Association in 1905, started initiating broader old-age pension plans. These voluntary schemes grew rapidly and enjoyed wide popularity into the early 1920s, serving for a while as competition to the welfare capitalism developed by employers. The second result, however, pulled in the other direction. Semi- and unskilled workers, under the influence of socialist leaders and state federations of labor, sought more secure protection and advocated state intervention to legislate welfare provision.[22] At the time, the AFL, under the leadership of Samuel Gompers, who maintained old craft-union suspicions of state intervention, continued to support voluntary union pensions. Gompers saw such voluntarism as the basis of union strength and freedom.[23] But by 1917, the AFL leadership had split over the proper role of unions, and some factions opposed Gompers and began advocating compulsory state-instituted social insurance schemes. An even stronger challenge to voluntarism came from William Green, secretary-treasurer of the United Mine Workers as well as a member of the AFL Executive Council with Gompers, arguing for a health, disability, and old insurance program with the costs borne jointly by the employee, the employer, and the state. "Why," asked Green, "should the working people themselves bear this financial burden? . . . Industry and society at large should be required to bear their share of the burden."[24] Labor leaders repeatedly launched such arguments in the coming years, especially in the pages of the *American Labor Legislation Review*.[25] Officially, however, the Gompers-led AFL remained opposed to state pension legislation into the early 1920s. By 1920, union membership had reached all-time highs, and union pension funds were strong. As the decade wore on, however, the strength of voluntarism was undermined by falling union membership, which resulted partly from increasing welfare capitalism (now backed by state legislation) in the northern states.[26] By the middle of the decade, with a falling membership base and thus depleted voluntary contributions, union pension plans became untenable.

Labor thus came to accept the idea of state-backed social insurance on a compulsory contributory model. The AFL's position on state intervention began to shift after Gompers's death in 1924 and Green's election as his successor. By the end of the decade, the AFL had reversed its position regarding state support and come to terms with a contributory scheme.[27] A number of court cases in the 1920s further encouraged this reversal, as workers made a series of legal claims to noncontributory employer pension funds. The majority of early welfare capitalist plans had been noncontributory and discretionary, paid out on the prerogative of the employer. Following appeals of entitlement by a number of groups of workers, the courts gradually accepted private pensions as a contractual right rather than merely discretionary compensation, forcing employers away from noncontributory plans. After 1923, new welfare capitalism pension plans were overwhelmingly contributory and insured.[28]

The contributory principle remained an issue for some reformers when debating social security in 1934–35. Underconsumption was seen as one of the major causes of the depression (a theory with which Roosevelt agreed). Some observers, including supporters of the Lundeen Bill (an alternative social security proposal funded entirely out of an inheritance tax), saw compulsory contributions as likely to sap disposable income, further stifling consumption, and prolonging the depression.[29] Roosevelt, no doubt partly because of his unsuccessful bid for a contributory pension bill while serving as governor of New York, nevertheless went ahead with a contributory scheme.[30] By late 1934, Edwin Witte, executive director of the Committee on Economic Security, which was in charge of implementing the SSA, confidently concluded that "the question of whether insurance should be contributory or non-contributory has almost ceased to be discussed. . . . [I]n the eyes of the workers and of the public in general the contribution is the feature which distinguishes insurance from relief [and] creates a right to benefits."[31] Witte was especially right to note the significance contributions would have for workers' sense of independence.

As passed, the SSA consisted of three different measures, each operating under a different set of principles: an old-age pension and an unemployment insurance plan, each financed entirely by a regressive payroll tax with no government contribution, as well as federal funding for a host of means-tested and state-administered programs.[32] Most accounts of the origins of the SSA agree that the labor movement had little influence on the passage of the legislation. In the early 1930s, organized labor focused its energies on labor legislation, such as the National Industrial Recovery Act and the Wagner Act. The workers who joined mass strikes that flooded the streets of American cities in 1934 were responding to wage cuts and unemployment rather than actively seeking redistribution.[33] The only sector of the labor movement that did organize and campaign for welfare reform was the railroad workers, whose successful bid for the federalization of company pensions with the 1934 and 1935 Railroad Retirement Acts was subsequently overturned by the US Supreme Court.[34]

Despite their absence from the reform process, the language and practice of paying contributions opened up new forms of agency and self-understanding to workers, a phenomenon that found its primary expression in a new sense of working-class political engagement. Recent analysis of opinion polling results has shown the popularity of the SSA among workers in the years immediately after its passage.[35] Historians have also pointed to the results of the 1936 election as proof of workers' endorsement of the program. For a moment, the Democratic Party became the "workers' party." Roosevelt was personally identified as having passed the National Industrial Recovery Act, Wagner Act, and SSA, and he did best in working-class neighborhoods.[36] Eric Davin's case study of working-class political activity in 1930s Pittsburgh reinforces such analyses. Davin concludes that the period featured unprecedented class-consciousness in the United States. Countering neo-Marxist historians who regretted the absence of radicalism in those years, Davin argues that the changes of the 1930s galvanized a coherent and visible working-class self-identity that chose to express itself electorally in the pursuit of a "workers' democracy."[37] (The context of the

Great Depression undoubtedly made possible such political self-expression, which had not previously been available to workers.)

Labor increasingly entered national politics. As historian Nelson Lichtenstein has described, the SSA gave workers "a sense of citizenship," a legitimated place in the liberal polity. Labor's appropriation of the language of consumerism was central to this phenomenon. Lichtenstein sees the New Deal as having worked an "imaginative revolution." Mass consumption complemented production as a foundational component of capitalism and reinvigorated democracy: "The New Deal and the new labor movement took the nascent consumer culture of the twentieth century and made it a political project."[38] In contrast to earlier fears expressed by the advocates of the Lundeen Bill, workers viewed social security as means of helping alleviate the problem of underconsumption. As George Lipsitz has written, "By assuring workers they would have more money available in their old age, social security made it possible for them to engage in less saving and more spending in the present."[39]

This was not simply a matter of massaging workers' "consent" into the liberal-capitalist fold. Analyzing Chicago's industrial classes during the Great Depression, Lizabeth Cohen has found that while workers were never anticapitalist, reforms such as the SSA enabled them to forge a new political identity that did not necessarily mean a loss of sense of membership in a distinct working class, as was evidenced in the innumerable letters sent to Roosevelt and his advisers explicitly on behalf of "working-class people." By voting Democratic, backing the New Deal, and supporting "cross-ethnic working class institutions" such as the Congress of Industrial Organizations, many workers felt that they were affirming an enriched working-class political identity. The SSA, Cohen has argued, was central to this belief: "Despite all the limitations of the Act," such as "the exclusion of many kinds of workers, the small benefits, the administration of much of the system by the states, and the regressive payroll tax that funded it—the Social Security Act made a strong impression on workers who had never before been offered any security by the federal government."[40]

A new sense of political activity and security forged new expectations of the federal government. Old paternalistic expectations, previously situated in the ethnic community or the craft brotherhood, were projected onto the state. In so doing, workers forged a novel notion that they were entitled to benefits from government. Alongside a pattern of state security grew a new claim to rights.[41] Whereas the contributory principle of national insurance violated Australian workers' sense of independence, that principle provided Americans with a way of reinventing the old craft-union ethos of independence. This independence, however, was highly gendered and racialized. As

Nancy Fraser and Linda Gordon have noted, a clear stratification of social security programs existed. Old-age insurance and unemployment insurance were considered first-track programs that disproportionately served white workingmen. Their stipends were relatively high, were offered without means testing, and were received as a matter of entitlement. Because contributions were paid, these first-track programs were not even considered welfare and were spared the pauper-like branding of "dependence."[42] In contrast, second-track benefits, among which Aid to Dependent Children (later Aid to Families with Dependent Children) became the biggest and most well-known, continued "the private charity tradition of searching out the deserving among the many chiselers."[43] Such programs were only partly funded by the federal government, were administered by the states, and were means-tested. The stipends were so low that they placed recipients below the poverty line. These second-track programs particularly targeted women and "minority men," especially after Roosevelt compromised with southern Democrats and excluded domestic and agricultural labor in southern states to guarantee the SSA's passage. As Suzanne Mettler notes, the reconfigured "sense of citizenship" that came out of the New Deal—that is, the "self-governing" sense of independence bestowed by the practice of paying contributions—only reconstituted the political identities of white working men, entrenching the breadwinning male as the subject of American citizenship. Those not included—women and "minority men"—were left as "state citizens," practically and symbolically outside the national polity and exposed to the imbalance of state-run services and support.[44]

Australian Workers and National Insurance

As with the SSA in the United States, the National Health and Pensions Insurance Scheme the conservative Lyons government enacted in 1938 (but never implemented) was no knee-jerk reaction to the Great Depression. It was the culmination of more than two decades of federal government flirtation with a contributory insurance program, and its failure cannot be attributed to the opposition by labor. Rather, opposition from state governments, the medical profession, the farming and women's lobbies, and ultimately disagreement within the cabinet over funding allocation with the likelihood of war in mid-1939 were responsible for the "strange death" of national insurance.[45] However, Australian workers opposed national insurance because the compulsory contribution violated workers' established political identity that was informed by the existing old-age pension and arbitrated wage institutions.

Australian governments since before the First World War had considered contributory social insurance as a measure that might alleviate what liberal reformers thought to be the moral deficiencies and untenable costs of the country's initial welfare program. In 1908, the commonwealth government had introduced an old-age pension scheme that was means-tested to target those most in need. The program was funded entirely from general revenue, which set the development of Australia's social policy on a different trajectory from that of Europe and Britain (and later the United States), where social welfare was established on insurance plans funded by employer, employee, and in some instances government contributions. Early on, government actuaries realized the potentially crippling cost of this means-tested pension scheme, especially as commonwealth revenue amounted to just a fraction of what it became during the Second World War, when the federal treasury rather than state governments finally began receiving most income tax. Contributory-based social insurance plans remained loosely attached to both Labor and non-Labor policy platforms in the interwar years. Between 1913 and 1936, six reports on social insurance schemes were prepared, including one submitted by a royal commission in 1923–27, while the conservative Bruce-Page government tried and failed to implement a program in 1928.[46] The fiscal crisis of the early 1930s again drew attention to the cost of the old-age pension. Economists and treasury officials promoted a contributory scheme as necessary to offset the pension's drain on general revenue, correcting "the mistake of '08."[47]

The proposed scheme was more than a matter of fiscal expediency, however. As Rob Watts has described, it was couched in an ethos of "social liberalism" that was common to both Labor and non-Labor in the interwar period. Reformers expressed concern about the "demoralizing" and "pauperizing" effects of the existing means-tested pension. Contributions, conversely, would encourage "self-respect" among the working class. Treasurer R. G. Casey, who had responsibility for piloting national insurance, thought it an "irreducible minimum component of a 'modern society.'"[48]

The measure passed in July 1938 established compulsory insurance to be administered by "approved societies" for all workers earning under seven pounds a week (well above the commonwealth basic wage of less than two hundred pounds per year)—roughly half the working population. Contributions entitled the wage earner to old-age, sickness, disability, and widow's pensions and medical benefits, covering low-income earners under one equitable scheme. Policymakers ignored the broad international experimentation with social insurance programs in the interwar years, including that of the United States, and relied exclusively on the British example and expertise. (The Australian plan was largely designed by Sir Walter Kinnear, on loan from the Insurance Department in the British Ministry of Health.) This approach contrasted markedly with the research that had gone into developing Australian social and wage policies at the turn of the century.[49] In keeping with Australians' interest in the New Deal, newspapers enthusiastically reported on the SSA's progress, though only to demonstrate how far Australia had fallen behind in social provision.[50] MPs referred to the American model on only a handful of occasions in the long parliamentary debate to pass the bill. The only major intersection between the two plans was when the US government requested Kinnear's services in mid-1938 to help with difficulties in the SSA.[51]

Organized labor's opposition to the plan and in particular to the contributory principle began before the 1937 election (in which the incumbent Lyons put forth the NI as a major policy) with a series of pamphlets rehearsing a redistributive argument that "those most able should pay" for social welfare.[52] John Murphy has characterized this statement as signaling the Labor Party's fundamental disagreement with the contributory model and affirmation of its commitment to the existing trajectory of social policy: "If Labor had been noncommittal on its position to the contributory principle in the 1920s," then John Curtin, the leader of the federal Labor opposition, "had now clarified this stance, laying the intellectual ground work for the reforms in the 1940s."[53]

Curtin's arguments against the contributory principle hinged on two key objections that workers maintained throughout the public debates over national insurance. The first was a rejection that workers should pay for what had already been established as a "right" with the 1908 Old-Age Pensions Act. Both the Australian Workers Union (AWU) and the Australian Council of Trade Unions vehemently protested that government was dissolving the workers' right.[54] The protest made by the Sheet Metal Workers Union at its April 1938 federal convention was typical, declaring the plan "a drastic inroad on the social rights of the Australian people. . . . The maintenance of the workers in old age and incapacity by the State is the inalienable right of the people and must be pressed by the whole labor movement."[55] Labor took contributions to be an attack on worker's self-dependence, which was already safeguarded by pensions and arbitrated wages. Pamphlets opposing the idea warned workers against the "specious language" and "demagogic phraseology" of "self-help" in which reformers framed NI.[56] Again, the response from the Sheet Metal Workers Union was typical: "The specious plea that contributory pensions will mean 'self-respect' for the insured, whereas non-contributory pensions reward the 'thriftless' completes [*sic*] distorts the position of and maligns the great majority of the population."[57]

The second objection to the contributory principle related to its incompatibility with the neighboring institution of arbitrated wages. With its capacity to shift costs, the presence of arbitration muddied arrangements to pay for the plan in a fair way. Curtin argued early on that if workers were to contribute to the scheme, their contributions should be included in the basic wage.[58] Labor's demands immediately prompted employers to retort that Curtin's request meant that employers would end up paying the entire amount.[59] Workers, in turn, argued that employers would absorb the costs by increasing prices, meaning that the workers would pay anyway. The existence of wage arbitration, with its ability to shift costs, thus "exerted a powerful gravitational pull over the policy firmament."[60]

The stalemate also exerted a powerful pull over workers' political imagination and mode of self-understanding. Francis Castles's description of Australia's unique "wage earners welfare state" assists in interpreting workers' attitude toward the contributory principle. Australian social policy necessarily took a different trajectory from that of Europe following the establishment of wage arbitration in the early twentieth century because it built assumptions about the maintenance of fair wages into future social policy decisions. Later policies necessarily had to be residual rather than universal, flat rate rather than earnings related, and paid from general revenue rather than targeted contributions.[61] This functionalist interpretation irritates policy historians because it dissolves the contingency inherent in policy development.[62] But in attempting to understand the historical self-understanding of Australian workers, Castles was right to highlight the deeply ingrained assumption about fair wages projected by the wage legislation established thirty years earlier. Time and again throughout this debate, organized labor and workers protested the "attack" contributions would make on living standards. The liberal claim that the contributory principle promoted workers' independence and self-help gained no traction with Australian workers. Independence was already tied to wage security (as was entitlement to the pension). For workers to find national insurance acceptable, "the existing architecture of policy—both the age-pension and arbitrated wages—had to be either built around, renovated or demolished, and what had already been constructed shaped both what could be imagined and what could be achieved."[63]

The resonance of such views with individual workers became especially visible when the union movement suddenly abandoned its protest against the plan. In August 1938, the Lyons government began putting in place the machinery to operate the program, including inviting friendly societies and unions to become "approved societies" to help in administration. The trades halls and labor councils in the states embraced this offer, as did the AWU and Australian Council of Trade Unions, encouraging smaller affiliated unions to create approved societies or have workers join larger national ones.[64] The vitriolic protest against the NI evaporated from the AWU's mouthpiece, the *Australian Worker*, and was replaced by advertisements justifying the creation of approved societies.[65] Union officials insisted that they still objected to the idea of contributory national insurance but felt because the plan had become law, they had a duty to protect workers. Affiliate unions and individual workers disagreed. The AWU's July 1939 annual general meeting reflected a general sense of betrayal, with one delegate moving that the "Executive of the AWU be censured for endorsing the National Insurance Scheme as the AWU should be the last to support such a rotten measure." Another declared that the plan "was not in the interests of the people of Australia," while a third described it as lacking "any genuine benefit to the workers" and demanded "the repeal of this political trick."[66]

The high point of worker agitation came in the form of a remarkable campaign in which individual workers printed, distributed, signed, and sent letters to federal members of parliament. Echoing Curtin's arguments from the previous year, these letters objected to the NI's "drastic lowering of the already low standard of living of the majority of people of Australia" and voiced resentment that the scheme had not been passed by referendum and had thus been "imposed upon the people without their consent."[67] Such complaints ignored the fact that Lyons had made the policy part of his successful platform in the previous election. The movement quickly spread up the Australian east coast as workplaces, small businesses, and individuals joined in. By November, 250,000 letters had been sent from Victoria alone.[68] It is difficult to ascertain the driving forces behind the campaign, and evidence indicates that an unlikely mix of the Communist Party, social credit organizations, and even the doctors' lobby facilitated the distribution of letters to workers.[69] Whatever the effort's origins, members of parliament took it seriously. The opposition taunted Casey for receiving more letters than Hollywood superstar Clark Gable. Robert Menzies, who later served seven terms (in two stints) as Australia's prime minister, responded to every letter he received.[70]

These experiences are consistent with a broader literature that has described the political self-understanding of Australian workers in this period. Stuart Macintyre has demonstrated how an "ingrained attachment to independence and self-sufficiency" that ran "through the whole working class" stifled state governments' attempts to implement any unemployment relief program in the 1920s and continued to hinder such plans even into the 1930s.[71] Despite being steeped in the language of self-reliance, the contributory model of national insurance was similarly castigated. Labor deemed appeals to self-reliance as specious precisely because workers already understood themselves as self-dependent citizens. Writing in 1933, Frederic Eggleston, an ALP sympathizer and advocate of progressive social reform, famously described "the average worker" as a "self-contained man."[72]

Paradoxically, however, the invisible paternalism established by the early century wage legislation and the old-age pension is precisely what enabled workers to maintain this independent self-understanding. Wage regulation underwrote the sense of self-sufficiency. As W. K. Hancock noted in 1930, "To the Australian, the State means collective power at the service of individualistic 'rights.' Therefore he sees no opposition between his individualism and his reliance upon government."[73] Hancock's observation might lead to the belief that workers should have gravitated toward national insurance, but he was referring to precisely the wage institutions and legislation that serviced Australian workers' "individualism." The contributions compelled by national insurance upset the balance of this existing arrangement.

Peering slightly into the future reveals the delicacy of this balance. Ann Firth has shown that the Australian welfare state created by Labor governments and economists in the 1940s was designed on the recognition of male workers' conceptions of themselves as independent breadwinners and thus emphasized full employment rather than wealth distribution, soothing primary fears of joblessness and appealing to the sense of masculine independence.[74] Something of a congruence exists with the way white, male American workers came to conceive of themselves politically following the SSA's implementation. Institutional reform shaped these subjectivities. The legitimation of the independent, breadwinning male identity in Australian social policy in the 1940s had broader social implications, of course, but it garnered the support of male wage earners in a way national insurance could not. Taking its cues from the existing policy paradigm, the 1940s welfare state, which remained means-tested and funded from general revenue, reaffirmed the existing compact between workers and the state, whereas the contributory principle threatened that arrangement.

Conclusion

Over the past two decades, American and Australian labor historians have challenged older understandings of their countries' working classes by deploying a range of analytic tools to understand the construction of workers' political identity through discursive practices. This approach has helped overcome an older problem in which by maintaining essentialist conceptions of a working class, labor historiography puzzled over the seemingly anomalous experience of labor in liberal societies such as the United States and Australia. A comparative analysis of the political experiences of American and Australian workers adds a dimension to this revision process.

Labor historians' slowly increasing appropriation of poststructuralist analysis has been accompanied by a healthy critique of "class" as a category of historical and social analysis. While this has eased the overt class politics of some labor history, as the gender and race turn has demonstrated, clear and pressing political projects nevertheless abound in the subdiscipline. The comparative approach used here, with its focus on the way institutions help constitute workers' self-understandings, points in one such direction. Historical comparison of workers' subjectification in the United States and Australia emphasizes the possibilities of working-class experience in liberal-capitalist societies, which need not adhere to or fulfill Marxian prophecies. Such insights link up to broader theoretical projects regarding the possibilities of institutional alternatives within capitalist society. As Roberto Unger has written, ideas about achieving institutional alternatives remain inhibited by theoretical assumptions that have shaped much of classical social theory. Similar to the essentialist ways labor historians have until recently thought about class, capitalism and its historical alternatives such as feudalism and socialism are still too often assumed to be indivisible systems, standing or falling as a whole and appearing to possess law-like characteristics. Such "false necessities," to use Unger's term, derail the possibility of imagining more democratic, enriching forms of social life and the subjectivities they would entail.[75] Comparative, historical reflection on the mutable self-understandings and experiences of workers as they have been shaped by institutional change offers one way of helping break though such impasses.

Notes

1. The claim is, of course, not without contest. For an overview of debates surrounding other dominant intellectual traditions in these polities, see, Joyce Oldham Appleby, *Liberalism and Republicanism in the Historical Imagination* (Cambridge: Harvard University Press, 1992) (for the United States); Graham Maddox, "Australian Democracy and the Compound Republic," *Pacific Affairs* 73 (2000): 193–207 (for Australia).

2. Louis Hartz, *The Liberal Tradition in America* (New York: Harcourt, Brace, 1955); Hugh Collins, "Political Ideology in Australia: The Distinctiveness of a Benthamite Society," *Daedalus* 114 (1985): 147–69.

3. As classically formulated in Gøsta Esping-Andersen, *The Three Worlds of Welfare Capitalism* (New York: Wiley, 2013).

4. Francis Castles, *The Working Class and Welfare: Reflections on the Political Development of the Welfare State in Australia and New Zealand, 1890–1980* (Sydney: Allen and Unwin, 1985), 102–9.

5. Werner Sombart, *Why Is There No Socialism in the United States?* (London: Macmillan, 1976); Albert Métin, *Socialism without Doctrine* (Sydney: Alternative, 1977).

6. For an overview of "essentialist" readings of class in American labor historiography before the 1980s, see Herbert Gutman, *Power and Culture: Essays on the American Working Class* (New York: New Press, 1992), 342–44; Stuart Macintyre, "The Making of the Australian Working Class: An Historiographical Survey," *Historical Studies* 18 (1978): 233–53 (for Australia). Until the middle of the twentieth century, a "radical-nationalist" interpretation of Australian history upheld the labor movement as the prime mover of social progress and reform.

7. See, for example, Mike Davis's indicatively titled *Prisoners of the American Dream: Politics and Economy in the History of the U.S. Working Class* (London: Verso, 1986); K. D. Buckley and E. L. Wheelwright, *No Paradise for Workers: Capitalism and the Common People in Australia, 1788–1914* (Melbourne: Oxford University Press, 1988).

8. For an overview of these critiques, see Macintyre, "Making of the Australian Working Class"; Michael Kazin, "Struggling with Class Struggle: Marxism and the Search for a Synthesis of U.S. Labor History," *Labor History* 28 (1987): 497–514.

9. Frank Bongiorno, "Australian Labour History: Contexts, Trends, and Influences," *Labour History* 100 (2011): 12. These explorations have not occurred without critical reflection, however. See Sean Scalmer, "Experience and Discourse: A Map of Recent Theoretical Approaches to Labour and Social History," *Labour History* 70 (1996): 156–68. Greater resistance arose in America: see, for example, Bryan Palmer, *Descent into Discourse: The Reification of Language and the Writing of Social History* (Philadelphia: Temple University Press, 1990).

10. For an overview of these research directions, see Lenard R. Berlanstein, *Rethinking Labor History: Essays on Discourse and Class Analysis* (Urbana: University of Illinois Press, 1993); Donna T. Haverty-Stacke and Daniel J. Walkowitz, eds., *Rethinking U.S. Labor History: Essays on the Working-Class Experience, 1756–2009* (New York: Continuum, 2010); Nick Dyrenfurth, "Rethinking Labor Tradition: Synthesising Discourse and Experience," *Labour History* 90 (2006): 177–99.

11. Kazin, "Struggling with Class Struggle," 509.

12. See Peter Clayworth, this volume.

13. Nikolas Rose, "Identity, Genealogy, History," in *Questions of Cultural Identity*, ed. Stuart Hall and Paul du Gay (London: Sage, 1996): 128–50. *Subjectification* is used here not to imply domination or subordination but as a critical tool to designate processes of being made up.

14. Dyrenfurth, "Rethinking Labor Tradition," 185.

15. Nikolas Rose, *Inventing Ourselves: Psychology, Power, and Personhood* (Cambridge: Cambridge University Press, 1998).

16. Gary Gerstle, *Working-Class Americanism: The Politics of Labor in a Textile City, 1914–1960* (New York: Cambridge University Press, 1989).

17. Carole Pateman, "The Patriarchal Welfare State," in *The Welfare State Reader*, ed. Christopher Pierson and Francis Castles (Cambridge: Polity, 2006): 134–74.

18. Lloyd Churchward, *Australia and America* (Sydney: Alternative, 1979), 140.

19. See Jacob S. Hacker, "Bringing the Welfare State Back In: The Promise (and Perils) of the New Social Welfare History," *Journal of Policy History* 17 (2005): 125–54. On the compromises the Roosevelt administration made to guarantee the passage of the SSA, see Ira Katznelson, *Fear Itself: The New Deal and the Origins of Our Time* (New York: Liveright, 2013).

20. Colin Gordon, *New Deals: Business, Labor, and Politics in America, 1920–1935* (New York: Cambridge University Press, 1994), 241.

21. Ibid., 240–61.

22. Jill S. Quadagno, *The Transformation of Old Age Security: Class and Politics in the American Welfare State* (Chicago: University of Chicago Press, 1988), 51–76.

23. On Gompers's opposition to any sort of compulsion in labor relations, see Archer, this volume.

24. Samuel Gompers, "Voluntary Social Insurance vs. Compulsory," *American Federationist* 23 (1916): 33–57, 669–81; William Green, "Trade Union Sick Funds and Compulsory Health Insurance," *American Labor Legislation Review* 7 (1917): 91–110.

25. For example, "Recent American Opinion in Favor of Health Insurance," *American Labor Legislation Review* 6 (1916): 345–52.

26. Union membership peaked in 1920 at just over 5 million, almost 20 percent of the nonagricultural workforce. By 1929 it had declined to 3.6 million, barely 10 percent (Quadagno, *Transformation*, 54–55).

27. Ibid., 71, 108; Gordon, *New Deals*, 245.

28. Gordon, *New Deals*, 254.

29. Mark H. Leff, "Taxing the 'Forgotten Man': The Politics of Social Security Finance in the New Deal," *Journal of American History* 70 (1983): 359–81.

30. Quadagno, *Transformation*, 109.

31. Quoted in Colin Gordon, *Dead on Arrival: The Politics of Health Care in Twentieth-Century America* (Princeton: Princeton University Press, 2009), 93.

32. Jill S. Quadagno, "Welfare Capitalism and the Social Security Act of 1935," *American Sociological Review* 49 (1984): 632–47.

33. J. Craig Jenkins and Barbara G. Brents, "Social Protest, Hegemonic Competition, and Social Reform: A Political Struggle Interpretation of the Origins of the American Welfare State," *American Sociological Review* 54 (1989): 891–909.

34. Jon R. Huibregtse, *Working in the Americas : American Railroad Labor and the Genesis of the New Deal, 1919–1935* (Gainesville: University Press of Florida, 2010), 92–105.

35. Eric Schickler and Devin Caughey, "Public Opinion, Organized Labor, and the Limits of New Deal Liberalism, 1936–1945," *Studies in American Political Development* 25 (2011): 162–89.

36. Rhonda F. Levine, *Class Struggle and the New Deal: Industrial Labor, Industrial Capital, and the State* (Lawrence: University Press of Kansas, 1988).

37. Eric Davin, *Crucible of Freedom: Workers' Democracy in the Industrial Heartland, 1914–1960* (Lanham, Md.: Lexington, 2012).

38. Nelson Lichtenstein, *State of the Union: A Century of American Labor* (Princeton: Princeton University Press, 2013), 25–26; Lizabeth Cohen, "The New Deal State and Making of Citizen Consumers," in *Getting and Spending: European and American Consumer Societies in the Twentieth Century*, ed. Susan Strasser, Charles McGovern, and Matthias Judt (Cambridge: Cambridge University Press, 1998), 111–26.

39. George Lipsitz, "Consumer Spending as State Project," in *Getting and Spending*, ed. Strasser, McGovern, and Judt, 131.

40. Lizabeth Cohen, *Making a New Deal: Industrial Workers in Chicago, 1919–1939* (New York: Cambridge University Press, 1990), 272, 285–87.

41. Ibid., 285.

42. Nancy Fraser and Linda Gordon, "A Genealogy of Dependency: Tracing a Keyword of the U.S. Welfare State," *Signs* 19 (1994): 309–36.

43. Ibid., 321.

44. Suzanne Mettler, *Dividing Citizens: Gender and Federalism in New Deal Public Policy* (Ithaca: Cornell University Press, 1998).

45. Rob Watts, *The Foundations of the National Welfare State* (Sydney: Allen and Unwin, 1987), 21–25.

46. T. H. Kewley, *Social Services in Australia, 1900–1972* (Sydney: Sydney University Press, 1973), 130–69.

47. See, for example, F. A. W. Gisborne, "Australia's Pension Burden," *Australian Quarterly* 3 (1931): 93–101. For an overview of these debates, see Watts, *Foundations*, 9–13.

48. Quoted in Rob Watts, "Light on the Hill: The Origins of the Australian Welfare State, 1935–1945," (PhD diss., University of Melbourne, 1983), 94.

49. John Murphy, "Path Dependence and the Stagnation of Australian Social Policy between the Wars," *Journal of Policy History* 22 (2010): 463.

50. See, for example, *Sydney Telegraph*, 22 July 1838.

51. *Melbourne Age*, 31 May 1938.

52. John Curtin, *Labor's Challenge: Why Australia Should Vote out the Lyons Government: Case against an Incompetent Coalition* (Canberra: Australian Labor Party, 1937); W. H. Mackenzie and Matt Hyde, *National Insurance, a Burning Question: Lyons Government and the Experts, Another Barefaced Swindle* (Sydney: State Unemployed and Relief Workers' Council of NSW, 1937); T. Wright, *A Real Social Insurance Plan* (Sydney: Communist Party of Australia, 1937).

53. John Murphy, *A Decent Provision: Australian Welfare Policy, 1870–1949* (Surrey: Ashgate, 2011), 191; Australian Labor Party, *Why Labor Opposed the Lyons Government's National Insurance Scheme and How it Could be Improved* (Canberra: Federal Parliamentary Labor Party, 1938).

54. *Sydney Australian Worker*, 30 March 1938.

55. Federal Council Meeting Minutes, 19 April 1938, Papers of Sheet Metal Workers Union, N24–51, Noel Butlin Archives Centre, Australian National University.

56. *Melbourne Argus*, 20 April 1938; Mackenzie and Hyde, *National Insurance*, 33.

57. Federal Council Meeting Minutes, 19 April 1938, Papers of Sheet Metal Workers Union, N24–51, Noel Butlin Archives Centre, Australian National University.

58. *Melbourne Argus*, 25 November 1937, 30 April 1938.

59. *Sydney Taxpayers' Bulletin*, May 1938; *Sydney Morning Herald*, 2 May 1938.

60. Murphy, *Decent Provision*, 202.

61. Ibid., 201.

62. Rob Watts, "Ten Years On: Francis G. Castles and the Australian 'Wage-Earners' Welfare State,'" *Journal of Sociology* 33 (1997): 1–15.

63. Murphy, *Decent Provision*, 201.

64. *Brisbane Courier Mail*, 27 October 1938.

65. For unions withdrawing protest, see *Melbourne Argus*, 27 August 1939; *Adelaide Advertiser*, 5 November 1938.

66. Australian Workers' Union, *Official Report of the 53rd Annual Convention* (Sydney: Australian Workers' Union, 1939), 109–15.

67. For an example, see *National Insurance: A Short Summary of Some Important Provisions of the National Health and Pensions Insurance Act 1938 and the Method of Securing Its Repeal* (Sydney: Electoral Campaign, Non-Party Political NSW Division, 1938).

68. For a detailed account of the campaign, see *The People Demand the Repeal of the N.H.I. Act: The Story of the Birth and Growth of a New Movement* (Melbourne: General Practitioner, 1938); *Melbourne Argus*, 22 November 1938.

69. Watts, "Light on the Hill," 196; *Workers' Voice*, 8 October 1938; *Brisbane Courier Mail*, 24 November 1938. The physicians' journal, the *General Practitioner*, published a pamphlet celebrating the campaign.

70. *Commonwealth Parliamentary Debates: Representatives*, 22 September, 25 November 1938. See also *Melbourne Argus*, 26 November 1938; *Adelaide Advertiser*, 23 November 1938; Letter from Kew Branch of the United Australia Organisation, MS 4851/12, National Library of Australia.

71. Stuart Macintyre, *Winners and Losers: The Pursuit of Social Justice in Australian History* (Sydney: Allen and Unwin, 1985), 59–78.

72. Frederic Eggleston, *State Socialism in Victoria* (London: King, 1932), 331.

73. W. K. Hancock, *Australia* (London: Benn, 1930), 73.

74. Ann Firth, "The Breadwinner, His Wife, and Their Welfare: Identity, Expertise, and Economic Security in Australian Post-War Reconstruction," *Australian Journal of Politics and History* 50 (2004): 491–508.

75. Robert Mangabeira Unger, *The Left Alternative* (London: Verso, 2009).

Controlling Consumption

A Comparative History of Rochdale Consumer Cooperatives in Australia and the United States

GREG PATMORE
NIKOLA BALNAVE

By international standards, the consumer cooperative movements in Australia and the United States have been relatively weak. However, in defiance of the usual assumptions about collectivism in Australia and the United States, the US movement has been stronger than the Australian movement, with continuous national organization since 1916 and greater labor movement support, particularly during World War I and the late 1930s–1940s.

This chapter focuses on Rochdale consumer cooperatives, which date back to 1844, when a group of "pioneers," dominated by skilled and supervisory trades, in Rochdale, England, started the movement to combat low wages, high prices, and poor-quality food. The principles for the Rochdale cooperatives included the provision of capital by members at a fixed rate of interest; cash purchases only and no credit; a dividend on purchases, or *divvy,* based on profits to be divided among members in proportion to the amount of purchases; and management based on democratic principles—one member, one vote rather than one vote, one share.[1]

The Australian and US cooperative movements exchanged ideas and people. Although the Australian movement focused primarily on the UK cooperative movement, the general manager of the Newcastle and Suburban Co-operative, undertook a three-month international study tour in 1954 to investigate retailing developments such as self-service, and this tour included meetings with US cooperators. More recently, in 2015, Ellen Michel from the US Cooperative Grocer Network gave evidence on US developments to an Australian Senate Committee Inquiry on Co-operatives and Mutuals.[2]

The chapter begins by examining some of the reasons for the growth and decline of consumer cooperatives before turning to a comparative narrative history of the movements in Australia and the United States. While at no point reaching the heights of their European counterparts, both consumer cooperative movements played an important role in particular locations such as coal mining and rural areas and were particularly popular during periods of social unrest and rising prices. Weak labor movement support and tensions within the cooperative movements, however, diminished their potential growth and sustainability.

Why Cooperatives Grow and Decline

Cooperative historians have suggested a number of factors that assist the formation and growth of Rochdale consumer cooperatives. Price inflation and its impact on real wages and purchasing power is one key factor. As prices rise, consumers look for ways to reduce their grocery bills. By cutting out the private retailer and redistributing the surplus back to consumers, cooperatives can lower prices. "Periods of unrest," when disenchantment with the prevailing economic and social order leads to an interest in alternative ways of controlling both consumption and production, is another factor. Such periods include the Great Depression of the 1930s and the counterculture movements of the 1960s and 1970s.[3] A favorable legal environment that provides legal recognition and even tax concessions can also assist the growth of cooperatives.

Support for cooperatives has historically come from farmer groups and the labor movement. Farmers have established not only agricultural cooperatives but also Rochdale consumer cooperatives in rural areas to buy in bulk, ensure continuity of supply, and keep prices down. Where farmers are well organized, farmers' political parties and lobby groups have provided legislative support for cooperatives. Labor movements may also support consumer cooperatives to protect real wages by keeping prices down and preventing profiteering. Union organizers have promoted the formation of cooperatives as a counter to the influence of company stores or expensive general stores. This link between the movements is strong in the United Kingdom, where the Co-operative Party is affiliated to the Labour Party. Immigration can influence the formation and growth of consumer cooperatives, with British immigrants and Finnish immigrants, for example, bringing the idea of consumer cooperatives to Australia and the United States, respectively.[4]

Rochdale consumer cooperatives have experienced declines for a number of reasons, including economic prosperity, demographic changes, and competition from the non–cooperative retailing sector. The decline of working-class communities in mining areas and the waning rural population as a consequence of mechanization in agriculture and economies of scale brought about by the consolidation of rural properties have had a negative impact on consumer cooperatives. Increasing car ownership in rural areas created further difficulties for cooperatives reliant on their remoteness for success.[5]

Direct competition from the non–cooperative sector presented a major challenge, particularly where Rochdale cooperatives posed a threat to the financial viability of these private-sector storekeepers. Price wars, bribery, and collusion with wholesalers aimed at crippling and bankrupting cooperatives occurred, and consumer cooperatives bid against each other in a competitive market. To meet these issues in Great Britain the Co-operative Wholesale Society began trading in 1864, and the Scottish Co-operative Wholesale Society began trading in 1868.[6]

Consumer cooperatives also faced indirect competition associated with the changing nature of retailing, such as the rise of chain stores, cash and carry, supermarkets, and shopping centers. The cooperatives had to find capital funds to attract and maintain business, and the cash gains made through regular dividends were initially important in attracting and maintaining members but lost their appeal, particularly in the postwar period, when large private retail supermarkets could offer immediate specials or discounts at the point of sale. Where dividends have fallen out of fashion, concessions have been given to cooperative members in the form of price cuts, member-only specials, and competitions offering prizes.[7]

The Nineteenth Century

Interest in the idea of cooperatives first appeared in the United States in the late 1820s. A decade and a half later, John Kaulback, a Boston tailor and member of the New England Association of Mechanics, promoted the idea of a buying club to procure basic goods as a way to promote attendance at association meetings. The group opened a store in 1845 and in January 1847 created the Workingmen's Protective Store, which operated in twelve locations. While the founders knew little about Rochdale principles, they adhered to the principles of equal voting and cash sales. By October 1852, the movement had become the New England Protective Union, covering both farmers and workers, with 403 stores and a wholesaler. However, the effort declined in the face of internal discord, competition from non–cooperative retailers, and the disruption arising from the US Civil War. Nevertheless, three of these stores remained in operation in 1888.[8]

The ideas of the Rochdale movement began to attract interest in Australia and the United States in the 1850s. One significant influence was the work of George Jacob Holyoake, an English cooperator, whose pamphlet, *Self-Help by the People: History of Co-operation in Rochdale*, was first produced in a summary form in the *New York Tribune* before the Civil War. The *Sydney Empire* newspaper published an August 1858 review of the pamphlet. During the US Civil War, an estimated one hundred cooperative stores opened for business, with many of them drawing from Rochdale principles. The earliest known Australian Rochdale consumer cooperative formed in Brisbane and registered in August 1859 under the New South Wales Friendly Societies Act (before Queensland separated from New South Wales).[9]

Following the Civil War, movements among farmers and workers encouraged consumer cooperatives in the United States. In rural areas, railway construction assisted the development of agriculture and settlement, allowing farmers and their cooperatives access to wholesalers and manufacturers. The Grange, founded in Washington State in December 1867, aimed to remove middlemen and bring consumers, farmers, and manufacturers into "direct and friendly relations." The Grange sponsored Rochdale cooperative stores, which spread across New England, the Midwest, the South, and the Pacific Coast. The Grange movement lost its momentum by the mid-1880s, but some stores continued to operate.[10]

Some cooperatives operated under the umbrella of labor unions such as the Knights of St. Crispin and the Knights of Labor. The Knights of Labor's 1878 constitution called for "distributive cooperatives," and by 1883 they had organized between fifty and sixty cooperative stores, primarily in towns where the only retailer was a company store. While they operated generally on Rochdale principles, they were closed organizations that admitted and traded only with members of the Knights. The organization shifted its focus to a "cooperative" industrial system in 1884 and collapsed in the 1890s, but some of its cooperative stores continued to operate.[11]

Cooperatives attempted to establish a national body, forming the Cooperative Union of America in September 1895 in Cambridge, Massachusetts, to serve as an educational and coordinating body for local cooperatives. The Cooperative Union joined the International Co-operative Alliance and issued a newspaper, but it had only fourteen members, all of them in the Northeast, and faced financial difficulties. The Union collapsed in 1899 following the dissolution of the Cambridge Cooperative Association, its major sponsor.[12]

While broader nineteenth-century attempts to establish consumer cooperatives failed, independent consumer cooperatives operated in various locations for varying periods. The Union Cooperative Association No. 1 in Philadelphia, the first known cooperative store in the United States based on Rochdale principles, organized in December 1862, with its first outlet opening in April 1864 with twenty-three members. The association eventually opened two more stores, but membership and sales did not match the cost of expansion, and effort ended in 1866.[13]

Waves of interest in Rochdale consumer cooperatives also occurred in Australia in the second half of the nineteenth century. Despite the long economic boom that followed the Australian gold rushes, Rochdale consumer cooperatives peaked in the 1860s against the background of unemployment and urban poverty. Concerns about living standards and disillusionment with the existing political system led to a second wave of interest in the late 1880s and early 1890s. More than fifty societies registered in New South Wales between 1886 and 1900. Many were short-lived, and when officials collected the first statistics in 1895, only nineteen societies still existed.[14]

Nevertheless, Rochdale cooperatives became significant in several localities. British immigrants to Australia played an important role in bringing the Rochdale principles to coal-mining districts, where retail cooperatives became common. In the Lithgow Valley near Sydney, miners established a Rochdale cooperative store in 1891 that operated for three years before it ceased trading during the depression. Ten Rochdale cooperatives in the Hunter Valley formed between 1886 and 1893; although six collapsed during the 1890s depression, two remained in operation at the end of World War I. In metropolitan areas, the Adelaide Co-operative opened for business in 1868 and went on to become one of Australia's longest-surviving Rochdale cooperatives, while the Newcastle and Suburban Co-operative, which became Australia's largest Rochdale consumer cooperative, opened its first store in August 1898.[15]

Despite some local successes, the future of consumer cooperatives in Australia and the United States did not look very promising at the end of the nineteenth century. While some US cooperators moved to establish a wholesaler in California, no cooperative wholesalers or federations existed elsewhere. Consumer cooperatives tended to run small retail businesses with virtually no contact with other cooperatives. In Australia, the interest in consumer cooperatives had also waned. In New South Wales registrations subsided from 1895 until 1905 in the face of depression and drought.[16]

1900–1945

The consumer cooperative movements in Australia and the United States made major advances by the end of World War II, despite fluctuating interest during the first half of the twentieth century. US cooperatives gradually expanded between 1900 and 1910, fueled by criticism of the high prices set by monopolies. Socialist and farmers' groups promoted cooperatives as a means of redressing injustice and eliminating waste, and by 1905, the nation's 343 cooperatives included 138 in the Midwest and 98 in the Far West. Nevertheless, the movement remained uncoordinated.[17]

One particularly notable feature of the cooperative movement during this period in the United States was the role played by ethnic groups such as Finns in Michigan, Minnesota, and Wisconsin. While political differences existed within the American Finnish community, they were more radical than most other immigrant communities and were strongly influenced by socialist and eventually communist ideals. They arrived too late to obtain the best homestead land and were further radicalized by having to find work in mines and lumber camps. They played an active role in the 1907 Mesabi Iron Range strike and other work stoppages, which led to the blacklisting of many workers, who then had no option other than farming marginal land. One Finnish cooperative, the Farmers' Cooperative Company, was founded in Hancock, Michigan, in 1914, after a copper-mining strike. By contrast, Finnish immigration to Australia was insignificant and had no links to the formation of Rochdale cooperatives there.[18]

As in the United States, concerns about rising prices contributed to a rise in interest in consumer cooperatives in Australia during the decade after 1905, with fifty-five new societies registered in New South Wales alone. For example, Sydney's Balmain Co-operative was established in 1902 and by 1921 had fourteen thousand members in several Sydney suburbs. By the end of 1914, however, only forty-five cooperatives remained in New South Wales, and four of them faced liquidation.[19]

Immigration also played a key role in Australia, particularly in coal-mining areas, where British immigrants brought with them the idea and principles of the Rochdale movement. In 1901, miners established cooperatives in the mining towns of Lithgow, New South Wales; and Collie, Western Australia. In November 1912, miners established a cooperative in the coal-mining town of Wonthaggi in Victoria. The following year, Australian had fifty-one consumer cooperatives, including twenty-five in New South Wales, eight in Victoria, and eight in Western Australia.[20]

Coal-mining consumer cooperatives played a crucial role in the formation of the New South Wales Co-operative Wholesale Society (NSWCWS), founded by four Hunter Valley consumer cooperatives in 1912. The local Rochdale consumer cooperatives faced serious challenges, including price cutting by competitors and the refusal of some wholesalers to supply the cooperatives to avoid jeopardizing relationships with existing businesses. The NSWCWS faced boycotts by flour millers and oil companies prior to World War I. In addition, manufacturers, importers, and the agents of overseas companies refused to include the NSWCWS on their wholesale lists. Nevertheless, the NSWCWS attracted an increasing number of societies as affiliates and launched the *Cooperative News*, the main journal for the cooperative movement, in 1923. A slump in membership occurred between 1924 and 1934, but the number of affiliates subsequently increased significantly, with the society growing from fifteen affiliates in 1934 to thirty-seven in 1945.[21]

The economic and political conditions associated with World War I and its aftermath encouraged the establishment and growth of cooperatives in the United States, where they found support from both unions and farmers concerned about rising prices, profiteering, and a declining standard of living. In January 1916, Dr. James Warbasse and his wife, Agnes, held a meeting in their Brooklyn, New York, home to launch the Cooperative League of the United States, which promoted cooperative education and brought together the cooperative movement. James Warbasse served as the league's president from 1916 until 1941, while Agnes served as educational director from 1916 to 1928. The league produced the *Cooperative Consumer* and organized its first national conference in September 1918, attracting 185 delegates from 386 cooperatives. In 1922 the league adopted the "Circle Pines" seal showing two pine trees surrounded by a circle.[22]

Despite the optimism at the end of World War I, consumer cooperatives in the United States faced major challenges during the 1920s. The postwar economic recession devastated Seattle's cooperatives, for example, and in an increasingly antiunion environment, employers established company unions that supplanted bona fide unions. Scandals resulted when private promoters created bogus cooperatives and siphoned off the money, and as cooperatives failed, organized workers became disillusioned. Even when prosperity returned in the mid-1920s, consumers turned to installment plans to buy goods, and cooperative members demanded more access to credit, forcing cooperatives to increase their financial liabilities. The number of the cooperatives declined, and cooperative wholesaling generally collapsed in the early 1920s. Many regional wholesalers and the National Cooperative Wholesale Association went into liquidation, as did many of the associated local cooperatives.[23]

The Australian experience with World War I and the 1920s differed from that of the United States. While little activity occurred during the war, the subsequent boom and its aftermath in Australia provided the conditions for a renewed interest in consumer cooperatives, particularly given concerns regarding rising prices and declining living standards. In 1923 Australia had 152 consumers' societies with a membership of 110,000. On the legislative front, the Country Party, which focused on farmers and rural communities and generally aligned with the Liberal Party and its predecessors rather than the Labor Party, played a significant role in the passage of the New South Wales Co-operation Act of 1924, which covered a range of cooperatives including Rochdale consumer cooperatives. The legislation created a registrar of cooperative societies and detailed "model rules" to assist in their formation.[24] The Labor Party, however, showed limited interest in cooperatives. One important dimension of the Australian system of compulsory arbitration involved efforts to link the basic wage or equivalents to prices for particular periods. Such wage indexation muted labor's support for consumer cooperatives, providing an alternative means of protecting the interests of workers as consumers. Rochdale cooperatives became a feature of rural areas, particularly in fruit-growing or poultry-breeding districts or in towns at important railway junctions.[25]

However, efforts to form a national organization for cooperatives were ineffective. In April 1920, the Reverend Frank Pulsford, a Congregationalist minister in Sydney and the author of the influential *Co-operation and Co-Partnership* (1913), organized the All-Australian Co-operative Congress in Sydney, with representatives of seventy-eight cooperatives in attendance, but the conference ended without making any major decisions. Deep divisions among the Australian Rochdales had grown entrenched. Federalists believed in the need for a central organization such as the NSWCWS, while individualists preferred autonomous local consumer cooperatives with far looser links to other consumer cooperatives. For example, according to Gary Lewis, at the time of World War II, the Adelaide Co-operative was individualist, and the other major Rochdale metropolitan cooperative in South Australia, the Port Adelaide Industrial Co-operative, was federalist.[26]

The cooperative movement in both countries faced economic challenges during the 1930s depression. Workers confronted wage cuts, work rationing, and mass unemployment. Australia's Balmain Co-operative, for example, went into voluntary liquidation in 1936. However, the collapse of cooperatives was less severe than the United States experienced during the early 1920s. The Great Depression generally encouraged criticism of the prevailing business system and the search for alternatives based on service rather than profit, and members of some cooperatives voted to leave any surplus funds in the cooperative to ensure financial stability. Between 1929 and 1934, the Cooperative League estimated that membership of consumer cooperatives in the United States grew 40 percent. Lewis has calculated that while the membership of Rochdale cooperatives in New South Wales fell from sixty thousand in 1929 to twenty-four thousand in 1933, the number of consumer cooperatives grew in New South Wales beginning in 1935. This growth was spurred in part by such external influences as a 1935 Australian tour by Japanese Christian cooperator Toyohiko Kagawa and the spread of the ideas of Canadian clergyman Dr. Moses Coady.[27]

The US cooperative movement consolidated its position during the early 1930s. In February 1933, six regional associations combined to form National Cooperatives, a joint buying organization, as the first step toward a national organization. New regional wholesalers formed in Texas, Washington, and Illinois. The Cooperative League saw its membership grow from 155 societies with 77,826 members in 1927 to 1,500 local associations and more than 750,000 members in 1935. E. R. Bowen, a former sales executive for a farm machinery company, became chief executive of the league on 1 January 1934 and broadened the organization to embrace farmers' purchasing associations, increased publicity for the cooperative cause, and improved its financial position, reducing its dependency on Warbasse's philanthropy. As in Australia, Kagawa and Coady also provided significant external influences.[28]

The US cooperative movement enjoyed a favorable political climate under President Franklin Roosevelt, who in June 1933 set up a Consumers Advisory Board that included Warbasse to protect consumer interests under the Codes of Fair Competition created under the National Industrial Recovery Act. Roosevelt's New Deal posed an early problem for the consumer cooperatives since the Codes of Fair Competition prohibited rebates and discounts as unfair trade practices. On 23 October 1933, following protests from the cooperative movement, Roosevelt issued an executive order exempting all "bona fide and legitimate cooperative organizations" from the code prohibitions providing that they paid patronage refunds out of actual earnings rather than as discounts at the time of purchase.[29] Roosevelt also supported the broader cooperative cause via the 1934 Federal Credit Union Act, which recognized that credit unions had fared well during the depression and provided an opportunity for all citizens to organize credit unions and rural electricity cooperatives.[30] Roosevelt sent a July 1936 mission to Europe to investigate cooperative developments there. He was particularly interested in cooperatives as a "middle way" in Sweden, where they "existed happily and successfully alongside private industry."[31] The mission's report was anticlimactic, expressing doubts about consumer cooperatives as a panacea for the United States. While it made no specific recommendations for government assistance, the report did recommend a survey of consumer cooperatives and the establishment of an agency to assist them.[32]

This favorable climate resuscitated consumer cooperatives in some areas where they had virtually disappeared. In California, for example, several factors contributed to the revival. In 1932, members of the state's unemployed population organized self-help cooperatives to trade labor for food, clothing, and housing. Author Upton Sinclair ran for governor in 1934 with the slogan "End Poverty in California" (EPIC) and developed EPIC clubs throughout the state to support his campaign. While he lost, the clubs became an outlet for dissatisfaction with the economic system and fueled the formation of buying clubs and cooperatives. Kagawa's visit to the Bay Area also influenced Christians to look at cooperatives as a faith-based alternative to the existing system of distribution. A number of these buying groups and cooperatives around San Francisco formed Pacific Cooperative Services, which incorporated in January 1937 as an umbrella buying organization that provided liability protection. Further cooperatives, in turn, formed in other areas, including Berkeley.[33]

By the time the United States entered World War II, its cooperative movement had reached unprecedented levels of influence and membership. The number of local retail cooperatives affiliated with the fifteen regional wholesale cooperatives that formed National Cooperatives. reached 2,328 by 1940, an increase of 13.7 percent over the previous year. The Cooperative League estimated that in 1942, the United States had a total of 3,100 cooperative stores with a membership of 485,000. The Cooperative League experienced a major change in leadership after Warbasse and Bowen clashed over Bowen's decision to extend the definition of consumer cooperatives to include cooperative purchasing by farmers' organizations. This change shifted the majority of the league membership from industrial workers to farmers and led to an internal split between Bowen and Warbasse factions. Warbasse resigned as president of the league in 1941 and was replaced by Murray Lincoln, who had a background in the farmers' distributive cooperatives and was a founder of the Nationwide Insurance Group and who remained in office until 1965.[34]

World War II brought the same opportunities and challenges for consumer cooperatives as for other businesses—labor shortages and difficulties with obtaining goods such as gasoline. Cooperatives in both Australia and the United States supported nationwide rationing to ensure an equitable distribution of goods and assisted in drives for war bonds. In the United States, transitory cooperatives developed in the Japanese American war relocation camps and the civilian public service camps for conscientious objectors. The Cooperative League also gained considerable kudos for its assistance to war-ravaged Europe through a "freedom fund" and later the Cooperative for American Remittances to Europe (CARE).[35]

Australia also experienced an expansion in the influence of consumer cooperatives during World War II, in part as a result of concerns about price increases, shortages of goods, and the fairness of rationing. Some cooperatives expressed interest in forming a peak Australian organization of cooperatives, although at least three previous Australian Co-operative Congresses had not led to any permanent umbrella group. In December 1943, representatives of producer and consumer cooperatives from six states met in Canberra as the Commonwealth Consumers Co-operative Conference. Those present saw the Australian cooperative movement as having a vital role in postwar reconstruction, suggesting that cooperative principles should form the basis of that reconstruction. The conference passed a series of resolutions, calling for the representation of consumer cooperatives on all commonwealth government boards dealing with the retail and wholesale trade and the establishment of a permanent secretariat in Canberra, the Co-operative Federation of Australia, and state cooperative federations. While, many of the hopes emerging from this conference never reached fruition, the conference represented a high point for the Rochdale consumer cooperative movement in Australia.[36]

The Australian Rochdale movement was weakened by its failure to form alliances with the farmer/producer cooperatives or with the labor movement. Farmer cooperative formed the Australian Producers' Wholesale Co-operative Federation in 1919 to trade with the English Co-operative Wholesale Society. The NSWCWS, which focused on consumption rather than agricultural production, was excluded from this relationship with the English Co-operative Wholesale Society and repeatedly clashed with the Australian Producers' Wholesale Co-operative Federation on issues such as national organization and cooperative legislation. The uncomfortable relationship between the agricultural producer cooperatives and the Rochdale consumer cooperatives continued into the postwar period.[37]

In contrast to their counterparts in the United Kingdom, Australia's Rochdale cooperatives developed no formal political link to the country's Labor Party. The Australian cooperative movement regularly appealed for greater ties to the labor movement, urging unions to invest funds in cooperatives in preparation for industrial action. In turn, some Rochdale cooperatives provided credit to striking workers and allowed closed shops. However, calls within the Rochdale movement for unions of cooperative employees and a Co-operative

Party did not please trade unions or the Labor Party, which expressed concerns about the political effectiveness of the Rochdale movement in challenging capitalism and fears that the cooperatives reinforced capitalism through "business co-operativism." Despite claims to the contrary, some unions believed that co-operatives differed little from the private sector in the treatment of employees. The union movement saw solutions to concerns about higher costs of living in the realm of political action through the Labor Party and industrial tribunals.[38]

At the local level, some trade unions, trade unionists, and members of the Communist Party or the Labor Party were active in their cooperatives. For example, local unions played an important role in the establishment of the Port Adelaide Industrial Co-operative in 1896, and Jim Healy, a notable labor activist and communist secretary of the Waterside Workers' Federation, served on the board of the North Sydney Co-operative. The Labor Party at times supported the consumer cooperative societies: in 1937 in South Australia, for example, the Labor Party adopted a resolution to give support to retail cooperatives and held a conference with them in April at the Adelaide Trades Hall to see how this could be done.[39]

While labor movement support for consumer cooperatives in Australia was generally weak throughout the period, the US labor movement gave stronger support during World War I and the Great Depression. At its November 1916 convention, the American Federation of Labor (AFL) appointed a committee to investigate cooperatives, and the following year, the committee reaffirmed its support for cooperation and called for the appointment of a lecturer to promote consumer cooperatives. While affiliates did not provide sufficient funds for the appointment of the lecturer, the AFL lobbied the federal government to exempt cooperatives from income tax on accumulated savings.[40]

Unionists played a key role in organizing cooperatives between 1917 and 1922. Coal miners and railway workers were particularly active in organizing consumer cooperatives, with particular successes recorded by the United Mine Workers in Illinois, Ohio, and Pennsylvania. In 1918, formed the Seattle Consumers Cooperative Association, and by October 1919 it claimed 1,460 members, eight grocery stores, a coal yard, and two tailor shops. The post–World War I economic downturn, financial management issues, and inadequate capitalization contributed to the Seattle association's demise in 1920, however. The high point of interest in cooperatives was the November 1919 Farmer-Labor Conference held in Chicago, which brought together representatives from farm organizations, unions, and cooperatives. It adopted the "National Cooperative Manifesto" and appointed a joint board for developing cooperatives. A second conference in February 1920 sought to bring together consumer cooperative and eliminate speculators. The All-American Cooperative Commission formed as a result of these conferences, but it failed to gain endorsement from the AFL and received a lukewarm response from the Cooperative League. Nevertheless, the United States had twenty-two hundred active consumer cooperatives by the end of 1920.[41]

The US cooperative movement also found a renewed level of support from the trade unions during the late 1930s. The AFL welcomed the resurgence of the consumer cooperative movement, noting that workers benefited by cutting out the middle man, ensuring high-quality goods, and reducing prices by minimizing waste. Bowen addressed the November 1936 AFL Convention in Tampa, Florida. The AFL published a 1937 pamphlet, *An Idea Worth Hundreds of Dollars*, that promoted the Rochdale principles and encouraged members to contact the Cooperative League. In Racine, Wisconsin, and elsewhere, union locals also played a crucial role in organizing consumer cooperatives.[42]

Communist interest in capturing the US cooperative movement was evident as early as 1921 but came to a head at the 1930 Congress of the Cooperative League, when communist delegates withdrew not only from the Congress but also from the cooperative movement. While some splits occurred at a regional level and some cooperatives joined the communists, the bulk of the cooperative movement remained committed to the principle of political neutrality. In Wisconsin, the Cooperative Central Exchange, a Finnish wholesaler, responded to the communists by changing its name to the Central Cooperative Wholesale, changing its label from the red star to the twin pines, and encouraging non-Finns to join. The communists formed their own wholesaler, the Workers' and Farmers' Cooperative Unity Alliance. By 1934, the Central Cooperative Wholesale had thirty-four stores in Wisconsin, while the alliance had only four.[43]

The growth of consumer cooperatives attracted concern in the established business community. In 1936, the US Chamber of Commerce watched the growth of consumer cooperatives with concern, noting that it was "improper for government agencies to extend preferential treatment" to cooperatives, which were "but another form of competitive force" seeking to win consumers' patronage.[44] The well-resourced National Tax Equality Association, founded in 1943, attacked cooperatives as "tax dodgers" and declared them "unpatriotic."[45] The tax group remained a major problem for the US cooperative movement after the war with one Cooperative League officer describing Vernon Scott, the association's executive vice president, as "the cooperative movement's worst enemy in America."[46]

The US and Australian cooperative movements differed in regard to women's guilds. The Northern States Cooperative Women's Guild, which formed in 1930, was the only regional American guild organization. The guilds initially had only Finnish members and were found primarily in Minnesota, Michigan, and Idaho. After the failure of an attempt to form a national guild, the main activity focused on the Women's Committee of the Cooperative League, established in 1942. Several cooperative women's associations focused on cooperative education, but they did not organize along the same lines as the women's guilds.[47]

In contrast, many cooperatives in Australia's coal-mining and metropolitan areas formed women's guilds to educate women in cooperative principles and promote the cooperative movement. The Australian women's guilds formed a national organization in 1936, with all guilds affiliating by 1945. In New South Wales, the guilds went beyond the supportive role expected by the NSWCWS, with some guilds frequently challenging the male-dominated NSWCWS by criticizing their leadership and organizing conferences to promote alternative paths for the Rochdale movement. The divisions along gender lines persisted into the post–World War II period.[48]

1945 to the Present

From the high point of the 1940s, consumer cooperatives in Australia and the United States generally declined. Postwar prosperity, with its relatively low levels of unemployment and inflation, removed the main economic factor that had driven individuals to form and maintain cooperatives. They also faced increased competition from private chain stores, such as Safeway in the United States and Coles and Woolworths in Australia, which offered consumers a wider range of goods at competitive prices. Cooperatives in smaller rural communities lost business to larger regional or urban centers, where the volume of business justified large supermarkets. Advertising, cars, and better roads gave urban residents the incentive and means to shop elsewhere. Smaller rural communities at best grew marginally and often declined. In the Australian coal-mining communities that had sustained the cooperatives, mines closed and the working-class aspect of these towns evaporated. High levels of credit, particularly in rural areas, and cases of mismanagement also posed problems.[49]

Some cooperatives both in Australia and the United States collapsed spectacularly. The Newcastle and Suburban Co-operative, which had become Australia's Rochdale cooperative, achieved a peak membership of 95,000 in 1978 but closed just three years later in the face of major competition from Woolworths and Coles. In the United States, California's Berkeley Cooperative, peaked at 116,232 members in 1982 but began shutting stores in 1981 to cut costs. A 1987 plan under which employees and consumers would each own and manage half the cooperative proved unsuccessful, and in 1988 the cooperative filed for bankruptcy and closed its last three stores. This collapse was paralleled on the East Coast by the 1991 dissolution of Maryland's Greenbelt Cooperative, which had a peak membership of 116,018 in 1986.[50]

A small number of Rochdales survived in Australia in rural areas such as Denmark in Western Australia, Junee in New South Wales, and Nuriootpa in South Australia. These cooperatives have become franchisees for the Independent Grocers of Australia network to ensure wholesale supplies. They have been joined by at least two dairying cooperatives on the mid-northern coast of New South Wales that have transformed themselves into retail cooperatives. The survival and prosperity of these establishments has resulted in large part from "localism," which is fueled by a sense of place. The cooperatives played an active role in the community and in turn encouraged residents to "shop local" rather than at other regional centers. At least one rural US Rochdale cooperative in Sault St. Marie, Michigan, survived until May 2012 but then closed after a Wal-Mart Super Center opened nearby and roadwork disrupted traffic to the cooperative.[51]

These problems for the consumer cooperatives occurred against the background of a weakening of the level of political and industrial support for the movement following World War II. The movement's nonpolitical stance created suspicions on both the right and left in Australia, particularly during crises such as the Labor Party split of the 1950s. Some Rochdale consumer cooperatives did not explicitly encourage union membership, and with the exception of Frank Walker and Bob Debus in New South Wales during the 1980s, Labor governments generally maintained lukewarm attitudes toward the cooperative movement,.[52]

In the United States, active support from the AFL and Congress of Industrial Organizations for the cooperative movement peaked in the late 1940s, with unions encouraging members to join cooperatives and in a few cases providing funds to assist cooperatives. Political controversy continued: Republicans in particular raised concerns about whether cooperatives should receive aid through tax concessions and direct financial assistance. While Democratic president Harry S. Truman was sympathetic to the cooperative movement, not until three decades later, when his fellow Democrat, Jimmy Carter, took office, did a major initiative develop in support of cooperatives. In 1978, following lobbying from the Cooperative League and with Carter's support, Congress established the federally funded Cooperative Bank to provide cheap finance to cooperatives. The Reagan administration initially moved to close the Cooperative Bank as part of a plan to cut the budget but agreed to privatize the bank in 1981 after the cooperatives raised close to two hundred million dollars in capital for the bank.[53]

While many of the older Rochdale cooperatives did not survive, disillusionment with capitalism during the late 1960s and 1970s led to the formation of new consumer cooperatives in both countries. Protesters against the Vietnam War, environmentalists, community control advocates, and civil rights activists saw cooperatives as a symbol of the counterculture they sought to build. Some of these cooperatives have prospered by focusing on organic foods and locally produced goods. In the United States, current examples include the GreenStar Cooperative Market in Ithaca, New York, which was founded in 1971 and had eight thousand members in 2011, and the New Pioneer Food Co-op in Iowa City, which was also founded in 1971 and has more than eleven thousand members. As in earlier eras, these consumer cooperatives established regional associations and then formed a national group, the National Cooperative Grocers' Association, in 1999. The association currently has 143 food cooperatives that operate 190 stores in thirty-eight states, with combined annual sales of more than $1.7 billion and more than 1.3 million customer-members. In 2014, Minnesota had the largest number of these stores (25), followed by Washington (19), Wisconsin (14), and California (12).[54]

Another important difference between the Australian and US cooperative movements is the survival and strength of national cooperative organizations. In the United States, the Cooperative League became the National Cooperative Business Association in 1985, and its membership still covers all forms of cooperatives. It conducts education programs and lobbies Congress on behalf of cooperatives. In 1991, the association persuaded Congress to establish the Rural Cooperative Development Grants Program to encourage new cooperative businesses in rural areas. Nine years later, the association achieved another milestone when the Internet Corporation for Assigned Names and Numbers created a new top-level Internet domain, .coop, exclusively for cooperatives.[55]

In contrast, two conventional retail supermarket chains control 80 percent of the Australian grocery market, only a small number of food co-operatives currently exist in Australia, and the Australian movement has failed to maintain an effective national organization. Reflecting the decline in consumer cooperatives, the NSWCWS closed in 1979, and the women's guilds folded. The Co-operative Federation of Australia remained weak and fluctuated in its level of activity before becoming moribund in 1986, with the Co-operative Federation of New South Wales forming the Australian Association of Co-operatives, which collapsed in 1993 as a result of financial problems associated with its internal banking services to members. The Australian Association of Co-operatives had made some bad loans to the struggling New South Wales Rochdale consumer cooperative at Singleton, which also went into liquidation. The Co-operative Federation of New South Wales was subsequently reconstituted, but it now restricts its activities to lobbying governmental agencies and providing advice on legal and financial matters. It joined with other state cooperative associations in 1993 to form a national body, now known as Co-operatives Australia, which performs a similar role at a national level. These peak bodies represent more than just consumer cooperatives. The United Nations International Year of Co-operatives in 2012 promoted further moves toward organization, including the establishment of the Business Council of Co-operatives and Mutuals in 2013 and of a new cooperative wholesaler.[56]

Conclusion

The Rochdale consumer cooperative movements in Australia and the United States at no point achieved the success of some of their European counterparts. However, in some locations, such as coal-mining and rural areas, they played an important role and were particularly popular during periods of social unrest and rising prices. Specific immigrant groups such as the British in Australia and the Finns in the United States were important in transmitting and promoting the idea of consumer cooperatives in their new homes. While many traditional Rochdale consumer cooperatives collapsed in both countries, the national organization survived in the United States, and the resurgent food cooperative movement that followed the political discontent of the 1960s and 1970s has become more firmly established in the United States than Australia.

The support of farmers and workers was crucial for the formation and growth of consumer cooperatives. The relationship with farmers, however, has proved problematic if the interests of consumer cooperatives clash with those of agricultural cooperatives, as has occurred in Australia. Farmers' political conservatism can also clash with the more radical viewpoints of the urban working class, although Australia's Country Party played a positive role in passing legislation that assisted cooperatives. Labor movement support was weak in both countries except during World War I and the late 1930s–1940s, when unions saw consumer cooperatives as useful in combating profiteering and price increases. US consumer cooperatives gained political support from Democratic presidents such as Roosevelt, Truman, and Carter. In contrast, Australian unions saw the solution to rising prices and profiteering in their links with the Labor Party and industrial tribunals rather than in consumer cooperatives.

The consumer cooperative movements faced hostility and competition from the non–cooperative retailers and their supporters in both countries and had difficulty obtaining supplies from non–cooperative wholesalers. In the United States, groups such as the Chamber of Commerce and the National Tax Equality Association, along with their Republican allies, criticized government assistance to the cooperatives through taxation benefits. The growth of non–cooperative supermarket chains presented problems for the Rochdale consumer cooperatives, particularly in regard to traditional membership incentives such as dividends, the need for capital investment in new facilities, and economies of scale in marketing and wholesaling. Internal divisions also weakened the consumer cooperative movements. Where consumer cooperatives have survived in Australia and the United States, they have developed strong links with their local communities and an appeal that focuses on shopping locally, sustainably, and healthily.

Notes

1. Nikola Balnave and Greg Patmore, "Rochdale Consumer Co-operatives in Australia: Decline and Survival," *Business History* 54 (2012): 986.

2. *Newcastle Morning Herald*, 12 June 1954; Economics References Committee, Cooperative, Mutual, and Member-Owned Firms, 2015, available at http://parlinfo.aph.gov.au/parlInfo/search/display/display.w3p;query=Id%3A%22committees%2Fcommsen%2F7f80cc46-c08e-4cda-946a-d495e6882061%2F0012%22.

3. John Curl, *For All the People: Uncovering the Hidden History of Cooperation, Cooperative Movements, and Communalism in America* (Oakland, Calif.: PM, 2009), 348; Herbert Heaton, *Modern Economic History*, 3rd ed. (Adelaide: Workers' Educational Association of South Australia, 1925), 305.

4. Nikola Balnave and Greg Patmore, "Practical Utopians: Rochdale Consumer Co-operatives in Australia and New Zealand," *Labour History* 95 (2008): 98, 100; Curl, *For All the People*, 347; Steven. J. Keillor, *Cooperative Commonwealth: Co-ops in Rural Minnesota, 1859–1939* (St Paul: Minnesota Historical Society Press, 2000), 310–11.

5. US Department of Labor, *Consumer Cooperatives*, January 1957.

6. Johnston Birchall, *Co-op: The People's Business* (Manchester: Manchester University Press, 1994), 81–87; Martin Purvis, "Stocking the Store: Co-operative Retailers in North-East England and Systems of Wholesale Supply *circa* 1860–77," *Business History* 40 (1998): 55–78.

7. Alexander Carr-Saunders, Philip Sargent Florence, and Robert Peers, *Consumers' Co-operation in Great Britain: An Examination of the British Co-operative Movement*, 3rd ed. (London: Allen and Unwin, 1940), 121.

8. E. W. Bemis, "Cooperation in New England," in *History of Cooperation in the United States*, ed. H. Adams (Baltimore: Johns Hopkins University Studies in Historical and Political Science, 1888), 4:18–26; Keillor, *Cooperative Commonwealth*, 15; Steven Leiken,

The Practical Utopians: American Workers and the Cooperative Movement in the Gilded Age (Detroit: Wayne State University Press, 2005), 3; Florence Parker, *The First 125 Years: A History of Distributive and Service Cooperation in the United States, 1829–1954* (Superior, Wis.: Cooperative Publishing, 1956), 3–4.

9. Balnave and Patmore, "Rochdale Consumer Co-operatives: Decline and Survival," 987–88; *Sydney Empire*, 26 August 1858; Leiken, *Practical Utopians*, 5–6.

10. Keillor, *Cooperative Commonwealth*, 38–39; Parker, *First 125 Years*, 10–15.

11. Parker, *First 125 Years*, 16–21.

12. Ibid., 23–24.

13. E. W. Bemis, "Cooperation in the Middle States," in *History*, ed. Adams, 141–43; Parker, *First 125 Years*, 25–26.

14. Balnave and Patmore, "Rochdale Consumer Co-operatives: Decline and Survival," 988.

15. Ibid., 988–89; Gary Lewis, *A Middle Way: Rochdale Consumer Co-operatives in New South Wales, 1859–1986* (Sydney: Australian Association of Co-operatives, 1992), 52; Greg Patmore, "Localism and Labour: Lithgow 1869–1932," *Labour History*, no. 78 (2000): 61.

16. Balnave and Patmore, "Rochdale Consumer Co-operatives: Decline and Survival," 988–89; Parker, *First 125 Years*, 34–35.

17. Keillor, *Cooperative Commonwealth*, 221–25; Robert Neptune, *California's Uncommon Markets: The Story of Consumers Cooperatives, 1935–1976* (Richmond, Calif.: Associated Cooperatives, 1977), 4–6; Parker, *First 125 Years*, 39–54.

18. Keillor, *Cooperative Commonwealth*, 310–11; Leonard Kercher, Vant Kekber, and Wilfred Leland, *Consumers' Cooperatives in the North Central States* (Minneapolis: University of Minnesota Press, 1941), 18–33, 262, 264; Olavi Koivukangas, "Finns," in *The Australian People*, ed. James Jupp (Cambridge: Cambridge University Press, 2001), 353–55.

19. William Kennedy McConnell, "Consumers' Co-operation in New South Wales," *Economic Record* 5 (1929): 263–64.

20. Nikola Balnave and Greg Patmore, "Rochdale Consumer Co-operatives in Australia: A Case of Rural Survival," *Journal of Co-operative Studies* 41 (2008): 15–18; Frank Pulsford, *Co-operation and Co-Partnership* (Sydney: Worker Trade Union, 1913), 44–50.

21. Balnave and Patmore, "Rochdale Consumer Co-operatives: Decline and Survival," 989.

22. *New York Times*, 24 February 1957; Parker, *First 125 Years*, 56–58, 108.

23. Consumers' League of New York, *Consumers' Cooperative Societies in New York State* (New York: Consumers' League, 1922), 16–18; Dana Frank, *Purchasing Power: Consumer Organizing, Gender, and the Seattle Labor Movement, 1919–1929* (Cambridge: Cambridge University Press, 1994), 145; Parker, *First 125 Years*, 81–89, 93–99.

24. Balnave and Patmore, "Rochdale Consumer Co-operatives: Decline and Survival," 988, 991–92; William Bayley, *History of the Farmers and Settlers' Association of New South Wales* (Sydney: Farmers and Settlers' Association, 1957), 118–19; Brian Costar, "National Party of Australia," in *The Oxford Companion to Australian History*, ed. Graeme Davidson, John Hirst, and Stuart Macintyre (Oxford: Oxford University Press, 1998), 455; Lewis, *Middle Way*, 61–64, 76–82.

25. Nikola Balnave and Greg Patmore, "Localism and Rochdale Co-operation: The Junee District Co-operative Society," *Labour History* 91 (2006): 56; Balnave and Patmore, "Rochdale Consumer Co-operatives: Case of Rural Survival," 19.

26. Lewis, *Middle Way*, xvii, 61–64, 76–82, 178–79.

27. Balnave and Patmore, "Rochdale Consumer Co-operatives: Case of Rural Survival," 18; Lewis, *Middle Way*, 133, 146, 160–62.

28. Lizabeth Cohen, *A Consumers' Republic: The Politics of Mass Consumption in Postwar America* (New York: Vintage, 2004), 49–50; Joseph Knapp, *The Advance of American Cooperative Enterprise, 1920–1945* (Danville, Ill.: Interstate, 1973), 379–84, 389–90; Florence Parker, "Consumers' Cooperation in the United States," *Annals of the American Academy of Political and Social Science* 191 (1937): 97–98; *New York Times*, 29 September 1935.

29. Knapp, *Advance*, 377–78.

30. J. Carroll Moody and Gilbert Fite, *The Credit Union Movement: Origins and Development, 1850–1970* (Lincoln: University of Nebraska Press, 1971), chap. 7.

31. Franklin Delano Roosevelt, *The Public Papers and Addresses of Franklin D. Roosevelt*, vol. 5, *The People Approve, 1936* (New York: Random, House, 1938), 226–27.

32. Knapp, *Advance*, 391.

33. Robert Neptune to Wallace Campbell, 20 February 1937, Box 111, Local and Regional Cooperatives: Associated Cooperatives File, Cooperative League of the United States of America Records, 1936–1939, Harry S. Truman Library and Museum; Neptune, *California's Uncommon Markets*, chap. 1; Harlan Randall and Clay Daggett, *Consumers' Cooperative Adventures: Case Studies* (Whitewater, Wis.: Whitewater, 1936), 150–90.

34. Wallace Campbell, *Consumer Cooperatives in America* (Chicago: Cooperative League of the United States of America, 1943), 6; *Berkeley Co-op News*, 21, 28 November 1965; Parker, *First 125 Years*, 161–65; *New York Times*, 17 April 1941.

35. Knapp, *Advance*, 497–98, 521–25, 531; Parker, *First 125 Years*, 166–67. The organization subsequently renamed itself the Cooperative for Assistance and Relief Everywhere.

36. Balnave and Patmore, "Rochdale Consumer Co-operatives: Decline and Survival," 989, 992–93; Lewis, *Middle Way*, 181–85.

37. Balnave and Patmore, "Rochdale Consumer Co-operatives: Decline and Survival," 990–91.

38. Ibid., 991.

39. Ibid.

40. AFL, *Report of Proceedings of the Thirty-Seventh Annual Convention Held at Buffalo, New York November 12 to 24, Inclusive 1917* (Washington, D.C.: AFL, 1917), 308–10; AFL, *Report of Proceedings of the Thirty-Eighth Annual Convention Held at St. Paul, Minnesota June 10 to 20, Inclusive 1918* (Washington, D.C.: AFL, 1918), 132; AFL, *Report of Proceedings of the Fortieth Convention Held at Montreal, Quebec, Canada June 7th to 19th, Inclusive 1920* (Washington, D.C.: AFL, 1920), 176–80.

41. Wallace Campbell, *The Consumers' Cooperative Movement: A Factual Survey* (New York: League for Industrial Democracy, 1937), 41; Frank, *Purchasing Power*, 145–52; Parker, *First 125 Years*, 59–80.

42. AFL, *An Idea Worth Hundreds of Dollars* (Washington, D.C.: AFL, 1937; AFL, *Report of Proceedings of the Fifty-Sixth Annual Convention Held at Tampa, Florida November 16 to 27, Inclusive 1936* (Washington, D.C.: AFL, 1936), 159–60, 554–56; *American Federationist*, August 1937.

43. Keillor, *Cooperative Commonwealth*, 311; Parker, "Consumers' Cooperation," 97.

44. Chamber of Commerce of the United States, *Cooperative Enterprises Operated by Consumers* (Washington, D.C.: Chamber, 1936), 3.

45. Knapp, *Advance*, 497–98, 521–25, 531; Parker, *First 125 Years*, 166–67.

46. Wallace Campbell to Fred Toothill, 26 August 1949, Box 71, Foreign Countries: England File, Folder 2, Cooperative League of the United States of America Records, 1936–1939, Harry S. Truman Library and Museum.

47. International Co-operative Women's Guild, *Report of the Committee, 1937–1946* (London: Guild, 1947), 43–44; Wallace Campbell to Emily Freundlich, 26 March 1947, Box 71, Foreign Countries: England File, Folder 1, Cooperative League of the United States of America Records, 1936–1939, Harry S. Truman Library and Museum; Parker, *First 125 Years*, 201–3.

48. Balnave and Patmore, "Rochdale Consumer Co-operatives: Decline and Survival," 989–90.

49. Ibid., 994–96; Cooperative League of the United States of America, *Cooperatives, 1959–1960* (Chicago: League, 1960), 27–30; US Department of Labor, *Consumer Cooperatives*, January 1957.

50. Balnave and Patmore, "Rochdale Consumer Co-operatives: Case of Rural Survival," 18–19; Daniel Copper and Paul Mohn, *The Greenbelt Cooperative: Success and Decline* (Davis, Calif.: Center for Cooperatives, 1992); Curl, *For All the People*, 192–203.

51. Balnave and Patmore, "Rochdale Consumer Co-operatives in Australia: Case of Rural Survival," 18–19; "Soo Co-op Grocery to Close," *Soo Evening News*, 10 May 2012, available at http://www.sooeveningnews.com/article/20120510/NEWS/305109971.

52. Balnave and Patmore, "Rochdale Consumer Cooperatives in Australia: Decline and Survival," 994.

53. Berkeley Historical Society, *A Conversation with Robert Neptune: Pioneer Manager of the Consumer Cooperative of Berkeley and Long-Term Manager at Associated Cooperatives* (Berkeley: Berkeley Historical Society, 1996), 22–23; Harry Truman to Howard Cowden, 17 November 1949, Box 58, Cowden, Howard A., File, Folder 2, Cooperative League of the United States of America Records, 1936–1939, Harry S. Truman Library and Museum; Parker, *First 125 Years*, 329–33.

54. Curl, *For All the People*, 214–18; *GreenLeaf*, September 2011, https://www.ncga.coop/; New Pioneer Food Co-op, http://www.newpi.coop/; David J. Thompson, "What's Next for California's Consumer Co-ops?," in *What Happened to the Berkeley Co-op?*, ed. Michael Fullerton (Davis, Calif.: Center for Cooperatives, 1992), 90.

55. Curl, *For All the People*, 250–51; National Cooperative Business Association, CLUSA International, http://www.ncba.coop/.

56. Stuart Alexander, "Australian Market," available at http://www.stuartalexander.com.au/aust_grocery_market_woolworths_coles_wholesale.php; Balnave and Patmore, "Rochdale Consumer Cooperatives: Decline and Survival," 993.

PART 6

Transnational Working-Class Politics

Anarchy at the Antipodes

Australian Anarchists and Their American Connections, 1885–1914

TOM GOYENS

In the autumn of 1885, an American immigrant from Rhode Island, Frederic Upham, delivered a lecture, "What Is Anarchy?," to a gathering of Melbourne freethinkers.[1] Also at that time, Melbourne-born David Alfred Andrade subscribed to *Liberty*, a Boston-based anarchist journal, and became a regular correspondent.[2] These events led to the founding of Australia's first anarchist group in 1886 and attest to the connections between Australian anarchists and their counterparts in the United States.

One of the most exciting directions in today's field of radical history is documenting the transnational dimension of international anarchism since the 1870s. The anarchists' critique of the state makes them unique among transnational actors. Local and regional movements are linked to hubs or individuals in different countries. This "transnational turn" in anarchist studies should not become an exit from existing tracks of analysis, such as the local or regional level. The transnational dimension should be a coequal branch of the scales of analysis that promise a more wholesome picture of the anarchist movement. A recent volume, *Reassessing the Transnational Turn*, cautions scholars not to discard the nation-state altogether.[3] If forging transnational networks constituted a conscious strategy, anarchists were also well aware of the power of the state. In fact, the nation-state itself could act transnationally through coordinated surveillance and other police efforts.

Particularly illuminating is anarchism's local movement culture fostered by employment (mining or textile towns), ethnic ties, or the clustering of exiles. Beyond its local flavor, movement culture embodied a shared experience of living an anarchist vision, debating that vision, reporting on current affairs, and commemorating a shared past.[4] Language is a natural cohesive that reinforces a locally shared identity and sustains long-distance connections throughout the radical diaspora.

This means that the local anarchist movement was never just that; its local existence was predicated on the fact that it also constituted a node in a global network. As historian Davide Turcato has pointed out, the anarchist press and the role of itinerant speakers may be the most enlightening ingredients for mapping the transnational dimension of anarchism.[5] Press and orators are the media in which the local, regional, and transnational exist symbiotically. This insight has led Turcato and others to counter the oft-repeated charge that anarchism lacks continuity, is ungrounded, and therefore is ineffective and irrational: they point to transnational networks that allow repressed movements in one place to shift activities elsewhere, only to reappear on their original terrain of activity. This dynamic demonstrates not discontinuity but an organic steadiness that is all but invisible in examinations of only one country or region.

The symbiotic relation between the local and transnational within the anarchist movement is an appropriate context in which to examine Australian anarchism. Here, too, the anarchist press and transoceanic communications are critical dimensions. In a biography of Errico Malatesta, Max Nettlau, a celebrated historian of anarchism, stresses the role of the anarchist press in creating a "sphere of intellectual exchange [that] ranged from Portugal to China and New Zealand, and from Canada to Chile and Peru. This made every formal organization, however loose and informal it was, really unnecessary."[6]

This chapter explores the extent and significance of connections between key figures in Australian anarchism and their US counterparts between 1885 and the First World War.[7] A small anarchist movement in the colonies that appeared to lack enduring organizations was sustained by new ideas because Australian anarchists belonged to a transnational network. They were "rooted cosmopolitans," to use sociologist Sidney Tarrow's term: embedded locally, mostly in Melbourne and Sydney, but consciously connected transnationally.[8] And while anarchists comprised a small contingent within Australian radicalism, they were part of the conversation for a freer and more just society. As historian Bruce Scates remarks, "Studying the losers is a way of opening up a wider field of possibilities, of escaping a view of the past that is often narrow and teleological."[9]

The Melbourne Anarchist Club

The founding of the Melbourne Anarchist Club on 1 May 1886 may seem at first glance a local, isolated story.[10] The immediate context, however, also reveals a colonial and transnational dimension. During the late 1880s and 1890s, a collapsing land boom and excessive borrowing abroad caused an economic depression with global dimensions. Social dislocation and high unemployment fueled a search for national identity. Politics was often oppositional and fragmented. Socialism presented a radically new vision in this late colonial society.[11] The main sources of inspiration for Australian socialists were Britain and the United States—not surprising, as historian Verity Burgmann notes, since Australia had a "derivative culture": "Australian socialists suffered from a cultural cringe, a tendency to hero-worship leading British and American . . . socialists."[12]

Even before the Melbourne Club, anarchist ideas circulated within many different reform organizations. For example, half of the members of the Workingmen's Political Reform Association became anarchists.[13] The Victoria branch of the Australasian Secular Association, led by troublemaking immigrant Joseph Symes, was another notable domicile for closeted anarchists. Here, freethinkers of all stripes battled against a colonial government that sought to enforce a puritanical "code of respectability" with the help of churches and the press.[14] Parallels with the United States exist in this regard, although Australian society was far less religious than American society, as historian Robin Archer has shown.[15] Socialist and anarchist ideas also flourished among German immigrants in South Australia (particularly in Adelaide) and Melbourne. In March 1886, the Allgemeiner Deutscher Verein (General German Association) formed in South Australia, although little is known about anarchists within the group. Almost two years later, the Verein Vorwärts (Forward Association) was formed in Melbourne, and English-speaking anarchists established contacts with the new group.[16]

The Anarchist Club's split from the Australasian Secular Association thus reflected local and colonial circumstances. The founding members included David Alfred Andrade and his brother, Will; the US-born Upham; British-born John William Fleming; Laurence Petrie; and John Arthur Andrews, who was born in Bendigo, Victoria. David Andrade (1859–1928) was the leading figure. He was born in Collingwood (now a Melbourne suburb) to storekeepers who had come from Middlesex, England.[17] He had been attracted to the libertarian thought of Pierre-Joseph Proudhon, who talked about transforming society without a state via voluntary associations and a mutualist ethic that retained some form of property. For Andrade and Proudhon, connecting atheism to anarchism was easy: as Andrade declared in 1886, "Anarchy, in short, is to politics what atheism is to theology."[18] The club met regularly until 1889 and welcomed all radicals, whatever their differences. They were united by a commitment to individual liberty, hostility to church and state, and a passion for education through critical reading and lectures.

During its brief existence, the club probably never had more than one hundred members, but it nevertheless left a mark on the local political landscape. Within the Melbourne labor movement, the club embodied an "opposite pole of attraction" to the craft conservatism of the Trades Hall Council.[19] Andrade and his associates attacked the state and particularly the Victoria government's tariff policy and its role in education, the economy, and health policies. (Andrade later became active in the movement against compulsory vaccinations.)[20] Members also set up a cooperative home, an idea pushed by Andrade, but the venture soon collapsed. Fleming remembered decades later that many club members subsequently left for America, although little is known about them.[21] In April 1887, club members launched their own newspaper, *Honesty*, copies of which were sent to America—specifically, to Boston.[22]

Andrade and *Liberty*

Although the international connections of the club and some of its members have received little attention, they existed even before the club was founded.[23] David Andrade was a subscriber to and correspondent for *Liberty*, which emerged under editor Benjamin Tucker as the foremost exponent of individualist anarchism in the United States. Some Melbourne anarchists did not subscribe to this philosophy, just as immigrant anarchists in the United States espoused revolutionary anarchism.[24] In 1886 and 1887, Andrade sent five reports from his home in South Yarra to Boston in which he sketched the state of anarchism in Australia.[25] Such connections allowed both sides to be plugged into a global community. It provided support and legitimacy for the Australians because local issues were framed in a wider debate about human nature, natural rights, and the role of the state. After all, if an anarchist philosophy speaks to universal aspects of the human condition, movements should be able to exist in all corners of the world. The Melbourne anarchists imagined their audience as wide as possible despite geographical limitations—the club's manifesto was addressed to "the People of Australasia."[26] An excited Andrade told Tucker about the prospect of having anarchist clubs spring up across the continent and join together in the imaginary Australasian Association of Anarchists.[27]

Tucker was equally enthusiastic: "Anarchism is nowhere more active than in Australia," which he called "that little continent."[28] Periodicals and a global postal service thus provided one of the enduring connecting tissues for a far-flung radical movement.

English secularist and anarchist Henry A. Seymour was another figure who connected Tucker and the Australians. From 1885 to 1888, Seymour edited *The Anarchist* in London and published Mikhail Bakunin's *God and the State*, which had been translated by Tucker, to introduce Bakunin to an American (and by extension, Australian) public. All three individualist anarchist papers shared an affinity with the writings of Bakunin, Proudhon, Herbert Spencer, and Max Stirner. Each editor placed advertisements in the other papers. Andrade read aloud the manifesto of Seymour's English Anarchist Circle at the second meeting of the Melbourne Anarchist Club.[29] In 1887, Tucker wrote that "it is sufficient description of *Honesty*'s principles to say that they are substantially the same as those championed by *Liberty* in America."[30] In 1888, more than one-eighth of *Liberty*'s book and pamphlet patronage came from Melbourne.[31] Interestingly, Andrade's writings, including "What Is Anarchy?," which appeared in the May 28, 1887, issue of *Liberty*, also appeared in the leading German-language anarchist paper, *Freiheit*, edited by Johann Most, the most notorious anarchist speaker and editor in the United States and an opponent of Tucker.[32]

Haymarket

Three days after the founding of the Melbourne Anarchist Club, the Haymarket bombing on the evening of 4 May 1886 in Chicago shocked the United States and reverberated around the world. The first news about Haymarket came as a twenty-three-word "cablegram" received at one o'clock on the afternoon of 5 May and printed in Perth, Sydney, and Brisbane papers that same day. The cable made no mention of anarchists, only "foreign Socialists."[33] The first cable that explicitly mentioned anarchists as the perpetrators was received on 6 May and printed the next day.[34] Subsequent telegrams were woefully incorrect, putting the attendance at the Haymarket meeting at fifteen thousand.[35] The first mail report in June also stated inaccurately that two bombs had been hurled and that the "rioters" were "well armed, replied, and poured volley after volley into the midst of the officers."[36]

Melbourne anarchists criticized these accounts and expressed sympathy for the Chicago anarchists who had been arrested and charged with conspiracy. As more information trickled in, Australia learned that in the moments after the explosion, Chicago police had opened fire and killed an unknown number of civilians and that those arrested had been accused of criminal conspiracy, including bomb making. As is now known, several anarchists did make bombs, and rhetoric about explosives and insurrection was quite common among Johann Most's followers.[37] Andrade himself recommended revolutionary violence a month before Haymarket, but he later abandoned such views.[38]

The Melbourne anarchists stepped up their protests against the state and the press after they learned of the guilty verdict and death sentences for the defendants in August 1886. They most likely obtained this news from correspondence with American comrades, since no mainstream Australian paper reported on the trial or verdict. The Melbourne anarchists condemned the "base intrigue of the authorities as they stained [with blood] that memorable meeting held in Chicago last May."[39] They even adopted a resolution, published in *Liberty* and directed at the governor of Illinois, in which they called the trial a "legal murder."[40] The news by cable that the four defendants had been executed on 11 November 1887 was not reported until 14 November.[41] Andrade declared the affair "one of the foulest crimes that ever stained the bloodiest pages of American history."[42] On 11 November 1888, the Melbourne anarchists gathered on the busy Queen's Wharf on the Yarra River, a public space and old center of commerce, and delivered speeches about the Haymarket martyrs while selling copies of *Honesty* and the *Australian Radical*. Sydney anarchists organized a similar event. The Haymarket executions entered the collective memory of the anarchists of the world to be commemorated annually. Whether in New York, Barcelona, Havana, or Melbourne, Haymarket memorials fused the local (Queen's Wharf) and the transnational (the martyrs and their ideals). "Our comrades in Sydney commemorated the event in a similar manner," reported *Honesty* in 1889, "and at all the principal centres in Europe and America similar steps were taken to keep up the remembrance of that day so eventful in the history of the struggle for labor's emancipation."[43]

Communist Anarchism

In 1888, the Melbourne anarchists split, not so much over the issue of violence as over the role of property and the fruits of one's labor in a future anarchist society. This split had consequences for the local and intercolonial anarchist movement, but the dispute also reflected divisions within international anarchism. During the 1870s and 1880s, all anarchists opposed the state, defended individual dignity, and excoriated the evils of "wage slavery" and monopolies of any kind. In the United States, militant anarchism arose around 1880 in the community of immigrant socialists who began to espouse revolutionary tactics and radical egalitarianism. Individualist anarchists such as Tucker sought to safeguard the principle of individual liberty. A common hero was Russian revolutionary Mikhail Bakunin, who had challenged Marx and the idea of a socialist state. Bakunin warned against using any hierarchical organizations to bring about the revolution, instead urging the formation of small voluntary groups propelled by a spirit of revolt. He believed that all means of production and distribution should be collectively owned (without a state, of course) and insisted that the fruits of one's labor be a measure of the time expended (as recorded by labor notes). Many European anarchists, however, believed that this so-called collectivist anarchism could never wholly eradicate all exploitation because it retained not only the principle of ownership—albeit collective—but a form of remuneration (labor notes).

Only after Bakunin's death in 1876 did anarchist thinkers such as Peter Kropotkin and Errico Malatesta advance communist anarchism, which would come to dominate anarchist thinking until the advent of anarchosyndicalism. Communist anarchists argued that production and distribution of goods should indeed be socialized (in fact, held by no one person), but unlike collectivist anarchism, the fruits of labor ought to be distributed at no cost to each according to his needs, not according to his labor. Private property—indeed, the concept of ownership—was abolished, although personal possessions would not be affected. Labor notes or any other form of remuneration, Kropotkin warned, would inevitably result in a system of state-backed currency. To the followers of Bakunin and individualists, communist anarchism seemed impossibly naive and nonvoluntary.

American individualist anarchists and their Australian counterparts, while never a uniform bunch, held several principles at odds with communist anarchism. Tucker and Andrade clung to the concept of private or collective ownership and the idea that able producers ought to enjoy the fruits of their labor. The will of the individual was sacrosanct in the face of any external authority. A need-based communist anarchist arrangement, Tucker believed, would leave no room for someone to opt out. Many individualists also rejected mass revolutionary action because it could lead to unwanted hierarchies. Nearly all individualists subscribed to evolutionary rather than revolutionary tactics and abhorred violent deeds or the arming of workers (as Most advocated). Individualist anarchists, especially in the United States, stressed personal consciousness and freedom of thought and were far more willing to challenge Victorian mores of gender relations and sexuality.

The pugnacious Tucker therefore had no stomach for communist anarchists, with whom he feuded constantly. Friends and foes remembered his style as cold and argumentative, featuring "a glittering icicle of logic," as one friend put it. Lizzie Holmes, a frequent contributor to *The Firebrand*, an Oregon-based communist anarchist publication, discerned "intolerance, severity, and invective" in Tucker's opinions.[44] So when David Andrade announced the launch of *Honesty* and expounded his philosophy in *Liberty*, Tucker was elated to have an ally in the remotest place possible. Because Andrade contacted a number of anarchist papers, including the London-based communist anarchist *Freedom*, news of the ventures in Australia spread quickly along the anarchist networks. In 1888, Tucker took issue with *Freedom*'s declaration that the "*habitat* of Individualistic Anarchism" seems to be "only in newly-settled countries" like Australia and the United States. Tucker took this statement to be implying that given enough time, individualist anarchists would outgrow their primitive ideas. "On hearing of this discovery," Tucker sneered, "the Individualistic Anarchist will straightway become Communists, no doubt." He did boast that individualist anarchism blazed a trail for anarchism in both countries: "If Liberty had not been started and Comrade Andrade had not begun to agitate, perhaps there would not have been a distinctive Anarchistic movement in either country today."[45] A month later, Tucker grew even more irritated with the European communist anarchists. In response to a reader's request, Kropotkin's paper, *La Révolte*, provided *Freedom* with a list of current English-language anarchist papers. The list included *Honesty* but left out *Liberty*. Tucker believed that the two papers espoused identical principles and did not understand why one should be included but not the other. He asked Andrade to set the record straight. He did so but added that the omission had occurred "owing to the marked hostility which Comrade Tucker shows to the Communist-Anarchist papers, and which we fail to see good cause for." "'Freedom' has a strong Communistic tendency, it is true," Andrade conceded, "but its Communism is more than counterbalanced by its vigorous and unremitting protests on behalf of individual liberty." Andrade reasoned that the communistic element could be taken on board voluntarily. Tucker disagreed; it was a slippery slope, and he ended his complaint with a "warning to the editor of 'Honesty.' Danger that way lies."[46] Andrade's writings continued to circulate in the international anarchist press. In 1888, *The Alarm*, a New York–based paper edited by Dyer Lum, published Andrade's column "Anarchy: Its Definition," taken from the *Radical*, an Australian paper edited by William Robert Winspear in the Hamilton suburb of Newcastle, New South Wales.[47]

The philosophical debates and subsequent split within the Melbourne Anarchist Club began when Fred Upham delivered a June 1888 lecture, "The Anarchism of Prince Kropotkin," based on an 1887 article by Kropotkin that had appeared in a British literary monthly, *The Nineteenth Century*.[48] Club members immediately launched into a debate. Andrade admired Kropotkin but could not agree with his support for mass uprisings and expropriation. Others, among them Scottish-born laborer Larry Petrie (1859–1901), favored expropriation and expressed support for *La Révolte*.[49] Also in attendance was John Arthur Andrews, a quiet and frail-looking man who had just returned to Melbourne from a yearlong stay in rural Dunolly, Victoria.

J. A. Andrews as International Correspondent

Jack Andrews (1865–1903) was Australia's leading voice of communist anarchism and was easily the most internationally connected activist in the Australasian anarchist movement. Both his parents were born in London, and once in Australia, his father became chief clerk at the Victoria Mines and Water Supply Department. Born in Bendigo, a hundred miles north of Melbourne, young Jack was often bullied at school. He entered Scotch College in 1879 and graduated in 1881. A year later, his father died. Andrews took a job in the same department with a good salary and discovered a talent for writing: he once won a prize for a poem on the eight-hour day. He then became interested in freethinking and socialism and grew increasingly disillusioned with his job until he was dismissed days before Christmas 1886. His physical and mental health deteriorated to the point where he may have considered suicide. He joined the Melbourne Anarchist Club but did not make his first visit until January 1887 and was initially unconvinced of the soundness of anarchism. After a restorative stay in Dunolly, he returned to a club absorbed in debate, only to leave as a journalist spreading the wisdom of communist anarchism.[50]

In 1889, Andrews became a correspondent for a number of international anarchist publications. He knew several languages, including Latin and Chinese, and began soaking up the ideas of Kropotkin as they appeared in *La Révolte*.[51] While Andrade resided in South Yarra, just east of downtown Melbourne, Andrews lived in Richmond, also east of Melbourne but north of the Yarra River. From there, he penned "Communism and Communist-Anarchism" and sent it to Tucker, who published it in May 1889. Andrews explained the principle "to each according to his needs" and reassured his skeptical readers that communist anarchism's "revolutionary aspect is howled at by some, but the revolution is simply throwing off the yokes instead of waiting for them to rot off."[52] The article became Andrews's last for *Liberty*. According to Bob James, Andrews also published his work in two Portuguese anarchist papers.[53]

In 1890, an economic downturn descended into full-blown depression, throwing thousands out of work. Andrews had tramped his way to Sydney, where he joined German-born anarchist and florist Joseph Schellenberg at his farm in nearby Smithfield. They and others set up the Communist Anarchist Group, which affiliated with the Australian Socialist League and issued a manifesto.[54] In August, Andrews sent a report on the maritime strike to Most, who published it in *Freiheit* in October 1890. Andrews believed that Melbourne was on the verge of a general strike and revolution and that the anarchists were educating workers as well as operating soup kitchens for the unemployed.[55] *Freiheit* later published Andrews's "Anarchismus in Australien," which he may have translated himself.[56] Most had by this time tempered his insurrectionary rhetoric and veered toward communist anarchism. In fact, Most found his own Australian correspondent and distributor of printed materials, including *Freiheit* subscriptions. In 1891, C. Weinhold, based in Adelaide's German community, purchased pamphlets from New York and collected funds to support Most's partner, Helene Minkin, while Most was incarcerated.[57] Little is known about the German anarchists in Adelaide, but by 1896, they seemed to have been the only coherent anarchist association in Australia. "There is no consolidated party whatever to back us up," Andrews reported to American readers, "except in Adelaide where there is a small groupe of German Anarchists who contributed £4 [to Andrews's *Reason*] and do their best to push on the circulation in that city."[58]

Andrews struggled to make a living. He was forced to tramp for months at the beginning of 1892 but continued writing and agitating. He found time to correspond with historian Max Nettlau, who cultivated a keen interest in global anarchism. Writing in a frank, personal style, Andrews described his precarious and solitary existence in a land of struggling anarchists: "The movement in Australia appears more disintegrated than it has ever been." Maintaining connections with comrades in Australia and abroad was essential not only tactically but also psychologically: "If I can keep in active communication with others interested in the movement it will keep me going."[59] Andrews's letters illustrate that he had access to a variety of foreign anarchist papers, either through personal subscription or through Australia's radical groups. He read the Spanish paper *El Combate* (Bilbao), *La Révolte*, and *Les Temps Nouveaux* (Paris). In return, he sent copies of Australian papers and pamphlets to Nettlau and other outlets abroad. Andrews soon began disseminating his own ideas in anarchist papers in Europe and the United States.

Throughout the early 1890s, Andrews lacked steady work and published several short-lived papers such as *Reason* and *Revolt*, usually with the most primitive means at hand. He joined the Active Service Brigade, founded in 1893 as a radical direct-action organization for the unemployed and a constant headache for conservatives.[60] He published polemical pieces defending anarchism in the mainstream and labor press. In December 1894, he was arrested and charged with seditious libel, and he was convicted and sentenced to five months in jail the following year. Authorities confiscated all his papers, pamphlets, and drafts. In the fall of 1895, after his release, he moved back to Melbourne and began writing regular reports and essays for *Les Temps Nouveaux*, the successor to *La Révolte* edited by Jean Grave. Andrews also became a regular correspondent for *The Firebrand*. For two years he dispatched regularly lucid articles on anarchist organization, revolution, property, and communism as well as reports on the movement in Australia. In 1897, he was offered a position with *The Firebrand* but was unable to pay for the voyage to the United States.[61]

Andrews's correspondence with anarchists in the United States and Europe provides a window into the workings of a remarkably integrated global anarchist network at least at the level of exchanges of news and ideas. The editorial offices of anarchist papers were not simply locales for expediting a product; rather, and perhaps to a greater extent, they were destinations and clearinghouses for a large amount of printed material from all corners of the globe that was serialized, translated, advertised, or forwarded to other periodicals. A cursory glance at the "letters" section of any anarchist periodical of the era hints at the truly polyglot and transnational logistics behind the production of each issue. In 1896, *The Firebrand* inserted a brief notice by Andrews asking "the comrades in this country" to refute an assertion, made in the *Melbourne Age*, that American socialist Eugene Debs and Illinois governor John Peter Altgeld are anarchists.[62] A month later, *The Firebrand*'s editors responded to an inquiry concerning the paper's opinion on a French radical colony in New Jersey by endorsing their Australian correspondent's views on the matter.[63]

In a polyglot anarchist media network, language was often the most practical approach for assessing the movement's strength. While news about international anarchism or general social and political affairs was arranged under country headings, anarchist press ventures were grouped by language, so that the heading "Italian Language" included papers from the United States, Argentina, Tunisia, and Italy. Translators played a pivotal role and were always in demand. Anarchists had long discussed the idea of a central translation bureau, which was revived in the mid-1890s when German anarchist Alfred Sanftleben (1871–1952), also known as Slovak, set up a service at his residence in Zürich by placing announcements in the major anarchist newspapers, including *Freiheit*, *The Firebrand*, and *Les Temps Nouveaux*.[64] Sanftleben's home became a clearinghouse for translated books and pamphlets. Andrews, too, made use of it. In 1896, Sanftleben sent Andrews a book along with a letter requesting information on the movement in Australia and copies of radical papers. Sanftleben placed a similar request in *Les Temps Nouveaux*. Andrews then composed a report in English and sent it to Sanftleben for translation, even though Andrews was fluent in French. As a correspondent, Andrews also sent an English-language report, "Our Movement in Australia," to *The Firebrand*, where it was published in May.[65] The edited French version appeared in *Les Temps Nouveaux* in July.[66] Andrews died of tuberculosis on 26 July 1903 in Melbourne. His talents as a writer and translator made him one of the more compelling Australian anarchists, but his constant struggle to avoid penury and his early death prevented him from becoming a true international traveler for anarchism in the manner of Pietro Gori or Peter Kropotkin.

Chummy Fleming and May Day

Shortly after the founding of the Melbourne Anarchist Club, several of its members, including Andrews (who overcame a stutter), conducted open-air speeches on the banks of the Yarra River. When the economic depression of the early 1890s created a mass of unemployed workers, especially in the cities, several Melbourne anarchists made significant connections with the jobless, whom Andrews told that class divisions in society historically were not the cause but the result of the formation of the state.

One of the most active, persistent, and loudest tub-thumpers was Andrews's friend John William "Chummy" Fleming (1864–1950). Born in England to an Irish working-class father and English mother, Fleming learned the trade of bootmaker before coming to Australia in 1884.[67] If Andrews wielded an eloquent pen, Fleming transformed his radical temper into fiery speeches with strength and courage. He was later remembered as the "most tenacious and enduring agitator" in the history of Australian anarchism, partly because he outlived everyone else.[68] When three unemployed protesters were arrested in Melbourne in 1885, Fleming resolved to free them, announcing a meeting on the Queen's Wharf. Money collected there paid the fine for one of the protesters. Andrade and Upham also spoke but abandoned these activities when the government, aided by the Harbor Trust, began cracking down. Fleming was unfazed and returned to the wharf despite frequent harassment and beatings by thugs. "I have fought an uphill fight," Fleming boasted, "but dogged determination has crowned my labor with success."[69] He attracted thousands of listeners, many of whom bought anarchist literature from him. On 17 August 1890, five thousand people gathered around Fleming's "flaming flag of Anarchy."[70]

In 1889, the Second International had proclaimed that an annual celebration of labor would be held beginning on 1 May 1890. This initiative was rooted in the older campaign for an eight-hour workday that had galvanized American workers beginning in 1886. In Australia, however, workers had been celebrating a Labour Eight-Hour Day since the 1850s but had done so on different dates—21 April in Victoria.[71] This traditional Labour Day was exclusively a celebration of Australian craftsmen; unskilled workers were excluded. On 21 April 1890, therefore, a group of unemployed workers disrupted Melbourne's official procession, prompting Fleming to unfurl a banner that screamed, "Feed on Our Flesh and Blood You Capitalist Hyenas: It Is Your Funeral Feast."[72] One angry passerby promptly tore it to pieces. In 1913, Fleming, now aged forty-nine, was still setting up his booth and adorning it with his red flag to address the crowd, but by this time, he noted, "I was not mobbed nor interrupted."[73] During World War I, when Australia participated on the side of the British, Fleming continued his orations. He sent a short report to *The Blast*, which was located in San Francisco and edited by Emma Goldman's lifelong companion, Alexander Berkman: "Recently I addressed an out-of-door meeting. There were present about ten thousand people. You can see by the enclosed newspaper clippings how brutally the soldiers attacked me, smashed the platform, burned the red flag and injured my back."[74]

The celebration of *another* day of labor on 1 May that would include all workers regardless of skill therefore became a statement about the solidarity of labor. Not well-groomed craftsmen but Queensland shearers at the Barcaldine camp inaugurated Australia's May Day march in 1891.[75] In Melbourne, Fleming, who had rejected the parochially traditional Labour Day, founded May Day in 1892 as what Andrews declared "a protest," even "a warning to tyrant[s]."[76] These events unfolded in the midst of an economic depression accompanied by a wave of strikes in Australia's key industries from 1890 to 1894. Depression and unemployment also crippled the United States, where, according to Robin Archer, "state repression was greater . . . than it was in Australia."[77] Emma Goldman, fast becoming the most publicly active anarchist in America, also addressed crowds of up to three thousand unemployed New Yorkers in 1893, defending the hungry person's right to take bread; she was eventually arrested and briefly jailed. Radical movements always diminish—but rarely disappear—during economic hard times. One of the main differences between Goldman's and Fleming's public agitation was the fact that Fleming increasingly resembled an activist without a movement, whereas Goldman was the voice of an American movement still capable of stagecraft and fund-raising. "Towards the end of 1895," Bob James has written, "Fleming participated in an attempt to revive the Melbourne Anarchist Club. This came to nothing. Crowds had dwindled also on the Yarra Bank, but authorities continued to harass speakers."[78] In 1909, Fleming asked Nettlau to "please only send three *Freedoms* it is about all I can sell. I will forward some money soon."[79] This disparity was implicit in one Melbourne paper's warning of an alleged anarchist threat: "Special emissaries have been sent to these colonies from the head-quarters of the Socialists in America and England to rouse up the working class."[80]

In 1907, Fleming invited Goldman for a two-year tour of Australia to begin in 1909. Renowned lecturers connected dispersed movements with the goal of invigorating deflated branches. For example, Kropotkin twice visited the United States, and Gori and Malatesta made successful propaganda tours there as well.[81] In fact, Andrade had once suggested to Tucker that Edwin Cox Walker, editor of *Lucifer, the Light-Bearer,* come to Australia to reform the "law-ridden Australasians," though he never did.[82]

Goldman had already visited Britain, France, and Canada, and in 1908 she was thrilled with the prospect of going to Australia: "I am strongly contemplating giving up everything," she wrote to a friend, "and going to Australia, travelling a few years alone."[83] Fifteen hundred pounds of literature were sent to Victoria in advance.[84] "Comrades in Sydney and Adelaide are anxious for you to come," raved Fleming, "and are organizing into committees to raise funds and arrange meetings. You can look forward to a successful tour."[85] Fleming kept Americans abreast of the Australian movement (as Andrade and Andrews had done) by sending letters to Goldman's *Mother Earth* magazine.[86] Goldman's pending visit was reported in all of Australia's major papers: "An Apostle of Unrest. To Visit Australia," screamed one headline.[87] Her initial departure date, 23 January 1909, was postponed after she was arrested for disturbing the peace.[88] The next chance came in March, but Goldman canceled at the last minute, worried about her pending loss of citizenship and the government's attempt to exile her for life. Fleming tried to bring her over as late as December 1909, but she never went and was deported ten years later anyway.[89] Fleming resumed his Yarra bank speeches and held true to his anarchism until his death—"the last of the Mohicans," as Stuart Christie called him.[90]

Conclusion

The formative years of Australian anarchism show that despite the movement's modest size, a number of key figures—Andrade, Andrews, Fleming—consciously cultivated a transnational dimension. Their connections with Americans were neither incidental nor trivial; instead, such links deeply affected and informed their words and actions at home. As "rooted cosmopolitans" in a wider anarchist network, they spread the tenets of anarchism—including the notion that parliamentary methods and labor politics were corrupt and futile—to a "wide circle of working-class people."[91] As far as historians can determine, none of the key figures in Australian anarchism traveled to the United States and experienced firsthand American labor conditions and politics, as did labor activists P. H. Hickey and Harry Bridges, for example.[92] One reason may be that anarchism in Australia initially arose not as a social movement but as a politico-philosophical exchange in letters and periodicals between men such as Andrade and Tucker.

Different immigration patterns in the United States and Australia partly explain why anarchism declined in Australia as early as 1901 but continued to grow in the United States. While immigrants to both countries in 1890 overwhelmingly came from Northern and Western Europe, the United States received a far larger contingent from Germany, and a handful of Germans in American cities started and sustained an anarchist movement beginning in 1880. Even in Australia, German immigrants in Adelaide served as the heart of the anarchist movement. While Andrews once observed that in Sydney, "the anarchists themselves . . . were nearly all foreigners," the massive influx of Southern and Eastern European immigrants into the United States from 1900 to 1920 had no parallel in Australia.[93] Jewish and Italian radicals sustained and expanded American anarchism into a major radical movement before 1917.[94] The White Australia campaign, and nationalism in general also likely played a role in the diminishing appeal of any radical internationalist alternatives.[95] Even some Australian anarchists, among them Petrie, were far from consistent in their opposition to racism, especially its anti-Chinese variant.[96]

Progressive Australian social legislation between 1901 and 1914 may also have kept workers aloof from the anarchist message. In 1901, John Dwyer, a leading figure in the Active Service Brigade, sent two letters to London's *Freedom*. "We here *have* what some people consider Utopia," Dwyer explained, listing factory and arbitration acts, an eight-hour day and minimum wage, labor bureaus, and an old-age pension. Perhaps claiming too much, Dwyer asserted that despite being "few in number," anarchists "in Australia have been practically the means of forcing ideas and circumstances equally in our favor." Whereas the voices of anarchism grew louder in America, Dwyer pointed out, in Australia "we Anarchists don't do too much yelling, but we are there everytime."[97]

Notes

The title of this chapter comes from Benjamin Tucker, "On Picket Duty," *Liberty* (Boston), 20 February 1886. I thank Shawn P. Wilbur, who has made *Liberty* available online (http://travellinginliberty.blogspot.com/2007/08/index-of-liberty-site.html), and Wendy McElroy, who created an index to the paper (https://web.archive.org/web/20060903022232/http://tmh.floonet.net/articles/ind_int2.html). I thank the National Library of Australia for creating the Trove digitized newspaper database (https://trove.nla.gov.au/newspaper). I also thank Bob James for making available his own and others' work on Australian anarchism (http://www.takver.com/history/indexbj.htm). All of James's works cited in this chapter are available at this site.

1. *Liberty* (Boston), 20 February 1886.

2. Ibid., 14 November 1885, 20 February 1886.

3. Constance Bantman and Bert Altena, eds., *Reassessing the Transnational Turn: Scales of Analysis in Anarchist and Syndicalist Studies* (New York: Routledge, 2015).

4. See Jesse Cohn, *Underground Passages: Anarchist Resistance Culture, 1848–2011* (Oakland, Calif.: AK, 2014).

5. Davide Turcato, "Italian Anarchism as a Transnational Movement, 1885–1915," *International Review of Social History* 52 (2007): 407–44.

6. Quoted in ibid., 412.

7. I do not present an overview of Australian anarchism; its history has been written elsewhere. See Sam Merrifield, "The Melbourne Anarchist Club, 1886–1891," *Bulletin of the Australian Society for the Study of Labour History*, November 1962, 32. See also Sam Merrifield, "The Formation of the Melbourne Anarchist Club," *Recorder*, July 1964; Andrew Markus, "White Australia? Socialists and Anarchists," *Arena* 32–33 (1973): 80–89; Bob James, ed., *A Reader of Australian Anarchism, 1886–1896* (Canberra: James, 1979); Bob James, *Anarchism and State Violence in Sydney and Melbourne, 1886–1896: An Argument about Australian Labor History* (Newcastle East, N.S.W.: James, 1986); Bob James, *Anarchism in Australia: An Anthology* (Parkville, Vic.: James, 1986); Verity Burgmann, "One Hundred Years of Anarchism," *Arena* 74 (1986): 104–14; Bruce Scates, *A New Australia: Citizenship, Radicalism, and the First Republic* (Cambridge: Cambridge University Press, 1997); G. Cresciani, "The Proletarian Migrants: Fascism and Italian Anarchists in Australia," *Australian Quarterly* 51 (1979): 6.

8. Sidney Tarrow, *The New Transnational Activism* (Cambridge: Cambridge University Press, 2005).

9. Bruce Scates, "'Millennium or Pandemonium?' Radicalism in the Labour Movement, Sydney, 1889–1899," *Labour History* 50 (1986): 72.

10. Announcements appeared in local papers, including the conservative *Argus* (Melbourne) on 5, 19 June 1886.

11. See Scates, *New Australia*.

12. Verity Burgmann, *"In Our Time": Socialism and the Rise of Labor, 1885–1905* (Sydney: Allen and Unwin, 1985), 7.

13. Merrifield, "Melbourne Anarchist Club." See also Merrifield, "Formation."

14. See F. B. Smith, "Joseph Symes and the Australasian Secular Association," *Labour History* 5 (1963): 34.

15. Robin Archer, *Why Is There No Labor Party in the United States?* (Princeton: Princeton University Press, 2007), 177.

16. Burgmann, *"In Our Time,"* 108, 149–51. For more on Germans in Australia, see Jürgen Tampke, *The Germans in Australia* (Port Melbourne, Vic.; Cambridge University Press, 2006); R. B. Walker, "German-Language Press and People in South Australia, 1848–1900," *Journal of the Royal Australian Historical Society* 58 (1972): 121–40.

17. Andrew Reeves, "Andrade, David Alfred (1859–1928)," *Australian Dictionary of Biography,* available at http://adb.anu.edu.au/biography/andrade-david-alfred-5024/text8359. See also Sam Merrifield, "David Alfred Andrade," *Recorder,* March 1965.

18. David Andrade, "What Is Anarchy?," *Liberty* (Boston), 28 May 1887. This was originally a lecture given in May 1886 in Melbourne.

19. Burgmann, "One Hundred Years," 104.

20. See *Bendigo Advertiser,* 15 May 1891.

21. J. W. Fleming to Max Nettlau, 14 May 1933, Max Nettlau Papers, International Institute for Social History, Amsterdam.

22. *Liberty* (Boston), 2 July 1887.

23. The Australasian Secular Association received anarchist literature from abroad as early as 1884. See James, *Anarchism and State Violence,* chap. 4.

24. See Wendy McElroy, "Benjamin Tucker, *Liberty,* and Individualist Anarchism," *Independent Review* 2 (1998): 421–34; James J. Martin, *Men against the State: The Expositors of Individualist Anarchism, 1827–1908* (1953; Colorado Springs: Myles, 1970).

25. These reports appeared in *Liberty* from February 1886 to May 1887. The last piece Andrade published in *Liberty* was "The Gospel in Australia," 6 October 1894.

26. David Andrade, "The Melboume [*sic*] Anarchist Club Manifesto," May 1886, available at http://www.takver.com/history/raa/raa02.htm.

27. David Andrade, "The Melbourne Anarchists' Club," *Liberty* (Boston), 30 October 1886. He also spots a hopeful sign in New Zealand in the figure of Joseph Evison, editor of the *Rationalist.*

28. Benjamin Tucker, "Anarchy's Growth in Australia," *Liberty* (Boston), 15 September 1888.

29. James, *Anarchism and State Violence,* chap. 4.

30. *Liberty* (Boston), 2 July 1887.

31. Benjamin Tucker, "Anarchy's Growth in Australia," *Liberty* (Boston), 15 September 1888.

32. "Der Anarchismus," and "Was ist Anarchie?" *Freiheit* (New York), 11 June 1887. Most mistakenly identified David Andrade as an "English anarchist."

33. "Socialism in Chicago," *Inquirer and Commercial News* (Perth), 5 May 1886; "Rioting in Chicago," *Evening News* (Sydney), 5 May 1886; "Riots in Chicago," *Telegraph* (Brisbane), 5 May 1886.

34. See, for example, "The Labour Movement in America," *South Australian Register* (Adelaide), 7 May 1886.

35. "A Serious Riot," *Daily News* (Perth), 6 May 1886. The organizers anticipated a crowd of perhaps twenty thousand, but according to Paul Avrich, "no more than two or three thousand had gathered on the square" (*The Haymarket Tragedy* [Princeton: Princeton

University Press, 1984], 199). James Green writes that three thousand workers had assembled (*Death in the Haymarket: A Story of Chicago, the First Labor Movement, and the Bombing That Divided Gilded Age America* [New York: Anchor, 2006], 183).

36. "The San Francisco Mail: Arrival of R.M.S. Alameda," *Evening News* (Sydney), 5 June 1886.

37. Avrich, *Haymarket Tragedy*, 227–32, 282; Timothy Messer-Kruse, *The Trial of the Haymarket Anarchists: Terrorism and Justice in the Gilded Age* (New York: Palgrave Macmillan, 2011), 77–78, 119.

38. Michael Vandelaar, "The Haymarket Affair 'Down Under,'" in *Haymarket Scrapbook*, ed. Dave Roediger and Franklin Rosemont (Chicago: Kerr, 1986), 233.

39. Quoted in ibid., 234.

40. "A Protest from Australia," *Liberty* (Boston), 9 April 1887.

41. For example, "Anarchists Hanged," *Telegraph* (Brisbane), 14 November 1887; "Execution of the Chicago Anarchists," *South Australian Advertiser* (Adelaide), 14 November 1887.

42. Quoted in Vandelaar, "Haymarket Affair," 234.

43. "On the Lookout," *Honesty*, February 1889, available at http://www.takver.com/history/aia/aia00005.htm.

44. All quoted in Paul Avrich, "Benjamin Tucker and His Daughter," in *Anarchist Portraits* (Princeton: Princeton University Press, 1988), 146.

45. Benjamin Tucker, "On Picket Duty," *Liberty* (Boston), 25 February 1888.

46. Benjamin Tucker, "Anarchy and Its Organs," *Liberty* (Boston), 14 April 1888.

47. *New York Alarm*, 1 September 1888; *Libertarian Labyrinth*, available at http://library.libertarian-labyrinth.org/items/show/3449. On Winspear, see Verity Burgmann, "The Mightier Pen: William Robert Winspear," *Rebels and Radicals*, ed. Eric C. Fry (Sydney: Allen and Unwin, 1983): 163–77.

48. Peter Kropotkin, "The Coming Anarchy," *Nineteenth Century*, August 1887, 149–64.

49. Burgmann, *"In Our Time,"* 30; Bob James, "Larry Petrie (1859–1901)—Australian Revolutionist?"

50. Bob James, "J. A. Andrews (1865–1903)—A Brief Biography"; Andrew Reeves, "Andrews, John Arthur (1865–1903)," *Australian Dictionary of Biography*, http://adb.anu.edu.au/biography/andrews-john-arthur-5028. See also Merrifield, "Melbourne Anarchist Club."

51. James, "J. A. Andrews."

52. John Arthur Andrews, "Communism and Communist-Anarchism," *Liberty* (Boston), 18 May 1889.

53. James, "J. A. Andrews."

54. Joseph Schellenberg, "Anarchism versus Socialism," *Evening News* (Sydney), 12 May 1892. Curiously, Schellenberg identified Andrews as a "female comrade."

55. *Freiheit*, 11 October 1890.

56. J. A. Andrews to Max Nettlau, 22 March 1892, Max Nettlau Papers, International Institute for Social History, Amsterdam.

57. *Freiheit*, 10, 24 October 1891. Nothing is known about Weinhold except that a man by that name was among the passengers on the MMS *Yarra* who arrived in March 1890 at Albany in Western Australia from Marseilles (*Morning Herald* [Sydney], 4 March 1890). By 1895, one "H.V." of Adelaide subscribed to *Freiheit* (*Freiheit*, 24 August, 7 December 1895). Hans Voit is another figure in the Adelaide German anarchist community who corresponded with Austrian anarchist Rudolph Grossmann (Pierre Ramus Papers, International Institute for Social History, Amsterdam).

58. J. A. Andrews, "Our Movement in Australia," *The Firebrand* (Portland, Ore.), 31 May 1896.

59. J. A. Andrews to Max Nettlau, 22 March 1892. Max Nettlau Papers, International Institute for Social History, Amsterdam.

60. Burgmann, *"In Our Time,"* 63–65. See also Andrews's articles in *Tocsin*, 17 May–28 June 1900, available at http://www.takver.com/history/aasv/aasv_app1.htm.

61. Reeves, "Andrews, John Arthur."

62. *The Firebrand* (Portland, Ore.), 13 December 1896.

63. Ibid., 10 January 1897, 4.

64. See, for example, "Bureau of Translation," *The Firebrand* (Portland, Ore.), 12 July 1896.

65. Andrews, "Our Movement in Australia."

66. *Les Temps Nouveaux* (Paris), 11–17 July 1896, available at http://gallica.bnf.fr/ark:/12148/bpt6k64891097.

67. Paul Avrich, "An Australian Anarchist: J. W. Fleming," in *Anarchist Portraits*, 260–68. The *Australian Dictionary of Biography* gives Fleming's birth year as "1863?" However, FamilySearch reveals that John William Fleming was born in Derby, England, on 4 April 1864. See "England Births and Christenings, 1538–1975," index, *FamilySearch* (https://familysearch.org/pal:/MM9.1.1/NYWF-RQB), John William Fleming, 31 March 1867; Family History Library microfilm 1041158, 1041168.

68. Quoted in Avrich, "Australian Anarchist," 260.

69. J. W. Fleming, "Progress of Anarchism at the Melbourne Wharf," *Honesty* (Melbourne), February 1889, available at http://takver.com/history/aia/aia00003.htm.

70. *Table Talk* (Melbourne), 29 August 1890.

71. Len Fox, "Early Australian May Days," *Bulletin of the Australian Society for the Study of Labour History* 2 (1962): 38 n. 4.

72. Scates, *New Australia*, 32–33.

73. Avrich, "Australian Anarchist," 265.

74. *The Blast* (San Francisco), 4 March 1916, reprinted in Alexander Berkman, *The Blast*, intro. Barry Pateman (Edinburgh: AK, 2005), 172.

75. Fox, "Early Australian May Days."

76. Scates, *New Australia*, 33.

77. Archer, *Why Is There No Labor Party?*, 117. Employers increasingly had the courts and law enforcement do their bidding in suppressing unions and labor activists. During the 1892 Homestead Strike near Pittsburgh, Henry Clay Frick hired Pinkerton guards

to break it, resulting in a bloody gun battle. Anarchist Alexander Berkman attempted to murder Frick but failed. During the 1894 Pullman strike near Chicago, US attorney general Richard Olney, a corporate lawyer on retainer with major railroad companies, supported the General Managers Association. He had President Grover Cleveland dispatch federal troops to end the strike.

78. Bob James, "Chummy Fleming (1863–1950): A Brief Biography."

79. J. W. Fleming to Max Nettlau, 4 May 1909, Max Nettlau Papers, International Institute for Social History, Amsterdam.

80. "Amongst the Anarchists," *Table Talk* (Melbourne), 20 May 1892.

81. See Turcato, "Italian Anarchism."

82. David Andrade, "Anarchy in Australia," *Liberty* (Boston), 20 February 1886.

83. Quoted in Bob James, "Emma Goldman: The Australian Connection."

84. Emma Goldman, *Living My Life* (1931; New York: Dover, 1970), 2:437.

85. Quoted in Bob James, "Emma Goldman: The Australian Connection."

86. "International Notes," *Mother Earth* 5 (1910): 61–64.

87. *Advertiser* (Adelaide), 10 September 1908.

88. Emma Goldman, "The End of the Odyssey," *Mother Earth*, April 1909, quoted in *Emma Goldman: A Documentary History of the American Years: Making Speech Free, 1902–1909*, ed. Candace Falk, Barry Pateman, and Jessica Moran (Urbana: University of Illinois Press, 2005), 2:418.

89. The US government revoked her ex-husband's citizenship, thus jeopardizing her status. See Goldman, "End of the Odyssey."

90. Quoted in Avrich, "Australian Anarchist," 266.

91. Burgmann, "One Hundred Years," 107.

92. See Peter Clayworth, this volume; Robert Cherny, this volume.

93. J. A. Andrews, "Anarchism and the Social Movement in Australia," *L'Humanité Nouvelle*, 1898, quoted in James, "J. A. Andrews." For the 1920s, see Cresciani, "Proletarian Migrants."

94. See Kenyon Zimmer, *Immigrants against the State: Yiddish and Italian Anarchism in America* (Urbana: University of Illinois Press, 2015).

95. Archer, *Why Is There No Labor Party?*, 58.

96. Verity Burgmann, "Racism, Socialism, and the Labour Movement, 1887–1917," *Labour History* 47 (1984): 39–54. In 1888, Petrie declared that "depravity is the natural result of association with Chinamen" (43).

97. John Dwyer, "A Letter from Australia" [7 August 1901], *Freedom* (London), October 1901.

An Agitator Abroad

P. H. Hickey, Industrial Unionism, and Socialism in the United States, New Zealand, and Australia, 1900–1930

PETER CLAYWORTH

Patrick Hodgens Hickey (1882–1930) was a labor activist whose life illustrates the transnational migration of workers and their ideas during the early twentieth century. Hickey was one of the most prominent and controversial labor leaders during New Zealand's "Red Fed" era. In those years (1907–14), a major workers' revolt broke out against the country's compulsory arbitration system. From the speaker's platform and in print, Hickey advocated revolutionary industrial unionism and socialism. Most of New Zealand's militant labor leaders were originally from Australia or the United Kingdom, although they included several North American propagandists. Hickey, in contrast, was from New Zealand, where he grew up during a time of industrial peace under the arbitration system. His political and industrial ideologies had their origins in his youthful travels around the United States, which introduced him to mining, union agitation, and class warfare. Beginning in 1916, Hickey spent a considerable portion of his activist career in Australia. His life and work show the mobility of workers' political and industrial ideas and activism, highlighting how workers created international webs and transmitted their experiences and ideologies from one geographical and industrial context to another.[1]

The Red Feds and Transglobal Networks

Hickey was a prominent leader of the New Zealand Federation of Labour (NZFL), the union peak body known colloquially as the Red Feds. The development of the NZFL was firmly linked to the mobility of working people and their ideas in the late nineteenth and early twentieth centuries. International investment and imperial adventures opened up a transglobal labor market to European workers. The expansion of the British Empire and of the continental United States placed "white" English-speaking workers at a distinct advantage in a market built on land and resources obtained relatively cheaply from indigenous populations. Steamships and railways made travel easier, faster, and less expensive. Prior to the First World War, many restrictions on travel had yet to be universally applied. Cheaper and more efficient printing, mail, and telegraphic systems aided the spread of information by working-class people. Webs of connection developed around the planet, particularly between Anglophone workers in industries such as mining and transport. Militant labor activists became a strand in the broader net of workers and working-class ideologies. Hickey was part of a global movement where the doctrines of revolutionary industrial unionism were spread by traveling activists and through rapidly improving communication systems.[2]

British immigrants brought unionism to New Zealand in the second half of the nineteenth century. Weakened by the defeat of the 1890 maritime strike, New Zealand unions initially welcomed the reforming Liberal government's compulsory arbitration system, established in 1895. By 1907, after a protracted period of industrial peace, some unionists were disillusioned with arbitration. They believed Arbitration Court decisions were too favorable to employers, while wage awards failed to keep up with inflation. Older union leaders were hesitant to take direct action, but their reluctance was not shared by a coterie of young Australian activists newly arrived in New Zealand. Economic downturn and industrial strife in early twentieth-century Australia had induced many experienced union activists to cross the Tasman expecting to find a workers' paradise. Disappointed with the reality of New Zealand's industrial relations, many of these migrants formed the backbone of the Red Fed movement, bringing to it their experience of industrial conflict.[3]

While the NZFL was founded on British unionism and powered by energetic Australian militants, its doctrines of revolutionary industrial unionism were largely North American in origin. As Robin Archer discusses in this volume, the turn of the century saw considerable exchange of ideas between North America and Australasia. American progressive thinkers and unionists took a direct interest in New Zealand's social and industrial reforms, while many

American ideas influenced New Zealand.[4] Henry George's single-tax ideas had a strong impact in the 1880s and 1890s, while Edward Bellamy's utopian socialist *Looking Backwards* was a best seller. The Knights of Labour formed branches around New Zealand, influencing the Liberal government's reforms. The early twentieth century brought more radical North American activists, including American socialist Robert Rives Lamonte and two Canadians, Socialist Party of Canada agitator H. M. Fitzgerald and militant J. B. King of the Industrial Workers of the World (IWW).[5] Pat Hickey was part of this flow, bringing the revolutionary influences of the Western Federation of Miners (WFM) and the Socialist Party of America (SPA).

Background and Early Travels

Pat Hickey was born on 19 January 1882 on a farm at the junction of the Motueka and Wangapeka Rivers, in backcountry Nelson, on New Zealand's South Island. His parents, Thomas Hickey and Mary Jane Hodgens Hickey, were Irish immigrants. Pat, the third son and fourth of seven siblings, grew up in a staunchly Catholic, pro-Fenian household. Following Thomas's accidental death in 1890, the Hickeys moved to the rural village of Foxhill. With no Catholic schools in the vicinity, Pat attended state primary schools. After leaving school at the age of fourteen, he worked briefly as a clerk before becoming a sawmill laborer to avoid being bound to a desk.[6] Hickey's early jobs were not unionized, and he showed no interest in unions or socialism. He was eager to travel, unsuccessfully attempting to enlist for the South African war.[7]

Hickey wanted to visit County Cavan, Ireland, seeking an inheritance Thomas Hickey claimed to have left there. Leaving New Zealand in March 1900, Pat sailed for San Francisco, assuming that the United States would be a cheap departure point for Ireland. Work was initially plentiful in California, but wages were low and conditions often poor.[8] Hickey became an itinerant worker, part of the "floating army" of labor for the agriculture, logging, construction, mining, and milling industries.[9] In Central and Northern California, he learned that mining and smelting provided the best-paid work for itinerant laborers. Hickey became a true hobo, "beating the trains" through Idaho, Oregon, Wyoming, Colorado, Utah, and Nevada. Jumping trains was an uncomfortable and dangerous form of transportation. In the winter, the extreme weather made outdoor work impossible, while mining jobs were hard to find as a consequence of a series of miners' strikes. Hickey eventually found work at a copper mine in Shasta County, Northern California, but he returned home three months later with almost empty pockets.[10]

Mining and Class War: Choosing Sides?

After returning to New Zealand in 1901, Hickey went to Buller, on the South Island's West Coast. He worked at the Denniston mines as a trucker, pushing trucks to and from the coal face, then graduated to loading trucks. The miners' work hierarchy resembled the Australian shearers' work hierarchy.[11] Trucking and loading, though low-ranked occupations, were steps to a hewer's job. The hewers, who worked the coal face, were the highest-ranked and most influential workers and unionists. Hickey's first American odyssey introduced him to underground mining, but he did not become a hewer until 1905. He only gained influence in the miners' unions after becoming an experienced hewer.[12]

Hickey became a miner when a network of Anglophone mining communities existed around the globe. The mining communities of Scotland, Wales, and England (including Cornish metal miners) were linked to mining communities in the United States, Canada, South Africa, Australia, and New Zealand. English-speaking miners had an advantage under this system. Traveling the world, they found employment combined with a shared language and vocabulary, work practices, leisure activities, and union culture. Mining unionism often provided space for militant activism and discussion of socialist ideas.[13]

Before becoming a traveling activist, Hickey was simply an itinerant worker. He was not a union member during his first American journey and joined the Denniston union only because the mine was a closed shop.[14] His early travels did not radicalize him, but the United States provided Hickey with his first observations of open class warfare. New Zealand had no major strikes from 1893 to 1907, an industrial peace enforced from 1895 onward by the compulsory arbitration system. The American West, with its numerous miners' strikes, provided a stark contrast. Hickey and his traveling companions were not tempted to become strikebreakers despite days of hunger riding the mountain rails in midwinter.[15] They were repelled by the idea of scabbing rather than afraid of retaliation. Hickey commented, "We did not have a chance unless we would go scabbing and this of course we were determined not to start."[16] Though not yet committed to unionism, he sided with the striker rather than the scab.

Back to the United States

In 1903, the twenty-one-year-old Hickey booked passage to London and then made his way to Ireland. His County Cavan relatives informed him that the family inheritance was mythical: Thomas Hickey had left Ireland as a penniless orphan. Pat Hickey decided to return to the United States and make his own fortune.[17] He arrived in New York in June 1903, just as a wave of strikes swept the city. Italian tunnelers stopped work on the subway, while disputes involving carpenters, ironworkers, plasterers, cement floor workers, and teamsters halted New York's building boom.[18] Hickey headed for Youngstown, Ohio, finding work at the "Carnegie" steel mill.[19] There he met veterans of the infamous 1892 Homestead strike. Hickey later used Homestead to illustrate the brutality of capitalism, charging Andrew Carnegie with paying for philanthropy in workers' blood.[20]

After a month at the steel mill, Hickey headed west, traveling through Chicago, Kansas, and Colorado. As during his first American sojourn, Irish connections helped Hickey find work and accommodations.[21] Hickey passed through Colorado in October or early November 1903, while the Colorado Labor Wars were in full swing. WFM copper miners struck at Teller County and Telluride, while coal miners of the United Mine Workers of America struck at Trinidad. Unionists had armed confrontations with local deputies, employers' gunmen, and the National Guard. Hickey wrote, "The whole country was on strike here and the militia were guarding the company's properties." In Colorado, class warfare was not an abstract concept.[22]

The Western Federation of Miners

Hickey worked at a copper smelter in Northern California, then explored and prospected around the Aleutian Islands before working at a sawmill in Washington. By July 1905 he was at a copper mine in Bingham Canyon, Utah. After joining the strong WFM Local 67, he was nominated for the union finance committee and a delegation to the state union convention.[23] Hickey left Utah in September 1905 to avoid the winter, but his brief experience with Local 67 began his career in union leadership, agitation, and labor politics.[24] The WFM's strategy of combining industrial unionism with political support for socialist parties became the basis of his activist thinking.

From its foundation in 1893 through to 1905, the WFM endured bitter, often violent, struggles with employers and state forces. The union became more radical, promoting industrial unionism as enabling workers to gain control of the workplace and the products of their labor. The WFM sought to enroll all mining and metal-processing workers while supporting broader unionization outside the mining industry. At the turn of the century, workers in many Rocky Mountain mining towns held a considerable degree of power both in the workplace and in municipal administration through the combined strategy of industrial unionism and political engagement.[25] The WFM's original political strategy, which John P. Enyeart calls "union centered political action," involved organizing union members to support pro-labor candidates regardless of their party. Such a strategy encouraged all aspiring political candidates to take seriously the interests of unionized workers.[26]

Elizabeth Jameson has described a localized example of industrial unionism and union-centered political action in Cripple Creek, Teller County, Colorado. From 1898 to 1903, the WFM organized the majority of the district's wage workers. Unions insisted that local governments enforce the union pay scale and the eight-hour day. Many elected officials in the district's mining towns were active union members.[27] Union control of Cripple Creek was broken in 1904, with the WFM's defeat in the Colorado Labor Wars, but Hickey witnessed similar union power at Bingham Canyon. WFM members who also belonged to the SPA had a strong presence in Bingham's local government.[28]

The 1902 WFM convention voted to abandon general union-centered political action in favor of officially endorsing the SPA. Opponents of the endorsement believed that it would reduce union influence over political candidates. Supporters argued that the Socialists were the only party that could be trusted to deliver a just society for working people. Jameson has shown that despite official policy, many WFM members continued to vote for candidates from other parties. Regardless of whether or not they voted Socialist, most Rocky Mountain unionists supported a dual industrial and political strategy for social change.[29]

Days of Hope: Bingham Canyon Socialism

Hickey arrived at Bingham in mid-1905, an active time for the SPA local. Utah locals had been busy in 1904, promoting the presidential campaign of Eugene Debs and campaigning for Utah's own Socialist candidates.[30] In 1905 the Utah SPA was preparing for the November local government elections. Bingham went on to elect a Socialist mayor and Utah's first SPA-dominated municipal administration. Between 1901 and the early 1920s, at least 115 Socialist candidates were elected to public office in Utah, holding positions in more than two dozen towns and cities. Five Utah municipalities elected majority Socialist administrations.[31] Hickey, a foreigner, could not vote but may have helped the SPA's campaign preparations. He would have missed the election victory, having left for California in September.[32]

Hickey's newfound enthusiasm for industrial unionism would have been reinforced by the considerable power that the WFM and SPA wielded in the day-today running of the Bingham Canyon community. Bingham was relatively quiet during Hickey's stay, but members of Local 67 must have been infected by the heightened sense of class warfare brought on by the WFM's ongoing struggles.[33] At Bingham Hickey would have met veterans of the Colorado Labor Wars, whose enemies in the Cripple Creek fight, the Penrose brothers and Charles McNair of the US Reduction and Refining Company, were major investors in Bingham Canyon.[34] Militant class-conscious unionists saw themselves as fighting a class war that the workers would inevitably win. Hickey joined the revolutionary industrial unionist movement just as a new strategy for unity was being launched. The WFM was the major initiator of the IWW foundation conference, held at Chicago in June 1905, around the time Hickey was arriving in Utah. Local 67 passed resolutions supporting the IWW and formed the Bingham Canyon IWW Local 93.[35] Hickey later claimed to have met SPA leader Eugene Debs and WFM secretary William Haywood, two meetings that would have fired his enthusiasm.[36] When Hickey left the United States in 1906, he was optimistic, unaware of the schisms and disillusionment that would engulf the revolutionary industrial movement.

Hickey's experience with the WFM at Bingham appears to have been the key event in his conversion to revolutionary industrial unionism.[37] Traveling through the United States had shown him the real nature of class struggle. Throughout his working life, Hickey stood up for his working conditions, arguing with bosses or leaving a job if he believed he was being treated unfairly. He frequently applied the policy of spelling—working no harder than he had to and taking frequent rests during tough physical jobs. Hickey supported the idea, promoted by the WFM and other mining unions, that workers should gain as much control of their workplaces as possible.[38] The aggressive male approach of the WFM's "two-fisted men" appealed to Hickey, who was not afraid to defend himself physically. He respected the WFM as a union literally prepared to fight for its members while it emphasized the gendered, masculinist idea of the dignity of the workingman.[39]

Hickey's personal vision now expanded beyond a narrow concern for his own working conditions to advancing the interests of working people as a class. He adopted the WFM and SPA strategies of trying to establish workers' control over the economic system through both industrial unionism and socialist political activity. His views on the relative importance of industrial versus political struggle varied through the years, but the dual strategy remained at the heart of his thinking. Hickey's involvement with the WFM and the SPA gave him a worldview built around class struggle as highlighted by the rugged industrial relations of the American West.

A Prophet in His Own Country

In later years, Hickey proudly recalled returning to New Zealand in 1906 carrying the red card of the Socialist Party of America and his membership ticket in the "great American fighting union the Western Federation of Miners."[40] Hickey developed and disseminated his industrial and political ideas while involved in itinerant work, experiences comparable to those of young Harry Bridges.[41] Hickey came home at a time when a significant minority of workers were becoming disillusioned with New Zealand's compulsory arbitration system and its promoters, the moderate trade unions and the "progressive" Liberal government. Hickey thus found a ready-made audience for the messages he brought from the American class struggle. He returned to the Denniston coal mines as an experienced miner, obtaining work as a hewer. Hewers had higher status in the workplace and at union meetings than did less skilled workers, but Hickey still lacked the influence wielded by older, established unionists. Arriving from the United States, where some unionists defended their rights in armed combat, Hickey was shocked that Denniston miners accepted decisions imposed by the Arbitration Court. He believed that arbitration destroyed the unions' fighting spirit, removing power from the rank and file. The Arbitration Act made it illegal for employers to lock out workers and for registered unions to strike while under an award. Unionists now placed their faith in union officials, awards, and politicians' promises rather than in their own organized strength.[42]

Hickey could not convince the Denniston union to abandon arbitration in favor of industrial action. He switched tactics, working with a group of young miners, including recent Victorian immigrant Paddy Webb, to establish a Denniston branch of the New Zealand Socialist Party (NZSP).[43] In 1907, the NZSP had several largely autonomous branches scattered around the country. The Denniston branch distributed socialist and industrial unionist propaganda rather than running candidates for local or national political office. The party campaigned on issues such as abolishing the hated miners' medical test, building a Denniston hospital, and even establishing ladies' tennis courts.[44] Hickey and other Denniston socialists were still forming their ideas on socialism and revolutionary industrial unionism. They imported a large number of works from the Charles H. Kerr Company, a radical Chicago publishing house.[45] The Socialists also distributed Upton Sinclair's *The Jungle*, a novel that publicized socialist ideas.[46]

Fired from Denniston for campaigning against the medical test, Hickey found employment at the Runanga state coal mine in the Grey Valley.[47] He worked with Runanga miners' union leader Bob Semple to establish NZSP branches in the Grey Valley mining towns and in Greymouth, the local provincial center. Semple, an Australian immigrant, came to New Zealand after being blacklisted during the 1903 Gippsland mining strike.[48] Hickey wrote that another Runanga activist, Frank Hudson, "continually dinned into my ears the need of federation, not merely of miners, but of all workers."[49] Although introduced to revolutionary industrial unionism by the WFM, Hickey continued developing and refining his ideas on industrial organization. He built on his own experiences and the influence of activists such as Hudson and Semple.

Founding the Red Feds

In January 1908, Hickey found work in the Grey Valley coal mining town of Blackball after the Runanga mine management refused to renew his contract.[50] He was accompanied by his old comrade, Paddy Webb, fired from Denniston for organizing a speaking tour by British socialist Ben Tillett. Hickey and Webb established a Blackball branch of the NZSP and took leadership positions in the miners' union. The union had a number of ongoing disputes with the mine management, including the demand to extend the fifteen minutes allowed for "crib" (lunch) to half an hour. When a strike broke out over this issue, it made national headlines. The miners' eventual victory was a major propaganda coup for advocates of direct action.[51]

Hickey met Rose Rogers at Blackball in 1908. Their 1911 marriage further linked him to the mining and union communities. Rose's family was deeply committed to unionism and socialism. Her father, Walter Rogers, was secretary of the Blackball Miners' Union from 1902 to 1915. Her mother, Mary Fisher Rogers, made the family home a refuge for visiting labor activists. Rose, an activist in her own right, strongly supported Pat's political and industrial campaigns.[52]

Hickey's role in the Blackball strike brought him to national prominence. The strike victory was a direct challenge to the arbitration system. It provided the springboard for a campaign, spearheaded by Hickey and Semple, to establish a New Zealand Federation of Miners. This federation became the parent organization of the New Zealand Federation of Labour (NZFL), the Red Feds. As advocates of industrial unionism, the Red Feds sought to wrest labor movement leadership from supporters of trade unionism and compulsory arbitration. The Red Feds believed that trade unions organized around specific occupations divided the working class and that the only effective way of organizing was industrial unionism, with all workers in a particular industry united in an organization powerful enough to take on employers.[53] Compulsory arbitration kept unions dependent on the state while encouraging centralization and union oligarchy. Direct action gave workers power over their own unions, allowing them to fight to control their working conditions and establish socialism.[54]

A struggle developed between the Red Fed–affiliated unions and the organized employers, combined in the Employers' Federation. Federation secretary William Pryor understood the concepts of class war and industrial unionism and was a key figure in raising a fighting fund and organizing the Employers' Federation to combat the NZFL. The employers were backed by the Farmers' Union and by the Reform government after 1912. This struggle culminated in the Waihi Strike of 1912 and the Great Strike of 1913, perhaps the most violent confrontations in New Zealand's industrial history.[55]

Hickey recognized that the capitalist press was a powerful medium to which militant unionists had very limited access. He was instrumental in negotiating the federation's 1911 takeover of the *Maoriland Worker*, a struggling newspaper recently set up by the shearers' union. Hickey was a frequent contributor to the *Worker*, holding a number of roles on its staff.[56] The paper became the platform for a broad range of left-wing views and debates. It disseminated news of the transnational labor movement through articles and letters from around the globe, with an emphasis on Anglophone communities, including the United States.[57] The *Worker* also supplied overseas labor newspapers with information on the New Zealand movement, forming part of a transnational labor press.[58]

Industrial Unionism, the Socialist Party, and Electoral Politics

In his earliest reported speeches from late 1907, Hickey argued that workers should organize industrially while seeking political power by voting for socialist electoral candidates.[59] This approach matched the WFM strategies he had observed in the American West. With the growth in power of the New Zealand Federation of Miners and then the NZFL, Hickey and other young Red Fed activists became more skeptical about the value of electing parliamentary representatives. While the federation prioritized class war, activists worried that political candidates campaigning for votes might water down the emphasis on class struggle.[60] By 1910, Hickey was giving far greater priority to industrial over political action. In an October 1910 *Maoriland Worker* article, Hickey argued that because workers had only their labor to sell, they must combine to control the labor market. This "does not mean the policy of the IWW by a long way, but it does mean revolution." He defined revolution not as the violent overthrow of capitalism but as an evolutionary process creating "a complete change in the existing conditions." The industrial unionist was "a revolutionist" with "his eye fixed on the ultimate goal of the co-operative commonwealth." Hickey believed not that industrial unionists should eschew political action but rather that they should not concentrate on politics until the working class had complete industrial organization.[61]

Hickey had not completely abandoned his belief in workers' political action. He accepted nomination as Socialist Party candidate for the Ohinemuri seat in the December 1911 parliamentary election. He was an NZSP member, but endorsement by the Waihi Miners' Union and the NZFL appears to have strongly influenced his decision to accept. The NZFL supported eight candidates in the 1911 election. Despite giving priority to industrial organization, they shared the NZSP's concerns over a newly formed moderate New Zealand Labour Party.[62] The federation worried that moderates could seize the initiative within the labor movement if more militant socialists failed to contest the election.[63] Hickey campaigned hard, using the election campaign as a platform for advocating socialism and industrial unionism.[64] He failed to win the seat but finished a respectable second in a two-round contest.[65]

Events during 1912 led Hickey back to giving equal priority to both industrial and political action. William Massey's probusiness Reform Party took power that year, using violent and repressive methods to crush a strike by the Waihi miners. In the face of such power, Hickey felt that the working class had to use parliamentary elections to gain control of the economic, political, and military systems: "We must invade Parliament; we must wrest the sceptre of power from the hands of capitalism: we must openly declare the battle politically as well as industrially. . . . Let us get in and control the police club and the conscript's bayonet."[66]

As his support for political action grew, Hickey parted company with IWW activists. A small group of Wobblies from British Columbia, including John Benjamin King, set up an IWW local in Auckland in 1911. Recruiting resident socialists, including Tom Barker, they disseminated the Wobbly message around the country. The Auckland Wobblies followed the Chicago IWW, rejecting political action and treating union officials, "Labor fakirs," with suspicion. Hickey at first regarded the IWW as allies but came to see them as a disruptive element within the labor movement.[67]

The Red Feds were involved in two large-scale 1912 disputes centered on gold mines at Reefton and Waihi. A group of Waihi engine drivers who found the Waihi Miners' Union too militant formed a breakaway arbitrationist union with employer support. The Waihi Miners' Union, a Red Fed affiliate that had withdrawn from the arbitration system, went on strike rather than work with the arbitrationists. The Reefton miners were locked out in a dispute over the safe use of mining equipment.[68] Hickey journeyed around Australia from July to December 1912 on an NZFL fund-raising tour for the Reefton and Waihi miners. He talked to a wide range of union groups, traveling through the mining towns of New South Wales, Western Australia, Tasmania, and Queensland.[69] Hickey's efforts stimulated an Australian effort that contributed around a quarter of the total strike fund.[70]

Industrial Conflict, War, and Tasman Crossings

Following the violent defeat of the Waihi strike, Hickey worked as a key organizer of the Unity Conferences of January and July 1913. These conferences built a new and potentially powerful alliance between militant and moderate unions. Hickey was elected secretary of the United Federation of Labour, the peak body formed at the July Unity Conference. In this position he reluctantly became one of the leaders of the Great Strike, a nationwide industrial confrontation sparked in October 1913 by watersiders' (longshoremen's) and miners' strikes. Thousands of special constables were deployed around the country, with armed clashes occurring in the streets of Wellington and a brief general strike taking place in Auckland. By January 1914, the strike had been broken through this extensive use of state power.[71]

The strike's defeat greatly weakened the United Federation of Labour, with militants such as Hickey and Semple losing their jobs. Blacklisted by employers, Hickey resorted to laboring on a government road gang. A committed antimilitarist, he was saddened by the labor movement's failure to unite against the war that broke out in August 1914. In late 1915, he decided to move to Australia with Rose and their two-year-old son, Pat Jr.[72] Hickey believed that his job prospects would be better in Australia, where he had many connections, "from Premiers down," within the more powerful labor movement. He was also convinced that the Massey administration would soon introduce conscription, which he was determined to avoid. Hickey believed that the strength and influence of the unions would make Australian state power less repressive toward labor activists and less likely to implement conscription than was New Zealand.[73]

Hickey found work in Melbourne as an organizer for the Victorian Railways Union. He joined the Victorian Socialist Party and the Australian Labor Party. He and Rose were anticonscription activists in the 1916 and 1917 referendum campaigns. From April 1919 to April 1920, Hickey was an organizer with the Queensland Railways Union and founding editor of the union's journal, *Militant*.[74] Hickey continued promoting industrial unionism, including the One

Big Union campaign.[75] He was, however, now bitterly opposed to the IWW, considering their actions detrimental to a united Australian industrial movement. Hickey aired his criticisms in a vitriolic pamphlet, *Solidarity or Sectionalism? A Plea for Unity*, published by the Queensland branch of the Australian Workers' Union. He denounced sabotage as a weapon of despair, condemning the Wobblies as inexperienced young men who attacked all the Australian labor movement's political organizations and union leaders. Hickey claimed that the IWW disrupted existing labor organizations, flouted union rules, and launched unauthorized strikes.[76] Despite these views, Hickey called for the release of imprisoned Wobbly Tom Barker and condemned the government's suppression of the IWW.[77]

Hickey returned to New Zealand in 1920, working as a journalist and editor for the *Maoriland Worker*. He later worked as an organizer for the syndicalist-oriented Alliance of Labour. He ran unsuccessfully as Labour Party candidate for mayor of Wellington in 1921 and failed to win the Invercargill seat for Labour in the 1925 parliamentary election. In 1926, disillusioned with the New Zealand labor scene, Hickey and his family returned to Melbourne, and he and Rose managed hotels there and in rural Victoria. Renewing his involvement with the Australian Labor Party, Hickey was selected for the party's safe state seat of Dandenong in 1929. He resigned as candidate following a head injury and died of the resulting brain damage on 25 January 1930.[78]

Conclusion: A Career of Transnationalism

Pat Hickey's career as a worker and labor activist provides an example of the transnational lives led by many workers at the turn of the twentieth century. Mobility exposed workers to new ideas, which they then carried to other parts of the world. Hickey's American travels introduced him to levels of class conflict far more intense than those occurring in New Zealand, opening him to American versions of revolutionary industrial unionism and socialism. Mining experiences in the United States and New Zealand linked Hickey to trans-global mining communities and taught him skills that commanded respect in the workplace and union settings. The WFM and the SPA introduced him to the dual strategy of industrial unionism and political action. Hickey returned to New Zealand at a time when disillusionment with both arbitration and the Liberal administration meant that some workers were open to militant ideas. The Red Fed movement that Hickey helped initiate was itself a product of transnationalism, based on British unionism with a core of experienced Australian activists and a strong American ideological influence. The *Maoriland Worker* provided a further link in the labor movement network, transmitting information in and out of New Zealand. Hickey the activist used transnational working-class networks of communities and communications, as in his 1912 fund-raising tour of Australian mining towns. Connections with the Australian labor movement helped convince him to cross the Tasman in 1915. The strength of Australian unions and the Australian Labor Party made that country seem more hospitable to labor activists than wartime New Zealand, and Hickey's New Zealand union experience helped him get organizing jobs in Australia. His interest in industrial unionism and politics drew him into debates regarding IWW activities. Hickey's life shows how traveling could lead a worker to adopt influential ideas and become part of the networks that spread those concepts.

Notes

I thank Pat Hickey's relatives, Noelene McNair, Eileen Thawley, and John Weir, for access to their correspondence collections and other family material.

1. On Hickey, see E. Olssen, "Hickey, Patrick Hodgens," *Dictionary of New Zealand Biography: Te Ara—The Encyclopedia of New Zealand*, available at https://teara.govt.nz/en/biographies/3h22/hickey-patrick-hodgens. E. Olssen, *The Red Feds: Revolutionary Industrial Unionism and the New Zealand Federation of Labour, 1908–1913* (Auckland: Oxford University Press, 1988), analyzes Hickey's role in the New Zealand Federation of Labour. P. H. Hickey, *"Red" Fed Memoirs* (Wellington: New Zealand Worker, 1925), covers 1907–13, with limited autobiographical information. The most comprehensive biography of Hickey to date is J. E. Weir, "The 'Red' Feds: P. H. Hickey and the Red Federation of Labour" (unpublished manuscript, ca. 1970), MS 119, John Weir Papers, Acc 664, Macmillan-Brown Library, University of Canterbury.

2. On the transnational English-speaking working class in the early twentieth century, see Verity Burgmann, *Revolutionary Industrial Unionism: The Industrial Workers of the World in Australia* (Cambridge: Cambridge University Press, 1995), 37–38, 69–71; J. Bennett, *Rats and Revolutionaries: The Labour Movement in Australia and New Zealand, 1880–1940* (Dunedin, N.Z.: Otago University Press, 2004), 63–66; E. C. Fry, *Tom Barker and the IWW* (Brisbane: Industrial Workers of the World, 1999); J. Hyslop, "The Imperial Working Class Makes Itself White: White Labourism in Britain, Australia, and South Africa before the First World War," *Journal of Historical Sociology* 12 (1999): 398–421. On Hickey and transnationalism, see F. Shor, "Left Labor Agitators in the Pacific Rim of the Early Twentieth Century," *International Labor and Working Class History* 67 (2005): 148–63; P. Clayworth, "'By Tomorrow I May Be Flying': Patrick Hodgens Hickey, a Case Study in Transnational Labour Biography," in *Labour History and Its People: Papers from the 12th Biennial National Labour History Conference, ANU, 15–17 September 2011*, ed. M. Nolan (Canberra: Australian Society for the Study of Labour History/National Centre of Biography, 2011), 244–57.

3. Hickey, *"Red" Fed Memoirs*; Olssen, *Red Feds*; H. O. Roth, *Trade Unions in New Zealand: Past and Present* (Wellington: Reed, 1973), 17–41; J. Holt, *Compulsory Arbitration in New Zealand: The First Forty Years* (Auckland: Auckland University Press, 1986), 57–115; B.

Gustafson, *Labour's Path to Political Independence* (Auckland: Auckland University Press, 1980), 24–77; Len Richardson, *Coal, Class, and Community: The United Mineworkers of New Zealand, 1880–1960* (Auckland: Auckland University Press, 1995), 82–154.

4. P. Coleman, *Progressivism and the World of Reform: New Zealand and the Origins of the American Welfare State* (Lawrence: University Press of Kansas, 1987).

5. H. O. Roth, "American Influences on the New Zealand Labour Movement," *Historical Studies Australia and New Zealand* 9 (1961): 413–20; E. Olssen, "American Influences on the New Zealand Labour Movement, 1885–1920," in *The American Connection: Essays from the Stout Centre Conference*, ed. M. McKinnon (Wellington: Allen and Unwin/Port Nicholson, 1988), 25–37; R. E. Weir, *Knights Down Under: The Knights of Labour in New Zealand* (Newcastle upon Tyne: Cambridge Scholars, 2000).

6. Weir, "'Red' Feds," 25–27; J. N. W. Newport, *Footprints: The Story of the Settlement and Development of the Nelson Back Country Districts* (Christchurch: Whitcombe and Tombs, 1962), 297–98.

7. *Nelson Evening Mail*, 27 January 1900; *Nelson Colonist*, 29 January 1900.

8. P. H. Hickey, Journal, 1900–1903, in possession of P. Clayworth. Used by permission of Noelene McNair. The journal records Hickey's 1900–1901 journey, written after the events from detailed travel notes.

9. M. Walker, "'The Floating Army': Transient Labor in Early Twentieth Century California," paper presented at the Society for Historical Archaeology Conference, Albuquerque, New Mexico, 2008, available at www.academia.edu/1663544/_The_Floating_Army_Transient_Labor_in_Early_20th_Century_California; G. C. Woirol, *In the Floating Army: F. C. Mills on Itinerant Life in California, 1914* (Urbana: University of Illinois Press, 1992).

10. P. H. Hickey to Mary Jane Hickey, 1 August, 11 September 1900, 19 May 1901, Eileen Thawley Private Collection; Hickey, Journal, especially 24–25, 69, 83–84. The Thawley Collection consists of Thawley's transcriptions of Hickey's letters.

11. See Scott Stephenson, this volume.

12. On hewers' status, see R. C. Brown, *Hard Rock Miners: The Intermountain West, 1860–1920* (College Station: Texas A&M University Press, 1979), 70; N. Emery, *The Coal Miners of Durham* (Stroud: History Press, 1992), 44–47; T. G. Andrews, *Killing for Coal: America's Deadliest Labor War* (Cambridge: Harvard University Press, 2008), 162–67.

13. Brown, *Hard Rock Miners*; Richardson, *Coal, Class, and Community*; A. R. McCormack, *Reformers, Rebels, and Revolutionaries: The Western Canadian Radical Movement, 1899–1919* (Toronto: University of Toronto Press, 1977); J. Hyslop, *The Notorious Syndicalist: J. T. Bain, a Scottish Rebel in Colonial South Africa* (Johannesburg: Jacana, 2004).

14. P. H. Hickey to Mary Jane Hickey, September 1901, 21 September 1901, Thawley Collection; Hickey, *"Red" Fed Memoirs*, 6.

15. P. H. Hickey to Mary Jane Hickey, 19 May 1901, Thawley Collection.

16. Hickey, Journal, 52–53; see also 31.

17. P. H. Hickey to Mary Ann Hickey, 4, 20 April, 28 May 1903, P. H. Hickey Letters, Alexander Turnbull Library, Wellington; P. H. Hickey to Mary Jane Hickey, 18, 29 March, 3, 5, 14 April, 6, 23 May 1903, Thawley Collection.

18. P. H. Hickey to Mary Jane Hickey, 24 June 1903, Thawley Collection. On the strikes, see *New York Tribune, New York Evening World, New York Sun,* 21 May–21 June 1903.

19. P. H. Hickey to Mary Jane Hickey, 27 August 1903, Thawley Collection. Andrew Carnegie had sold his steel mill interests to US Steel in 1901, but Hickey and his Youngstown workmates apparently were unaware that the mill had new owners, perhaps because Carnegie protégés ran US Steel using Carnegie's industrial and business methods. See also C. S. Reback, "Merger for Monopoly: The Formation of U.S. Steel," *Essays in Economic and Business History: Journal of the Economic and Business Historical Society* 25 (2007): 105–16; D. Brody, *Steelworkers in America: The Nonunion Era* (Cambridge: Harvard University Press, 1960), 16–22.

20. *Nelson Evening Mail,* 31 December 1907.

21. See Elizabeth Malcolm and Dianne Hall, this volume.

22. P. H. Hickey to John Hickey, 15 November 1903, Thawley Collection. On the Colorado strikes, see Elizabeth Jameson, *All That Glitters: Class, Conflict, and Community in Cripple Creek* (Urbana: University of Illinois Press, 1998); Andrews, *Killing for Coal,* 239–44; V. H. Jensen, *Heritage of Conflict: Labor Relations in the Non-Ferrous Metals Industry up to 1930* (Ithaca: Cornell University Press, 1950), 118–59. On Hickey's Irish networks, see P. H. Hickey to Mary Jane Hickey, 11 September 1900, P. H. Hickey to John Hickey, 27 June 1903, Thawley Collection.

23. P. H. Hickey to Mary Ann Hickey, 15 August 1905, Hickey Letters, Turnbull Library; Shor, "Left Labor Agitators," 152.

24. Shor notes that Hickey appears in the WFM Local 67 minute books from 15 July 1905 to 16 September 1905 ("Left Labor Agitators," 152). Hickey's letters indicate that he was at Bingham Canyon by July 1905 and left Utah around late September (P. H. Hickey to Mary Ann Hickey, 15 August 1905, Hickey Letters, Turnbull Library; P. H. Hickey to Mary Jane Hickey, 16 August, 20 November 1905, Thawley Collection).

25. Jensen, *Heritage of Conflict,* especially 119–70; M. Dubofsky, *We Shall Be All: A History of the IWW* (New York: Quadrangle/NY Times, 1969), 36–87; D. R. Berman, *Radicalism in the Mountain West, 1890–1920: Socialists, Populists, Miners, and Wobblies* (Boulder: University Press of Colorado, 2007), 161–69.

26. John P. Enyeart, *The Quest for "Just and Pure Law": Rocky Mountain Workers and American Social Democracy, 1870–1924* (Stanford: Stanford University Press, 2009), 107–9, 126–29, 132–38.

27. Jameson, *All That Glitters,* 68–71, 76–77.

28. J. S. McCormick and J. R. Sillito, *A History of Utah Radicalism: Startling, Socialistic, and Decidedly Revolutionary* (Logan: Utah State University Press, 2011), 142.

29. Enyeart, *Quest,* 132–44, 200–202; Jameson, *All That Glitters,* 177–79, 186, 187–94; Berman, *Radicalism,* 100–115, 123–26, 138–50; McCormick and Sillito, *History,* 139–48.

30. Berman, *Radicalism,* 148–49, 348.

31. McCormick and Sillito, *History,* 188–89, 225–26.

32. P. H. Hickey to Mary Jane Hickey, 20 November 1905, Thawley Collection.

33. McCormick and Sillito, *History*, 141–42, 193; P. J. Mellinger, *Race and Labor in Western Copper: The Fight for Equality, 1896–1918* (Tucson: University of Arizona Press, 1995), 91–106. On 21 October 1905, shortly after Hickey's departure, five miners were accidentally killed at Bingham Canyon's Highland Boy mine. Local 67 narrowly voted not to strike over safety issues (*Arizona Republican*, 22 October 1905; Mellinger, *Race and Labor*, 99).

34. T. J. LeCain, *Mass Destruction: The Men and Giant Mines That Wired America and Scarred the Planet* (New Brunswick, N.J.: Rutgers University Press, 2000), 117–19.

35. Mellinger, *Race and Labor*, 105.

36. *Greymouth Evening Star*, 28 October 1907; Roth, "American Influences," 416; N. Jeffrey, "My Estimate of Bob Ross and Pat Hickey," in H. O. Roth, "Patrick Hodgens Hickey Biographical Notes," Roth Papers, Turnbull Library.

37. Hickey's only descriptions of his Bingham Canyon sojourn are in P. H. Hickey to Mary Ann Hickey, 15 August 1905, Hickey Letters, Turnbull Library; P. H. Hickey to Mary Jane Hickey, 16 August, 20 November 1905, Thawley Collection. For the WFM influence on Hickey and the New Zealand Federation of Miners, see Hickey, *"Red" Fed Memoirs*, 6; "Our Candidates," *Maoriland Worker*, 1 September 1911; P. H. Hickey, "The Birth and Growth of the NZ Federation of Labor, Pt. III," *Maoriland Worker*, 17 May 1912.

38. Hickey, Journal, 22, 24, 44, 45; P. H. Hickey to Mary Jane Hickey, 11 September 1900, 11 March, 17 December 1903, P. H. Hickey to John Hickey, 15 November 1903, Thawley Collection. On workers' workplace control strategies, see A. Green, *British Capital, Antipodean Labour: Working the New Zealand Waterfront, 1915–1951* (Dunedin, N.Z.: Otago University Press, 2001), 151–53.

39. For a gendered approach to the Wobblies, see F. Shor, "Gender and Labour/Working Class History in Comparative Perspective: The Syndicalist and Wobbly Experience in the USA, Australia, and New Zealand," *Left History* 11 (2006): 118–36.

40. Hickey, *"Red" Fed Memoirs*, 6.

41. See Robert Cherny, this volume.

42. Hickey, *"Red" Fed Memoirs*, 4, 7; P. H. Hickey, "The Birth and Growth of the NZ Federation of Labor," *Maoriland Worker*, 3 May 1912. Hickey's analysis of compulsory arbitration in New Zealand closely matches Stephenson's description (this volume) of Australian compulsory arbitration.

43. Len Richardson, "Webb, Patrick Charles," *Dictionary of New Zealand Biography: Te Ara—The Encyclopedia of New Zealand*, available at www.teara.govt.nz/en/biographies/3w5/webb-patrick-charles.

44. *Commonweal*, August, October 1907; Hickey, *"Red" Fed Memoirs*, 9.

45. Hickey, *"Red" Fed Memoirs*, 9; M. Derby, "'Subversive Literature for All the Family': Radical Literary Culture in New Zealand, 1900–1914," in *Trans Tasman Labour History: Comparative or Transnational? Proceedings of the Trans Tasman Labour History Conference*, ed. Ray Markey (Auckland: Auckland University of Technology, 2007), 23–31.

46. J. E. Duncan to H. O. Roth, 28 February 1954, in "John Edward Duncan," H. O. Roth, "Biographical Notes, Drayton–Dyer," Roth Papers.

47. Hickey, *"Red" Fed Memoirs*, 9.

48. Len Richardson, "Semple, Robert," *Dictionary of New Zealand Biography: Te Ara—The Encyclopedia of New Zealand*, available at www.teara.govt.nz/en/biographies/3s11/semple-robert; C. Hickey, "From Coal Pit to Leather Pit: Life Stories of Robert Semple" (PhD diss., Massey University, 2010), 29–51.

49. Hickey, *"Red" Fed Memoirs*, 19.

50. P. H. Hickey to Mary Jane Hickey, 12 January 1908, Thawley Collection.

51. Hickey, *"Red" Fed Memoirs*, 11–18; Olssen, *Red Feds*, 1–15; B. Wood, *The Great '08 Blackball Coal Miners' Strike, 27 February–13 May 1908* (Greymouth, N.Z.: Wood, 2008).

52. *Maoriland Worker*, 17 June, 20 October 1914; "Walter Rogers Obituary," *Maoriland Worker*, 3 November 1915; "Mary Rogers Obituary," *Maoriland Worker*, 21 February 1923.

53. This view of compulsory arbitration's impact on trade unions parallels Stephenson's description (this volume) of the Australian compulsory arbitration system.

54. Hickey, *"Red" Fed Memoirs*; Olssen, *Red Feds*; Roth, *Trade Unions*, 17–41.

55. "William Pryor Obituary," *Wellington Evening Post*, 27 February 1922; W. Pryor, *Organising and Defence Fund Schemes: A Plea for the Complete Industrial Organisation of All Employers of Labour in New Zealand* (Wellington: New Zealand Employers Federation, 1912); Olssen, *Red Feds*; H. E. Holland, "Ballot Box" [Frank O'Flynn], and R. S. Ross, *The Tragic Story of the Waihi Strike* (Wellington: Worker, 1913); M. Nolan, ed. *Revolution: The 1913 Great Strike in New Zealand* (Christchurch: Canterbury University Press/Trade Union History Project, 2005).

56. H. O. Roth, "Patrick Hodgens Hickey Biographical Notes," Roth Papers; Weir, "'Red' Feds," 173–80.

57. The *Maoriland Worker*'s American content in 1911 included "Appeal to Reason's Fight for Justice," 20 March 1911; "Western Miners, USA," 5 May 1911; "American Unionism," 19 May 1911; "Fighting for Freedom in Mexico," 2 June 1911; "A New Zealander in the States," 6 October 1911.

58. "A Tribute from America," *Maoriland Worker*, 15 September 1911. The *Worker* fulfilled a role comparable to that of the anarchist press Tom Goyens describes, this volume.

59. *Greymouth Evening Star*, 28 October, 4 November 1907; *Grey River Argus*, 28 October 1907.

60. Hickey, *"Red" Fed Memoirs*, 31–32.

61. P. H. Hickey, "Industrial Unionism," *Maoriland Worker*, 15 October 1910.

62. This New Zealand Labour Party of 1910 should not be confused with the New Zealand Labour Party formed in 1916 (which remains a significant political party today). The Labour Party of 1916 was a coalition of the Social Democratic Party (successor to the Socialist Party) and the United Labour Party (successor to the 1910 New Zealand Labour Party). See P. Franks and J. McAloon, *The New Zealand Labour Party, 1916–2016* (Wellington: Victoria University Press, 2016), especially 56–74.

63. P. J. O'Farrell, "The Workers in Grey District Politics, 1865–1913: A Study in New Zealand Liberalism and Socialism" (master's thesis, University of Canterbury, 1955), 209–16; P. J. O'Farrell, *Harry Holland: Militant Socialist* (Canberra: Australian National

University, 1964), 49; P. Rainer, "Company Town: An Industrial History of the Waihi Gold Mining Company, Ltd, 1887–1912" (master's thesis, University of Auckland, 1976), 170–73; "Political Action of Industrial Unionism," *Maoriland Worker*, 2 June 1911.

64. P. H. Hickey, "The Battle of Ohinemuri," *Maoriland Worker*, 5 January 1912.

65. *Appendices to the Journals of the House of Representatives*, Session 2, 1912, H-12, 2, 6; Gustafson, *Labour's Path*, 39–41.

66. P. H. Hickey, "In Australia," *Maoriland Worker*, 25 October 1912.

67. Olssen, *Red Feds*, 130–34; Fry, *Tom Barker and the IWW*; "IWW Notes," in H. O. Roth, "Biographical notes Earsman–Hurd," and "J. B. King," in H. O. Roth, "Biographical Notes, Hutchinson–King," both in Roth Papers.

68. Rainer, "Company Town"; Holland, "Ballot Box"; Ross, *Tragic Story*; S. Roche, *Red and Gold: An Informal Account of the Waihi Strike, 1912* (Auckland: Oxford University Press, 1982); Olssen, *Red Feds*, 133–60; C. Locke, "Rebel Girls and Pram-Pushing Scab-Hunters: Waihi's 'Scarlet Runners,' 1912," *Labour History* 107 (2014): 35–52.

69. *Maoriland Worker*, 2, 9, 16, 30 August, 13 September, 11, 25 October, 1, 22 November 1912.

70. Of £35,191 raised for the strike fund, £9,395 came from Australia (Holland, "Ballot Box"; Ross, *Tragic Story*, 194–98).

71. Olssen, *Red Feds*, 163–209; Nolan, *Revolution*, 10–19; Roth, *Trade Unions*, 34–39; Weir, "'Red' Feds," 268–72; Len Richardson, "The Workers and Grey District Politics during Wartime, 1914–1918" (master's thesis, University of Canterbury, 1968), 17, 32.

72. P. H. Hickey to Mary Jane Hickey, 1915, 19 November 1916, January 1918, Thawley Collection; A. Holland to S. Holland, 9 August 1914, P. J. O'Farrell Papers, Turnbull Library; Weir, "'Red' Feds," 321–40.

73. P. H. Hickey to Mary Jane Hickey, November 1915, Thawley Collection. As Hickey predicted, the New Zealand government introduced conscription in August 1916. On the effect of the strong Australian labor movement on state and federal governments during the Great War, see Archer, this volume; Shelton Stromquist, this volume.

74. H. O. Roth, "Patrick Hodgens Hickey Biographical Notes," Roth Papers; *Railways Union Gazette*, 21 August 1916; *Queensland Worker*, 3 April, 19 June 1919, 18 March, 15 April 1920.

75. Shor, "Left Labor Agitators," 159–63; C. Larmour, "The 'Y Club' and the One Big Union," *Labour History* 19 (1970): 26–36.

76. P. H. Hickey, *Solidarity or Sectionalism? A Plea for Unity* (Brisbane: Worker, 1918), 6–8, 16. The pamphlet was not released until early 1919.

77. P. H. Hickey, "No Bastille for Tom Barker," *Labor Call*, 11 May 1916. See also Burgmann, *Revolutionary Industrial Unionism*, 181–245; Verity Burgmann and Jeffrey A. Johnson, this volume.

78. Weir, "'Red' Feds," 350–67; H. O. Roth, "Patrick Hodgens Hickey Biographical Notes," Roth Papers.

Harry Bridges's Australia, Australia's Harry Bridges

ROBERT CHERNY

Born in Australia in 1901, Harry Bridges left home in 1919, arrived in the United States in 1920, and led Pacific Coast longshore workers from 1934 until 1977. His experience bears some resemblance to that of other working-class transnational activists discussed in this volume.[1] Sometimes seen as an exemplar of transnationalism for bringing Australian perspectives to the docks of San Francisco, Bridges and his union later provided inspiration and examples for Australian dockworkers. This chapter first examines Australia's significance for Bridges before turning to the ways Australians viewed Bridges.

Harry Bridges's Australia

Born in Kensington, a working-class suburb of Melbourne, on 28 July 1901, Bridges was baptized Alfred Renton Bridges.[2] Lessons learned in his parents' household pointed him along quite different paths, one marked by his mother, a different one by his father, and a third by a favorite uncle.

His mother, Julia Dorgan Bridges, was of Irish parentage, and she and her sisters, Ellen and Beatrice, were devout Catholics. Bridges's education came in Catholic schools, and Julia added lessons in Irish nationalism. Julia and Ellen considered themselves friends of Archbishop Daniel Mannix, who served a parish near Ellen's home from 1913 to 1917. Bridges remembered Mannix as "a great hero to my family."[3]

Harry's father, Alfred Bridges, was of English descent, unchurched but devoted to the British Empire. He bought and sold real estate and invested in rental housing in Melbourne's western suburbs. Young Alfred disliked working for his father when he had to collect rent and deliver eviction notices, especially when he faced the families of his classmates.[4]

Young Alfred was strongly influenced by his father's brothers, especially Henry Renton Bridges, who had married Julia's sister, Beatrice. Their family lived on a small farm near Yea, north of Melbourne, where Henry Bridges, known as Harry, worked as a wool presser during sheep shearing and belonged to the Australian Workers' Union, which represented agricultural workers. Australia's largest and wealthiest union, the Australian Workers' Union gave vital support to the Australian Labor Party (ALP) in rural areas. The *Yea Chronicle* described Harry Bridges, "the local organizer for the Labor Party," as taking "a most prominent part in electioneering matters" and as "a fearless speaker" and "a fair fighter."[5] Young Alfred so admired his favorite uncle that he began to call himself *Harry*. Charles, the third brother, was also an ALP activist and later held elective office in Sydney. Alfred, too, initially supported the ALP.[6] The ALP advocated trade-union issues, nationalization of monopolies, social welfare measures, and Australian nationalism. In 1910, it became the first social democratic party in the world to win a national electoral majority and majorities in both houses of parliament.[7]

Young Alfred, not yet known as Harry, attended a secondary school run by the Christian Brothers from May 1912 until February 1915 but did not graduate. While working for a stationery firm, he frequented the Melbourne docks, talked with seamen, studied seafaring, and dreamed of going to sea.[8]

By then, the world was at war. Greeting the war with cheerful optimism, Australians immediately sent troops in support of Britain. Henry Renton Bridges, young Harry's favorite uncle, volunteered and died on the battlefield in France in mid-1916, six weeks after English troops suppressed the Easter Rising. Archbishop Mannix publicly deplored British actions in Ireland, and throughout Victoria, Irish nationalism became increasingly coupled to criticism of the war—topics of intense discussion among the Dorgan sisters and their friends.[9]

By late 1916, the need for troops became so great that William Hughes, ALP prime minister, called a national referendum on conscription, hoping to avoid splitting his party. He failed. Labor spokesmen damned him as a class traitor. Mannix blamed conscription for the "disastrous proportions" the war had assumed and condemned conscription as "certain to bring evil in its train." Most of the British, Protestant elite and middle class supported conscription; opposition was strongest among the Irish and the working class. Harry's mother and aunt, Ellen, opposed conscription and disliked the war. When the referendum lost, the ALP voted no confidence in Hughes, leading him and his supporters to leave the ALP and form the Nationalist Party. Harry's father followed Hughes out of the ALP and, his nephew recalled, became "a very strong Tory."[10]

Events in 1917 helped to shape Bridges's political understanding. In the middle of the year, Melbourne and Sydney dockworkers cited high food prices and resolved to load food only onto ships bound for Britain and Allied ports. In mid-August, Melbourne dockworkers completely closed the port. Other unions joined the strike, then government railway shop workers in New South Wales struck over new work rules. Many others joined the stoppage, which came to be called the Great Strike. In Victoria, New South Wales, and Queensland, the number of strikers swelled to ninety-seven thousand. Hughes blamed enemy agents and the Industrial Workers of the World (IWW), and newspapers vied with government spokesmen in discerning the specter of the IWW's "general strike" intended to bring down the government and destroy capitalism. The strikes collapsed by late September.[11] At Bridges's home, his father's admiration for Hughes and Hughes's attacks on the strikers produced an antiunion atmosphere.[12]

During the Great Strike, Adela Pankhurst launched a series of demonstrations in Melbourne. Daughter of British suffrage leader Emmeline Pankhurst, Adela belonged to the Socialist Party of Australia and the Women's Peace Army. She led demonstrations against high food prices and in support of the strikers that also carried antiwar implications. Several times in September 1917, demonstrators surged through Melbourne, led by women carrying red flags (banned by the Hughes government) and singing "songs of revolt."[13]

In November 1917, a second referendum on conscription was held, even more bitter than the first. Mannix labeled conscription "slavery imposed by military domination" and claimed that "all the capitalists are conscriptionists."[14] The vote, like the first, went against conscription.

In December 1917, sixteen-year-old Harry Bridges went to sea and worked aboard ships for more than four years. At first, he lived at home and sailed between Victoria and Tasmania and later between Australia and New Zealand. His recollections of seafaring include no mention of the strike by the Australian Seamen's Union in mid-1919, but the small sailing vessels on which he worked were not covered by an arbitration award and effectively were not unionized, so the strike did not affect them.[15]

Bridges always took pride in having been a member of the Australian Seamen's Union, but the union's dues registers list no one named Bridges in 1917, 1918, or 1919. Though dues paid in Tasmania or New Zealand might not have been properly transferred to the union's ledgers, it is more likely that he did not pay dues regularly, if at all. His final voyage as an Australian seaman was on a larger vessel covered by the arbitration award, and he likely paid union dues on that voyage.[16]

In early 1920, hoping to see places he had read about in Jack London's novels, Bridges grabbed an opportunity to sign onto a ship bound for San Francisco. Arriving in April 1920, he paid the US immigration entry fee, did some sightseeing, applied for an American certificate as an able seaman, and joined the Sailors Union of the Pacific. He sailed from American ports for the next two years. In New Orleans in 1921, he took part in the unsuccessful nationwide strike by maritime unions and briefly joined the IWW. In 1922, he "went on the beach"—that is, began to work on the San Francisco docks.[17]

Bridges digested these early experiences slowly, as they became integrated with later experiences as a seaman and longshoreman. Fifty years later, the significance of the Great Strike loomed large for him: "I did not know what it was all about then, but later on I could look back and I could remember . . . No [labor movement] since 1917 has ever organized the power to shut down industry as Australian unions shut down this whole country in 1917 . . . [It] began my real working class education." If he read newspaper accounts of the events in Petrograd in November 1917, they made no impression on him. Later, on a voyage, he read John Reed's *Ten Days That Shook the World* and gained some understanding of the Bolshevik seizure of power. He didn't know that Thomas Walsh, head of the Australian Seamen's Union, and Adela Pankhurst Walsh supported the Communist Party of Australia (CPA) from the time of its founding in 1918. After leaving Australia, Bridges once bought Marx's *Capital* to read on a voyage, but—like others before and since—he gave up before finishing it. His brief membership in the IWW gave him experience with organizing and an understanding of the need for worker solidarity across the lines of race, but he took no further part in the IWW after leaving New Orleans.[18]

Though Bridges left Australia in 1919, Australia remained central to his self-identity through his entire life. He spoke with an Australian accent and loved to spin stories about his seafaring experiences. From his earliest days shipping from American ports, he recited the accomplishments of Australian unions. Soon after arriving in the United States, his discussion of the efficacy of the Australian Seamen's Union and his experiences as a member led his shipmates to elect him ship's delegate, a position comparable to a union shop steward. After becoming a longshoreman, he joined an unsuccessful effort to revive a union that had lost a disastrous strike in 1919 and found himself blacklisted. In 1933, he joined the newly chartered Local 38-79, International Longshoremen's

Association. There his accounts of Australian unionism caused others, one later recalled, "just naturally" to turn to Harry for leadership.[19]

Bridges rapidly emerged as a leader in Local 38-79. In 1934, a longshore strike spun off strikes by other maritime unions and eventually a four-day general strike in San Francisco. Holding office only as chair of his local's strike committee, Bridges became the strike's de facto leader. He subsequently was elected president of Local 38-79, then president of the International Longshoremen's Association's autonomous Pacific Coast District. In 1937, the Pacific Coast District broke away and was chartered by the Congress of Industrial Organizations as the International Longshoremen's and Warehousemen's Union (ILWU); Bridges became its first president.

Throughout the 1930s, Bridges looked to Australia for examples of effective unionism or labor politics. During the 1936 strike by the Maritime Federation of the Pacific, he declared that Australian shipping lines had better working conditions for ship stewards than did American lines. In 1937, he pointed to the ALP for his claim "that labour in the United States was realizing the necessity for political action, thus entering a phase which labour in other countries had passed years ago." In a book published in 1937 and apparently based on interviews with Bridges, Richard Bransten attributed Bridges's political outlook to his experiences at sea. An Australian university student who interviewed Bridges in 1938 noted that he considered the ALP a model for American labor and loved to talk about sailing the Bass Strait and Tasman Sea. In a 1940 article in the *New York Times Magazine*, Bridges attributed important parts of his political outlook to his experiences as a seaman.[20] Thus, his early life in Australia remained central to his self-definition, especially his politics, and to the way that he wanted others to see him.

As early as May 1934, Bridges's opponents charged that he was a communist. Bridges openly praised the Communist Party (CP) but always insisted that he never joined.[21] In 1939 Bridges faced a hearing by the US Immigration and Naturalization Service (INS) on the charge that he was a CP member and should be deported. In his testimony, he attributed his political views to his youth in Australia and experiences as an Australian seaman.[22] According to the Australian press, Bridges declared, "I formed most of my beliefs before the Communist Party existed. I came from Australia. The Australians are pretty progressive. Many of the things which Communists here now advocate are old stuff down there." The hearing officer, James M. Landis, dean of the Harvard Law School, concluded, "There is slight doubt but that Bridges' present conceptions as to the place of trade-unionism derive considerably from his Australian experiences and upbringing."[23]

Landis found in Bridges's favor, and Secretary of Labor Frances Perkins dismissed the charges against him, touching off a political firestorm. The INS was moved from the Department of Labor to the Department of Justice. In June 1940, the House of Representatives, voted 330–42 to deport Bridges; the bill died in the Senate only when Attorney General Robert Jackson agreed to have the FBI investigate Bridges, producing another INS hearing the following year.[24]

In 1940, amid these events, two articles about Bridges appeared in popular magazines. As in the INS hearing, Bridges pointed to his Australian childhood and youth to explain his political outlook. He reiterated those explanations many times over the next fifteen years as he fought off repeated attempts to prove that he was a communist and hence subject to deportation. Throughout the rest of his life, he repeated those stories when asked about the origin of his political views.[25] Thus, Bridges's life in Australia not only helped to form his views on labor and politics but also provided him with a valuable legal defense.

Australia's Harry Bridges

In 1943, Lon Jones, correspondent for the *Sydney Morning Herald*, reported that during a lecture tour of the United States, every audience asked "what Australians thought of Harry Bridges." His answer: "Australians, like Americans, think about Bridges according to which side of the political fence they happen to be on."[26] He might have added that the mainstream Australian press viewed Bridges the same way the US press presented him but that he was a hero to Australia's left-wing unions.

Bridges first appeared in the Australian press nearly two months into the 1934 strike. In late June, the Australian Press Association issued a release quoting E. O'Conner, an Australian in San Francisco, who stated that Bridges "heads the strike" and supplied background information—much of it inaccurate—on Bridges. O'Conner accurately described Bridges as having "a long record of efficient work on the waterfront" and as "a forceful speaker" who "has established leadership which the strikers accept, in the belief that he is incorruptible. They have lost their faith in other leaders." On 2 July, several papers published a brief account based on that release.[27]

That day, the *Melbourne Argus* published more accurate information than the Australian Press Association release based on a visit to Bridges's mother. When the reporter rang her doorbell and asked if she was Bridges's mother, she was startled because the family had received no letters from him for nearly a decade and knew nothing of his union activities.[28]

After San Francisco police killed two strikers and injured many more on 5 July and the San Francisco Labor Council voted for a general strike on 14 July, Bridges's name appeared frequently in the Australian press.[29] Those articles quickly came to mirror his treatment in the US press. By mid-July, Australian newspapers were calling Bridges "a sharp-nosed young Australian iron-man who rules the San Francisco longshore and seamen's forces"—a very different characterization than that of 29 June –2 July but similar to what the major San Francisco dailies were saying.[30] On 18 July with the general strike under way, Australian papers followed the Hearst press in saying, "The Communists are in the saddle today," and quoted Joseph Ryan, the national president of the International Longshoremen's Association, as saying that no settlement was possible because of "Harry Bridges and his Communists' control behind the scenes." On 20 July, as the general strike was ending, a Queensland paper published a more balanced article on Bridges, beginning with his statement, "I am not a Communist" and then quoting him on the dangers of longshore work, but that treatment was unusual.[31]

Throughout the mid- and late 1930s, the Australian press repeatedly interviewed Bridges's father. The *Sydney Labor Daily* carried a long interview with Alfred Bridges in 1937. In 1938, he told the *Melbourne Australasian* that while in Australia, his son "had not been a Labour representative, agitator, or organizer, as had been alleged in certain quarters," and that it was only after arriving in the United States that he had become "active in trying to improve the working conditions of the American seamen, which he had described as deplorable, compared with those existing in Australia." In 1941, when Harry Bridges was facing his second INS hearing, Alfred assured a reporter that "his son was not a Communist" but added, "if Harry returned to Australia, he would probably go into politics."[32]

When the 1941 INS hearing went against Bridges, he appealed, ultimately to the US Supreme Court, which ruled in his favor in 1945. During 1941–45, the Australian press speculated that he might return. The ALP had won at the federal level in 1941 for the first time since the split over World War I conscription. That split had made the ALP more Irish and Catholic than before; like Catholic parties elsewhere, the ALP was anticommunist. Nonetheless, the CPA maintained a strong presence in several Australian unions, and the tiny CPA challenged the ALP as the representative of workers.

In 1940, Australia's Department of External Affairs (the foreign ministry) opened a file on Bridges, and the Australian legation in Washington began sending information. In June 1941, the legation forwarded nine pages of information received from a "most reliable"—though unidentified—source and a two-page biographical summary. The material closely resembles that being provided at the time by the American Legion, the Industrial Association of San Francisco (an antiunion organization), and similar antiunion and anticommunist organizations.[33]

On 30 May 1942, the *Melbourne Argus* reported talk in Washington that "Australian authorities do not desire Bridges's appearance in Australia." Two days later, however, Jack Beasley, acting attorney general in the ALP government of John Curtin, announced, "There is no legal bar to prevent Harry Bridges . . . from returning to Australia." The *Canberra Times* quoted "highest official sources"—likely Beasley—as saying that "Bridges was still a British subject and a member of the Australian community and . . . therefore no legal bar could be placed in the way of his return." A controversial figure within Australian labor politics, Beasley, though close to the communists in the 1920s, later helped to oust CPA supporters from the ALP.[34]

Beasley's statement did not reflect the government's position. Two weeks later, an enciphered and unsigned cablegram, likely from foreign minister H. V. Evatt, to the Australian minister in Washington, with copies to "P.M.," was unambiguous: "I saw Mr. Cordell Hull [US secretary of state] and told him that having in view Bridges long residence and domicile in the United States we could not be expected to facilitate deportation to Australia. . . . In any case you know that Bridges would have no legal right to re-enter Australian territory (Potter v. Minahan and ex parte Walsh.) As there will be delay nothing need to be done but refrain from taking any positive step without prior reference to us."[35] Curtin's government, by intent or accident, was saying one thing to the press while preparing for something very different. Given the ALP's long struggle against communist influence in the Australian union movement, Bridges's reputation for closeness to the CP likely soured any possibility of a welcome from the governing ALP. Likely unaware of the ALP's position on his situation, Bridges sent congratulations to Curtin for the ALP win in the 1943 elections and to Evatt in 1951 for "leading a good fight against the Menzies pro-Fascist police state laws."[36]

After the US Supreme Court ruled in Bridges's favor in 1945, he became a naturalized US citizen. In 1949, however, US authorities brought him to trial and charged him with lying on his naturalization papers when he swore that he had never been a CP member. Convicted in 1950, he appealed. Had his appeal failed, he would have been denaturalized and subject to deportation. In 1953, the Supreme Court again ruled in his favor.

Between 1950 and 1953, Australian newspapers again buzzed with speculation that Bridges might return. This time, Australia had a Liberal-Country coalition government led by Robert Menzies. Menzies had entered politics as a Nationalist and then became part of the United Australia Party (a coalition of anti-ALP parties). In 1945, he led in organizing the Liberal Party, a center-right party drawing support from business and the middle class. The Country Party, now called the National Party, was and is a conservative party, strongest in rural areas. In US domestic politics, anticommunist initiatives by the Truman administration did not prevent the opposition Republicans from seeking more far-reaching measures; Australia's Menzies government similarly sought to extend the anticommunist actions of the ALP.

The Menzies government closely watched Bridges's trial and appeals, and External Affairs had an extensive, secret file on him. In late 1949, a memo from the first secretary of the Australian Embassy in Washington discussed the trial and noted, "The Ambassador and other members of the staff have to date taken a noncommittal stand on the question of Bridges' possible deportation when the matter has arisen in informal conversation, the suggestion being made however, that it might be possible that Bridges would have lost his Australian citizenship by virtue of his naturalization in the United States." When Bridges was convicted in April 1950, the *New York Times* reported from Sydney that according to a "highly placed Government official," "Australia will not take back Harry Bridges if he is deported." The report continued, "'He is America's baby, not ours,' this official said, 'I don't think we want him.'" No international agreement existed "whereby we would be legally obligated to receive a denaturalized American deportee who was born in Australia." If the United States were to request that Australia accept Bridges, the anonymous official continued, it "would be very embarrassing" for Menzies, then seeking to outlaw the CPA and bar communists from union office. "The only way that Bridges could be admitted," the official added, "would be as an immigrant. Australian laws prohibit the entry of convicted felons, suspected Fascists and Communists and other persons of doubtful character." External Affairs filed a clipping from the *New York Herald-Tribune* quoting a "high immigration official" in the United States as saying that Bridges, though potentially a stateless person, could remain in the United States if no other country would admit him.[37]

Nonetheless, a week after the *Times* article, immigration minister Harold Holt insisted that no decision had been made regarding Bridges's return. Two months later, however, the *Melbourne Argus* quoted a US Justice Department official as saying, "The Australian Government has said that Australia doesn't want him." By then, Holt had caught up to the US press reports; he now specified that Bridges should be regarded as a stateless person and any application for admission to Australia would be considered "in the light of the current immigration policy."[38]

As Bridges's appeals moved through the courts, the Menzies government began to worry that Bridges might enter the country covertly. On 5 February 1952, External Affairs sent a telegram marked "secret" to its embassy in Washington: "Information received from reputable source that strong efforts will be made by Communist party to arrange entry to Australia from America of Harry Bridges." Further, "Bridges may possibly endeavor [to] secure passage Australia as seaman."[39]

Two days later, John Anderton, a San Francisco attorney with close ties to the city's Australian consulate, told the FBI that "he had received a request from [name redacted] for whereabouts of subject and possibility of his sailing as an American seaman. [name redacted] authorities had obtained information from their intelligence sources as to such a possibility." Australian authorities apparently had asked Anderton to approach the FBI for assistance. According to the FBI report, Anderton "was politely informed of the confidential nature of Bureau information and that if the [name redacted] desired to make a formal request of the Bureau, it would be promptly forwarded." Anderton indicated that there would be no official request, and "in view of his past and present cooperation in other cases, [Anderton] was advised that BRIDGES activities are usually noted by the press and are a matter of public knowledge and he was referred to an article in a local paper showing BRIDGES in Hawaii."[40]

The next day, Norman N. Frewin, the Australian vice consul in San Francisco, informed the Australian embassy in Washington that Bridges was in Hawaii but planned to return soon to San Francisco. The coded teletype also noted that Bridges was a member of the Marine Cooks and Stewards Union and "ostensibly has sufficient seaman credential(s) to permit him to be signed as crew member." In fact, Bridges had not gone to sea since 1922; any membership in the union was entirely honorary. Frewin contacted shipping company officials to alert them and found that all "can be relied on to follow our wishes." One company official suggested that Bridges might try to stow away.[41]

On 14 February, the Australian embassy in Washington sent a confidential telegram to External Affairs in Canberra with Frewin's information and a request for advice about approaching the US Coast Guard. Two months later, an embassy official visited the Security Division of the Coast Guard, where his contact was "non-committal" but said "quite definitely that the seaman's documents which Bridges now held were no longer valid." The Coast Guard official did not promise to alert all Coast Guard offices. Two days later, the same embassy official spoke to the State Department's chief of security, who also did not seem greatly concerned but agreed to ask the FBI to inform him if Bridges applied for seaman's papers.[42]

Why was the Australian government was so deeply concerned that Bridges might show up there? On 7 February, Anderton attributed Australian authorities' concern to "possible economic and political unrest [location redacted] immediate future."[43] Australia had experienced a series of strikes during 1950 and 1951 as inflation eroded purchasing power and the Menzies government worked to hold down wages. More strikes loomed in early 1952. At the same time, both the Menzies government and the ALP were pushing Australian unions to bar communists from union leadership, and some major unions—including the Waterside Workers Federation (WWF), the Australian counterpart to the ILWU—were experiencing deep divisions over that issue.[44]

The Menzies government and its ALP predecessor were also likely aware of the extent to which Bridges and his union had become an inspiration for Australia's left-wing unions, especially the WWF, which was led by James "Big Jim" Healy between 1937 and his death in 1961. In 1942 Healy, a CPA member, led Australian dockworkers' efforts to gain wage increases and an end to the "bull" system of hiring (the Australian counterpart to the "shape-up" that had been the key issue in the 1934 strike) and its replacement by rotating gangs (similar to the ILWU's "low man out" rule).[45]

Healy also created and edited the *Melbourne Maritime Worker* as part of his efforts to unite Australia's far-flung dockworkers. The first issue, in April 1938, told of WWF members' refusal to load material that could be used for war munitions, especially scrap metal bound for Japan. The ILWU had begun similar efforts in 1936 directed at Italy and then late in 1938 (after the WWF's actions) at Japan. The third and fourth issues of the *Maritime Worker*, published in June and July 1938, presented "The Life Story of Harry Bridges," taken directly from but not attributed to Richard Branstein's *Men Who Lead Labor*, published in the United States in September 1937.[46]

The first direct contact between Bridges and Healy seems not to have come until 1940, when Healy sent Bridges a long letter with information about current WWF wages and working conditions and requested similar information about the ILWU; Bridges immediately replied with a copy of the current ILWU contract. Thereafter, the two men corresponded regularly, as did other officers of the two unions. With the end of World War II in sight, Healy tried to interest Bridges in a conference of the WWF, ILWU, and the Waterside Workers Union of New Zealand. Bridges expressed interest, but events in the United States prevented the ILWU from participating. In 1946, Bridges arranged a cable address to speed up communications between him and Healy and offered to phone Healy. Subsequent communications included regular exchanges of information on how each union was responding to issues it faced. Another frequent topic was the need for dockworkers around the Pacific to exchange information and coordinate activities; those discussions eventually led to a 1959 conference in Tokyo.[47]

Bridges made certain that each issue of the ILWU's newspaper, the *Dispatcher*, was airmailed to Healy and the WWF, and Bridges regularly commented on articles in the *Maritime Worker*. The *Maritime Worker* closely followed Bridges's various legal cases as well as the ILWU's accomplishments. The paper ran several articles by Bridges and sometimes reproduced articles from the *Dispatcher*. Healy eventually took the title of Bridges's regular column in the *Dispatcher*, "On the Beam," for a similar but unsigned feature in the *Maritime Worker*. In 1953, at the conclusion of the third Bridges case, Bridges sent his personal thanks to the WWF for its support. The WWF also compared the efforts of the Australian government and the mainstream Australian labor movement to oust communists from union leadership to the similar experience of the ILWU, which the Congress of Industrial Organizations had expelled in 1950 as communist-dominated. In advocating for pensions for WWF members, the *Maritime Worker* repeatedly cited the ILWU pensioners, who were significantly better off than their Australian counterparts.[48]

By the late 1950s, the overarching issue of mechanization dominated communication between the two unions. As the ILWU was engaging in both extensive internal discussions and bargaining on mechanization, Healy tried unsuccessfully to persuade the Menzies government to bring Bridges and his corporate counterpart, J. Paul St. Sure, to Australia. Similarly, when the ILWU invited Healy to attend its biennial conference to be held in Hawaii in 1961, the US State Department refused to issue him a visa, a refusal Healy attributed to his "associations"—that is, his CPA membership. Healy's comment about that refusal could as easily have been written by Bridges about the refusal of the Menzies government two years earlier: "Irrespective of who the individuals may be or their associations, neither Governments nor ship owners have viewed with any degree of equanimity the international association of trade unions."[49] Healy died later that year, but Bridges continued his close relationship with Healy's successor, and similar relations between the unions have persisted into the present.

In 1960, Bridges had led the ILWU into a modernization and mechanization agreement that was considered a model of its kind. US secretary of labor James Mitchell proclaimed that "next only to John L. Lewis, Bridges has done the best job in American labor of coming to grips with the problems of automation." Some even called Bridges a "labor statesman," though he disavowed the title. In 1967, a year after Menzies left the prime minister's office, Bridges applied to visit Australia as the guest of the WWF. The government of Harold Holt put up no obstacles. The Australian labor movement gave him a hero's welcome, and the Australian press treated him like a visiting celebrity.[50]

Conclusion

Harry Bridges's Australian experiences helped establish him as knowledgeable about unions and labor politics, and he later found it convenient to claim that his political outlook had been formed through his experiences in Australia rather than by exposure to the CP in the United States. Bridges brought Australian concepts of labor and politics to the docks of San Francisco in the early 1930s, and he injected Australian examples into discussions of US working conditions and politics throughout the 1930s.

Bridges was demonized in the US press, and the same process occurred in Australia as the Australian press drew on its American counterparts in presenting Bridges to Australians. Just as some business groups and conservatives in the United States saw Bridges as a dangerous radical, conservative Australian political figures let their fear of Bridges carry them into a quixotic campaign to prevent him from sneaking into their country. The WWF, however, looked to Bridges and the ILWU as inspiration and exemplar, and Bridges and his union worked closely with their counterparts in Australia. With the thaw in the Cold War and a decline in anticommunist rhetoric in both nations, Bridges could be celebrated in both places as a labor statesman.

Notes

Some research for this chapter was made possible by a fellowship from the National Endowment for the Humanities and by an appointment as a visiting scholar in the history department of the University of Melbourne. This chapter is drawn from a biography of Bridges that is currently in progress; parts have previously appeared in the *Pacific Historical Review*.

1. See, for example, Peter Clayworth's study of Patrick Hickey and Tom Goyens's account of the transnational ties among anarchists.

2. Baptism Register, St. Brendan's Church, Kensington.

3. Harry Bridges, interview by author, 19 December 1985, 29 January, 7 May, 2 September 1986; Harry Bridges, interview by Charles Einstein, tape 18, 21; Harry Bridges, interview by Noriko Sawada Bridges, tapes 1, HB; Harry Bridges to C. H. Fitzgibbon, 18 December

1963, item 98, Waterside Workers Federation of Australia Collection, N114, Noel Butlin Archives Centre, Australian National University. For Mannix, see Colm Kiernan, *Daniel Mannix and Ireland* (Morwell, Vic.: Alella, 1984); B. A. Santamaria, *Daniel Mannix: The Quality of Leadership* (Carlton, Vic.: Melbourne University Press, 1984); James G. Murtagh, *Australia: The Catholic Chapter* (Sydney: Angus and Robertson, 1959).

4. Bridges, interview by Noriko Sawada Bridges, tape HB; Bridges, interview by Einstein, tape 49.

5. Bridges, interview by Einstein, tape 4; Bridges, Henry Renton Nicholson, file, Personnel Dossiers for 1st Australian Imperial Forces ex-service members, series B2455, World War I Personnel Records Service, Australian Archives, Mitchell, Australian Capital Territory; John Merritt, *The Making of the AWU* (Melbourne: Oxford University Press, 1986), 341; *Yea Chronicle*, 24 August 1916.

6. Bridges, interview by Einstein, tapes 4, 46; Bridges, interview by Noriko Sawada Bridges, tapes 1, HB; Alec H. Chisholm, comp. and ed., *Who's Who in Australia*, 13th ed. (Melbourne: Herald and Weekly Times, 1947), 169; Bridges, interview by author.

7. Frank Bongiorno, *The People's Party: Victorian Labor and the Radical Tradition, 1875–1914* (Carlton, Vic.: Melbourne University Press, 1996), chaps. 1–2; Bede Nairn, *Civilising Capitalism: The Beginnings of the Australian Labor Party*, rev. ed. (Carlton, Vic.: Melbourne University Press, 1989); Ian Turner, *Industrial Labour and Politics: The Dynamics of the Labor Movement in Eastern Australia, 1900–1921* (Canberra: Australian National University, 1965), 17–22; Robin Gollan, *Radical and Working Class Politics: A Study of Eastern Australia, 1850–1910* (Parkville, Vic.: Melbourne University Press, 1960), 69–72, 78, 80–81, 128–50; Russel Ward, *The History of Australia: The Twentieth Century* (New York: Harper and Row, 1977), 75–82. *Labour History* 102 (May 2012) is devoted entirely to the ALP government of 1910–13.

8. Register, Christian Brothers' School, St. Mary's, West Melbourne; Bridges, interview by author; Bridges, interview by Noriko Sawada Bridges, tape 1; Bridges, interview by Einstein, tapes 5, 18, 49; *Essendon Gazette*, 5 July 1934.

9. Mannix's speech appeared in the *Advocate* on 6 May 1916; it is reprinted in L. L. Robson, *Australia and the Great War, 1914–1918* (South Melbourne: Macmillan, 1969), 62–63; Bridges, interview by Noriko Sawada Bridges, tape HB; Ward, *History*, 102, 118. See also Val Noone, "Class Factors in the Radicalisation of Archbishop Daniel Mannix, 1913–1917," *Labour History* 106 (2014): 189–204, which points to Mannix's service as a parish priest as a significant factor in his stance.

10. Ward, *History*, 113–14, 116–17, 121–22; Robson, *Australia and the Great War*, 72–76; Cyril Bryan, *Archbishop Mannix: Champion of Australian Democracy* (Melbourne: Advocate, 1918), 61–62; Laurence F. Fitzhardinge, *William Morris Hughes: A Political Biography* (Sydney: Angus and Robertson, 1979), 2:171–97, 213, 225–34; Michael McKernan, *The Australian People and the Great War* (West Melbourne: Nelson, 1980), 7; Ward, *History*, 111, 113; Turner, *Industrial Labour and Politics*, 83–84, 113–16; Bridges, interview by author; Bridges, interview by Einstein, tapes 3, 12; Thelma D. Bridges, on behalf of George Bridges, to author, 16 June 1990.

11. Rupert Lockwood, *Ship to Shore: A History of Melbourne's Waterfront and Its Union Struggles* (Sydney: Hale and Iremonger, 1990), 134–46, 151, 164–71; Charles Fahey and John Lack, "The Great Strike of 1917 in Victoria: Looking Fore and Aft, and from Below," *Labour History* 106 (2014): 69–97; Stuart Macintyre, *1901–1942: The Succeeding Age* (Melbourne: Oxford University Press, 1997), 170–71; McKernan, *Australian People*, 8; Fitzhardinge, *William Morris Hughes*, 2:271–74; Brian Fitzpatrick, *A Short History of the Australian Labor Movement* (Melbourne: Rawson's, 1944), 144; Ward, *History*, 120.

12. Bridges, interview by Noriko Sawada Bridges, tapes 1, 9; Bridges, interview by Einstein, tapes 8, 28.

13. *Melbourne Argus*, 16 August–10 October 1917; *Melbourne Age*, 24 August–26 September 1917; Macintyre, *1901–1942*, 171–72; Lockwood, *Ship to Shore*, 159–60, 172–78; Bridges, interview by Noriko Sawada Bridges, tape 9; Bridges, interview by Einstein, tape 3.

14. Bryan, *Archbishop Mannix*, 128–66, esp. 130, 158, 162; Bridges, interview by Noriko Sawada Bridges, tape 9; Bridges, interview by Einstein, tape 3.

15. Bridges, interview by Noriko Sawada Bridges, tapes HB, 2; shipping articles for the *Daisy Knights*, 7 December 1917, *Sara Hunter*, 7 January 1918, *Lialeeta*, 5 July 1918, *Southern Cross*, 30 January 1919, *Valmarie*, 28 February 1919, all in Mercantile Marine Office records, Articles of Agreement, VPRS 566/P, units 215–18, 227, Public Record Office of Victoria, Laverton Repository. See also Harry R. Bridges, application for certificate of service as able seaman, 21 April 1920, Sailors' Union of the Pacific Archives, San Francisco. For the strike, see Brian Fitzpatrick and Rowan J. Cahill, *The Seamen's Union of Australia, 1872–1972: A History* (Sydney: Seamen's Union of Australia, 1981), 50; Macintyre, *1901–1942*, 183. Shipping articles had a place to paste in the terms of the most recent arbitration award, but none of the articles for Bridges's vessels carried those provisions.

16. Bridges, interview by Noriko Sawada Bridges, tape 2; contribution books for New South Wales, Victoria, and South Australia, 1912–22, and transfer books for Tasmania, 1916–40, and New Zealand, 1916–22, items 34/3–5, 10, 12, 19, 20, Seamen's Union of Australia Collection, E183, Butlin Archives. I infer that Bridges paid union dues on his voyage to San Francisco not only because that ship was covered by the arbitration agreement but also because of his memories of being a union member and of joining the Sailors Union of the Pacific by transferring his membership from the Seamen's Union of Australia.

17. Bridges, interview by Noriko Sawada Bridges, tape 5; Bridges, interview by Einstein, tapes 5, 6; Bridges, interview by author; Harry R. Bridges, application for certificate of service as able seaman, 21 April 1920, and Harry Bridges membership records, both in Sailors' Union of the Pacific Archives.

18. *Sydney Maritime Worker*, 8 November 1967; "Biographical Notes on Members of the Victorian Socialist Party, Part II," *Recorder* (Melbourne Branch, Australian Society for the Study of Labor History) 82 (1976): 7; Fitzpatrick and Cahill, *Seamen's Union*, 53; Bridges, interview by author.

19. Bridges, interview by Einstein, tape 8; Bridges, interview by Noriko Sawada Bridges, tape 12; Bridges, interview by author; Marine Exchange Records, Maritime Museum Library, San Francisco; B. B. Jones quoted in Charles P. Larrowe, *Harry Bridges: The Rise and Fall of Radical Labor in the United States* (New York: Hill, 1972), 16.

20. *Sydney Morning Herald*, 10 December 1936, 20 August 1937; Richard Bransten [pseud., Bruce Minton] and John Stuart, *Men Who Lead Labor* (New York: Modern Age, 1937), 172–76; Alan Benjamin, "Some Want to Deport Him: Australia's Bridges," *Melbourne Herald*, 2 September 1938; Byron Darnton, "The Riddle of Harry Bridges," *New York Times Magazine*, 25 February 1940.

21. See Robert Cherny, "Harry Bridges and the Communist Party: New Evidence, Old Questions; Old Evidence, New Questions," paper presented at the annual meeting of the Organization of American Historians, 4 April 1998.

22. "Official Report of Proceedings before the Immigration and Naturalization Service of the Department of Labor, Docket No. 55973/217, In the Matter of: Harry Bridges: Deportation Hearing, Angel Island, San Francisco, California, August–September, 1939," typescript, Robbins Collection, Boalt Hall, University of California, Berkeley, 18:2865, 3052–53, 3056–58. Regarding his seafaring, see Robert Cherny, "Constructing a Radical Identity: History, Memory, and the Seafaring Stories of Harry Bridges," *Pacific Historical Review* 70 (2001): 571–600.

23. *Sydney Morning Herald*, 5 August 1939; James M. Landis, *In the Matter of Harry R. Bridges: Findings and Conclusions of the Trial Examiner* (Washington, D.C.: US Government Printing Office, 1939).

24. For the four Bridges hearings or trials, see Stanley I. Kutler, *The American Inquisition: Justice and Injustice in the Cold War* (New York: Hill and Wang, 1982), 118–51.

25. Darnton, "Riddle"; Theodore Dreiser, "Story of Harry Bridges," *Friday*, 4, 11 October 1940. For late-in-life examples, see Bridges's comments on the occasion of the fiftieth anniversary of the 1934 strikes, San Francisco, 30 June 1984 (tape in possession of author) or his comments at the recognition dinner sponsored by the Southern California Library for Social Studies and Research, Los Angeles, 11 February 1986 (observed by the author).

26. *Melbourne Argus*, 27 March 1943.

27. Most articles just reprinted the press release; see, for example, *Burnie Advocate*, 2 July 1934; *Hobart Mercury*, 2 July 1934.

28. Dorothy McNaught, interview by author, 2 July 1997; *Melbourne Argus*, 2 July 1934; *Essendon Gazette and Flemington Spectator*, 5 July 1934.

29. A Trove search for "Harry Bridges" returned about eighty articles in Australian newspapers during July 1934.

30. For example, *Perth Daily News*, 14 July 1934; *Rockhampton Morning Bulletin*, 16 July 1934.

31. *Townsville Daily Bulletin*, 18 July 1934; *Maryborough Chronicle, Wide Bay and Burnett Advertiser*, 20 July 1934. See also, for example, *Cairns Post*, 20 July 1934.

32. *Sydney Labour Daily*, 21 August 1937, Box 79, File F, Frances Perkins Papers, Columbia University; *Melbourne Australasian*, 26 February 1938; *Canberra Times*, 7 April 1941.

33. Chancery to Department, 29 February, 10 June, 1 July 1941, Series A981, Item MIG 3, Title Migration Restrictions: Deportation of Harry R. Bridges, Department of External Affairs File, Australian Archives, Canberra. On the campaign against Bridges in the late 1930s and early 1940s, see Kutler, *American Inquisition*; Robert Cherny, "Anticommunist Networks and Labor: The Pacific Coast in the 1930s," in *Labor's Cold War: Local Politics*

in a Global Context, ed. Shelton Stromquist (Champaign: University of Illinois Press, 2008), 17–48.

34. *Melbourne Argus*, 30 May 1942; *Canberra Times*, 1 June 1942; "John Albert (Jack) Beasley," *Australian Dictionary of Biography*, available at http://adb.anu.edu.au/biography/beasley-john-albert-jack-9461.

35. Cablegram to Australian Minister, Washington, 25 June 1942, with copies to P.M. and Minister E.A. on 26 June. I conclude that the cablegram was probably from Evatt based on the cablegram from Dixon, Australian Legation, Washington, to Department of External Affairs, 20 June 1942 (Department of External Affairs File), which refers to Evatt's recent meeting with Hull.

36. Harry Bridges to John Curtin, 31 August 1943, Harry Bridges to Jim Healy, 2 December 1951, Harry Bridges to Robert Menzies, 7 October 1960, all in ILWU History Series, Trade Unions Relations/Foreign—Australia File, ILWU Library.

37. O. L. Davis to Secretary, Department of External Affairs, 14 December 1949, 24 May 1950, *New York Times* (clipping), 5 April 1950, *New York Herald-Tribune* (clipping), 9 April 1950, all in Miscellaneous: Enquiry re Mr. Harry Bridges, file marked secret, Department of External Affairs, Series/Accession A1838/2, Item 1461/131, Australian Archives.

38. *Melbourne Argus*, 12 April, 19 June 1950; *Sydney Morning Herald*, 20 June 1950; *Canberra Times*, 21 June 1950.

39. File: Deportations: Bridges, Harry, File 609/1/2, Files of the Australian Embassy, Washington, D.C., 1952–53, Australian Archives.

40. FBI Director to SAC, San Francisco, 26 February 1952 (marked "Secret" and "Confidential"), SAC San Francisco to FBI Director, 13 February 1952, both in FBI File HQ39-915, Section 129. For information on Anderton, see *Hastings Community* 21 (1977): 33, available at http://repository.uchastings.edu/cgi/viewcontent.cgi?article=1051&context=alumni_mag. Anderton provided pro bono assistance to Australian war brides seeking divorces from their American husbands: see *Australian Women's Weekly*, 12 July 1947.

41. File: Deportations: Bridges, Harry, File 609/1/2, Files of the Australian Embassy, Washington, D.C., 1952–53, Australian Archives.

42. Ibid.

43. SAC San Francisco to FBI Director, 13 February 1952, FBI File HQ39-915, Section 129.

44. See, for example, *Sydney Morning Herald*, 24 January, 1 February 1952; *Newcastle Morning Herald and Miners' Advocate*, 29 January 1952; *Brisbane Sunday Mail*, 3 February 1952; *Wagga Wagga Daily Advertiser*, 5 February 1952; *Queensland Times* (Ipswich), 9 February 1952; *Brisbane Worker*, 11 February 1952; *Sydney Morning Herald*, 4, 16 January 1952.

45. Ray Markey and Stuart Svensen, "James (Jim) Healy," *Australian Dictionary of Biography*, available at http://adb.anu.edu.au/biography/healy-james-jim-10470.

46. Healy to Bridges, 8 May 1958, ILWU History Series, Trade Unions Relations/Foreign—Australia File, ILWU Library; *Maritime Worker* (Melbourne), 1 April 1938; Richard Alan Liebes, "Longshore Labor Relations on the Pacific Coast, 1934–1942"

(PhD diss., University of California at Berkeley, 1942), 183–84; *Maritime Worker*, 1 June, 1 July 1938; Bransten and Stuart, *Men Who Lead Labor*, 172–202.

47. The ILWU Library in San Francisco contains a thick file of correspondence between Bridges and Healy and more generally between the ILWU and WWF as well as other Australian unions. See especially Healy to Bridges, 20 January 1940, Bridges to Healy, 2 May 1940, 14, November 1951, 25 November 1952, 16 April, 18 September 1958, Bridges to WATFED, 25 January 1946. The ILWU Library also has a large file on the Tokyo conferences. At my request, Brett Goodin surveyed the WWF collection at the Butlin Archives and found nothing that was not represented in the files at the ILWU Library.

48. See, for example, *Maritime Worker*, 29 January, 16 July 1949, 11 February 1950, 23 February, 1, 22 November, 6 December 1952, 18 May, 22 September, 27 October 1953.

49. See, for example, Healy to Bridges, 8 May 1958, 20 November 1959, Bridges to Healy, 4 December 1959; see especially Healy to Bridges, 22 December 1959, 22 May 1961, all in ILWU Library.

50. "The Man Who Made the Most of Automation," *Time*, 27 December 1963; *Melbourne Age*, 27 September 1967.

Conclusion

Harvesting the Fruits of Transnational and Comparative History

SHELTON STROMQUIST
GREG PATMORE

Comparative history provides an opportunity for scholars to move beyond national boundaries and reflect on their own societies in new light. But such comparisons are not always straightforward. While both Australia and the United States have federal governments, the state played a more coercive role against organized labor and radicals in the United States than in Australia. Several factors softened the impact of the state on labor in Australia: a stronger trade union movement, the formation of labor parties, and a political consensus on regulating industrial relations at least until the 1980s. In the United States, unbridled hostility of large corporations toward organized labor governed state policy. Despite these differences, labor in both countries found political space to promote progressive policies and modify the harsh behavior of governments.[1]

Comparative analysis is also complicated by variations in local economic climate, the severity of depressions, and the impact of the two world wars on the two countries. While Australia and the United States have converged in recent years around neoliberal economic policy and changing industrial relations, the divergent impact of the recent global financial crisis on each illustrates enduring differences in their political economies.[2] Claims of convergence are belied by the rhetoric of the 2016 US presidential election, where the tide shifted again toward protection and away from support for global free trade.

These essays are comparative but also transnational in approach, reflecting the movement of people and ideas across national boundaries. Immigration facilitated the global transmission of ideas and cultures. Both Australia and the United States relied on large-scale immigration for settlement and economic development, and the essays presented here illustrate the transnational influence of the Irish in shaping the labor movements in both countries and the role of Jewish and Italian immigrants in sustaining and expanding the influence of anarchism before 1917. British immigrants in Australia and Finnish immigrants in the United States played crucial roles in developing and promoting consumer cooperatives.[3]

The fruits of comparative and transnational history are rich and often unanticipated. They yield insights that are unavailable when we limit ourselves to national frameworks examined in isolation. This volume has produced such findings, providing a starting point for new research in the labor history of both countries and in the global patterns and processes by which their histories are linked.

The United States and Australia joined the allied effort in World War I at different times and under different circumstances. Both countries lay geographically on the margins of the European war but became full-fledged combatants with critical roles in the war effort. But both also experienced deep political divisions over conscription and support for the war itself. The essays on working-class opposition to World War I illustrate these deep divisions, but the comparisons also highlight ambiguities that colored the opposition. In the United States, opposition to the war gestated for more than two years of neutrality, but then conscription came quickly and contributed to the severe persecution and repression of what had been a robust labor, socialist, and reform-minded opposition. The war ultimately proved devastating to these movements. Australia entered the war early and relatively unified. But referenda on conscription revealed deep political and social divisions that the war itself had not. The Industrial Workers of the World and women spearheaded that opposition and consequently suffered severe repression. The political space in which conscription was debated and ultimately defeated enabled a divided Labor Party and trade union movement to rebuild themselves and enter the postwar years far healthier than their American counterparts. But the legacy of wartime suppression of dissent outlasted the war and even intensified over the twentieth century. Each case illuminates aspects of the other in ways that would not otherwise be obvious.[4]

Observations about differences in the role of the state in Australia and the United States abound in the literature, but the roots of those differences in the regulatory environments of the early colonial United States and Australia have been little explored. Jennie Jeppesen's study of the use of convict labor in both countries clearly shows that despite similarities in their systems of labor coercion, convicts in colonial Virginia were privately owned and subject to little state regulation, while in Australia they remained the property of the state in a regulatory environment that placed significant limits on their abuse. This difference contributed to the development of an economy in which state regulation of labor was normative. The recent convergence in the coercive behavior of employers in key industries such as meatpacking suggests that this long tradition of labor regulation in Australia may be eroding in the face of the globally hegemonic influence of the antiregulatory neoliberal practices of American employers and their state allies.[5]

While it is customary to assume that the greater US ethnic diversity helps to explain the two countries' distinctive political and cultural histories, the essays in this volume that examine the Irish in Australia and the United States suggest more subtle differences and alternative grounds for differentiating the effects of ethnicity. The nature and extent of Irish immigrants' role in the labor movement and politics were very much a by-product of the national contexts in which they functioned. In Australia, the Irish found less cultural space for their own nationalist opposition to the British Empire; they were deeply influenced by a powerful Catholic Church presence in their communities; and they were drawn to support a working-class labor party and a hegemonic "White Australia" posture in which their influence was diluted. The United States offered a much larger Irish immigrant population greater political and cultural space in which its defensive, nationalist culture might flourish with greater autonomy than was the case in Australia. This produced strands of working-class culture that were both more conservative and more progressive, at some times virulently racist and at others spearheading progressive class-wide movements and political initiatives. This work, as James Barrett suggests, warrants a degree of caution in assessing immigrants' impact in both countries. "We risk misunderstanding" Irish Australians and Irish Americans "if we ignore the nuances in their narratives."[6]

The literature on labor conflict has taken for granted the idea that the United States experienced more protracted (and more violent) strikes than did Australia. While this may be true for some periods and some industries, the essays in this collection suggest that this overview requires modification. On the conflict-plagued railroads of the late nineteenth century, Australia, despite government ownership, was remarkably like the United States, though the violence of conflict in the United States still stands out. But a close comparison of Queensland and the northern Great Plains suggests strong parallels in the persistence of conflict in the late nineteenth century and management's concerted efforts to cut labor costs; the causes, however, are different than we thought. Competition was not the primary factor driving attempts to cut wages and attack union prerogatives; rather, the main factor was the shared experience of dramatically falling commodity prices and the railroad fiscal crisis it precipitated. A closer look at the impact of globalization and capital flight in recent times may similarly help us understand the convergence in industrial relations between the United States and Australia—and, for that matter, other long-established industrial economies. Here, too, we might benefit from the kind of rigorous comparative analysis that Bradley Bowden and Peta Stevenson-Clarke have presented. Similarities in class relations and conflict are also evident in the milieu of military service, where soldiers brought their experience as workers and members of working-class communities to bear on decisions regarding their deployment. Across time and geography, as Nathan Wise's essay suggests, remarkable similarities are evident in soldiers' capacity for collective protest in defense of ties of class and community both in the United States and in Australia.

In no area of comparative US-Australian labor history is the extant interpretation more entrenched than in the comparison of class institutions (unions, parties, cooperatives) and the role of the state in protecting and addressing the social and economic needs of workers. These essays turn the tables on this analysis in significant and unpredicted ways. Major national unions in each country (the Australian Workers' Union and United Auto Workers) came to practice forms of hierarchical organization that eroded union democracy; in this respect, their experiences, though rooted in quite different economies and political traditions, look quite similar. In the realm of cooperatives, despite the more individualist US political culture, American trade unions provided greater support and ultimately produced a more robust cooperative movement than Australia possessed. And in the realm of social policy, the political tradition in Australia, whereby workers looked to a more assertive state and stronger protection of workers' interests, undermined support for old-age insurance in the 1930s because of its proposed contributory principle. In the United States, that same principle (a contributory regressive tax) facilitated working-class support for the passage of social security insurance that became a foundational element of the New Deal welfare state.[7]

The linkages between the United States and Australia may be most clearly manifested in the crosscurrents of radical traditions and the transnational migration of working-class activists—but again in ways that are surprising and unanticipated. Australian anarchists in the formative nineteenth-century years of their movement looked to the United States for inspiration and the nourishment of a vital flow of ideas and transnational linkages. US dockworkers on the West Coast imbibed the experience and traditions of their Australian counterparts through the leadership of Australia's own Harry Bridges. That Bridges would later convey the inspiration of the American International Longshoremen's and Warehousemen's Union back to his own countrymen further illuminates the transglobal flow of radical traditions. And New Zealand miners found inspiration in the experience and leadership of their own Patrick Hickey and the new models of industrial unionism and militant collective action that he had learned from his years of work with the Western Federation of Miners in the United States. He also became a conduit for the transmission of those United States–New Zealand traditions to Australia during World War I.[8]

The original findings that these essays bring to the study of US and Australian labor history in many ways only scratch the surface of the rich possibilities awaiting transnational and comparative research. Despite the substantial differences in economic structure, the composition of the working classes, and political cultures and traditions of state intervention in labor relations and social welfare, much comparative ground remains to be more fully explored—the nature and extent of political dissent and democratic practice, the legacies of dependent labor, the imprint of colonialism and empire, the meaning and influence of racism on workers' capacity to act collectively, convergent industrial relations in an era of globalization, and shared traditions of radicalism and collective action. In an era of global corporate hegemony, such lessons have never seemed more relevant. The work ahead is both challenging and bracing, but as this volume reveals, the fruits of such transnational collaboration can be well worth the effort.

Notes

1. See, for example, the influence of labor and socialist movements on city government in both the United States and Australia in Shelton Stromquist, this volume.

2. The recent history of the meat industry offers a laboratory for neoliberal antiunion policies in both countries. See Marjorie A. Jerrard and Patrick O'Leary, this volume.

3. For immigrants as transnational carriers of ethnic identity, see James R. Barrett, this volume; Elizabeth Malcolm and Dianne Hall, this volume. On immigrant anarchists' global influence, see Tom Goyens, this volume; for consumer cooperatives as transnational institutions, see Greg Patmore and Nikola Balnave, in this volume.

4. These convergent and divergent patterns of dissent during World War I are examined in Robin Archer, this volume; Verity Burgmann and Jeffrey A. Johnson, this volume; Diane Kirkby, this volume; Stromquist, this volume.

5. The essays in this volume by Jennie Jeppesen and Jerrard and O'Leary bracket a chronology of labor regulation in Australia and the United States that highlights their historic differences and their recent convergence.

6. For the contrasting ethnic milieus of the two countries through the lens of Irish immigrant experience, see Malcolm and Hall, this volume; Barrett, this volume.

7. For the comparative patterns of state activism and the functioning of working-class institutions, see Scott Stephenson, this volume; Patmore and Balnave, this volume; Benjamin Huf, this volume.

8. For an original take on these striking transnational currents of radical ideas and organizing experience, see Goyens, this volume; Peter Clayworth, this volume; Robert Cherny, this volume.

Contributors

The Editors

GREG PATMORE is professor emeritus of business and labor history and chair of the Business and Labour History Group and the Co-Operative Research Group in the School of Business at the University of Sydney. He previously served as president of the Australian Society for the Study of Labour History and editor of its journal, *Labour History*, and he continues to serve on the journal's editorial board. He is the author of *Worker Voice: Employee Representation in the Workplace in Australia, Canada, Germany, the UK, and the US, 1914–1939* (2016) and *Australian Labour History* (1991).

SHELTON STROMQUIST is professor emeritus of history at the University of Iowa. He is a past president of the Labor and Working-Class History Association. His publications include *Labor's Cold War: Local Politics in a Global Context* (2008), *Reinventing "the People": The Progressive Movement, the Class Problem, and the Origins of Modern Liberalism* (2006), and *Solidarity and Survival: An Oral History of Iowa Labor in the Twentieth Century* (1993), and he is completing a comparative study of municipal labor and socialist politics, ca. 1890–1925.

The Authors

ROBIN ARCHER is director of both the postgraduate program in political sociology and the Ralph Miliband Program at the London School of Economics as well as emeritus fellow in politics at Corpus Christi College, Oxford. He is the author of *Why Is There No Labor Party in the United States?* (2008) and *Economic Democracy* (1995).

NIKOLA BALNAVE is a senior lecturer in the Department of Marketing and Management and a member of the Centre for Workforce Futures at Macquarie University. She has conducted extensive historical research on the management strategy of welfarism in Australia and on consumer cooperatives in Australia and New Zealand. She serves as president of the Australian Society for the Study of Labour History and as deputy editor of the society's journal, *Labour History*. She also serves as president of the Academic Association of Historians in Australian and New Zealand Business Schools.

JAMES R. BARRETT is professor emeritus of history and African American studies at the University of Illinois at Urbana-Champaign. His most recent book is *History from the Bottom up and the Inside Out: Ethnicity, Race, and Identity in Working-Class History* (2017), and he is also the author of *The Irish Way: Becoming American in the Multi-Ethnic City* (2013). He and Shelton Stromquist are currently coediting a collection of essays by labor historian David Montgomery.

BRADLEY BOWDEN is professor of employment relations at Griffith University. He is chair of the Management History Division of the American Academy of Management and editor in chief of the *Journal of Management History*. He has published numerous articles on Australian labor history, particularly working-class life and organization in Queensland and Brisbane. He is also a longtime member of the editorial board of *Labour History*.

VERITY BURGMANN is adjunct professor of politics in the School of Social Sciences at Monash University and director of the Roger Coates Labour History Project, an online resource of primary-source documents of Australian radicalism (www.reasoninrevolt.net.au). She is the author of numerous publications on labor movements, protest movements, radical ideologies, and environmental politics, among them *Globalization and Labour in the Twenty-First Century* (2016), *Climate Politics and the Climate Movement in Australia* (2012), *Power, Profit and Protest* (2003), *Green Bans, Red Union* (1998), *Revolutionary Industrial Unionism: The Industrial Workers of the World in Australia* (1995), *Power and Protest* (1993), and *"In Our Time": Socialism and the Rise of Labor* (1985).

ROBERT CHERNY, professor emeritus at San Francisco State University, is completing a biography of Harry Bridges. He specializes in American political history from the Civil War to World War II and in the history of California and the West. He is the author of *A Righteous Cause: The Life of William Jennings Bryan* (1985) and *Populism, Progressivism, and the Transformation of Nebraska Politics, 1885–1915* (1981) as well as coeditor of *California Women and Politics from the Gold Rush to the Great Depression* (2011) and *American Labor and the Cold War* (2004). His most recent book is *Victor Arnautoff and the Politics of Art* (2017).

PETER CLAYWORTH is an independent scholar who has previously worked as a researcher for the Waitangi Tribunal, a historian for the New Zealand Department of Conservation, and a writer for *Te Ara—The Encyclopedia of New Zealand*. He is currently writing a biography of union agitator Patrick Hodgens Hickey.

TOM GOYENS is associate professor of history at Salisbury University. His research focuses on immigrant anarchism in the United States. He is the author of *Beer and Revolution: The German Anarchist Movement in New York City, 1880–1914* (2007). His edited works include *Radical Gotham: Anarchism in New York City from Schwab's Saloon to Occupy* (2017) , Helene Minkin's memoir, *Storm in My Heart: Memories from the Widow of Johann Most* (2015). He has published articles on anarchism and social space in *Social Anarchism* and *Rethinking History: The Journal of Theory and Practice*. He is currently writing a biography of Johann Most.

DIANNE HALL is senior lecturer in history at Victoria University. She has published widely on history of religion, gender, violence, and race and the Irish in Ireland and Australia. She is author of *Women and the Church in Medieval Ireland* (2008) and coauthor of *Imperial Spaces: Placing the Irish and Scots in Colonial Australia* (2011). She and Elizabeth Malcolm are currently collaborating on a history of the Irish in Australia.

BENJAMIN HUF is a doctoral candidate at the Australian National University, where he teaches in the School of History. His research focuses on the intersections between theories of the state, economic sociology, and nineteenth-century British political thought. He has written for the *Australian Book Review*.

JENNIE JEPPESEN holds a doctorate from the University of Melbourne, where her research focused on transnational American-Australian convict history. She is currently examining the implications of race for notions of unfreedom and slavery and the impacts of lack of freedom on the children of convicts and indentured servants.

MARJORIE A. JERRARD is a senior lecturer in the Monash Business School. She has published articles and book chapters on the Australian and New Zealand meat-processing industries, trade union strategy, community unionism in Australia, and workforce diversity. Her work has appeared in *Labour History*, the *Journal of Industrial Relations*, the *Labour Studies Journal*, and the *Economic and Labour Relations Review*. Her current research involves trade unions in Victoria and Queensland and the Australasian Meat Industry Employees' Union and employers.

JEFFREY A. JOHNSON is a professor of history and director of American studies at Providence College. He is the author of *The 1916 Preparedness Day Bombing: Anarchists and Terrorism in Progressive Era America* (2017) and *"They Are All Red Out Here": Socialist Politics in the Pacific Northwest, 1895–1925* (2008).

DIANE KIRKBY is research professor (emeritus) at La Trobe University and adjunct professor of law and humanities at the University of Technology Sydney. She has written and edited several books, including *Voices from the Ships: Australia's Seafarers and Their Union* (2008), *Barmaids: A History of Women's Work in Pubs* (1997), and *Alice Henry: The Power of Pen and Voice* (1991). She is an elected fellow of the Academy of the Social Sciences in Australia and the Australian Academy of the Humanities and an honorary fellow of the American Society for Legal History. She is currently working on a history of international organizing among maritime workers as well as a history of women's leadership.

ELIZABETH MALCOLM is an honorary professorial fellow at the University of Melbourne. She has published extensively on Irish social, cultural, and medical history, and her most recent book is *The Irish Policeman: A Life, 1822–1922* (2006). She serves as an editor of the *Australasian Journal of Irish Studies*, and she and Dianne Hall are currently collaborating on a history of the Irish in Australia.

PATRICK O'LEARY is a lecturer in the Federation Business School at Federation University Australia. He has published articles and book chapters on the Australian and US meat-processing industries and neoliberal employer industrial relations strategies. His articles have appeared in *Labour History* and the *Employment Relations Record,* among other publications. His current research projects involve the pre–World War II history of the US, Australian, and Argentine meat-processing industries; regional employment relations in Australia; and strategic human resource management in Chinese and Australian green industries.

SCOTT STEPHENSON recently completed his PhD in the School of History at the Australian National University. His research focuses on democracy and oligarchy within the New South Wales labor movement. He has published articles in *Labour History* and the *Australian Journal of Political Science,* and he received the 2015 Gollan Prize for the best article published in *Labour History* by a graduate student or early career researcher in the preceding two years.

PETA STEVENSON-CLARKE is lecturer in accounting at RMIT University. Her research interests include corporate governance and reporting as well as management and accounting history. Her work has been published in the *Journal of Business Ethics, Accounting and Finance,* and the *Journal of Management History.*

NATHAN WISE is senior lecturer in the School of Humanities at Australia's University of New England. His research focuses on cultural representations of military labor. He is the author of *Anzac Labour: Workplace Cultures in the Australian Imperial Force during the First World War* (2014). His current book project is *The Pursuit of Justice: The Military Moral Economy in the USA, Australia, and Great Britain, 1861–1945.*

Index

THE WORKING CLASS IN AMERICAN HISTORY

Worker City, Company Town: Iron and Cotton-Worker Protest in Troy and Cohoes, New York, 1855–84 *Daniel J. Walkowitz*

Life, Work, and Rebellion in the Coal Fields: The Southern West Virginia Miners, 1880–1922 *David Alan Corbin*

Women and American Socialism, 1870–1920 *Mari Jo Buhle*

Lives of Their Own: Blacks, Italians, and Poles in Pittsburgh, 1900–1960 *John Bodnar, Roger Simon, and Michael P. Weber*

Working-Class America: Essays on Labor, Community, and American Society *Edited by Michael H. Frisch and Daniel J. Walkowitz*

Eugene V. Debs: Citizen and Socialist *Nick Salvatore*

American Labor and Immigration History, 1877–1920s: Recent European Research *Edited by Dirk Hoerder*

Workingmen's Democracy: The Knights of Labor and American Politics *Leon Fink*

The Electrical Workers: A History of Labor at General Electric and Westinghouse, 1923–60 *Ronald W. Schatz*

The Mechanics of Baltimore: Workers and Politics in the Age of Revolution, 1763–1812 *Charles G. Steffen*

The Practice of Solidarity: American Hat Finishers in the Nineteenth Century *David Bensman*

The Labor History Reader *Edited by Daniel J. Leab*

Solidarity and Fragmentation: Working People and Class Consciousness in Detroit, 1875–1900 *Richard Oestreicher*

Counter Cultures: Saleswomen, Managers, and Customers in American Department Stores, 1890–1940 *Susan Porter Benson*

The New England Working Class and the New Labor History *Edited by Herbert G. Gutman and Donald H. Bell*

Labor Leaders in America *Edited by Melvyn Dubofsky and Warren Van Tine*

Barons of Labor: The San Francisco Building Trades and Union Power in the Progressive Era *Michael Kazin*

Gender at Work: The Dynamics of Job Segregation by Sex during World War II *Ruth Milkman*

Once a Cigar Maker: Men, Women, and Work Culture in American Cigar Factories, 1900–1919 *Patricia A. Cooper*

A Generation of Boomers: The Pattern of Railroad Labor Conflict in Nineteenth-Century America *Shelton Stromquist*

Work and Community in the Jungle: Chicago's Packinghouse Workers, 1894–1922 *James R. Barrett*

Workers, Managers, and Welfare Capitalism: The Shoeworkers and Tanners of Endicott Johnson, 1890–1950 *Gerald Zahavi*

Men, Women, and Work: Class, Gender, and Protest in the New England Shoe Industry, 1780–1910 *Mary Blewett*

Workers on the Waterfront: Seamen, Longshoremen, and Unionism in the 1930s *Bruce Nelson*

German Workers in Chicago: A Documentary History of Working-Class Culture from 1850 to World War I *Edited by Hartmut Keil and John B. Jentz*

On the Line: Essays in the History of Auto Work *Edited by Nelson Lichtenstein and Stephen Meyer III*

Labor's Flaming Youth: Telephone Operators and Worker Militancy, 1878–1923 *Stephen H. Norwood*

Another Civil War: Labor, Capital, and the State in the Anthracite Regions of Pennsylvania, 1840–68 *Grace Palladino*

Coal, Class, and Color: Blacks in Southern West Virginia, 1915–32 *Joe William Trotter Jr.*

For Democracy, Workers, and God: Labor Song-Poems and Labor Protest, 1865–95 *Clark D. Halker*

Dishing It Out: Waitresses and Their Unions in the Twentieth Century *Dorothy Sue Cobble*

The Spirit of 1848: German Immigrants, Labor Conflict, and the Coming of the Civil War *Bruce Levine*

Working Women of Collar City: Gender, Class, and Community in Troy, New York, 1864–86 *Carole Turbin*

Southern Labor and Black Civil Rights: Organizing Memphis Workers *Michael K. Honey*

Radicals of the Worst Sort: Laboring Women in Lawrence, Massachusetts, 1860–1912 *Ardis Cameron*

Producers, Proletarians, and Politicians: Workers and Party Politics in Evansville and New Albany, Indiana, 1850–87 *Lawrence M. Lipin*

The New Left and Labor in the 1960s *Peter B. Levy*

The Making of Western Labor Radicalism: Denver's Organized Workers, 1878–1905 *David Brundage*

In Search of the Working Class: Essays in American Labor History and Political Culture *Leon Fink*

Lawyers against Labor: From Individual Rights to Corporate Liberalism *Daniel R. Ernst*

"We Are All Leaders": The Alternative Unionism of the Early 1930s *Edited by Staughton Lynd*

The Female Economy: The Millinery and Dressmaking Trades, 1860–1930 *Wendy Gamber*

"Negro and White, Unite and Fight!": A Social History of Industrial Unionism in Meatpacking, 1930–90 *Roger Horowitz*

Power at Odds: The 1922 National Railroad Shopmen's Strike *Colin J. Davis*

The Common Ground of Womanhood: Class, Gender, and Working Girls' Clubs, 1884–1928 *Priscilla Murolo*

Marching Together: Women of the Brotherhood of Sleeping Car Porters *Melinda Chateauvert*

Down on the Killing Floor: Black and White Workers in Chicago's Packinghouses, 1904–54 *Rick Halpern*

Labor and Urban Politics: Class Conflict and the Origins of Modern Liberalism in Chicago, 1864–97 *Richard Schneirov*

All That Glitters: Class, Conflict, and Community in Cripple Creek *Elizabeth Jameson*
Waterfront Workers: New Perspectives on Race and Class *Edited by Calvin Winslow*
Labor Histories: Class, Politics, and the Working-Class Experience *Edited by Eric Arnesen, Julie Greene, and Bruce Laurie*
The Pullman Strike and the Crisis of the 1890s: Essays on Labor and Politics *Edited by Richard Schneirov, Shelton Stromquist, and Nick Salvatore*
AlabamaNorth: African-American Migrants, Community, and Working-Class Activism in Cleveland, 1914–45 *Kimberley L. Phillips*
Imagining Internationalism in American and British Labor, 1939–49 *Victor Silverman*
William Z. Foster and the Tragedy of American Radicalism *James R. Barrett*
Colliers across the Sea: A Comparative Study of Class Formation in Scotland and the American Midwest, 1830–1924 *John H. M. Laslett*
"Rights, Not Roses": Unions and the Rise of Working-Class Feminism, 1945–80 *Dennis A. Deslippe*
Testing the New Deal: The General Textile Strike of 1934 in the American South *Janet Irons*
Hard Work: The Making of Labor History *Melvyn Dubofsky*
Southern Workers and the Search for Community: Spartanburg County, South Carolina *G. C. Waldrep III*
We Shall Be All: A History of the Industrial Workers of the World (abridged edition) *Melvyn Dubofsky, ed. Joseph A. McCartin*
Race, Class, and Power in the Alabama Coalfields, 1908–21 *Brian Kelly*
Duquesne and the Rise of Steel Unionism *James D. Rose*
Anaconda: Labor, Community, and Culture in Montana's Smelter City *Laurie Mercier*
Bridgeport's Socialist New Deal, 1915–36 *Cecelia Bucki*
Indispensable Outcasts: Hobo Workers and Community in the American Midwest, 1880–1930 *Frank Tobias Higbie*
After the Strike: A Century of Labor Struggle at Pullman *Susan Eleanor Hirsch*
Corruption and Reform in the Teamsters Union *David Witwer*
Waterfront Revolts: New York and London Dockworkers, 1946–61 *Colin J. Davis*
Black Workers' Struggle for Equality in Birmingham *Horace Huntley and David Montgomery*
The Tribe of Black Ulysses: African American Men in the Industrial South *William P. Jones*
City of Clerks: Office and Sales Workers in Philadelphia, 1870–1920 *Jerome P. Bjelopera*
Reinventing "The People": The Progressive Movement, the Class Problem, and the Origins of Modern Liberalism *Shelton Stromquist*
Radical Unionism in the Midwest, 1900–1950 *Rosemary Feurer*
Gendering Labor History *Alice Kessler-Harris*
James P. Cannon and the Origins of the American Revolutionary Left, 1890–1928 *Bryan D. Palmer*
Glass Towns: Industry, Labor, and Political Economy in Appalachia, 1890–1930s *Ken Fones-Wolf*

Workers and the Wild: Conservation, Consumerism, and Labor in Oregon, 1910–30 *Lawrence M. Lipin*

Wobblies on the Waterfront: Interracial Unionism in Progressive-Era Philadelphia *Peter Cole*

Red Chicago: American Communism at Its Grassroots, 1928–35 *Randi Storch*

Labor's Cold War: Local Politics in a Global Context *Edited by Shelton Stromquist*

Bessie Abramowitz Hillman and the Making of the Amalgamated Clothing Workers of America *Karen Pastorello*

The Great Strikes of 1877 *Edited by David O. Stowell*

Union-Free America: Workers and Antiunion Culture *Lawrence Richards*

Race against Liberalism: Black Workers and the UAW in Detroit *David M. Lewis-Colman*

Teachers and Reform: Chicago Public Education, 1929–70 *John F. Lyons*

Upheaval in the Quiet Zone: 1199/SEIU and the Politics of Healthcare Unionism *Leon Fink and Brian Greenberg*

Shadow of the Racketeer: Scandal in Organized Labor *David Witwer*

Sweet Tyranny: Migrant Labor, Industrial Agriculture, and Imperial Politics *Kathleen Mapes*

Staley: The Fight for a New American Labor Movement *Steven K. Ashby and C. J. Hawking*

On the Ground: Labor Struggles in the American Airline Industry *Liesl Miller Orenic*

NAFTA and Labor in North America *Norman Caulfield*

Making Capitalism Safe: Work Safety and Health Regulation in America, 1880–1940 *Donald W. Rogers*

Good, Reliable, White Men: Railroad Brotherhoods, 1877–1917 *Paul Michel Taillon*

Spirit of Rebellion: Labor and Religion in the New Cotton South *Jarod Roll*

The Labor Question in America: Economic Democracy in the Gilded Age *Rosanne Currarino*

Banded Together: Economic Democratization in the Brass Valley *Jeremy Brecher*

The Gospel of the Working Class: Labor's Southern Prophets in New Deal America *Erik Gellman and Jarod Roll*

Guest Workers and Resistance to U.S. Corporate Despotism *Immanuel Ness*

Gleanings of Freedom: Free and Slave Labor along the Mason-Dixon Line, 1790–1860 *Max Grivno*

Chicago in the Age of Capital: Class, Politics, and Democracy during the Civil War and Reconstruction *John B. Jentz and Richard Schneirov*

Child Care in Black and White: Working Parents and the History of Orphanages *Jessie B. Ramey*

The Haymarket Conspiracy: Transatlantic Anarchist Networks *Timothy Messer-Kruse*

Detroit's Cold War: The Origins of Postwar Conservatism *Colleen Doody*

A Renegade Union: Interracial Organizing and Labor Radicalism *Lisa Phillips*

Palomino: Clinton Jencks and Mexican-American Unionism in the American Southwest *James J. Lorence*

Latin American Migrations to the U.S. Heartland: Changing Cultural Landscapes in Middle America *Edited by Linda Allegro and Andrew Grant Wood*

Man of Fire: Selected Writings *Ernesto Galarza, ed. Armando Ibarra and Rodolfo D. Torres*
A Contest of Ideas: Capital, Politics, and Labor *Nelson Lichtenstein*
Making the World Safe for Workers: Labor, the Left, and Wilsonian Internationalism *Elizabeth McKillen*
The Rise of the Chicago Police Department: Class and Conflict, 1850–1894 *Sam Mitrani*
Workers in Hard Times: A Long View of Economic Crises *Edited by Leon Fink, Joseph A. McCartin, and Joan Sangster*
Redeeming Time: Protestantism and Chicago's Eight-Hour Movement, 1866–1912 *William A. Mirola*
Struggle for the Soul of the Postwar South: White Evangelical Protestants and Operation Dixie *Elizabeth Fones-Wolf and Ken Fones-Wolf*
Free Labor: The Civil War and the Making of an American Working Class *Mark A. Lause*
Death and Dying in the Working Class, 1865–1920 *Michael K. Rosenow*
Immigrants against the State: Yiddish and Italian Anarchism in America *Kenyon Zimmer*
Fighting for Total Person Unionism: Harold Gibbons, Ernest Calloway, and Working-Class Citizenship *Robert Bussel*
Smokestacks in the Hills: Rural-Industrial Workers in West Virginia *Louis Martin*
Disaster Citizenship: Survivors, Solidarity, and Power in the Progressive Era *Jacob A. C. Remes*
The Pew and the Picket Line: Christianity and the American Working Class *Edited by Christopher D. Cantwell, Heath W. Carter, and Janine Giordano Drake*
Conservative Counterrevolution: Challenging Liberalism in 1950s Milwaukee *Tula A. Connell*
Manhood on the Line: Working-Class Masculinities in the American Heartland *Steve Meyer*
On Gender, Labor, and Inequality *Ruth Milkman*
The Making of Working-Class Religion *Matthew Pehl*
Civic Labors: Scholar Activism and Working-Class Studies *Edited by Dennis Deslippe, Eric Fure-Slocum, and John W. McKerley*
Victor Arnautoff and the Politics of Art *Robert W. Cherny*
Against Labor: How U.S. Employers Organized to Defeat Union Activism *Edited by Rosemary Feurer and Chad Pearson*
Teacher Strike! Public Education and the Making of a New American Political Order *Jon Shelton*
Hillbilly Hellraisers: Federal Power and Populist Defiance in the Ozarks *J. Blake Perkins*
Sewing the Fabric of Statehood: Garment Unions, American Labor, and the Establishment of the State of Isreal *Adam Howard*
Labor and Justice across the America *Edited by Leon Fink and Juan Manuel Palacio*
Frontiers of Labor: Comparative Histories of the United States and Australia *Edited by Greg Patmore and Shelton Stromquist*

The University of Illinois Press
is a founding member of the
Association of American University Presses.

Composed in 10.75/13 Minion Pro
with Adrianna Extended Pro display
by Lisa Connery
at the University of Illinois Press
Cover designed by Jim Proefrock
Cover illustration: Miners at Speculator Mine, Butte, Montana,
ca. 1915. (Silver Bow Public Archives)

University of Illinois Press
1325 South Oak Street
Champaign, IL 61820-6903
www.press.uillinois.edu